Disability and Disadvantage

Disability and Disadvantage

EDITED BY

Kimberley Brownlee and Adam Cureton

OXFORD
UNIVERSITY PRESS

OXFORD

UNIVERSITY PRESS

Great Clarendon Street, Oxford OX2 6DP

Oxford University Press is a department of the University of Oxford.
It furthers the University's objective of excellence in research, scholarship,
and education by publishing worldwide in

Oxford New York

Auckland Cape Town Dar es Salaam Hong Kong Karachi
Kuala Lumpur Madrid Melbourne Mexico City Nairobi
New Delhi Shanghai Taipei Toronto

With offices in

Argentina Austria Brazil Chile Czech Republic France Greece
Guatemala Hungary Italy Japan Poland Portugal Singapore
South Korea Switzerland Thailand Turkey Ukraine Vietnam

Oxford is a registered trade mark of Oxford University Press
in the UK and in certain other countries

Published in the United States
by Oxford University Press Inc., New York

British Library Cataloguing in Publication Data

Data available

Library of Congress Cataloging in Publication Data

Brownlee, Kimberley, 1978–
Disability and disadvantage / Kimberley Brownlee and Adam Cureton.
p. cm.
Assembly of philosophers who contributed to this collection, which is the product of two
workshops held at the University of Manchester in May 2007 and the University of North
Carolina at Chapel Hill in September 2007.
Includes bibliographical references and index.
ISBN 978–0–19–923450–9
1. People with disabilities—Congresses. 2. Sociology of disability—Congresses.
3. Disabilities—Congresses. 4. Social justice—Congresses. I. Cureton, Adam Steven,
1981–II. Title.
HV1568.B76 2009
362.4—dc22   2009001720

Typeset by Laserwords Private Limited, Chennai, India
Printed in Great Britain
on acid-free paper by
CPI Antony Rowe, Chippenham, Wiltshire

ISBN 978–0–19–923450–9

10 9 8 7 6 5 4 3 2 1

Acknowledgements

WE are grateful to the excellent assembly of philosophers who contributed to this collection, which is the product of two workshops held at the University of Manchester in May 2007 and the University of North Carolina at Chapel Hill in September 2007. Both workshops were supported by a UK Arts and Humanities Research Council Grant. The University of Manchester workshop was hosted by the Manchester Centre for Political Theory (MANCEPT). We thank Alan Hamlin, Head of MANCEPT, and Charlotte Jackson, Elaine Edwards, and Victoria Riley in the School of Social Sciences Research Office for their assistance. The UNC workshop was held under the auspices of the Parr Center for Ethics. We received additional support from that centre, the UNC Department of Philosophy, and UNC Disability Services. We are particularly grateful to Jan Boxill, Director of the Parr Center, for her patience, encouragement and support for this project. We thank Adrienne Asch for responding to the papers presented at the UNC workshop. In addition to these two workshops, a Special Session on Disability was held at the 2006 American Philosophical Association Pacific Division Annual Meeting in Portland, Oregon. We thank Anita Silvers for the invitation to hold this session and Mary Mahowald for responding to the papers presented by Lorella Terzi, Christie Hartley, and Guy Kahane. We would also like to thank two anonymous referees for their comments and Peter Momtchiloff and Catherine Berry at OUP for their editorial work.

This project was conceived in an Oxford pub with Julian Savulescu who first encouraged us to pursue our interest in disability in this form. He has been a great source of encouragement throughout.

I (Adam) would also like to thank Tom Hill, who has inspired so much of my philosophical thinking. I am grateful to the National Science Foundation, the Polores Zohrab Liebmann Foundation, and the Institute for Humane Studies for their support. Thanks also to my family, especially Julie, for their unwavering patience and support.

Kimberley Brownlee   Adam Cureton
Manchester   *Chapel Hill, North Carolina*

Contents

Abbreviations

ADA	Americans with Disabilities Act
AID	artificial insemination by donor
DALYs	Disability Adjusted Life Years
EHA	Education for the Handicapped Act
IAAF	International Association of Athletics Federations
IDEA	Individuals with Disabilities Education Act
IVF	in vitro fertilization
PGA	Professional Golfers' Association
PGD	preimplantation genetic diagnosis
PTO	Person Trade-off
QALYs	Quality Adjusted Life Years
QOL	quality of life
SG	Standard Gamble
TBI	traumatic brain injury
TTO	Time Trade-off
WHO	World Health Organization

Notes on Contributors

NORMAN DANIELS is Mary B. Saltonstall Professor of Population Ethics and Professor of Ethics and Population Health, Department of Global Health and Population, Harvard School of Public Health.

ELLEN DANIELS ZIDE is Clinical Associate Professor and Assistant Director, Brain Injury Day Treatment Program, New York University School of Medicine.

LESLIE P. FRANCIS is Professor and Chair, Department of Philosophy, and Alfred C. Emery Professor of Law, University of Utah.

CHRISTIE HARTLEY is Assistant Professor of Philosophy, Georgia State University.

RICHARD HULL is Director of the Centre of Bioethical Research and Analysis, National University of Ireland, Galway.

GUY KAHANE is Deputy Director of the Oxford Uehiro Centre for Practical Ethics.

F. M. KAMM is Littauer Professor of Philosophy and Public Policy at The Kennedy School of Government and Professor of Philosophy, Department of Philosophy, Harvard University.

ROSALIND MCDOUGALL is a Doctoral Candidate at the Centre for Applied Philosophy and Public Ethics and the Centre for Health and Society, University of Melbourne.

DOUGLAS MACLEAN is Professor of Philosophy, University of North Carolina at Chapel Hill.

JEFF MCMAHAN is Professor of Philosophy, Rutgers University.

SUSANNAH ROSE is a Graduate Fellow, Edmond J. Safra Foundation Center for Ethics, and Doctoral Candidate, Harvard University Program in Ethics and Health

JULIAN SAVULESCU is Uehiro Professor of Practical Ethics and Director of the Uehiro Centre for Practical Ethics, Oxford University.

ANITA SILVERS is Professor of Philosophy and Department Chair, San Francisco State University.

LORELLA TERZI is Senior Lecturer in Philosophy of Education, Roehampton University.

DAVID WASSERMAN is Director of Research, Center for Ethics, Yeshiva University.

JONATHAN WOLFF is Professor of Philosophy, University College London.

Introduction

ADAM CURETON AND KIMBERLEY BROWNLEE

Disability and disadvantage are interrelated topics that raise important and sometimes overlooked issues in moral and political philosophy. Many of these issues strike at the core of traditional problems about what it takes to lead a good life, how we should treat others, and how society should be organized. Attending to the concerns raised by disability and disadvantage prompts a re-evaluation of core normative questions and identifies new problems for philosophical reflection. First, for example, focusing on the conditions required to provide justice for persons with disabilities can influence how we address longstanding problems about justly distributing the benefits and burdens of society. Second, understanding the particular circumstances and capacities of persons with specific disabilities can foster nuanced conceptions of the person within moral and political theory. Third, in the context of allocating healthcare resources, considering issues of disability may shed new light on well-known problems about medical need, comparative fairness, and desert by, for example, helping to highlight cases in which healthcare policies improperly discriminate against people with disabilities. Fourth, issues of impairment, disability, and disadvantage raise questions about what parents owe to their children, what virtues a parent should wish to possess, and what kinds of considerations ought to figure in reproductive choices. Finally, appreciating that impairment, disability, and related disadvantages are real possibilities for most of us at some stage in our lives can make us sensitive to our own vulnerabilities and dependencies on others. This in turn can trigger further reflection on the profound impact that social institutions have on the shape and quality of our lives, the damaging effects of social stigmatization, the potentially harmful messages conveyed by certain policies and actions, and the weight we tend to place on solidarity, group history, and common culture.

These are just a few ways in which examining the experience of disability and disadvantage can provide valuable, and sometimes surprising, insights into a variety of problems in moral and political philosophy. In recent years, issues of disability and disadvantage have begun to garner more attention from philosophers, perhaps due to an emerging appreciation that thinking about these topics can make important aspects of our lives more salient to us. Philosophers have also come to appreciate the strength of certain intuitions about how people with disabilities should be treated. Although our judgements about people with disabilities usually need to be interpreted and qualified, they tend to be ones with which a plausible moral theory or political theory must come to terms.

It is against this backdrop that we present this collection of original essays, the main aim of which is to expand the reach of philosophical reflection on disability while furthering the work of those who first began to see the primacy of these issues for moral and political philosophy. We caught a glimpse of the importance of issues of disability in moral and political philosophy ourselves when, studying together at Oxford, we sought to reconcile our own experiences as people with the same rare visual impairment with the way that traditional normative debates are usually conceived. We hope that the essays collected here encourage more philosophers to write and reflect about disability and related topics, as the contributions in this volume highlight exciting research areas in need of further investigation.

This collection brings together a number of thinkers who specialize in philosophical problems of disability as well as those who may be best known for their work in other areas of philosophy. Some of our contributors are younger philosophers while others are more established in their fields. We admire and respect all of these scholars and count it as a great privilege to have worked with them on this project. We were particularly fortunate to come to know most of them during a Pacific APA session and two conferences, at which nearly all of the essays in this collection were presented in one form or another. There are many other philosophers whose work has influenced all of us when it comes to thinking about disability and disadvantage. Suggestions for further reading on disability by these and other scholars can be found in the notes and references for the chapters.

Although many of the chapters address several distinct issues, they can be grouped roughly around their attention to certain core themes. Broadly in the order in which they are addressed, those themes include: (1) an analysis of the notions of *disability, disadvantage*, and *impairment* in ways that move beyond the so-called social and medical conceptions or 'models' of disability;[1] (2) reflections upon overlapping issues of social justice, distributive justice, and equality of wellbeing; (3) the conditions for full autonomy and inviolability; (4) notions of familial virtue; and (5) the normative terrain of reproductive decision-making. These themes play out in complex ways that can only be gestured at in the following brief chapter summaries.

In their chapter, Guy Kahane and Julian Savulescu offer an original conception of disability according to which, a disability is a stable personal trait that tends to diminish a person's wellbeing relative to some given context. Kahane and Savulescu take as their starting point the view that neither the social model nor the medical model of disability is adequate to resolve the range of moral and political problems for which a satisfactory theory of disability is required. The medical model is inadequate, they argue, since there is no reason to think that a trait is bad or in need of correction merely because it deviates from typical human functioning. The social model is faulty, on their view, because, even were we to remove all illegitimate social prejudice, there would remain a variety of disabling traits that we would have good reason to correct. Kahane and Savulescu propose instead a conception of disability closely tied to wellbeing. On their view, disabilities are traits that tend to decrease a person's wellbeing relative to certain circumstances. Three advantages that Kahane and Savulescu claim for their view are the following. First, it takes having a disability to be context-dependent—a trait that is generally disabling might not be disabling for a particular person if her wellbeing is not reduced as a result of having that trait. Second, their view is more inclusive than most in that

---

[1] In broad terms, the medical model regards a disability as a stable personal property that deviates from normal human functioning and, thus, a trait that we have reason to correct. The social model, by contrast, regards a disability as a stable personal trait that deviates from typical human functioning and tends to make a person's life go worse because of the social prejudices that exist against people with that trait.

it implies that we all have disabilities of various sorts. Third, it offers an appealing explanation for why there is strong reason to correct disabling traits, namely, that having them by definition makes our lives go worse. Although this conception of disability may seem overly broad, Richard Hull argues in his chapter that adopting a more inclusive conception of the disabling traits that most of us experience at some point in our lives may cultivate greater willingness to adjust social structures to reduce the cumulative disadvantages of functional loss and limitation.

Normal Daniels, Susannah Rose, and Ellen Daniels Zide take a different approach to understanding the concept of disability. They tease out a conception of disability from some empirical work on how persons who become impaired as adults respond to their new condition. Daniels et al. maintain that this evidence casts doubt on the widely accepted 'standard story' that people who experience a long-term impairment report that their lives are going better than do non-impaired people who merely imagine themselves having that impairment. (The basic idea in the standard story is that deaf people, for example, tend to regard their lives as going quite well while non-deaf people who imagine themselves becoming deaf think that their lives would not be going well.) According to Daniels et al. one problem with this view is that there is significant variation in how well people with certain types of impairments think their lives are going. People with severe depression and traumatic brain injuries, in particular, are much more likely to rate their lives as going worse than do people who merely imagine themselves with those conditions. In addition, the standard story risks giving the misleading impression that people are generally able to adapt successfully to most all types of physical and mental impairments, which may in turn suggest that disability is wholly accounted for by societal prejudice rather than by the impairments themselves. Given these reasons to doubt the standard story, Daniels et al. propose instead that we conceptualize disability as an impairment that leads someone to have fewer abilities than people without that impairment. To use their example, a paraplegic person with all sorts of assistive devices and community support may well have many of the same abilities as people without that impairment and so not be disabled in some respects. This account, they claim, not only makes sense of the empirical evidence of how people with disabilities evaluate the quality of their own lives, but it also rightly stresses that loss of functioning can result from both social and medical factors.

Lorella Terzi and Jonathan Wolff also consider conceptual questions in their chapters, but their main focus is on examining what is needed to secure equal social justice for all. In her chapter, Terzi draws upon some basic elements of the capability approach to distributive justice and suggests ways that this framework might address the needs of people with disabilities. The basic idea behind this framework is that everyone should be provided with whatever resources are needed to give them an equal opportunity to achieve certain valuable states (e.g. being well-nourished or healthy) and to perform certain valuable activities (e.g. running for public office or raising children). These beings and doings, or 'functionings' as Amartya Sen calls them, are regarded by proponents of this view as constitutive of individual wellbeing and so are taken to admit of the sort of interpersonal comparisons of wellbeing that distributive justice is sometimes thought to require. Terzi argues that this theory provides important insights into how we should think about distributive justice for the disabled. For one thing, it offers an intuitively compelling conception of disability that can explain why having a disability entitles one to just compensation. A person has a disability, on this view, when she has personal characteristics that make her unable to achieve certain valuable functionings at the same level that average people are able to achieve them in similar circumstances. And this approach encourages disabled people to be involved in the public deliberative process that Terzi believes should be used to determine which functionings matter from the standpoint of justice. Terzi stresses that this feature of the capability view she defends helps to respond to some of the worries about the capability approach that Jonathan Wolff raises in his chapter.

Wolff explores how issues of disability should be approached in a society consisting of equal moral persons. Wolff argues that bringing about a society of this sort requires us to remedy the effects that certain factors have on a person's life prospects. In particular, we must work to mitigate the way in which one's natural and social endowments, along with the basic structures of society, affect one's opportunities in life. Being disabled, Wolff suggests, can be understood as a state in which a person's natural endowments are impaired in such a way that she does not have genuine opportunities for secure (non-risky) functioning when considered against the background of the basic institutions and her place in the social lottery. This account lies within the capabilities approach to disability, but Wolff offers a few criticisms of the traditional versions of that view, including the one advocated by Lorella Terzi. Wolff prefers to talk about capabilities in terms of genuine opportunities for secure functioning, which are basically steps that it is reasonable to expect a person to take to achieve functionings that are not vulnerable to exceptional risk. Remedying a disability, on Wolff's account, can occur either by relieving a person's impairment or by affording him material resources. Wolff argues, however, that in most cases of disability we have more reason to change the basic structures of society in order to promote the equal recognition and acceptance of all persons.

The theme of social justice is carried forward by Christie Hartley, who sketches out in her chapter a contractualist account of justice that aims to explain and justify what society owes people with significant cognitive disabilities. As Hartley sees it, one of the main obstacles to constructing such an account is that contractualist positions usually regard society as essentially a fair system of cooperation where membership depends upon one's ability to participate in cooperative arrangements with others. The problem, as far as disabled people are concerned, is that people with cognitive disabilities may not be full members of society since they are unable to make the right sort of cooperative contribution to society. Hartley takes issue with this suggestion by offering a new way to understand fair cooperation as focused on establishing or maintaining worthwhile relationships rather than merely coordinating our efforts to produce some good. When fair cooperation is understood in this way, Hartley argues, a great many people with cognitive disabilities clearly participate in a variety of valuable cooperative arrangements, which in turn vouchsafes their status as full-fledged members of society who are owed equal justice. In particular, Hartley argues that people with cognitive disabilities can take part in relationships of engagement, which she describes as those in which two people recognize each other as responsive beings with whom communication is possible. According to Hartley, these relationships are valuable in themselves and often provide the basis for deeper relationships of respect, companionship, and friendship.

Like Hartley's chapter, Anita Silvers's chapter focuses upon people traditionally not included in accounts of social justice. Her essay is a continuation of her efforts to develop an account that gives due consideration to people not thought to fit the models of the person presupposed by dominant moral and political theories. These 'outliers', as she calls them, are people with characteristics that make them significantly different from the 'normal' or 'typical' person upon whom, as Silvers sees it, moral and political theories tend to focus. Rather than thinking of problems associated with 'atypical' people as issues to be worked out later, Silvers argues that we should recast issues of justice in a way that appreciates and embraces the many ways that people differ from each other. Her proposal is to think of justice as a matter of engendering trust amongst people with diverse characteristics, and thereby to emphasize that justice is a matter of promoting equal opportunity and human flourishing. Silvers argues that the main advantage of thinking of justice in this way, rather than along the model of a social contract, is that it allows us to adopt and combine three worthwhile strategies for dealing with problems of justice that arise from differences among persons; in particular, she suggests that some differences should be ignored, some mitigated, and some embraced from the point of view of justice.

Hartley and Daniels et al. give particular attention to severe cognitive impairment as a topic that raises distinct normative and conceptual issues. This focus on cognitive-related disabilities continues in the chapters by Jeff McMahan, Douglas MacLean, and Leslie Francis. Through an investigation of inter-related notions of autonomy, Francis argues that we should exercise due care when judging whether a person with an intellectual disability possesses or lacks autonomy. Francis shows that there is a variety of conceptions of autonomy and that at least some of them are matters of degree. According to Francis, context not only helps to determine which of the notions of autonomy is most relevant to a problem, but it can help to specify a threshold that a person must meet for certain judgements or actions to be autonomous. Francis argues that, when we distinguish correctly the various complex conceptions of autonomy, we see that many people with cognitive disabilities possess, to some degree, a variety of morally significant kinds of autonomy. This is especially evident, she thinks, when we reflect on the fact that, in many contexts, we do not judge a typical person's autonomy to be diminished when she makes use of certain assistive technologies such as calculators and notebooks or even when she seeks advice or information from other people. Indeed, we sometimes think that her autonomy is heightened when she avails herself of these forms of assistance. Similarly, in some contexts a person with minor mental retardation who relies on a caregiver for help in planning the week's meals may not differ greatly as far as autonomy is concerned from a busy professional who relies on a housekeeper for the same sort of help. Since many people with cognitive disabilities also make use of such assistive devices, albeit sometimes to greater degrees than the average person, and sometimes not by choice, Francis holds that these people are more autonomous in certain senses than we may tend to suppose.

Douglas MacLean takes up the vexing question of what attitudes we should have toward people with severe dementia. MacLean is particularly interested in the sorts of moral relationships that exist between people in the mid to late stages of Alzheimer's and the people who care for and about them. A difficulty in claiming that such people are owed our respect, in addition to our care and support, MacLean argues, is that they do not seem to have the sort of autonomy that respect is typically thought to require. The capacities to determine one's own ends, assess one's desires, make reasoned decisions, and much else diminish as Alzheimer's progresses; and there comes a point where some people with this disease seem no longer to be autonomous. If we are to justify affording them the sort of respect many tend to think they are owed, we must find some other basis for it. Identifying such a basis may also help to explain some other commonly held attitudes of respect that do not seem to be grounded in autonomy, such as respect toward the bodies of the dead and towards people who are permanently unconscious. MacLean proposes that we should conceive of moral persons, not as bundles of capacities that exist at particular times, but as organic beings who tend to live lives of a narrative structure, with our plot developments, rising action, and declining action. As our stories progress, we tend to gain some capacities and to lose others, but what makes us who we are is how these various pieces fit together as organic wholes. MacLean suggests that, if we think of others in this way then it becomes clearer why people who may have lost some of the capacities they once had are still owed respect. Although they may no longer have the capacities necessary for autonomy, we still should love and respect them for the totality of their lives.

Jeff McMahan addresses the issues of moral status, inviolability, and distributive justice in his chapter on the radically cognitively impaired. McMahan also takes up some of the conceptual questions raised in other chapters by questioning the common assumption that physical and cognitive disability are different dimensions of the same problem concerning a unitary group of people who all have equal moral status. In light of the marked difference between a radically cognitively limited human being and most other humans with respect to their psychological capacities and potential to realize the higher goods of wellbeing, McMahan doubts that such cognitively limited human beings should be called 'disabled' and he questions whether they have the same claims to equality of welfare. On his view, the inability of a radically cognitively limited human being to achieve higher levels of wellbeing is a feature of her individual nature rather than, as in the case of physically impaired persons, a contingent fact about the person's circumstances. As McMahan sees it, what is possible for the radically cognitively impaired in light of their nature should form the standard by which to assess their 'fortune' or how well their lives are going. By that standard, these people are well off if their wellbeing is relatively high on the scale that measures the range of wellbeing accessible to them given their psychological capacities and potential. McMahan goes on to argue that if there is a plausible principle of equality that applies to the cognitively normal and the severely cognitively limited, it is a principle of equality of fortune. According to this principle, in their fortune from moment to moment, a cognitively limited human should do as well by reference to her own capacities and potential as a cognitively normal human does by reference to his capacities and potential. Such a principle, McMahan argues, may be preferable to equalizing wellbeing and giving priority to the worst off. Not only does his requirement not involve the levelling down of wellbeing, but it also need not require that we always improve the objective wellbeing of those with severe cognitive limitations so long as they have achieved the same level of wellbeing relative to their capacities and potential as other people.

Like McMahan, Frances Kamm takes up the theme of distributive justice. In her chapter, she considers, how, if at all, disability should figure in decisions about distributing scarce healthcare resources. The basic problem she considers is that giving resources to the disabled is often less effective—produces a worse outcome—than giving those same resources to non-disabled people, especially when we are unable to correct the disability. Giving life-saving treatment to an otherwise healthy person, for example, will usually produce a better state of affairs in terms of wellbeing than giving it to a person with paraplegia. It may seem, however, that taking into account the goodness of outcomes in certain ways when making these sorts of decisions involves invidious discrimination by affording disabled people fewer resources than they might deserve, and doing so on the basis of their disability. Kamm aims to find a set of moral principles that both shows appropriate respect for persons and also accounts for our judgements in a variety of conflict cases involving people with disabilities where we must decide how to distribute healthcare resources. The first of two main principles she formulates tells us that, in cases where we are deciding how to distribute one sort of good, say that of saving someone's life, certain other goods are irrelevant to our choice, such as that of curing someone's sore throat. If we can save the life of only one of two people and one of them we expect to live for a few more years than the other one, because the latter person has a disability, this principle implies that our choice should not be affected by the few additional years of life. The other principle Kamm develops holds that we should treat people whose lives are worth living only in ways in which their identity does not count either in favour of or against them. According to her, when distributing life-saving treatment, this principle implies that we should not hold a person's disability for or against him; although if the treatment on offer is intended to address his sort of disability, then his having the disability can be relevant to our decision. The focus of Kamm's chapter is to develop these two principles and provide a detailed discussion about why, taken together, they form a part of a more or less justified way to distributing healthcare resources.

A final core theme of this volume, addressed most directly by David Wasserman, Rosalind McDougall, and Richard Hull, and indirectly by Douglas MacLean, is that of parental virtue (or familial virtue) and reproductive decision-making. David Wasserman's chapter explores an apparent moral asymmetry between actions that raise the chance of having a child with an impairment, which seem to be in most cases wrong, and actions that lower the chances of having a child with an impairment, which usually appear to be permissible or even sometimes morally required. Wasserman argues that endorsing this asymmetry can be incompatible with a parental ideal of 'unconditional welcome' which is an attitude many people think parents should have towards whatever child they produce. While he appreciates the initial plausability of this ideal, Wasserman offers an alternative that requires parents to be able to justify to their child any serious harm they expect the child to suffer as necessary or unavoidable for her or his overall good. According to Wasserman, parents have a justification of the required sort only if they regard such harm as necessary for the existence of any child they could have or for the kind of child they seek to have. Whereas Wasserman's justification requirement would oppose conduct that incidentally raises the odds of impairment, it would not oppose all conduct that knowingly raises those odds. The requirement would condone, however, many selective choices that the unconditional welcome rationale would condemn such as maintaining a genetic connection between parents and child or seeking to produce a particular kind of child.

In contrast to Wasserman's harm-based approach to parental decision-making, Rosalind McDougall sketches out a virtue-based approach to those choices. According to McDougall, the main problem with harm-based approaches to procreative decision-making is that, in light of the non-identity problem, the welfare of a potential child cannot have a direct influence on our decisions about whether to have her unless there is a significant risk that she will lead a life that is not worth living. Being brought into existence, in other words, is a harm only if one stands to lead a life that is not worth living. According to McDougall, if we are sure that a potential child will live a worthwhile life, the harm-based approach implies that her wellbeing should not figure directly in our decisions about whether or not to bring her into existence. McDougall thinks this is unacceptable. On her view, the wellbeing of our potential children should figure prominently in our decisions about whether to have them. Her alternative approach to procreative decision-making specifies a set of parental virtues, which in most cases derive from the aim of promoting the flourishing of one's actual and potential children. Correct procreative choices, she argues, are those that a virtuous parent would make. Three of the virtues she discusses are stable dispositions (1) to accept the characteristics of one's child that are conducive to her flourishing, (2) to be committed to fulfilling one's child's needs, and (3) to be moved to promote the development of one's child. After fleshing out this position, McDougall shows how her account can make sense of a variety of difficult parental choices having to do with the selection for or against children with disabilities. Thinking about what a virtuous parent would decide to do in these situations, she argues, offers a compelling account of how we all should approach these decisions.

In his chapter 'Projected Disability and Parental Responsibilities', Richard Hull develops a hybrid conception of disability as an interplay between medical and social factors and he argues that in all but a few cases it is quite unclear whether choosing a disabled child is wrong. Hull argues, first of all, that since social factors are a key aspect of disability, we have reason to change social structures so as to alleviate the disabling and disadvantaging effects of impairment. Second, even where social changes cannot alleviate all significant disability, he suggests that most persons with disabilities lead worthwhile lives that are far preferable to non-existence. This, he argues, casts doubt on the claim that parents can act wrongly by choosing to have a disabled child who will lead a genuinely worthwhile life rather than choosing not to have that child. Third, as noted above, Hull believes there is much to be said for moving beyond any rigid distinction between 'disabled' and 'non-disabled'. He advocates a more inclusive conception of the overlapping frailties and vulnerabilities that most people experience, which he thinks may cultivate greater willingness to adjust social structures to reduce the cumulative disadvantages of functional loss and limitation. Concerns about certain reproductive choices must be tempered, according to Hull, by an appreciation of the intensely personal nature of these choices, which are likely to affect us deeply and so can have profound effects on our own ability to flourish.

As these summaries indicate, the chapters in this collection advance debates on a variety of moral and political issues while opening up several paths for future research. First, although important work has been done to pin down the concept of *disability*, an interesting strategy, gestured at in several of the chapters, would conceive of disability as a family of distinct but related concepts concerning, including the notions of, disadvantage and vulnerability, that play interwoven and overlapping roles in moral, political, epistemic, personal, and social contexts. Second, it is worthwhile to reflect critically on the sorts of objections that disability rights advocates tend to make against certain kinds of theories and policies. Although some of these objections are made for largely political purposes, we should be sensitive to the fact that certain views can express hurtful or wounding messages to those with disabilities, so we need to be mindful of how we assess and present our views about disability. Third, proponents of a broadly Rawlsian approach to justice could consider more fully whether some of the disability-related criticisms against this approach can be adequately addressed from within that perspective, either on the basis of the basic view itself or with minor modification or supplementation.[2] Development of these and related debates makes all the more vivid the range of normative issues to which the concerns of this collection apply.

[2] See A. Cureton, 'A Rawlsian perspective on justice for the disabled', *Essays in Philosophy*, 9 (2008), 1.

1

The Welfarist Account
of Disability

GUY KAHANE AND JULIAN SAVULESCU

Consider the following list of actual and imaginary cases:

The deaf lesbians   A deaf lesbian couple who wanted to have a deaf child conceived their second child through Artificial Insemination by Donor (AID), using sperm from a friend with inherited deafness in his family. They argued that deafness is an identity, not a medical affliction that needs to be fixed. As they put it, 'Deafness is not a disability.' A hearing child would be a blessing, they said, but a deaf child would be a special blessing.[1]

Dwarfism   Two achondroplastic dwarfs request Preimplantation Genetic Diagnosis (PGD) to select an embryo with dwarfism. They argue that being little is not a disability, but only a difference. They claim that as their house and lifestyle have been modified for their short stature, they would be better able to rear a short child rather than a normal child—that if their child had achondroplasia, it would have a better life.[2]

We are grateful to the editors, Ingmar Persson, Jeff McMahan, David Wasserman, Dan Brock, Jo Wolff, an anonymous referee, and the participants in the 'Disability and Disadvantage Workshop' at Manchester University for very useful comments. We also greatly benefited from suggestions made by audiences at the Pacific APA meeting at Portland and at a workshop at Chapel Hill, University of North Carolina, where we presented some of the ideas of this chapter.

[1] See M. Spriggs, 'Lesbian Couple Create a Child who is Deaf Like Them', *Journal of Medical Ethics*, 28 (2002), 283.

[2] See D. M. Sanghavi, 'Wanting Babies Like Themselves, Some Parents Choose Genetic Defects', *New York Times* (December 5, 2006). According to a recent survey, selection of children with conditions such as deafness or dwarfism is not uncommon: 5% of 190 US PGD clinics allowed parents to select

Body integrity identity disorder   John is a want-to-be amputee. He does not identify with the body he was born with: a body with four limbs. He strongly desires to amputate his leg below the knee. John attends conferences with amputees and wants to be one of them. Although he has undergone extensive counselling and psychiatric therapy, this wish persists. John had pleaded for doctors to amputate his leg, but this request was declined, and he is now depressed. John is considering self-amputation.[3]

The ashley case   Ashley is a 9 year old from Seattle who was born with static encephalopathy, a severe brain impairment that leaves her unable to walk, talk, eat, sit up, or roll over. Ashley will remain at a developmental level of a three month old baby. In 2004, Ashley was given high-dose oestrogen therapy to stunt her growth, and her uterus and breast buds were removed to prevent menstrual discomfort and to limit the growth of her breasts. Ashley's parents argue that this treatment was intended 'to improve our daughter's quality of life and not to convenience her caregivers.'[4]

Colour blindness   A distinguished watercolour painter is afflicted by a rare disorder which causes him to go colour blind, no longer able to distinguish between red and green. The painter finds it difficult to continue his life's work, and becomes severely depressed.[5]

IQ reduction   A child is found to have a heart abnormality. Surgeons place the child on cardiac bypass to remove the lump. As a result of the bypass, the child's IQ drops from 180 to 150. The lump turns out to be benign and surgery was not necessary. When confronted by the parents, the surgeon says 'He has plenty of IQ points to spare.' The parents sue, arguing that the doctor 'disabled their child'.

embryos with these or similar conditions. (Sees S. Baruch, D. Kaufman, and K. L. Hudson, 'Genetic Testing of Embryos: Practices and Perspectives of U.S. IVF Clinics', *Fertility and Sterility* (2007).)

[3] See T. Bayne and N. Levy, 'Amputees by Choice: Body Integrity Identity Disorder and the Ethics of Amputation', *Journal of Applied Philosophy*, 22/1, (2005).

[4] D. Gunther and D. Diekema, 'Attenuating Growth in Children with Profound Developmental Disability: A New Approach to an Old Dilemma', *Archives of Pediatrics & Adolescent Medicine*, 160/10 (2006). See also http://ashleytreatment.spaces.live.com/.

[5] Such an example is discussed in Jonathan Glover, *Choosing Children: The Ethical Dilemmas of Benefic Intervention* (Oxford: Oxford University Press, 2006). The original case is described in Oliver Sacks, *An Anthropologist from Mars: Seven Paradoxical Tales* (London: Vintage, 1995). See also B. I. Cole and J. Nathan, 'An Artist with Extreme Deuteranomaly', *Clinical and Experimental Optometry*, 85/5 (2002), 300–5.

These cases raise difficult ethical questions. Is it permissible to deliberately create a child with deafness or dwarfism? Was it right to stunt Ashley's growth? Is it wrong to prevent John from getting the amputation he desires? Was it a misfortune for the gifted child to lose some IQ points, or for the painter to become colour blind? We can also ask whether the conditions described in these cases amount to a disability. Are deafness, dwarfism, and colour blindness disabilities? Is a drop from 180 to 150 IQ disabling?

These questions are related. As our brief descriptions suggest, some people already frame the ethical questions in terms of the concept of disability. They believe, for example, that it would be wrong to deliberately create a child with deafness or dwarfism *because* these are disabilities, whereas those who want to have children with these conditions believe that they can justify their choice simply by *denying* that they are disabilities.

Because of disputes such as these, claims about the concept of disability are now bitterly contested.[6] In this chapter we develop and defend a new account of disability. Our account is not a straightforward analysis of the existing concept of disability. Although concepts cannot be true or false, they can be defective in various ways. We argue that the everyday concept of disability is defective. It stands in the way of clear thinking about the cases we described. Disability advocates, and proponents of the 'social model' of disability, are also critical of the everyday concept. But their alternative proposal, while capturing something of normative importance, is not a useful substitute. We propose a new, third approach: a welfarist account of disability.

The welfarist account is revisionary: it preserves some aspects of the existing concept, and rejects others. As such, it faces a number of objections. The way it departs from common use will sometimes run against people's intuitions. We defend the welfarist account against these objections. Although it is not especially important whether the concept we define should be labelled 'disability' or something else, some such concept is needed for normative inquiry, to do the normative work that the existing concept of 'disability' is expected to do but can't.

---

[6] For a discussion of the acrimonious dispute between disability advocates and bioethicists, see G. M. Kuczewski, 'Disability: An Agenda for Bioethics' and peer commentary in *American Journal of Bioethics*, 1/3 (2001).

We end the chapter by returning to our list of cases to illustrate some of the normative work that needs to be done, and to show how our suggested account does that work. The advantage of the welfarist account is that it makes salient what is morally relevant in such cases. It cannot by itself provide answers to the difficult ethical questions these cases raise, but, unlike competing accounts, it sets us on the right path to answers.

1.1. The Everyday Concept

All of us possess the everyday concept of disability. We have no difficulty applying it to paradigmatic cases. Blindness, mental retardation, paralysis are usually classified as disabilities. Being shorter than average or short-sighted aren't. Then there is a range of more controversial cases. When we argue about such cases, one side to the disagreement might be confused about the implicit norms governing the concept, but it's also possible that the existing concept simply is not precise enough to supply an answer.

What is shared by the things that clearly fall under the concept of disability? An analysis of the concept should start from the observation that all of these paradigmatic cases of disabilities relate to stable physical or psychological conditions, conditions that lead to a lack of or deficiency in some motor, sensory or cognitive ability that most people possess. The important point is that the everyday concept has a definite *descriptive* component: there are empirical conditions that someone must meet if he or she is to count as having a disability. But the everyday use of disability also has an *evaluative* dimension. People are often described as *suffering* from a disability, and it would make no sense to ask, 'Yes, I know Smith has a disability but is that in any way bad?' Disability is taken to be a misfortune, something that makes life worse, and thus something that gives us reasons to try to avoid or correct it. In other words, the concept of disability is a *thick evaluative concept*—a concept that at once has specific descriptive content and commits speakers to certain valuations.[7]

---

[7] Bernard Williams introduced thick evaluative concepts in *Ethics and the Limits of Philosophy* (Cambridge, Press.: Harvard University Press, 1985), 141.

1.2. The Species Norm Account

In this chapter we will consider a range of competing accounts of disability. Since most of these are not properly understood as straightforward analyses of the everyday concept, we'll mark each of them with subscripted letters.

The Species Norm account, dominant in medical practice, defines disability as

Disability$_{SN}$
A stable intrinsic property of subject S that deviates from the normal functioning of the species to which S belongs

This account assumes that there are scientific truths about biological normality and function of a species, truths that can then be used as a standard against which to measure the characteristics of a particular organism. This is a problematic assumption that some reject, but we'll simply concede it here.[8]

Disability$_{SN}$ is not, however, the everyday concept of disability. It may capture the *descriptive* core of the everyday concept.[9] But the everyday concept also has an *evaluative* dimension—has normativity built into it. It implies beliefs about value and reasons. But although talk of deviation from a norm is talk about standards and how something ranks with respect to them, it is not normative talk in the sense that interests us in ethics. It is a form of attributive or functional value, the kind of value we refer to when we describe lawnmowers or knives as good or bad. Facts about functional value don't on their own imply facts about either intrinsic goodness or reasons for action.

We could get fairly close to an analysis of the everyday notion if we added this evaluative dimension to our formulation of disability$_{SN}$:

---

[8] Notice that, as it stands, this definition will not do. If someone has extraordinarily good vision or memory, she also deviates from normal functioning. So the definition needs to assume an asymmetry between two kinds of deviations, negative and positive. Cf. Boorse's well-known account of disease in 'On the Distinction between Disease and Illness', *Philosophy and Public Affairs* (1975).

[9] The descriptive aspect of the everyday concept is probably more specific than disability$_{SN}$ in including a reference to lack or limited *ability*. We'll discuss this below.

Disability$_{SN+E}$

A stable intrinsic property of subject S that deviates from the normal functioning of the species to which S belongs, and *simply because of that* makes S's life go worse, and therefore gives reasons to avoid, regret and correct it.

This concept is plainly defective. There are no intrinsic normative consequences to deviation from either biological or statistical norms. Such norms set *standards*, but they are not *normative*. It does not follow, simply from the fact that someone deviates from some biological or statistical norm, that there are any reasons to bring his functioning up (or down) to the norm, to prevent or 'cure' this condition, or to regret its occurrence.

Deviation from the species norm is not normative because there is no intrinsic connection between deviation from normal functioning and well-being. Such deviation is neither necessary nor sufficient for a negative effect on a person's life. Some people, for example, have ankyloglossia, a restricted lingual fraenum that prevents them from protruding their tongue tip beyond the edges of the lower incisors. This is hardly a misfortune, whereas loss of hearing or sexual function with old age is certainly consonant with the biological and statistical norm, but hardly less disabling for that. And when conditions that deviate from the norm lead to a reduction in well-being, and in enough cases they do, this is so not *because* they happen to be deviations from the norm.[10]

This mistaken implication that deviation from species norm must be bad has numerous pernicious consequences. Anita Silvers, for example, reports that

adults with upper limb phocomelia (congenitally anomalous arms), such as are occasioned by pre-natal exposure to thalidomide, often believe themselves to have

---

[10] For further arguments against Species Norm accounts, see Jeff MacMahan, 'Our Fellow Creatures', *Journal of Ethics*, 9 (2005), 353–80; *The Ethics of Killing: Problems at the Margins of Life* (Oxford: Oxford University Press, 2002), 209–28; and Anita Silvers, 'On the Possibility and Desirability of Constructing a Neutral Conception of Disability', *Theoretical Medicine*, 24 (2003), 479–81. The only normative view that comes close to justifying the move from deviation from species norm to normative conclusions is, perhaps, some version of Aristotelian ethics. But whatever the merits of such a view, it makes a substantive, not a definitional claim.

been injured as children by having had their natural digits amputated [and] been fitted with ineffective artificial arms... They see the process as extracting a high cost in suffering for the questionable goal of altering them merely to look a little less disabled.[11]

1.3. 'Germans' and 'Krauts'

Concepts can't be true or false. But they can be incoherent or defective in various ways. The everyday concept of disability is, we saw, a thick evaluative concept. Such concepts are especially prone to one kind of conceptual defect. It may be useful to diagnose this kind of error more generally.

Some of the clearest examples of thick concepts are racial and sexist epithets. One famous example is the word 'Kraut', as used in Britain for parts of the twentieth century.[12] The word 'Kraut' referred to people who are German, but it also expressed a negative valuation—hatred or contempt. Needless to say, the mere fact that a person is of German origins isn't sufficient, of itself, to make it the case that this person deserves contempt. If someone asserts 'Many Krauts are admirable', he may be making a semantic mistake, but hardly an evaluative one. You can't bring normative truths into existence simply by defining or using a word in some way.

'Kraut' is a defective concept. It establishes, by semantic fiat, a link between a certain empirical property and false normative conclusions.[13] What can we do when we discover that a concept is defective in this way? Most obviously, we can simply give up using the concept, and pressure those who do use it to stop. Indeed, we no longer use the word 'Kraut'. But, as we'll see, sometimes it is better to *correct* a defective concept, and in what follows we'll consider several ways of correcting the everyday concept of disability.[14]

---

[11] Silvers, 'Neutral Conception of Disability', 475.

[12] This example was first discussed by Michael Dummett in *Frege: Philosophy of Language* (Cambridge, Mass., 1973), 432.

[13] It is often claimed that, for many thick evaluative concepts, descriptive and evaluative elements are inextricably intertwined. One can grasp one only by accepting the other, and vice versa. But we doubt that such a claim could be defended with respect to the everyday concept of disability.

[14] One way of correcting it is to replace it with the neutral, descriptive concept of disability$_{SN}$. Such a concept is probably useful in various biological and medical contexts. But deviating from some

1.4. The Social Model Account

Disability activists and advocates often reject what they call the dominant 'medical model' of disability. What they reject is what we called disability$_{SN+E}$. We saw that they are right to do so. What they want to put in its place is what they call the 'Social Model'.

What is the Social Model? Disability activists sometimes claim, for example, that disability is

a social discrimination that limits opportunities of persons of difference ... [and] results only when physical difference is not accommodated by society.[15]

Or that

Disadvantages are ... effects not of biomedical conditions of individuals, but rather of the socially created environment that is shared by disabled and nondisabled people. This environment ... is so constructed that nondisabled people are privileged and disabled people penalized. Disability is a social problem that involves the discriminatory barriers that bar some people but not others from the goods that society has to offer.[16]

So far as we can tell, there is no single agreed formulation of the social model account of disability.[17] But the above statements suggest the following formulation:

Disability$_{SM}$
A stable intrinsic property of subject S which (1) deviates from the normal functioning of the species to which S belongs (i.e. a disability$_{SN}$) *and* (2) which tends to reduce S's level of well-being *because* members

standard doesn't, of itself, have any negative significance. However we want to call this notion, it is of no special use in normative contexts.

[15] T. Koch, 'Disability and Difference: Balancing Social and Physical Constructions', *Journal of Medical Ethics*, 27 (2001), 370–1.

[16] R. Amundson, 'Disability, Ideology, and Quality of Life: A Bias in Biomedical Ethics', in D. Wasserman, J. Bickerbach, and R. Wachbroit (eds.), *Quality of Life and Human Difference: Genetic Testing, Healthcare, and Disability* (Cambridge: Cambridge University Press, 2005).

[17] For a critical survey of the Social Model, see Tom Shakespeare, *Disability Rights and Wrongs* (Abingdon and New York: Routledge, 2006). One widely cited formulation of the social model is that of the Union of Physically Impaired Against Segregation (UPIAS), which defines *impairment* as 'lacking part or all of a limb, organ or mechanism of the body' and *disability* as 'the disadvantage or restriction of activity caused by a contemporary social organisation which takes little account of people who have physical impairments and thus excludes them from participation in the mainstream of social activities' (UPIAS, 1976).

of the society to which S belongs are prejudiced against such deviation from the normal.[18]

Note that this isn't an analysis of the everyday concept. It's a suggested replacement.[19] The descriptive content is kept, but the evaluative dimension is revised. In fact it's pretty much claimed that it's *because* of the entrenched use of the defective concept of disability$_{SN+E}$, use of this concept, in a sense, is self-confirming: disability$_{SN}$ *is* bad because *treated* as bad. It's contingently bad because (contingently) treated as necessarily bad.

The concept of disability$_{SM}$ is a species of a wider concept, the concept of a

Discriminated Trait
A stable property of subject S which tends to reduce S's level of well-being *because* members of the society to which S belongs are prejudiced towards people with this property[20]

Deviation from the human norm is merely one possible object of unjust attitudes. To the extent that a disability$_{SM}$ makes a person's life worse than it could otherwise be, it makes it worse in the same way that dark skin colour can make life worse in a racist society. Many people in the deaf community, for example, claim that the only way in which being deaf makes life worse is because deaf people are victims of 'audism', prejudice against the deaf.[21]

No doubt, disability$_{SM}$ singles out a genuine and pervasive form of prejudice that is a matter of great moral urgency, and disability advocates may be right in thinking that, in the context of their political and legal struggle, it is useful to use 'disability' to refer to such prejudice. We suspect, however, that this might be counterproductive. Revising the everyday

---

[18] Another possible formulation would replace 'normal functioning of the species to which S belongs' with 'the statistical norm in the society to which S belongs'. For our purposes, we can ignore this distinction.

[19] This is why it is a mistake to object that, because disability$_{SM}$ would apply to a black person in a racist society, 'it is clear that the social model gives an incorrect account of what 'disability' means.' (For this objection, see S. Sheldon and S. Wilkinson, 'Termination of Pregnancy for Foetal Disability: Are There Grounds for a Special Exception in Law?', *Medical Law Review*, 9 (2001), 103.)

[20] For an attempt to define wrongful discrimination, see Richard Arneson, 'What Is Wrongful Discrimination?' *San Diego Law Review*, 43 (2006), 775. Arneson argues that 'wrongful discrimination occurs only when an agent treats a person identified as being of a certain type differently than she otherwise would have done from unwarranted animus or prejudice against persons of that type.'

[21] See Harlan Lane, 'Do Deaf People Have a Disability?' *Sign Language Studies*, 2/4 (2002).

concept to refer to an entirely different normative phenomenon is likely to elicit unnecessary misunderstanding and resistance.[22] And, as we shall now argue, the everyday concept, even if defective, might partly track a genuine normative property that is not captured by disability$_{SM}$. It is not, however, very important what meaning we assign to the word 'disability'. What is important is that we have at hand concepts that accurately map the normative territory.

1.5. The Welfarist Account

In this section, we'll start with some general reflections on well-being and harm, and construct, out of these reflections, a number of specific evaluative concepts that we need anyway in thinking about normative questions. One of these concepts also happens to be a good candidate for a revised concept of disability. It is also, we believe, a concept that better captures what is best preserved in the existing concept.

The concept of disability$_{SM}$ is a species of discrimination. But discrimination is a species of the far broader concept of *the harmful*:

The Harmful
X is harmful iff X leads, in circumstances C, to a reduction in person S's level of well-being[23]

What does it mean to say that something leads to a reduction in well-being? One natural understanding is counterfactual: had X not been present, S's

---

[22] A point recognized by some proponents of the social model. See Ron Amundson and Shari Tresky, 'On a Bioethical Challenge to Disability Rights', *Journal of Medicine and Philosophy*, 32/6 (2007), 543.

[23] This is a widely held understanding of the concept of harm. Joel Feinberg, for example, claims that 'for A to harm B, he must cause B's personal interest to be in a worse condition *than it would have been* in had A acted differently.' ('Wrongful Life and the Counterfactual Element in Harming', *Social Philosophy & Policy*, 4 (1987)). Two cautionary remarks: (1) Some philosophers want to claim that a person can be harmed if something causes them to be in a condition that reduces well-being, even if there is no (nearby) possible world in which they come to exist without this harm. (2) It is extremely difficult to specify this counterfactual in a way that would not let in many counterexamples. This is a problem, not just for our welfarist account, but for any normative view that makes use of the concept of harm—for example for tort law (see L. Katz, 'What to Compensate? Some Surprisingly Unappreciated Reasons Why the Problem Is So Hard', *San Diego Law Review*, 40 (2003), 1347–53, and for attempts to account for the badness of death (see McMahan, *The Ethics of Killing*, ch. 2, esp. pp. 98–117). Unfortunately, we do not have space here to further discuss this difficulty.

well-being would be higher. X makes S worse-off than he would have otherwise been.[24]

Now a person could be said to be better off if he feels less pain, achieves more of his aim and projects, or enjoys deep relationships. That is, his life goes better if it includes more of the components of well-being—if it includes more of what is *intrinsically good* for the person. As we've defined the harmful, however, it refers rather to what is *instrumentally bad* for a person—something not bad in itself but bad through its effects. The harmful is what *leads to* harm.[25] Some conditions, however, are both harms *and* harmful. Pain, for example, is bad in itself but, if strong enough, also stands in the way of a person's pursuit of his projects.

The harmful is a very broad category. In thinking about normative questions, we can't do everything using concepts as thin as well-being and the harmful, just as we can't do all of our thinking about empirical matters using the concept of a physical object. We need more specific notions. One such notion is that of a discriminated trait. Others are danger, obstacle, disadvantage, incapacity, and disease. And, we'll suggest, one such notion can be properly labelled disability.

If we focus on cases where what makes a life worse has its primary causal source in an abiding intrinsic property of a person, we get

Harmful Trait
A stable intrinsic property of subject S that leads to a reduction of S's level of well-being in circumstances C

One thing that can be harmful in this way is the contents of a person's mental states. If someone believes that smoking is good for them, then this belief, through its many obvious behavioural ramifications, will have the causal effect over time of reducing his level of well-being. This belief may be a stable intrinsic property of him. It's a harmful belief. There can similarly be harmful desires and feelings. Beliefs and desires are *reasons-responsive*

[24] As we understand the harmful, it's a comparative notion: it refers to what makes life *worse*. Someone can have an extremely good life and be harmed by a small reduction of that very high level of well-being. If you feel extremely happy and we make you only mildly happy, you're harmed.

[25] The phrase 'lead to' can be understood both causally and non-causally. If I don't have some capacity, then it is logically impossible for me to exercise this capacity, and this may in turn prevent me from enjoying certain goods. Lacking the capacity is an instrumental evil, even if it we don't want to say that it *causes* me not to enjoy certain goods.

attitudes.[26] They are formed, maintained, and later influence behaviour, through the exercise (adequate or poor) of reason. It is better to put the way the contents of such attitudes affect well-being in a separate category.

So we need a slightly narrower concept, a concept that refers to the effect on well-being of the *abiding physical and psychological traits* of a person—features of her body and broader cognitive, sensory and affective dispositions—and excludes the contents of their mental states (though such traits will often *cause* a person to have various mental states).

This narrower concept gives us a third account of disability. This is our Welfarist account.[27] According to this account:

Disability$_W$
A stable physical or psychological property of subject S that leads to a reduction of S's level of well-being in circumstances C

We'll now clarify various aspects of the welfarist account. As we go along, we'll consider various ways of qualifying this initial formulation. We'll endorse some possible qualifications, and reject others.

1.5.1. Makes no reference to normality

Note that when we refer to a 'stable physical or psychological property' of a person, we are *not* referring to 'impairment', if this notion is taken to

---

[26] See Scanlon, *What We Owe to Each Other* (Cambridge, Mass.: Harvard University Press, 1999), ch. 1.

[27] Our welfarist account is in several ways similar to John Harris's view. Harris also denies any role to normality or species functioning. He defines disability as a 'harmed condition' or more precisely, 'a physical or mental condition that constitutes a harm to the individual, and which a rational person would wish to be without' ('One Principle and Three Fallacies of Disability Studies', *Journal of Medical Ethics*, 27/6 (2001), 384.) Although the difference between the two accounts might be terminological, we suspect that they are more substantial. (1) Harris's reference to harm strongly suggests a claim about reduction in well-being, and if something threatens to reduce someone's well-being, then she indeed has prudential reasons to try to avoid it. Harris, however, seems to define harm, and thus well-being generally, as what an agent who is procedurally rational would wish after reflection on the facts. We do not accept this subjectivist account of harm, well-being, and rationality. And, in any case, we prefer not to write any account of well-being into our definition of disability. (2) Harris's view makes no reference to context. This suggests that Harris takes disability to be *intrinsically bad*—to be, not a harmful condition but *a* harm. By contrast, the fact that a condition is a disability$_W$ doesn't *imply* that there are reasons to change this condition. Changing this condition is only one possible means to avoiding a reduction in well-being. So, to use Harris's terminology, it needn't be a condition that a rational person would wish to be without. And in different circumstances, the condition might even be a benefit. This is an insight of the Social Model that our welfarist account readily accommodates but to which Harris's view leaves no space.

be synonymous with disability$_{SN}$. We refer, quite simply, to *any* intrinsic property of the agent (qualified only in the sense explained above, that leaves out the contents of mental states).[28] Disability$_{SN}$ is not a notion of a *specific* kind of harmful thing. It's not the notion of a kind of harmful thing at all.

The concept of disability$_W$ makes no reference to biological or statistical normality. Whether or not a condition is normal or deviates from normality is not an intrinsic property of a person. This means that a lot of things may fall under disability$_W$ that don't fall under the everyday concept. Illness, for example, would count as a disability$_W$.[29] Harmful character traits—perhaps having a weak will, excessive stubbornness, a lack of confidence, a disposition to addiction, or recklessness—would all count as disabilities$_W$.

1.5.2. Has an intrinsic normative dimension

According to the everyday use, if something is a disability, then it is a misfortune to those who suffer from it and gives reasons to correct it. In a sense, the same is true of whatever counts as a disability$_W$. Although we didn't use explicit evaluative and normative terms in our formulation of disability$_W$, the concept of well-being is an intrinsically normative concept. If something leads to a reduction in someone's well-being, then that thing is bad for that person.

There is, however, a crucial difference from the everyday use. If something reduces well-being, then what is intrinsically bad is the harm it does—the reduction of well-being. But what reduces well-being is only instrumentally bad. And this means that while we may have some reason to correct it *as a means* to removing the harm, we can equally remove the harm by changing the circumstances. There is no intrinsic reason to correct a condition that counts as a disability$_W$.

1.5.3. Relative to person and context

As the above formulation makes clear, disability$_W$ is relative to both persons and circumstances. The everyday concept doesn't have this relativity. It not

---

[28] What counts as a property of a person as opposed to a property of his environment? This is not a clear distinction, nor is it clear that it marks an important normative boundary. Intuitively, we count glasses, contact lenses, and prosthetic legs as external to a person; hair and fingernails as internal. But what about an artificial heart? Or a mechanical eye that would provide perfect vision to an otherwise blind person? These are interesting questions that we cannot take up here.

[29] See Boorse, 'Disease and Illness' (n. 8 above) for the distinction between illness and the non-evaluative notion of disease.

only mistakenly implies that deviations from the species norm are bad, but also seems to imply that they are bad in themselves, quite independently of context.

The concept of a disability$_W$ is, by contrast, context-dependent. What makes leading a good life harder in one circumstance may make it easier in another. The atopic tendency which leads to asthma in the developed world protects against worm infestations in the undeveloped world. Colour blindness may be a disadvantage today but in human history some colour blind hunters may have had an advantage at spotting camouflaged prey. Deafness would be a positive advantage in an environment of extremely loud and distracting noise. Sitting in a wheelchair can be an advantage if one is waiting in a long queue.[30]

Internal and external factors often interact. For a wealthy and healthy person, blindness may not make a significant difference to well-being. A poor person can be made much worse by being blind. But, holding a person's blindness constant, we can ask whether poverty would reduce or increase her well-being. Holding her poverty constant, we can ask whether her blindness would reduce or increase her well-being. The two factors will obviously interact but we can still ask intelligibly what their causal contribution is, as long as we're clear enough about the context.

The less detailed and determinate our specification of 'circumstances C', then less useful it would be to designate a condition as a disability$_W$. This is why on our account it often makes little sense to ask of some condition, 'Is this a disability$_W$?' In order to judge which conditions constitute a disability$_W$, we need to know what class of people is being referred to, and to predict what the context or environment is likely to be. There is no context-independent answer to such a question.

We deliberately defined disability$_W$ to be relative to a specific person. When we consider questions about well-being, that's the normative ground level—the well-being of the 'average' or 'common' person has no independent moral standing. Nevertheless, in various contexts we need to speak in generalities. Certain foods, substances, temperatures, etc., are harmful to most human beings. That doesn't change the point that many things can be harmful to one person but not to another, harmful to a person at one time but not in another, and harmful in one set of circumstances and not in

---

[30] See Silvers, 'Neutral Conception of Disability' (n. 10 above), 478.

another. Folate is generally beneficial to people, important for health and the prevention of birth defects, but if given to a person with Vitamin B_{12} deficiency, it can be lethal.

We need to choose the level of magnification that is most useful for us to negotiate the world. If we want to speak accurately when we describe something as harmful, we at least need to be specific about the person, circumstances, and breadth of causal effect we intend to refer to. We will be more or less specific for different purposes, in the context of different normative questions. We cannot be as specific in political or legal contexts as we can be in first-person prudential ones. For such purposes, we may find useful a more coarse-grained concept that is framed in terms of what tends to be harmful for populations:

> Disability$_{WP}$
> A stable physical or psychological property that leads to a reduction of level of well-being for *most people from category Y* in circumstances C

Such a concept might be more useful for deciding on large-scale policies or laws.[31] But it will *not* be useful, and might even be an obstacle, when we want to answer normative question about a particular person, in particular circumstances.

1.5.4. It's ubiquitous

One example of a disability$_W$ is asthma. Asthma makes breathing more difficult in certain environments commonly encountered in the developed world. It's a consequence of our account of disability that, in this and similar ways, *all of us* can be said to suffer from disabilities$_W$—conditions inherent to our nature which reduce our well-being and make it more difficult to realize a good life. Asthma, a lame foot, pig-headedness, and weakness of will are all disabilities$_W$.

We tend to associate disability with visible and overt features of people's bodies, or with very severe mental limitations. But genetics, biology, and psychology will identify many other internal features of people to be

---

[31] Feinberg writes in a similar vein that 'Interests vary from person to person ... Some interests are so singular and eccentric that only a handful of persons possess them. Other interests are so widespread as to be almost universal, yet none of these ... is possessed by everyone without exception. The criminal law, however, must employ general rules that are applicable to everyone, and are reasonably simple.' J. Feinberg, *Harm to Others* (Oxford: Oxford University Press, 1987), 188.

impediments to well-being. It may turn out, for example, that having poor impulse control is a far greater obstacle to a good life than being deaf or missing an arm.[32] That is, having poor impulse control may be a *far greater* disability$_W$ than losing an arm, even if the intuitions of many will militate against this claim. The fact that certain properties of people are more salient than others may distort our understanding of the weight they have in shaping people's lives.

1.5.5. Degree, threshold, or threshold-and-degree concept?

Disability$_W$ is best understood as a degree concept. The degree comes simply from the amount of well-being lost by the presence of the disabling condition. Disability$_W$ thus encompasses even conditions that cause only insignificant or moderate harm. On our account, everyone suffers from disability$_W$ to some extent, in some respects.

The everyday concept, by contrast, is *both* a threshold and a degree concept. That is, light deviations from species norm, such as short-sightedness, don't count as disabilities. Only more significant deviations, such as very poor sight or blindness, meet this threshold. But once something counts as a disability, it's often compared in seriousness to other disabilities. Paraplegia, for example, is said to be a more serious disability than deafness.

This deviation from common usage is likely to offend some people's intuitions. They might object that it would be absurd to describe someone with an IQ of 150 as disabled just because some condition prevents her from having an IQ of 180 (assuming for a moment that higher IQ makes life go better). To see why we are not impressed by this complaint, consider the difference between unpleasant experiences and suffering. We all go through unpleasant experiences of various degrees throughout our lives. But obviously, some unpleasant experiences are too weak or fleeting to merit much attention. That's why we have the concept of suffering. Suffering is not a *different* kind of experience. It's just a painful experience that is above a certain threshold of intensity and length. Our account of disability is like the concept of an unpleasant experience; the everyday account, like that

---

[32] For dramatic evidence on the importance of impulse control, see Y. Shoda, W. Mischel, and P. K. Peake, 'Predicting Adolescent Cognitive and Self-Regulatory Competencies from Preschool Delay of Gratification: Identifying Diagnostic Conditions', *Developmental Psychology*, 26/6, (1990), 978–86.

of suffering. For practical purposes it is useful to have a way to refer to strong unpleasant experiences, or to especially harmful conditions. But it is important to see that the line that such distinctions draw is arbitrary.

People who, by our definition, suffer from significant disability$_W$ may require special facilities or financial support. Some people might prefer to use the word 'disadvantage' to refer to mild forms of disability$_W$. If we wanted to match the everyday use more closely, we could restrict disability$_W$ to conditions that cause severe effect on well-being:

Disability$_W$
A stable intrinsic property of subject S that that leads to a *significant* reduction of S's level of well-being in circumstances C

But we prefer to use the term 'disability' in a broader, more revisionary sense. This broader sense is more inclusive. Many conditions currently described as disabilities will be described as disabilities$_W$ on our definition. But many other, milder conditions common to all of us will also merit this label. This might contribute to resisting the way being labelled 'disabled' becomes a stigma, placing people with disabilities in an undesirable category distinct from most other people.[33] On our account, everyone has disabilities of one kind or another.

This is, in part, a terminological matter. It makes no difference, however, to the normative issues. What is important to see is that, just like unpleasantness and suffering, cases of serious disability$_W$ are continuous with many widespread forms of milder disability$_W$. If there is a distinct category of 'the disabled', that's only an arbitrary classification drawn for certain practical uses.[34] The suffering is no different from other people who undergo unpleasant experiences. It is just that their experiences are worse, and deserve more urgent attention.

1.5.6. Its application depends on our account of well-being

On its own, disability$_W$ doesn't tell us what falls under it. It doesn't have 'thick' descriptive content of the kind that disability$_{SN}$ has. To

---

[33] David Wasserman brought this point to our attention.

[34] As Silvers notes, the sharp increase in disabilities among US children (one in twelve in the 2000 census) is partly due to a broadening of the definition of disability, now taken to include mild asthma and attention deficit disorder (Silvers, 'Neutral Conception of Disability', 484). There can be various pragmatic reasons for broadening or narrowing down a definition. But it is not as if the scientific community suddenly discovered that mild asthma is a more severe deviation from the species or statistical norm than was previously believed.

apply disability$_W$ to something, we need to conduct two separate inquiries, one normative and one empirical. First, we need to adopt some account of well-being. Then we need to identify the causal factors that influence a person's well-being in a certain set of circumstances.

It is thus a substantive question, not determined by definition alone, whether the paradigmatic cases of disability in the everyday sense—deafness, blindness, and cognitive handicap—are disabilities$_W$. We ourselves are inclined to believe most of these are, in the conditions holding at present and in the foreseeable future. But a case needs to be made, and it needs to be made case by case. And note that although a general case can be made about the status of, say, deafness, as a disability$_W$ for most people in the common circumstances holding in our world, it may still be true that an opposite case can be made for a particular person, in special and specific circumstances. Nevertheless, it may be that, although the everyday concept is defective, our use of it is at least partly responsive to factors that genuinely reduce well-being, at least in present circumstances. It may thus be that, although disability$_W$ is a revisionary account, its extension *in the present world* will to a substantial extent overlap the extension of the existing concept.

1.6. The Relation of the Welfarist Account to the Everyday Concept of Disability

Like the social model, disability$_W$ isn't an analysis of the everyday concept. In the previous section, we've gone through many ways in which it diverges from it. The welfarist account preserves much of the evaluative dimension of the everyday concept, but drops its descriptive dimension. It refers to instrumental, not intrinsic badness, and the badness is relative to person and circumstance. Like the everyday concept, it refers to a stable physical or psychological condition, but there is no reference to either biological or statistical normality. And what this gives us is an evaluative concept that is not defective—a bit like starting to use 'Kraut' to refer to all people who deserve our contempt, regardless of whether or not they are German.

But why should we replace the existing concept with disability$_W$? Why not just drop the concept?[35] The first thing to say is that we *need* a concept such as disability$_W$, as defined above, whether or not we want to call it disability or disadvantage or something else. Although claims about harm, disability, danger, and so forth are reducible to claims that employ only the concepts of well-being and causation, in actual life we cannot manage by thinking and speaking only at that bare level. We also need richer, more specific concepts which relate internal physical and psychological states to external social and natural environmental states, via the concept of well-being. Disability$_W$ is one such concept.

In early Christianity, the word 'acedia' was used to describe monks in desert monasteries who, in certain periods, found it hard to adhere to the strict monastic work schedule. This was seen as a vice, a disposition to reject a great spiritual good. We do not need a concept with this precise descriptive and evaluative content. But we do need a way of referring to an analogous form of depression, and the concomitant difficulty to respond to what has value is a genuine misfortune, and sometimes a vice. The people who coined and used the term 'acedia' were responding to a genuine empirical phenomenon with genuine normative significance, but, from our present perspective, we want to say that they only partly understood it, and in many ways misunderstood it. We want to suggest that the everyday use of 'disability' is also partly responsive to a genuine phenomenon. We need a concept to refer to this phenomenon.

Finally, there are good reasons to use the word 'disability' to refer to this normative phenomenon. In deciding how to revise an existing but defective concept, we should consider not only the intrinsic merit of competing proposals but also the *expected consequences* of their adoption, *given* the prevalent use and associations of the existing term.

If the entrenched use of a word is evaluative, it may be dangerous to try to replace it with a purely descriptive term. People may find it hard to use 'Kraut' to simply mean German and nothing else. Even if people officially disavow the normative implications of a defective term, their use of it may still carry these pernicious associations. So it is better, if possible, to preserve the normative side but correct the descriptive one.

---

[35] Anita Silvers (ibid.) argues that in order to defuse the tensions between disability advocates and bioethicists, we should adopt a normatively neutral conception of disability. Silvers seems to have in mind something like disability$_{SN}$.

We need to adjust both descriptive and evaluative aspects in the way that preserves what's correct while making salient the mistake entrenched in the existing use. This is what the welfarist account does. We think that it is inclusive in just the right way. Not everyone disabled in the everyday sense would count as having disablity$_W$, and most people who count as normal have, to some degree, disabilities$_W$. Our account leaves out the irrelevant reference to normality and makes salient the normative continuity between stronger forms of disability$_W$ and the ubiquitous milder forms that everyone has.

1.7. The Relation of the Welfarist Account to the Social and Species-Norm Views

Disability$_W$ and disability$_{SN}$ Disability$_W$ preserves the evaluative import of the existing concept. But it deviates greatly from its descriptive content. Some people think that this is too radical a departure. That it's too inclusive of things that, intuitively, don't seem like disabilities at all. They therefore prefer to think of disability$_W$ as stating only a necessary condition for something's counting as a disability.[36] Some further condition must be met to get disability proper. But what would complete the definition? One answer is to go for a hybrid concept, to combine disability$_W$ and disability$_{SN}$.[37] This would give us:

Disability$_{W+SN}$

A stable intrinsic property of subject S that (1) deviates from the normal functioning of the species to which S belongs (i.e. a disability$_{SN}$) *and*

---

[36] We owe this suggestion to Ingmar Persson.

[37] Something like this view is endorsed by Jonathan Glover in *Choosing Children* (n. 5 above), 8–13. Glover's hybrid view contrasts disability with normal functioning only when deviation from the norm involves a reduction in human flourishing, and instead of a fixed biological standard or one set by the existing population, Glover takes this standard to be set by any reasonably sized group with a high-level of functioning, whether past or present. But what is the intrinsic moral significance of the existence of an actual past or present reference group of sufficient size? Imagine a future where, although advances in medicine have the power to make us live longer, healthier, and happier lives, we cannot enjoy these benefits because a burst of solar radiation has imposed an upper limit to our functioning. We would all suffer from a regretful disabling condition, even if no past or present group has ever actually enjoyed these benefits. But if we allow the mere possibility of higher functioning to determine whether a condition counts as a disability, then it seems that the reference to a statistical standard is redundant.

(2) leads to a reduction of S's level of well-being in circumstances C (i.e. a disability$_W$)

This concept is narrower than the everyday use because it excludes forms of disability$_{SN}$ that don't tend to reduce well-being. But it's obviously closer in its descriptive content to the everyday notion.

However, it's doubtful we need such a concept. The problem is precisely that there is no deep connection between conditions (1) and (2). It's not the fact that it deviates from a species norm that makes a property detrimental to well-being, even if the two conditions may sometime overlap. (It's a bit like using 'Kraut' to refer only to those Germans that *happen* to deserve contempt.)

There is another way in which disability$_W$ and disability$_{SN+E}$ may connect. There are some philosophers who seem to hold that a person's well-being is to be assessed in terms of his or her meeting standards of functioning proper for the species to which S belongs.[38] If this is one's view of well-being, then disability$_W$ may *imply* disability$_{SN-E}$. But this would not be definitional, but a substantive result. Our account is compatible with such a view, even if we ourselves reject it. This is as it should be—the welfarist account serves to direct inquiry in the right direction, to debate about the nature of well-being, and away from pointless and all too common terminological controversy.

Disability$_W$ and disability$_{SM}$ What about the relation between disability$_W$ and disability$_{SM}$? It may be useful to narrow down disability$_W$ so that it refers only to the effect a condition has on well-being that we get when we *subtract* the effect it has through social prejudice:

Disability$_{W-SM}$
A stable intrinsic property of subject S that tends to reduce S's level of well-being in circumstances C, *excluding* the effect that this condition has on well-being that is due to prejudice against S by members of S's society due to the deviation of this property from the normal functioning of the species to which S belongs.

---

[38] Some neo-Aristotelian accounts of human flourishing, such as those of Nussbaum and Foot, could be interpreted as claiming that. See Philippa Foot, *Natural Goodness* (Oxford: Oxford University Press, 2003), and Martha Nussbaum, *Women and Human Development* (New York: Cambridge University Press, 2000).

Or better, since there's nothing special about attitudes to deviation from species norm, we can define disability$_W$ to refer to the effect of a condition has on well-being when we subtract the effect on it due to discrimination against a trait of whatever kind. We can call this Disability$_{W-DT}$.

We adopt this qualification. It relieves us from having to claim that having dark skin colour in a racist society is a disability$_W$. This is not *ad hoc* given that the distinction makes a normative difference. Natural evil is to be prevented if possible. But someone is responsible for moral evil. It calls for a different response. There is moral priority to changing people's prejudices rather than the objects of their prejudice. There is no such priority to changing environment as opposed to people's traits when the harm is natural.[39]

1.8. Well-being, Social Arrangements, and the Social Model

This revision of disability$_W$ is, however, unlikely to satisfy the proponents of the Social Model. According to them, the harm referred to under disability$_{SM}$ captures all or at least most of the harm caused by the conditions that count as disabilities in the everyday sense. For conditions such as deafness, blindness, or paraplegia, if we subtract disability$_{SM}$ from disability$_W$, we get zero, or close to zero. In this section we will consider this objection.

Let's reconsider disability$_{SM}$:

Disability$_{SM}$
A stable intrinsic property of subject S which (1) deviates from the normal functioning of the species to which S belongs (i.e. a disability$_{SN}$) *and* (2) which leads to a reduction of S's level of well-being *because* members of the society to which S belongs are prejudiced against such deviation from the normal

To apply this definition, we need to know what is meant by 'prejudice'. Prejudice presumably involves negative attitudes and behaviour towards

---

[39] This is not to suggest, of course, that disabilities$_W$ might not result from morally culpable behaviour. If someone deliberately maims another, then there *is* someone that is morally responsible for the existence of a disability$_W$. The point though is that we don't need to know the source of the harmful condition to decide that it is harmful.

people with the trait in question. And these must be unjustified attitudes. There are plenty of cases where we have very good reasons to have negative attitudes towards people with certain intrinsic traits—reasons, for example, to feel contempt precisely for people with prejudiced attitudes.[40]

Now unjust beliefs, attitudes, and behaviour are bad not only because of their effects on the people discriminated against but also in themselves. We can hold people responsible for such attitudes. Such attitudes *ought* to be corrected. The condition to which disability$_W$ refers to needn't be bad in itself. It is bad only because of its effects. We have reason to correct it only as a *means* to reducing its harmful effects. But there is no normative priority to correcting this condition as opposed to changing the surrounding circumstances. So if unjust attitudes play a significant role in these circumstances, it is these attitudes we should first aim to correct, not the disability$_W$. And, it might be objected, the way we have defined disability$_W$ obscures this point.

Let us develop this objection. We first need to highlight one consequence of the context-dependence of disability$_W$. According to our definition,

> Disability$_W$
> A stable intrinsic property of subject S that leads to a reduction of S's level of well-being in circumstances C

But this means that whenever a condition X is a disability$_W$, it would be true not only that

(A) If S didn't have X, her well-being would be higher

But also that

(B) If S was no longer in circumstances C, her well-being would be higher

At the extreme, the Social Model is the claim that the innocent reference to 'circumstances C' is simply a way of concealing the fact that circumstances

---

[40] Except in those case where prejudice and discrimination is unconscious or akratic, prejudice would involve false beliefs—either empirical or normative or both. This is not to say that discrimination involves mere cognitive error of some kind. In many cases, the prejudiced person *ought* to know better. In any case our concern here is not with responsibility for prejudice but with its harmful consequences.

C are the circumstances of social prejudice. And, as we saw, if that were true then there would be priority to changing 'circumstances C' rather than condition X.[41]

It might be thought that according to both the welfarist account and the Social Model, a condition is a disability only contingently, not necessarily. After all, both hold that

(1) In some possible situation, having condition X wouldn't reduce well-being

This seems to simply follow, on the welfarist account, from the relativity to circumstances C. But this claim needs to be qualified in two ways.

First, this would be true only with respect to the instrumental badness of a condition. But many such conditions are arguably also intrinsically bad, to varying extents. Severe cognitive handicap places necessary limits on the kinds of goods accessible a person, limits that would hold in all circumstances. Having a certain level of intelligence is, if not intrinsically good, a necessary condition to certain goods necessary for a good life. (More complicated are the cases of blindness and deafness, which deprive one of access to a range of great aesthetic goods. While such sensory capacities are *necessary for access* to such goods, it's far less clear that enjoyment of these is *necessary for a good life*.)

Second, the possible world referred to in (1) must be one that includes the individual S. The fact that there are possible worlds in which X is harmless or even beneficial would be irrelevant if in these possible worlds S couldn't exist. The change in surrounding environment needs to be *identity-preserving* if it is to make S better off—identity-preserving in the sense relevant to prudential and moral considerations, which need not be identical to metaphysical personal identity.

Setting these qualifications aside, the first thing to note is that for many conditions, (1) is true only in an uninteresting sense. It refers to circumstances that might be *conceivable*, but which bear no realistic relation to the existing world. Paraplegia may not make a difference to well-being if we all possess powers of levitation and telekinesis. Being deaf or mute would make little difference if we were all telepathic. In other words, the

---

[41] But it doesn't follow that we *must* change society rather than the person. Sometimes the morally correct thing to do, in the face of injustice, is to adjust oneself to a defective reality.

mere truth of (1) with respect to a condition establishes little of genuine interest. We need to work with a weaker claim, the claim that

(2) In some *realistic* possible situation, having X wouldn't reduce S's well-being

Now what counted as realistic a thousand years ago was far narrower than what counts as realistic today. Technological development and consequent changes to our form of life mean that what counts as a realistic alternative to the present world can't be held fixed.

So far, no word about the social. We need to add that if we are to move closer to the Social Model. So consider

(3) In some realistic possible *social* arrangement, having X wouldn't reduce S's well-being[42]

No doubt, this claim would still encompass much of what reduces the quality of life of disabled people (disabled, that is, both in the everyday sense and in the welfarist sense). Such a claim will hold only for a given condition, in given contexts, but let's concede, at least for argument's sake, that much of the effect of many conditions on well-being might fall under (3), so long as we don't forget that (3) refers only to a subset of (2).

As an illustration, consider an example from Anita Silvers. She points out how a simple change in automobile styles has affected the mobility of people who need wheelchairs to move:

[I]f two-door sedans are available, an individual with a folding wheelchair can drive independently, pulling the chair into the car behind the driver's seat. But the design of four-door cars precludes this manoeuvre. Consequently, the rarity of the once common two-door automobile has attenuated the mobility of many wheelchair users who can get into a two-door but not a four-door car.[43]

---

[42] Notice the work still done by the restriction to realistic possibilities: excluded are possible worlds in which the family is abolished or the circumstances pertaining in Ancient Greece.

[43] In A. Silvers, D. Wasserman, and M. B. Mahowald, *Disability, Difference, Discrimination: Persepectives on Justice in Bioethics and Public Policy* (New York: Rowman & Littlefield, 1998), 63. Alison Davis, who has spina bifida, claims that 'If I lived in a society where being in a wheelchair was no more remarkable than wearing glasses and if the community was completely accepting and accessible, my disability would be an inconvenience and not much more than that. It is society which handicaps me, far more seriously and completely than the fact that I have spina bifida.' (Quoted in C. Newell, 'The Social Nature of Disability, Disease and Genetics: A Response to Gillam, Persson, Holtug, Draper and Chadwick', *Journal of Medical Ethics*, 25/2 (1999), 172.)

Having paralysed legs doesn't affect well-being, or even mobility, on its own. It does so only in a given context. Its effect on well-being is instrumental, and contingent. It's not intrinsic or necessary. If we could all fly, our mobility would not be affected by whether or not we can make use of our legs. And, as Richard Hull points out, walking people's mobility would be severely constrained in a city designed for people who could effortlessly jump to great heights.[44]

To the extent that limits on mobility have negative effects on well-being, many of these effects would be due to external conditions that can be described as 'social', and similar claims can be made about barriers to perceptual access to information in the case of deafness and blindness.

Those who oppose the Social Model tend to dismiss (3) far too quickly. They seem to think that, in order to reject the Social Model, we *have* to show that (3) is false. And those who defend the Social Model often mistakenly assume that (3) implies, or amounts to the truth of, the Social Model.[45]

However, the very fact that a person's well-being is reduced because of her social environment—because of the beliefs, attitudes and behaviour of others, and because of the distribution of resources in her society—doesn't yet show that this person is discriminated against. For this to be true, these beliefs, attitudes, and social arrangements also need to be *mistaken* and *unjust*.

Let's first set aside *explicit prejudice*—being mistreated simply because one is different.[46] No doubt this is a component of the reduction in well-being due to the social environment, but the Social Model, as some of its critics fail to see, is not the claim that if we correct prejudice in this narrower sense then no detrimental effect on well-being will remain.[47] The real dispute, however, is about social arrangements of the kind described by Silvers. So to get to the social model, we need to defend

[44] R. Hull, 'Defining Disability—A Philosophical Approach', *Res Publica*, 4/2 (1998), 199–210.

[45] Amundson and Tresky (n. 22 above), for example, contrast 'socially caused' and 'no one's fault' (p. 533), given the impression that what is socially caused must be someone's fault.

[46] See again Arneson (n. 20 above).

[47] In his criticism of the Social Model, John Harris may fail to see this, as he seems to take the Social Model to refer only to 'social exclusion, discrimination, ostracism and hostility'—'Is There a Coherent Social Conception of Disability?' *Journal of Medical Ethics*, 26 (2000), 98.

(4) In some realistic possible *and more just* social arrangement, having X wouldn't reduce well-being[48]

But it's a mistake to argue that

(i) If condition C didn't hold, the fact that people have X wouldn't make their life any worse than those who don't have X
(ii) Condition C is social in nature

Therefore

(iii) The holding of condition C is a prejudice against people with C

Even if condition C was utterly fixable by social arrangement, it still wouldn't follow that the holding of condition C is unjust or discriminatory, if there exist good reasons *not* to distribute resources to fully fix it.[49]

1.8.1. *The 'social model' and distributive justice*

Claim (3) doesn't imply claim (4). For (4) to follow, we also need to accept an extreme conception of distributive justice:

Absolute Welfare Equality
Any social arrangement which results in some members of a society having, through no fault of their own, less welfare than others is unjust

Even if we accepted this extreme view, it would not follow that there exist realistic alternative social arrangements on which people with a disability$_W$ have *exactly* the same level of well-being that others now enjoy. Absolute Welfare Equality is more likely to be achieved by a far greater reduction of the well-being of others than an increase to those with a disability$_W$.[50] (An

---

[48] It might be objected that our restriction of relevant possibilities to 'realistic' ones could be used to preserve status quo or injustice. No doubt this is a genuine danger. Someone might claim that the demand for equal access to facilities or education is 'unrealistic'. But, as the text indicates, we intend something else by 'unrealistic', though it would be difficult to give the term a precise definition.

[49] This point is not captured by Richard Hull's distinction between *impairment-induced disability*, which refers to 'the loss or limitation of ability or opportunities to take part in the life of a community on an equal level with others due to impairment; and *socially induced disability*, that refers to 'the loss or limitation of ability or opportunities for people with impairments to take part in the life of the community on an equal level due to . . . economic, political, social, legal, environmental and inter-personal barriers.' ('Defining Disability', 203). Commenting on this distinction, Sheldon and Wilkinson remark that socially induced disabilities 'have the same status as sex discrimination' (ibid. 105). But this overlooks the point that not all such barriers need be unjust.

[50] Cf. Parfit's famous Levelling Down objection in 'Equality and Priority'.

example: If all people and newborn were made deaf, equality with deaf people would be easily achieved. And this is a realistic 'social' change that can be easily achieved today.)

Consider some examples. The sizes of many doors, beds, and cars are too small for extremely tall people. It hardly follows that the prevalence of these sizes amounts to a prejudice against such people. Here the statistically normal does matter. It matters not directly, in evaluations of well-being, but in the context of considerations of distributive justice, broadly understood. It is through such considerations that people's well-being might be reduced because, due to social causes, they deviate from the statistically normal. But, by definition, this reduction would not be *unjust*. Trivially, by being determined by considerations of distributive justice, it would be not just neutral but *just*.

Now whether and when this would be so depends on our conception of distributive justice. But pretty much any plausible conception will allow such cases. If Gulliver becomes a citizen of Lilliput, justice would require the Lilliputians to make some allowance to make Gulliver's life go well, even if he radically diverges from the normal. But it would be absurd to claim that justice requires them to ensure that Gulliver's life would be in *no way* constrained by his different dimensions. Of course, if they could somehow achieve that at no expense, then they should. But even if they could achieve that at immense cost, it seems unjust to invest so much to improve Gulliver's prospects by greatly reducing those of everyone else.[51] Where exactly the line should be drawn is a tough question and it's not one we want or need to answer. The point of this example is the rather banal one that not all reduction of well-being due to social factors amounts to discrimination—amounts to a discriminated trait or disability$_{SM}$.[52] The very label of the 'Social

---

[51] Note that it wouldn't make the slightest difference whether Gulliver and the Lilliputians belong to the same or to a different species, and, if they belonged to the same species, which of them was closer to the species norm.

[52] The authors of *From Chance to Choice* make a similar point (A. Buchanan, D. Brock, N. Daniels, and D. Wickler (Cambridge: Cambridge University Press, 2000), 288 ff.). However, the example they use to make it has proven offensive to some and is liable to be misunderstood; it is vigorously criticized by Amundson and Tresky (n. 22 above, 553 ff.). It's important, however, to distinguish the conceptual claim that social arrangements that disadvantage some group needn't be unjust and the political claim, which we take Amundson and Tresky to defend, that the specific disadvantages that disability advocates are fighting to remove are indeed unjust. We do not mean to dispute this latter claim. Its truth depends on many empirical considerations and on what theory of justice we adopt.

Model' embodies this conflation. A better label would be the 'Social Injustice Model'.

Debates about the nature of well-being mean that there will be some controversy about the application of disability$_W$. This, by the way, is also true of disability$_{SM}$, since it also makes use of the concept of well-being. But now it emerges that debates about the distribution of well-being are such that the boundary between disability$_{W-SM}$ and disability$_{SM}$ will also be controversial. This is yet another reason not to write 'social prejudice' into our definition of the concept of disability.[53]

1.9. Objections to the Welfarist Account

1.9.1. It prejudges the normative issues

The everyday concept has an evaluative dimension. Disability$_W$ preserves this dimension, but it may be objected that it trivializes it. Since on our definition it's tautological that disability$_W$ is bad for those suffering from it, it might be thought to foreclose certain genuine normative questions about disability. The normativity is written into the concept.

While this objection is correct as it stands, it is not a genuine problem. Our definition doesn't foreclose any genuine normative question. On the contrary, it makes it impossible to move from a certain neutral relational empirical property to a tendentious normative conclusion simply through a semantic detour. But the conceptual tie between well-being, value, and reasons is acknowledged by any sane normative view.

What our definition does do is shift the normative question to where the action really is, the question of well-being. This is where normative debate should take place. But once we've settled on an account of well-being and the empirical facts are in, there is no further intrinsic normative issue about disability$_W$ that remains open. There are of course

---

[53] Jo Wolff has pressed upon us the difficulty of drawing this line. Consider, for example, a case where present social arrangements, while greatly reducing the prospects of a minority with some condition X, are due, not to present prejudice and injustice, but to such prejudice in the distant past. Suppose, for example, that a great monument was built long ago without consideration for people with condition X, who consequently cannot access and enjoy it. But to change this situation now might require destroying a valuable artefact. Should we say that the harm incurred by inability to access the monument is due to discrimination?

other normative considerations that might weigh in: considerations about other people's well-being, distributive justice, desert, or whatever else one's moral theory recognizes. But these other considerations were there anyway.

1.9.2. It will be impossible to agree about its application

The extension of disability$_W$ is determined by the empirical facts plus whatever is the true account of well-being. But regarding many conditions it may be extremely hard to obtain the relevant empirical facts, or to determine the normative ones. And even if we form a firm opinion, others are often likely to have different views, both about the empirical facts, and, most certainly, about well-being. So even if everybody will adopt the concept disability$_W$, there will be much disagreement about its application to any particular case. No such problem arises with disability$_{SN}$.

To some extent this fear is exaggerated. The main competing theories of well-being—hedonism, desire-satisfaction, and the variety of objective good theories—offer conflicting accounts of the nature of well-being, but still largely agree about the particular things that make life go better or worse. Thus, for example, hedonism and desire-satisfaction theories typically claim that significant relationships and achievements are good because they give us pleasure or satisfy our strong desires. Objective good theories typically recognize the value of pleasure and pain and think that our informed desires often track what is independently good. This is not surprising, since these are all competing accounts of our everyday concept of well-being, and as such are likely to preserve many of our pre-theoretical beliefs about well-being—beliefs that are indeed diverse, but also share a large core.

1.9.3. It is far too inclusive

Whatever its exact extension, disability$_W$ will almost certainly cover a more *extensive* range of cases than the everyday concept. On our account, disability is ubiquitous. We pointed out some advantages of this inclusiveness: the welfarist account is more resistant to stigmatization, and it gives due recognition to the effect on well-being of inner conditions that are less salient to the ordinary eye.

But some still think our account is far too inclusive. Wouldn't it be absurd to describe the child who ended up having 150 IQ instead 180

IQ as suffering from a disability? But the absurdity might simply be a semantic complaint. Our semantic intuitions don't agree with this way of using the term 'disability'. This isn't surprising, or a problem. Disability$_W$ is an explicitly revisionary concept. Some existing semantic intuitions are bound to militate against it. If we revised 'Kraut' so that it referred to all vicious people, it would sound equally awkward, for those who have been accustomed to using the previous jingoistic concept, to apply 'Kraut' to some English person.

There is a more substantive constraint that we should, however, introduce to our formulation of disability$_W$. When we judge whether or not a condition of a person is a disability$_W$, we ask whether his well-being would be higher if he hadn't had this condition. But, of course, there are many ways in which we could be different than we are now and which would make our lives go better. It would be pointless, however, to describe all of these as disabilities$_W$. Being short-sighted can make life somewhat more difficult, and is to this extent a very minor setback. Losing one's leg in an accident is a real misfortune. But not being able to paint like Picasso or write like Shakespeare are not any kind of misfortune, even if these are capacities we could have had in some possible world.

The lesson is that our counterfactual condition needs to be qualified. We need to compare S's level of well-being, given condition X, with those nearby possible worlds in which she exists and circumstances C hold, and those nearby possible worlds in which it doesn't. We need to exclude far-fetched, improbable, and unrealistic possibilities.[54]

What counts as realistic or probable changes over time? It's not a disability$_W$ for (most) of us not to have the creative powers of a genius. But if in the future it was discovered that transcranial magnetic stimulation of the frontal lobes dramatically increases one's ability to realize one's creative potential, then being deprived of such stimulation could be reasonably described as a disability$_W$.[55]

---

[54] See Jeff McMahan's defence of a 'realism condition' as a constraint on assessments of fortune in *The Ethics of Killing*, 133, 142, and 145 ff.

[55] This restriction comes close to formulating disability not in terms of well-being proper, but in terms of what Jeff McMahan calls *fortune*, a concept that appropriately piggybacks on top of that of well-being (ibid. 145 ff.).

1.10. Well-being, Disability, and Ability

It might be objected that our definition of disability$_W$ is too broad in another sense. The everyday notion of disability, as the word suggests, refers to a lack of ability. The blind cannot see, the deaf cannot hear, etc. If these conditions tend to reduce well-being, they do so, presumably, by depriving those who suffer from them from certain abilities. Their lives don't go as well as they could because there is a range of things that they can't do.

Our definition makes no reference to ability. Of course if blindness tends to reduce well-being, and does so because it is a lack of a certain range of abilities, then blindness would count as a disability$_W$. But so would various other well-being reducing conditions that reduce well-being regardless of ability. If a condition shortens one's life, or makes one unattractive to members of the opposite sex, or tends to cause strong headaches, it would count as a disability$_W$. Is this a problem?

We could define a fourth notion of disability that would simply refer to a condition that prevents a person from having a certain ability or set of abilities:

Disability$_a$
A stable intrinsic property of subject S that prevents S from Ving (in circumstances C)

This account makes no reference to either well-being or to species or statistical norm. But such a notion of disability doesn't seem useful. There is a vast amount of things we can't do and, presumably, facts about us that explain why we can't. But very few of these 'inabilities' matter. Being unable to wiggle one's ears isn't a disability. And someone blind may not be able to see, but may be able to hear far better than a seeing person, to read Braille, etc. Whereas it's true by definition that deafness is a disability$_a$, it takes substantive work to show that deafness is a disability$_W$.

Furthermore, we need a way of properly *individuating* and *counting* abilities, their degree, and their lack. We need, for example, to put some constraint on the notion of 'ability' for it to do any interesting work. What is it exactly, for example, that people of very low intelligence aren't able to do? And do we want to say that those who die young are *unable* to live longer?

(1) We might simply add this as a further condition to our formulation of disability$_W$. We *could* define a notion of disability$_{W+a}$ which would refer to stable condition that tends to reduce well-being *and* does so because its existence prevents the person from having a range of abilities. Such a restriction might be useful for various purposes. It would single out *one* way in which a condition might be harmful.

If lacking certain kinds of abilities or modes of 'functioning' was all there was to well-being, then disability$_{W+a}$ would simply follow from disability$_W$ plus this substantive view about well-being. But as this is an extremely implausible view—a view that leaves no space, for example, for the intrinsic value of pain or knowledge or longevity. Depression counts as a disability$_W$ not only because depressed people may find it harder to engage in various activities but also because depressed people are disposed to *feel bad*. And lack of an ability can contribute to well-being. For those who are addicted to alcohol or who cannot control their urge to eat, it may be a benefit to take substances or have surgery that restricts their ability to act on these harmful urges. So we need something like our broader notion of disability$_W$ in any case. So we see no good reason, except the desire not to offend semantic intuitions, to narrow down the welfarist account in this way.[56]

(2) A more interesting suggestion would be to define disability, not in terms of lack of abilities that *in fact* lead to reduction of well-being, but in terms of lack of *opportunities* for realizing well-being, whether or not these opportunities would have been taken.[57] It might be claimed, for example, that whereas someone deaf might have as good a life as someone hearing, even as good a life as she would have had had she been hearing, what makes deafness a disability is that it nevertheless restricts the range of opportunities for well-being this agent had in her life. This would give us

---

[56] Disability$_a$ bears obvious resemblance to Amartya Sen's capability approach. As Sen himself insists, the list of relevant capabilities needs to be restricted to *valued* or *valuable* ones. For discussion of whether this doesn't just turn the view into an account of well-being, see L. W. Sumner, 'Utility and Capability', *Utilitas*, 18 (2006).

[57] The model for this suggestion would be opportunity for welfare accounts of equality. See R. Arneson, 'Equality and Equality of Opportunity for Welfare', *Philosophical Studies*, 55 (1989).

Disability$_{OW}$

A stable physical or psychological property of subject S that decreases
S's range of opportunities for realising well-being in circumstances C

If the claim is simply that having less opportunities (or opportunities of a
certain sort) makes a life go worse, then this claim is not best stated in
terms of *opportunities* for well-being. This would rather be a substantive
claim about well-being itself, and as such would already be compatible
with our initial definition of disability$_W$. But if this claim is genuinely
about opportunities for well-being, why should we be interested in such
opportunities, independently of whether or not they were realized?

We might be interested in the range of available opportunities in the
context of questions about justice, where it is common to regard differences
in well-being that are entirely due to people's own choices as lying outside
the scope of distributive justice. But we are not now discussing questions
about justice, and someone's life could go well despite being unjustly
limited in his opportunities. We might also be interested in opportunity
for well-being in the context of *ex ante* prediction of the impact a certain
condition would have on a person's life. But if we are trying to make such
predictions, we might as well employ the concept, not of opportunities
for well-being, but of *expected* disability$_W$. That is, we'll need to assess the
probability of various circumstances holding in this person's life, and how
this condition would affect her well-being in each such circumstances.
If our questions are about a future person who has not even yet been
conceived, then they would be open-ended indeed. If we do not know
anything about the person's personality, preferences, or projects, we will
have to use fairly coarse-grained measures to assess how a condition would
affect his life—we would need to use something like disability$_{WP}$. We'd
need to make such coarse-grained assessments because of our epistemic
limitations. But when we make *ex post* assessments of how a condition has
affected a life, the only concept we need is disability$_W$.

1.11. The Welfarist Account at Work

We can now return to the list of cases we started with. These, we believe,
nicely illustrate the way in which disability$_W$ will sometimes conform to

the everyday use, and the ways in which it will sometimes surprisingly depart from it. In those cases where the welfarist account agrees with the everyday concept, it will give a better explanation of *why* a condition is harmful. In those cases where it departs from it, it will better highlight what is of normative significance.

In order to apply the concept of disability$_W$, we need an account of well-being. We then need some way of telling whether a given condition, in a given context, reduces well-being. What constitutes a good life is a difficult philosophical question. According to hedonistic theories, it consists of having pleasant experiences and being happy. According to desire fulfilment theories, what matters is having our preferences fulfilled. According to objective good theories, certain activities are intrinsically good—developing deep personal relationships and talents, gaining knowledge, and so on.[58] The welfarist account is neutral with respect to such philosophical disputes about the nature of the good life. But although there is this philosophical disagreement, there is considerable consensus about the particular traits or states that make life better or worse. Few if any would deny that chronic pain tends to make a life worse, or that joy makes a life better. All plausible moral theories have to make such judgements—judgements about harms and benefits. Our welfarist account doesn't rely on some controversial conception of well-being. All it asks us is to apply the same concepts we already employ in everyday situations.

The concept of well-being is likely to be plural and open-ended. It may be that different forms of life are equally good, or, perhaps, that the amount of well-being realized in each is 'on a par' without being equal. But there are plenty of cases where we *can* rank the goodness of lives. We do so in numerous moral decisions in everyday life. Few would deny that, in most cases, we can at least give rough answers to questions about well-being, and if this is the case, then we can also give rough

---

[58] To the extent that the capability approach of Sen and Nussbaum is best understood as a substantive account of well-being (for problems for this reading, see Sumner, 'Utility and Capability'), then accounts of disability that draw on this approach, such as Lorella Terzi's contribution to this volume, are best understood as variants of the welfarist view. Indeed the view of disability Terzi develops is quite close to the one defended in this chapter, even if it is couched in somewhat different vocabulary. However, we deliberately avoid endorsing any substantive account of well-being—whether disability is best understood in welfarist terms, and whether this or that view is the correct account of well-being, are two distinct and partly independent questions.

answers to questions about disability$_W$. In this section we'll examine a number of interesting cases and give such rough answers. But these are just rough answers. There are no general armchair answers to questions about disability$_W$.[59]

1.11.1. Deafness and dwarfism

Deafness and dwarfism are obviously disabilities$_{SN}$. But are they also disabilities$_W$? It is arguable that deafness is instrumentally bad in two senses. First, deafness reduces the goodness of a life by preventing access to the world of sound. A deaf person cannot hear music or the human voice. To be sure, in a world without sound, deafness would not be bad. It is the exercise of a capacity to hear that is valuable, not the capacity itself. But the capacity to hear is, obviously, a necessary condition for enjoying those intrinsic goods that are necessarily auditory. And in *our world*, there are plenty of such goods. Second, deafness also reduces the chances of realizing a good life because it makes it harder to live, to achieve one's goals, to engage with others in a world which is based on the spoken word. Being able to hear isn't a necessary condition for such activities and goods. But it is nevertheless significantly harder to move in the world, harder to respond to emergencies where the alarm is aural, and so on.[60] These difficulties are partly due to social circumstances, but, as we've pointed out earlier, this needn't mean that they are all due to injustice.

These general claims, however, are compatible with the claim that for particular people, in particular circumstances, deafness is not a disability$_W$. Indeed, for adults whose life projects are closely tied with their condition, and who will need to make a difficult and painful transition to the world of hearing, remaining deaf might be preferable to becoming hearing. For these people, *hearing itself* would count as a disability$_W$.

[59] Anita Silvers claims that in her 'neutral framework' for thinking about disability, bioethicists will have to 'base their beliefs about the difficulties of living with a disability on facts rather than fears. It will be unethical to assume without empirical confirmation that people do better by risking medical intervention than by adapting to life with a disability' (p. 476). This claim also holds of the welfarist account, which is in no way neutral. We should point out, however, that empirical inquiry can decide such questions only when guided by normative answers to questions about well-being.

[60] On the night of 10 April, 2003, a school for deaf and mute children in Makhachkala in Russia caught fire. Twenty-eight children aged 7 to 14 died and more than 100 were injured. Rescuing the children was hampered because 'each child had to be awakened individually and told in sign language what to do.' (AFP, 'School fire kills 28', *Herald Sun* April 11, 2003).

Similar considerations apply to dwarfism. To us this seems at most a mild disability$_W$, continuous with different limitations on well-being that all of us have (it makes no difference to well-being whether a person's short stature is due to genetic abnormality or to normal genetic variance). We doubt that achondroplasia does much to reduce the quality of a person's life once we subtract the consequences of prejudice.

1.11.2. Body integrity identity disorder

In most cases, losing one's limb would be a significant disability$_W$, and it would consequently be a serious prudential mistake to try to amputate one's own limb, or even simply to risk losing it. But in the case of some would-be amputees, it might actually be a disability$_W$ to *possess* a healthy limb, in the context of an otherwise incurable depression. Similar remarks apply to sex change operations in people with gender dysphoria. In these different contexts, the same condition might amount in one case to a harm and in another to a benefit, and what would count as 'correcting' a disability would be very different. Once we drop the instinctive reliance on normality as a normative guide, this result shouldn't be so surprising. It's not intrinsically bad to have only one leg just as it is not intrinsically bad to have 'only' two.

Of course, to lose a leg is potentially to lose a degree of mobility, and consequently some degree of well-being. To what extent this is a loss will depend on the sophistication of the prosthetic legs available (most would-be amputees apparently have no qualms about using prosthetic limbs), and, as technology advances, the negative effect on mobility will continue to diminish. But whatever the negative effect, such an operation would arguably amount to a benefit overall, when contrasted with the harm caused by *keeping* the leg.[61]

This is just a hypothesis. To properly assess it, we'll need to engage in serious empirical footwork. It can't be decided from the armchair, from sketchy case descriptions, let alone by gut reactions. We need to overcome gut responses to surgery or to the 'deformation' of the human figure, and to ask instead what effect such surgery would plausibly have on particular people's well-being.

[61] In this respect want-to-be amputees are arguably no different from people who desire to have a sex change.

1.11.3. The 'Ashley treatment'

On both our welfarist account and on the Species Norm view, Ashley was born with a severe disability.[62] But their verdicts radically diverge when we turn to the effect in Ashley of the treatment devised by her doctors. On the Species Norm view, the treatment would greatly increase Ashley's disability—driving her even further from the human norm. On our view, in the *context* of Ashley's brain impairment, and assuming that the claims made for the effects of the treatment on Ashley's well-being are correct, the treatment would be not disabling but enhancing.

We think that the concept of disability$_W$ does a better job, and sheds more light on the Ashley case, than that of disability$_{SN}$. As for disability$_{SM}$, it has been claimed by some that Ashley's condition is detrimental only because of adverse social circumstances and that it is only these circumstances that need to be changed—for example by providing further support for the parents to lift or transfer Ashley, and so forth. This claim is implausible. Not all the detrimental aspects of Ashley's condition are due to lack of social support, nor should it be simply assumed that changes to the social circumstances are always to be preferred.[63]

1.11.4. The colour blind painter

The context-dependence of disability$_W$ is nicely illustrated by the example of colour blindness. Generally this is seen as a very mild disadvantage because it has little impact on a person's life. Colour blind people experience the world differently, but this has virtually no impact on their lives. Although it involves some disadvantage, colour blindness constitutes only a mild disability$_W$. But consider now our colour blind painter. Such a person might be prepared to spend vast sums of money to correct his colour vision. This represents the value of colour vision to that particular person in his context. For such a person, colour blindness might be a significant disability$_W$.

1.11.5. IQ reduction

Is it a disability$_W$ to have 150 instead of 180 IQ? As we conceded earlier, this might sound odd. But being less intelligent might have a far greater

---

[62] It's actually unclear whether, on the welfarist account, Ashley's initial state is really a disability$_W$, if Ashley couldn't have existed without this condition, and removing it wouldn't make *her* better off.

[63] S. M. Liao, J. Savulescu, and M. Sheehan, 'The Ashley Treatment: Best Interests, Convenience, and Parental Decision-Making', *The Hastings Centre Report*, 37/2 (2007), 16–20.

impact on a person's life than having only three limbs. What kind of impact this might have on well-being is largely an empirical question, and there is at least some evidence that can help us answer it.[64] Let us just point out two general considerations. First, intelligence is at least partly a positional good. The negative impact on a life of such a drop in intelligence would to a large extent depend on the intelligence levels of the people around him. In our world the negative impact might be minor. In a world where most people have 180 IQ, it would be substantial. Second, it makes a difference at what point in one's life one suffers the drop in IQ. For the mature painter, becoming colour blind might be debilitating. For a professional mathematician, a significant drop in IQ might be equally devastating. It might not be as harmful if it happens to an infant, if there is a reasonable range of life plans still open to her which will realize a good life.

1.12. Conclusion

Discussion of disability has sometimes taken the form of a sterile debate between essentialists who think that deviation from a species norm or other standard of normality is intrinsically bad and always merits correction, and those disability advocates and proponents of the Social Model who claim that the disadvantage due to disability is almost entirely due to social prejudice. As we have argued, proponents of the Social Model are right to think that conditions are disabling only in a certain set of circumstances. But essentialists are also partly right given that, in the circumstances obtaining in our world and in the likely future, even if we were able to largely remove the effects of social prejudice it would still be better if many commonly recognized disabilities were prevented or corrected.

In this chapter we presented, developed, and defended the welfarist account of disability. This account is not an analysis of the everyday concept. The everyday concept is defective, and our account is one way of correcting it. It singles out a normative concept we need anyway, and which preserves what is worth preserving in the existing notion. Our

---

[64] See e.g. G. D. Batty, E. L. Mortensen, et al., 'Childhood IQ in Relation to Later Psychiatric Disorder Evidence from a Danish Birth Cohort Study', *British Journal of Psychiatry*, 187 (2005) 180–1; and R. Veenhoven, 'Findings on Happiness and Intelligence', *World Database of Happiness* (2003), from www.eur.nl/fsw/research/happiness.

account shifts the debate to what really carries the normative weight in this area: the concept of well-being.

If we want the welfarist account to most closely overlap the existing concept, we could formulate it to include the threshold limit and the relation to lack of ability. However, since these constraints don't mark genuine normative distinctions, our own preference is for a broader notion:

Disability$_{W-DT}$

A stable physical or psychological property of subject S that tends to reduce S's level of well-being in circumstances C, when contrasted with a realistic alternative, *excluding* the effect that this condition has on well-being that is due to prejudice against S by members of S's society due to the deviation of this property from the normal functioning of the species to which S belongs

This formulation singles out a widespread source of harm. It gives no weight to normality or to typical species functioning. We all suffer from various disabilities$_W$, to varying degrees, and we all have reasons to try to remove or reduce them, whether by changing ourselves or by changing our environment.

2

Disability, Adaptation, and Inclusion

NORMAN DANIELS, SUSANNAH ROSE, AND ELLEN DANIELS ZIDE

2.1. Introduction

In 2004 one of us (N.D.) attended a presentation by trainees (i.e. patients) in a prominent brain trauma treatment program where another of us (E.D.Z.) works as assistant director of clinical services. The presentation marks the mid-point of a twenty-week cycle or training period. In front of an audience of family, friends, and treating professionals, trainees describe their impairments and the motor, sensory, cognitive, and emotional problems they cause. They explain what compensatory skills they have learned in the training program. They then express their hopes for how what they have learned will enable them to carry on with their new, often dramatically altered, plans for their lives. A striking point about these emotionally moving presentations is that the trainees must focus on the permanence of the limitations that result from their brain injuries in order to invoke the lifelong coping strategies they must apply.

The presentation provoked several questions that are the focus of this paper. How does adaptation to the same kind of permanent impairment, and the disability that results from it, vary across individuals? Perhaps more important for policy purposes, does adaptation vary across different kinds of impairments? Specifically, if brain-injured trainees with cognitive and emotional impairments must focus awareness on their limitations in order to function better, does that make adaptation and satisfaction with the results different than it is for people with sensory or motor deficits? Similarly, how does the constellation of cognitive and affective symptoms of people with clinical depression influence the adaptive process?

The answers to these questions have implications for what we term the 'standard story' about adaptation that is commonly found in the literature on health state evaluations. The standard story is that people with long-term experience of a condition give higher evaluations of what life is like—that is, higher ratings of the utility they experience in it—than people with no direct experience of the health state and for whom the evaluation of the health state is merely hypothetical. Arguably, assuming the standard story is generally true, people with ongoing experience with a condition provide higher utility ratings because they commonly adapt well to their illnesses and disabilities. They have had time to learn techniques and skills that help them cope with the loss of certain functions. They may also have altered their expectations and preferences so that what they can do provides gratification or satisfaction with life compared to what they might have had without any impairment. In contrast, people who merely imagine themselves in such conditions focus only on the losses they would experience and do not envision such positive adaptation. If, however, the standard story is not so standard, and, for example, people with brain injuries or depression have more difficulty adapting because of the nature of their impairments and of the treatments and rehabilitation appropriate to them, then the gap between evaluations based on experience and merely hypothetical ones might not be similar to other cases of disability.

The challenge to the standard story is of empirical importance because, from both treatment and policy perspectives, we need to understand the factors affecting adaptation to chronic illness and other impairments in order to provide better care. But it is also of normative importance. The gap between people experiencing disability and those asked to evaluate it hypothetically has received considerable attention in the literature on the ethical issues raised by cost-effectiveness analysis, since judgments about the priority assigned to preventing or treating a given impairment will vary depending on whose evaluations are used. A challenge to the standard story thus has some implications for the construction and use of cost-effectiveness analysis.[1] Though we touch briefly on this matter later,

---

[1] At one level, the focus on this issue of whose evaluations to use is misguided since it would be ethically unacceptable to deny lifesaving treatment to those with prior disabilities simply because the

we are here primarily concerned about the implications of the challenge to the standard story for how we should conceptualize disability and for how we should think about advocacy on behalf of people with disabilities.

Suppose there is considerable variation in the quality of adaptation and satisfaction with it across impairments, as the poignant but necessary awareness of their deficits in the case of brain-injured trainees suggests. Then, we shall argue, it seems less likely that that disability should primarily be seen solely or even primarily as the consequence of social exclusion, as some historically important versions of a purely social model of disability claim (Oliver 1996).[2] On such views, it is not a deficit in functioning (an impairment) that causes disability, but the social exclusion of people with such impairments. If, contrary to the standard story, different impairments produce different levels of adaptation, then we would have to determine whether the variation in adaptation is better explained by variation in the levels or kinds of exclusion, as the social model would have it, or by both the impairment and exclusion, as critics of the purely social model would claim. In fact, we shall argue that more attention must be paid to the impairments that impact functioning and contribute to disability than is allowed in the purely social model.[3] This implication does not presuppose a necessary connection between the standard story and extreme forms of the social model. But it does presuppose that the standard story makes it seem more plausible that the whole focus of advocacy should be on social exclusion since, regardless of the kind of impairment, people standardly and successfully adapt with time to the impairments they have. If, however, variation in impairment is associated with variation in adaptation, it seems more plausible that the impairment has something to do with the disability to which people must adapt.

To explore this claim, we first describe two (disguised) cases of brain-injured patients who received intensive treatment. These illustrative cases

disability would remain after the life was saved; this is true regardless of whose evaluations are used. At another level, the issue is connected to a deeper problem for cost-effectiveness analysis that we return to later.

[2] Though Oliver's (1996) statement of the social model is stronger than versions we take less exception to, his formulation greatly advanced advocacy for people with disabilities in the United Kingdom and is reasonably viewed as a leading statement of that polar position, even if it is no longer representative of those who emphasize social contributions to disability (as we do, too).

[3] Our argument supports a view closer in spirit to the WHO International Classification of Functioning, Disability and Health (ICF) to which we briefly return later.

suggest why the standard story may not so readily apply for these kinds of impairment. We then survey the social science literature on health state evaluations to assess the evidence for the standard story We also highlight several studies investigating quality of life and/or health state utilities specific to brain injury and clinical depression, since we do not want to rest our case against the generality of the standard story on disguised cases alone. Finally, we turn to some of the implications of challenging the standard story for the conceptualization of disability and for the focus of advocacy.

2.2. Brain Injury, Impairment, and Adaptation: Two Cases

To illustrate what kinds of impairment are involved in brain injury, we begin with descriptions of N.E. and G.Z. We describe some aspects of the treatment in the Brain Injury Day Treatment Program they both went through, explaining why it is so important to build awareness of impairments in order to permit the use of coping strategies. We also note some of the factors that bear on differences in the outcomes for them and outcomes, concluding with some lessons that might be drawn from these cases.

N.E. sustained a closed head injury in a motor vehicle accident in the first year of graduate studies in architecture. She was an accomplished and highly competitive undergraduate student and was employed successfully for two years, in preparation for her graduate studies. After her injury and initial hospitalization, she spent approximately a year in a combination of in-patient and out-patient rehabilitation, relearning how to walk, feed, and care for herself with a combination of occupational therapy, physical therapy, and speech therapies.

N.E. had the classic constellation of neuro-behavioral and cognitive deficits that are associated with a moderately severe frontal lobe injury. She was inattentive, impulsive, and irritable (disinhibitive phenomena), had difficulty formulating clear, targeted, and organized statements; and required assistance to safely accomplish most activities of daily living because of her deficient executive function—roughly, organizational—skills. Her frontal lobe injury caused her to be unaware of her deficits and her memory difficulties caused her to forget that she was unaware. Because she would forget that she had deficits, she would also forget that she needed to use compensatory strategies to work around her problems. Moreover, her combined unawareness and memory difficulties also made her resistant to the coaching suggestions she required to become more aware of her cognitive limitations and to re-learn how to self-monitor her behaviour.

N.E.'s rehabilitation in a therapeutic community setting helped her to become more aware of her difficulties, while drawing inspiration from her peers. Gradually she learned how to compensate for some of her more basic deficits, including her impulsivity and irritability, as well as her attentional deficits. In turn, she was gradually able to process information more accurately and formulate her responses in a more clear and concise manner. N.E's behaviour became more controlled and her interpersonal relationships more mature; she reported that her friends from before her injury were now viewing her more as the 'old N.' (though she continued to feel inadequate around them).

N.E.'s single focus after rehabilitation was to return to graduate school. During her rehabilitation, under the staff's direction, she enrolled in an undergraduate course in psychology (her undergraduate major). She received significant support from the coaching staff, including help with preparing a study plan, reading and discussing assignments, and outlining her papers. Though she successfully completed the single course, she was also able to accept that she must postpone a return to her studies and focus instead on learning how habitually to apply her strategies in her daily life so that she would become more self-reliant and able to work.

Unawareness has the ability to insulate individuals from the enormity of their losses. Eventually, as N.E. became more aware, she also became more depressed and filled with a sense of dread because she was forced to accept the painful reality that her intellectual ability, which she had always relied on, was now diminished. Her career path was also inextricably altered and, in turn, her financial and personal security dramatically reduced.

N.E. was helped by staff to shift into a clerically-based vocational trial in a work setting. With the assistance of a vocational coach from the program, she developed a set of marketable skills that earned her a part-time (12 hour/week) position. The part-time position permitted her to have enough time to practice and make habitual the compensatory skills she required to live more competently and self-reliantly.

Since her discharge from the program, N.E. claimed that she 'released' her 'fixation' on her prior career and has continued to be successfully employed on a part-time basis. Nevertheless, she again returned to school, applied on her own to a graduate program, and put into place a full slate of accommodations (e.g. a reduced course load, tutoring both at school and at home to help her organize her schedule). Despite the accommodations, she was forced to withdraw from one of her two courses, and, while she successfully completed the other course, has now withdrawn from the program. This recent failure in graduate school unleashed a generalized regression in N.E.'s functioning, including a sense of failure, embarrassment, and lowered self-esteem. According to the clinicians guiding her rehabilitation, her future stable emotional adjustment will depend upon her ability to make peace with her limitations and find value in her current capabilities and accomplishments.

There are some important similarities and differences between N.E. and G.Z., who sustained a severe traumatic brain injury in a motorcycle accident. He was 27 years old and owned a highly successful investment brokerage company with close to 200 employees, including many of his family members. He was a 'risk taker' by self-description and accustomed to 'life in the fast lane.' Although never interested in academics, he was a college graduate (business). He characterized himself as the 'kid who never sat still,' someone who was adept at reading people, but with no altruistic interests or any tolerance for deficiencies in others. At the time of his injury his marriage of three years was dissolving, and he was separated from his wife and 6-month-old child.

As is characteristic of many frontal lobe injured patients, G.Z. was entirely unaware of changes in his behavior and thinking. His injury, in particular his disinhibition syndrome, nevertheless caricatured aspects of his pre-injury personality style. It rendered him highly impulsive, irritable, emotionally unregulated and vulnerable to errors in judgment. It was his good fortune to have a very trusting relationship with his parents and to be sufficiently malleable upon entering rehab (at the insistence of his parents) that he could take 'on faith' the recommendations of the rehabilitation professionals for problems he could not see himself.

Accustomed pre-injury to single-trial learning, reliable judgment, and a remarkable ability to 'trouble shoot,' G.Z. had to adjust to the tedious, slow pace of rehabilitation. He also had to adjust to the fact that unexpected changes or any kind of stress caused him, post-injury, to become impulsive, cognitively overloaded, or 'flooded' with emotions. The effect was to make him incapable of thinking clearly—or safely. Over the course of his intensive treatment over a two-year period, however, he developed an awareness of his multiple cognitive and neurobehavioral deficits. He became a diligent student of rehabilitation, reliably using strategies and seeking coaching from his parents once he realized—and accepted—that he was often unaware, in the moment, of how he was coming across and that his combination of his deficits made him likely to make poor decisions.

While he accepted the fact that he could never resume his business, once he left rehabilitation he was prone to become involved in what he called 'kidstuff' work, which nevertheless was beyond his current capabilities (given his constellation of deficits, which included neurofatigue, disinhibition syndrome, frontal lobe unawareness, memory and reasoning difficulties). Eventually, after several failures, he re-entered individual therapy. He trained as a volunteer peer counsellor and serves as a role model to current patients.

G.Z. is an example of a survivor of brain-injury who was able to transform his attitude about himself and achieve a new ego–identity. While he acknowledges that 'I may never be the star I once was,' he also says, 'I am productive. I feel my life has meaning—maybe more than before, because I'm helping people.' He would tell you he feels healthy, whole, and self-respecting. G.Z. is one of the few to achieve this level of self-acceptance and adjustment to the significant limitations imposed by his injury—as the story of N.E. illustrates. One factor that helped him is family support. He values highly what he is still able to achieve in that regard: he's remarried and a very involved and respected father. He also has sufficient financial resources to be able to support his family, while working as a volunteer, and he can still access the specialized kind of ongoing psychological counseling ('maintenance therapy') that helps him maintain his optimal adjustment.

Both N.E. and G.Z. illustrate the importance of receiving treatment that addresses the neurobehavioral deficits and cognitive impairments produced by their brain injuries. For many brain-injured patients this includes a frontal lobe unawareness syndrome that makes them unable to detect the profound—or subtle—behavioural and cognitive changes that alter their interpersonal and intellectual functioning. Rehabilitation that prematurely rushes patients back into their customary family roles, school, and work settings may cause them to experience unnecessary failure. Most importantly, patients must be helped to develop an awareness and understanding of the nature of their deficits, namely, the permanence of a brain injury and the fact that rehabilitation is *not* 'restorative.' Rather, it can only help to ameliorate problems in functioning. This awareness is pivotal to their becoming willing to adopt the necessary, *lifelong* compensatory strategies and developing realistic expectations, based on the limitations imposed by the injury. This holistic model also addresses the patient's acceptance of their changed circumstances, gradually helping them recover a sense of confidence and competence, which are the building blocks for a stable emotional adjustment (which includes the calm acceptance of the permanence of the brain injury, maintaining a positive outlook, and improvement of one's morale and self-esteem).

Nevertheless, there is no certainty, as N.E. reveals, about what makes it possible for some rehabilitants to become the genuine 'winners' (and not just survivors). The 'winners' are the ones who are able to change their 'yardsticks' for how they measure their current achievements, no longer measuring themselves against their past accomplishments. They can learn to find meaning in their current capabilities and feel productive, even if the work is dramatically below their previous level—as G.Z.'s voluntary work clearly is. Nor is it clear just what personality characteristics allow for this transformation; some are just better equipped to make peace with their devastating losses and accept their existential situation. Some are helped by their spirituality. We also know that family members must be active partners in the process, for *their* acceptance of limitations and realistic expectations is often critical. Money also helps, as G.Z.'s case shows. Some patients are 'luckier' for they have retained enough of their previous personalities to be still recognizable to their loved ones; this consistency in personality often makes it easier for trainees' loved ones to emotionally connect and be supportive. Many, such as those whose impairments radically transform their personalities, are just not that fortunate.[4]

---

[4] There is an extensive literature on 'resiliency,' which is defined in one review article as: 'a dynamic process encompassing positive adaptation within the context of significant adversity' (Luthar, Cicchetti, and Becker 2000: 543). Though we cannot discuss this topic extensively here, Luthar et al. and Carver (1998) discuss the factors that may be associated with positive adaptation to adversity.

Several key lessons emerge. Both N.E. and G.Z. underwent similar intensive training to focus awareness on their impairments so that they could invoke appropriate, learned coping strategies. Even with the coping strategies, their impairments mean radically changed capabilities and significantly altered plans of life. Neither can function in the cognitive and socially complex ways they did before their injuries. N.E. and G.Z. adapted less and more successfully, respectively, to these changes for reasons that have more to do with differences in temperament and resources than treatment or the nature of their injuries.

2.3. Health State Evaluations and the Standard Story

2.3.1. Mixed evidence

Case studies like those of N.E. and G.Z. give us reason to question the standard story that people actually living with an illness or disability rate the health utility[5] of that condition as higher than people with no direct experience of the health state and who are merely considering what life would be like in that condition. But anecdotal evidence cannot counter evidence from proper studies. So how strong and comprehensive is the evidence for the standard story?

In reviewing the literature on this subject, we find that the most often cited studies are ones that confirm this standard story. One of the most famous of these studies found that people paralyzed in an accident were only moderately less happy compared to the happiness of a control group, and, more strikingly, compared to a group of lottery winners (Brickman, Coates, and Janoff-Bulman 1978). Another seminal study by Sackett and Torrance (1978) found that people on dialysis provided higher valuations of life on dialysis than did the general public who imagined what life would be like on dialysis (the *hypothetical* condition). There are other studies that find similar results with various health conditions, including cancer (Dominitz and Provenzale 1997; Hall et al. 1992; O'Connor 1989; Slevin et al. 1990),

---

[5] Health state valuations are primarily conducted by administering an assessment of *health state utility* regarding a specific disease or disability state. 'Utilities are cardinal values that are assigned to each health state on a scale that is established by assigning a value of 1.0 to being healthy and 0.0 to being dead. The utility values reflect the quality of the health states and allow morbidity and mortality improvements to be combined into a single weighted measure' (Torrance 1986: 8).

having a colostomy (Boyd et al. 1990), Gaucher Disease (Clarke et al. 1997), and rheumatoid arthritis (Hurst et al. 1994).

However, not all studies support the *standard story*. De Wit, Busschbach and De Charro (2000) reviewed the literature on the differences in health state valuations, and they write:

> the results of the 38 studies [reviewed] do not facilitate an unequivocal conclusion on the subject. Twenty-seven of the 38 studies concluded that patient values are different or sometimes different from other groups' values. Eleven studies found no differences in values between rater groups. The studies reporting differences in valuations found in general that patients gave higher values than other groups: 22 studies reported higher patient values, two reported lower patient values, and three studies found contradictory results.   (De Wit et al. 2000: 110)

Another study, which conducted a meta-analysis of thirty-three studies, concluded that there are no statistical differences between the utility ratings of patients and the general population (Dolders et al. 2006). This is the first study, to our knowledge, to analyze statistically the results of many studies on this subject. It is interesting to note that the standard story is not fully supported in this analysis. These studies indicate that the standard story may accurately represent some health conditions in some studies, but not all conditions may be included in this representation. For example, other studies have not found statistically significant, consistent differences in average ratings between patients with a condition and other people's hypothetical ratings, including health state valuations for suffering a stroke (Dorman et al. 1997; Wolfson et al. 1982) and schizophrenia (Revicki, Shakespeare, and Kind 1996).

2.3.2. *Why do experience-based and hypothetical evaluations differ according to the standard story?*

In this section, we leave aside the fact that there is only mixed empirical evidence for the standard story and examine what mechanisms might underlie it in those cases where it does apply. Understanding these mechanisms may help us understand better why some kinds of disability, such as brain injury or depression, might differ in ways that affect the pattern of adaptation. Accordingly, where the standard story seems to apply, why is there a gap in health state evaluations between people with experience and the general public? Several reasons have been discussed in the literature: patient adaptation, and other factors, such as response shift and methodological issues (Ubel, Loewenstein, and Jepson 2003).

2.3.2.1. Patient adaptation   One key reason patients may rate their health state utilities as higher than the general public does is that people with the condition adapt well to it, and so have a good quality of life. Therefore, their health state valuations are relatively high. People who only hypothetically consider the same condition may underestimate the prospects of such positive adaptation (for discussion of methodology, see page 67, note 7).

Some researchers have speculated whether or not patients with medical conditions are really experiencing good adaptation and mood. Riis et al. (2005) investigated three possible sources of this discrepancy which relate to adaptation to illness: 'misestimation of the impact of illness or disability by healthy people, overstatement of [positive] mood experiences by patients, and understatement of [negative] mood experiences by healthy people [which they then project onto others, including people with disabilities]' (p. 4). These authors conclude that among the end-stage renal patients receiving hemodialysis and the healthy matched control participants studied, 'there was little indication that patients exaggerate their mood. In fact, their expectations and recollection were quite accurate' (p. 7), and patients appeared to have adapted well to their illness. Importantly, however, 'healthy people grossly underestimate sick people's measured quality of emotional experience' (p. 8). This study supports the notion that people with a disability cope well with their disability and that other people without the condition may fail to accurately predict this positive adaptation.

Another study by Damschroder, Zikmund-Fisher, and Ubel (2005) assessed whether the 'failure of non-patients to consider a patient's ability to adapt to a chronic illness' is at the heart of findings in previous studies that show non-patients rate quality of life (QOL) as lower than patients diagnosed with chronic diseases. The researchers believe that non-patients may focus too heavily on the shock of imagining the impact of an initial diagnosis of paraplegia and may not be considering the longer-term outcomes. These researchers asked participants to respond to survey where they conducted person trade-off (PTO) decisions regarding treatment decisions to save the lives of patients with either pre-existing paraplegia or new onset of paraplegia. In order to urge participants to fully consider the possibility of adaptation to paraplegia, a portion of the

359 participants were randomized to an 'adaptation exercise.' This exercise asked participants to think about how they personally adapted to negative life events, and also how they would emotionally cope to being paraplegic over time. Interestingly, the adaptation exercise significantly closed the gap between the value people placed on saving disabled people versus saving healthy people, and between saving the lives of people with a pre-existing condition versus a new-onset of a disabling condition; this effect was most profound for increasing the value of saving people with new onset of paraplegia. This study suggests that 'asking non-patients to do an adaptation exercise before giving QOL ratings may help close the gap in ratings between patients and citizen non-patients' (p. 267). Furthermore, another study found that helping general public participants appreciate how one can adapt to an illness did increase their ratings of QOL of particular disabilities—supporting the fact that healthy respondents do tend to underestimate the power of adaptation to illness, but their perceptions might be changed given a chance to consider methods of positive adaptation (Ubel, Loewenstein, and Jepson 2005).

2.3.3. Focusing illusion

Another hypothesis about the gap posits a 'focusing illusion': if healthy people who are asked to consider the QOL associated with various health states focus on narrow aspects of the disease, particularly on how they think their lives will change as a result of a disease, but they do not focus on all the aspects of their lives which would remain practically unchanged, they may rate the condition worse than those who experience it and are not so focused. However, Ubel and colleagues (Ubel et al. 2001; Ubel, Loewenstein, and Jepson 2005) did not find evidence that healthy participants use the focusing illusion in their responses to evaluating hypothetical chronic disabilities.

2.3.3.1. *Response shift*[6] Sprangers and Schwartz (1999) claim that a response shift is a mediator of adaptation to illness and 'involves changing

---

[6] In this paper, we are using the term 'response shift,' which is used by certain authors in the literature as we describe above. However, according to personal correspondence with Peter Ubel (Nov. 27, 2007), using this term has been criticized by some researchers because it uses one label to describe very different mechanisms, including circumstances where people actually do not adapt (such as scale recalibration) and others where people actually do adapt well.

internal standards, values and the conceptualization of quality of life' (p. 1507). For example, people with a disability may compare their well-being to others who are perceived to be worse-off than themselves; by using such 'downward social comparison,' people with the disability may think of themselves as better-off and therefore report good ratings of well-being. This contributes to response shifts based on scale recalibration—people are using a different basis (a worse one) for evaluations of their health/well-being. Another illustration of a response shift is when people with medical problems shift their focus to other parts of their life; for example, a physically disabled person might focus more on academic interests, and this change in focus might be adaptive. Response shifts may explain why people who experience health problems rate their quality of life as higher than hypothetical patients rate the same condition, and as higher than what medical professionals think they have.

However, response shifts can also be maladaptive. In cases where people will suffer an inevitable decline, or if they feel they have little control of the salient features of the downward social comparison, then they will feel worse. Such a negative response shift is more likely to occur when people are depressed, and conversely, less likely to occur if someone is particularly optimistic (Sprangers and Schwartz 1999). Although this has not been empirically assessed, we speculate that people with brain injuries may not be cognitively able to engage in such comparisons. And, even if they can, they may experience worsened sense of well-being when comparing themselves to others because they may not have a good functional prognosis. Furthermore, people with brain injuries may have deficits that impact multiple, or most, aspects of their lives, making it difficult for them to focus on components of their lives that they feel compare positively to other people's lives. An adaptive response shift is less likely to occur in this circumstance.

2.3.3.2. Study methodologies   Some researchers have claimed that the methods used for evaluating health state utilities may contribute to inaccurate utility ratings (Ubel et al. 2003; Dolders et al. 2006). Potential methodological problems are related to: inconsistencies due to limitation in human judgment (such as framing effects, anchoring effects, labeling effects, and outcome description effects), and inconsistencies due to situation-specific variables (including information on the prognosis of the condition, descriptions of hypothetical patients, mode of presentation of the health states to respondents; Froberg and Kane 1989). For example, labeling effects occur when the label used to describe the hypothetical health state alter the average utility ratings assigned to a health state. In the study conducted by Sackett and Torrance (1978), the disease label used in the health state descriptions did affect utility ratings, but the direction of the relationship between the label and the utility rating was not consistent. For example, 'cancer' resulted in lower utility ratings than did an unlabeled illness resulting in the same level of disability. However, the label 'tuberculosis' seemed to have little effect on ratings. Additionally, the actual scales used for rating health state utilities may inadvertently alter people's ratings, producing inconsistent, and potentially inaccurate results (Dolders et al. 2006). There are several common methods used to assess health state utilities, including the Standard Gamble (SG), Time Trade-off (TTO), and Person Trade-off (PTO) methods. Although the specific methods may vary, we want to present some of the general assessment methods used in the studies we discuss.[7]

So far, we have been discussing inter-group variation in utility ratings; that is, the differences between people with a disabling condition and those hypothetically considering life with such a condition. However, it is important to note that there is evidence that *intra*-group variability in utility ratings is also high, which has methodological implications as

---

[7] SG utility ratings are created by asking people to choose their preference between two health states. 'The first alternative offers the certainty of staying in the described health state for the remainder of the respondent's life. The second alternative is a gamble with specified probabilities for both the positive outcome of the gamble (a normal health state for the remainder of the time) and the negative outcome (immediate death)' (De Wit et al. 2000: 112). The TTO method asks people if they would give up some proportion of the remainder of their lives in order to 'improve an impaired health state to normal health' (De Wit et al, 2000: 112). PTO utility elicitation is derived from asking people to consider a choice between two treatment programs—for example, one will save the lives of 100 healthy people, and the other will save the lives of people with new onset of paraplegia. People choose an indifference point where they would consider the number of people in each category where the outcomes would be equally good (Damscroder et al. 2005).

Additionally, health state valuations can be assessed directly from people experiencing certain medical conditions or disabilities by evaluations of quality of life. 'Health-related quality of life (QOL) refers to the extent to which a person's usual or expected physical, emotional and social well-being are affected by a medical condition or its treatment' (Cella 1995). QOL is *subjective*, meaning that QOL is an individual patient's interpretation of his or her own functioning. It is important to note that QOL assessments are distinct from the utility assessments described above in many respects. One important distinction is that QOL instruments are used to directly assess people with a medical condition or disability, and are not typically used in eliciting evaluations from the general public about hypothetical conditions.

well as practical ones. For example, Sackett and Torrance (1978) found a large standard deviation (.30 on a 0–1 scale) for the distribution of health preferences by the study participants (both chronic renal failure patients and members of the general public). In referring to this study and others, Froberg and Kane assert the following:

> Since empirical evidence suggests that these individual differences cannot be adequately explained by variables such as age, sex, socio-economic status, religion, illness, and other personal characteristics, the more important questions may involve the implications of using an average weight to represent a particular population. Perhaps, we should be as concerned about the variability of preferences within groups as we have been about variability between groups.   (1989: 587)

This quote brings us back to the beginning of our paper where we asked whether adaptation varies across individuals who have the same kind of impairment. Indeed, these studies do seem to demonstrate that people with long-term conditions vary in their stated quality of life and assigned utility ratings, and this variation is important to consider when accurately capturing the range of people's adaptation. Taking the average or other summary scores of utility or quality of life measurements may miss this important point: some people do well adapting to a disability and some people do not.

The standard story may also rest upon a sample bias across the studies on this topic. Specifically, it is possible that the types of medical issues and disabilities used in the studies may not be representative of all conditions. In fact, one criticism relevant to the current focus on long-term disability is that many of the studies on utility ratings focus on short-term medical illnesses, and relatively few on long-term disabilities. Additionally, we have emphasized the fact that there is an absence of studies comparing personal and hypothetical utility ratings of traumatic brain injury and major depression.

2.3.4. Why would TBI and depression be different?

There are some conditions that may deviate significantly from the standard story. Specifically, people suffering from depression or traumatic brain injury (TBI) may rate their health state as lower than people hypothetically imagining the situation.

2.3.4.1. Depression   Appealing to a cognitive conceptualization of psychopathology, clinical depression is the result of an individual having

'a negative view of the self, the world, and the future, and perceiv[ing] the self as inadequate, deserted, and worthless' (Beck and Weishaar 1995: 239). Depression tends to be associated with pessimistic views about one's life and with low ratings of quality of life (Papakostas et al. 2004). However, people who do not have experience with depression may underestimate the negative effects of this disease and therefore provide higher health state utility ratings than people with the condition would provide. In fact, in a study by Williams and colleagues (1995; EuroQoL Group I), participants from the general population (based on TTO utility valuations) seemed to underestimate the seriousness of depression and mood disorders, rating depression similarly to less severe forms of disability (such as not being able to wash or dress oneself). It is also important to note that depression is by definition associated with a loss of subjective well-being (Paul Dolan, personal correspondence, June 2007); therefore, depressed individuals would be predicted to rate themselves low on utility ratings (which are intended to evaluate well-being or happiness).

In an extensive search of the literature, no studies were found which directly compare health state utilities for depression between people with depression and the general public. In the absence of such a study, we looked for clues in the literature that suggest such a difference. One study, conducted by Revicki and Wood (1998) did assess the health state utilities of depression among seventy people diagnosed with major depressive disorder. They found that the severity of the depression is significantly inversely related to utility ratings. Specifically, using the SG technique, major depression was given an average utility rating of .30 and '25% of patients rated this state as worse than or equivalent to death' (p. 25).[8] Interestingly, the patients rated their own health states at .74, which, according to these authors, is higher than some medical conditions, but lower than others (p. 34). It is also important to remember that the participants in this study were undergoing treatment for depression, and, on average, people without such treatment may rate their own health state utilities as even lower than did these participants.[9] Predictably,

---

[8] The utility ratings for moderate depression were between .55 and .63, and mild depression was rated the highest, with a range of .64–.73.

[9] We emphasize 'on average' in this statement so as not to discount the possibility that some people who receive treatment for depression may gain more insight into their condition or potentially become more depressed.

people with more serious depression rated their current health state utilities as lower than people with less severe disease. Importantly, the authors conclude that 'the utility state for severe depression was .30 suggesting that patients valued this health state lower than utilities reported in the literature for chronic medical diseases . . . and that patient preferences for severe to moderate depression [are] lower than or comparable to those for serious medical diseases' (p. 33).

Bennett and colleagues (Bennett et al. 2000) have described the use of a new measure of direct utility for depression, the McSad. At this time, however, this instrument has been used to directly assess utility among people with depression, but not (to our knowledge) in comparison with the general population. Interestingly, on a scale of 0–1 (indicating death to perfect health), the respondents (who had a six-month history of depression) rated the utility of having mild depression as .59, moderate depression as .32, and severe depression as .09—the latter is strikingly low; for people who reported a *lifetime* duration of severe depression, they rated the utility of their health state as even lower, merely .04. These two studies demonstrate that people with depression may suffer considerably from this disease; however, we do not know if the general public would rate depression differently than people suffering from this condition. Future empirical studies need to be conducted to test our hypothesis that people with depression will provide lower average utility ratings than people hypothetically considering this health state.

2.3.4.2. Traumatic Brain Injury To our knowledge, there are no studies that compare health state utilities related to traumatic brain injury between experienced and hypothetical evaluators. We believe that this is also a gap in the literature and needs to be empirically explored. However, in reviewing the literature on QOL associated with TBI, one may reasonably hypothesize that people with TBI may rate their QOL as lower than people from the general public who are asked to imagine what life is like with TBI. We outline our rationale below.

Unlike people with physical disabilities which leave cognitive processes intact, people with TBI who learn to adapt to their illness may, in fact, rate their QOL as lower than those who may not be adapting as well with their injury. This may be the case because a crucial part of the rehabilitation process is that TBI patients *focus on their deficits* in order to better manage them. Ben-Yishnay and Daniels-Zide state that

due to the impairments of both the cognitive and emotional functions of the person with brain injury, a particular task of therapy is to help the person become aware of and understand the nature and the functional consequences of his or her problems as much as possible in concrete, detailed terms. Awareness and understanding of one's deficits, thus, helps the person bear the restrictions.   (2000: 116)

However, learning to cope by focusing on one's deficits might have negative, as well as positive consequences. One may be able to function better in society because coping skills can better be invoked, but a possible result is that as one grows more aware of the deficits, depression may result. In a review article of QOL assessment in TBI, particularly relating to rehabilitation, Johnston and Miklos state that 'therapists try to make the persons with TBI more aware of their cognitive limitations, on theory that this will help them to compensate, but the patients may dislike this. . . . TBI is associated with decreased QOL and depression. Studies have reported very low life-satisfaction among persons with TBI' (2002: S33). The authors state that estimates of major depression range between 25% and 61%, and estimates of other psychiatric symptoms (anxiety, hostility, emotional distress, post-traumatic symptoms) are also high. Importantly, many patients report that these symptoms do not diminish, and may even worsen with time. In another study, the authors conducted literature and summarize the findings in the following statement:

[a]ffective distress may also be a reaction to the stressors and negative consequences of TBI (eg, cognitive difficulties, physical impairments, inability to work, impulsive behaviours that affect social interactions, discrimination, isolation). Individuals with TBI are more likely to experience 'reactive' depressions over time as they gain insight into their impairments. Affective distress of this kind appears to have no relationship to severity of injury or demographical variables.   (Cantor et al. 2005: 529)

Another study, by Wallace and Bogner (2000), found evidence to support a significant positive relationship between traumatically brain-injured patients' awareness of deficits and symptoms of depression/anxiety; in other words, when a brain-injured person is more aware of his deficits he is more likely to report distress. And, as we reported above, it might be reasonable to predict that TBI patients, particularly those who have depression, might rate their health state as low given the relatively low utility ratings provided by people suffering from major depression.[10]

2.3.4.3. The need for further research: There is much room for more and better quality research, comparing health state evaluations both across conditions and across the populations with and without experience of them. To assess the standard story properly, we would have to have more studies comparing hypothetical evaluations with ones based on experience across conditions—like depression and traumatic brain injury—where no direct evidence can be found. More studies investigating the source of an evaluation gap, where it exists, are needed to clarify what is at work: Failure to anticipate adaptation by hypothetical evaluators? Focusing illusions? Difference in perspective on the loss of opportunities or capabilities? Furthermore, it is important to note that the studies available in the literature assess a range of health states, and they include both short-term and long-term conditions. Because we are most interested in adaptation to chronic illness, we believe that more studies need to be conducted to fully tease out how the standard story explains long-term disabilities.

2.4. Implications for Conceptualizing Disability

The cases we describe of people with brain injuries and our review of the literature on health state evaluations suggest that the standard story may not be so standard after all. The cases suggest that people with brain injuries may experience a very different and varied course of adaptation than people with certain other disabilities, and people with depression may rate their conditions worse than those thinking about it hypothetically—though our literature review failed to find direct evidence of comparative studies for either category of conditions. In addition, the studies that do make a comparison across experienced and hypothetical evaluators for various conditions show mixed results, not uniform support for the standard story.

---

[10] However, it is important to note that this conclusion is tentative. People with coexisting medical conditions and depression may report different utility ratings and quality of life than people with only one of these disorders. Studies need to be conducted in order to accurately assess how people with TBI would rate the health state associated with their depression.

There is also far less citation of the studies that do not support the standard story, so the evidence for it looks stronger than it is. Indeed, the standard story may largely be a result of some of the ways in which the issue is framed for respondents, including the fact that hypothetical evaluators may underestimate the importance of adaptation. In short, we should be cautious about treating the standard story as so standard, and we later return to highlight some points about further research that it would be important to undertake. As we noted earlier, a better understanding of the process of adaptation across different impairments could improve patient care.

Our interest, however, lies primarily in the normative and conceptual implications of this challenge to the standard story. One context in which the standard story has acquired the status of received knowledge is in the literature on the ethical implications of cost-effectiveness analysis for people with disabilities. If, as in the standard story, people with disabilities rank the utility of living with their condition higher than the community as a whole, then community-based ratings may not only be mistaken about the quality of life with such a disability, but they may be based on stigmatizing or stereotyped community views of disability that will lead to forms of discrimination against people with disabilities. This charge was the basis of the original denial by Secretary of Health and Human Services, Louis Sullivan, of Oregon's application for a Medicaid waiver in 1992 (Fox and Leichter 1993). The contention was that the use of community-based ratings of health states risked importing anti-disability bias and stigma into the prioritizing of condition–treatment pairs for funding and thus violated the Americans with Disabilities Act.

The concern about discrimination in cost-effectiveness analysis is based on the following kind of case: a life-saving intervention aimed at a person with a prior disability would gain less health benefit per dollar spent if the hypothetical or community evaluations were used than if experienced evaluations are used. We thus risk discriminating against saving the lives of those whose lives are well worth saving if we use the more negative evaluations that derive from hypothetical judgments. Conversely, if we use the more positive evaluation of those who experience the conditions and adapt to them, then judgments about preventive interventions for these conditions will be given less importance than they would have if we used the more negative hypothetical evaluations. To get ethically justifiable outcomes, where the standard story applies, we would have to consider the prior disabling condition of those whose lives can be saved by an intervention as irrelevant to judgments about whom to save. We would also have to insist that, where prevention is at issue, we should judge the hypothetical evaluation as capturing a concern about a real loss that is worth preventing even if people with experience ignore the loss in their evaluations. Where the standard story is not true for some conditions, then we might well adhere to our ethically justifiable outcomes anyway. The standard story might thus seem largely irrelevant to when we judge a life worth saving or a health state worth preventing, as we noted earlier.

The concern that cost-effectiveness analysis is committed to discrimination against people with disabilities actually has a deeper source than the issue of whose evaluations of health states to use.[11] Consider two very different choices we might face. Suppose we imagine two people, A and B, in equally poor health. A can be treated and end up in moderate health while B can be treated and end up in good health. If we are healthy and are asked to imagine ending up in the situation of A or B, we clearly would think it worse to end up as A—that outcome involves a bigger loss of health. Suppose, however, that we are asked to imagine that we are A and that we face the same need for treatment as B. Now we would not agree that B should have priority over us in receiving treatment—it is equally important to each of us that we get the treatment we need, even if the outcome is different. The point goes beyond the case of lifesaving treatments and is quite general. Yet cost-effectiveness analysis imposes the constraint that we arrive at mathematically consistent answers to these two questions based on very different situations. Mathematical consistency here comes at the expense of forcing us to ignore A's perspective—or we have to make an ad hoc exception to the implications of the methodology. The deeper ethical issue facing cost effectiveness analysis thus does not turn on whose evaluations of health states we use, and thus is not affected by our challenge to the standard story.

We turn instead to the main point of challenging the standard story. If the standard story is not true, or if it is true only for some disabilities, then we may want to reject, or at least to modify and strongly qualify, a widely

---

[11] One of us (ND) is indebted to discussions with Erik Nord that are drawn on in this paragraph; similar points are contained in a presentation Erik Nord made, based on these discussions, at a workshop on cost-effectiveness analysis sponsored by ISPOR in Philadelphia, November 9, 2007.

held theory of how we should conceptualize disabilities. Were the standard story generally true, we might think it more plausible that physical and mental impairments can generally be adapted to quite successfully. That is, regardless of the kind of impairment they may have, people adapt in a typical (standard) way. In effect, the impairments do not seem to matter much; regardless of what they are, they are manageable. If they do not matter or influence the situation very much, then it seems to make it more plausible that the fundamental source of disadvantage in the case of disabilities is not impairment but the social exclusion of people perceived to have disabilities. The disadvantage that attaches to having impairments is, on this view, not the result of the impairments but of social attitudes and policies that exclude people with them from various education, work, and life opportunities.

One codification of this view is commonly referred to in the disability literature as the 'social model' (Oliver 1996, see n. 2 above). Proponents of the social model note that people have impairments but deny that these impairments are the source of disability or disadvantage. Thus Oliver (1996: 35, cited in Terzi 2004: 143) says 'disablement has nothing to do with the body.' Oliver (1996: 22, cited in Terzi 2004: 143) contrasts impairment, seen as the lack of 'part or all of a limb, or having a defective limb, organism or mechanism of the body' with disability, which is 'the disadvantage or restriction of activity caused by a social organization which takes no or little account of people who have physical impairments and thus excludes them from participation in the mainstream of social activities.' Another defender of the view rejects the idea that disability is susceptible to medical treatment and argues that 'it is mainly a cultural and socio-political problem' since not all people with 'losses, diseases, or illnesses etc. experience disablement' (Reindal 2000, cited in Harris 2000: 97).

The social model has had some very positive social consequences, not only in the United Kingdom where it emerged, but elsewhere in the worldwide disability rights movement. It helped galvanize advocates into focusing on and altering the social exclusion policies that create disadvant-age, directing attention outward from people with disabilities to the social environment that victimizes and excludes them. Quite commonly, the social model is articulated as a rejection of a 'biomedical model' in which a physical or mental departure from normal functioning (an impairment) is viewed as 'the' cause of disability. The incompleteness of this narrow version of a biomedical model does not mean that all biomedical models need assign only one cause to disability and disadvantage.

Conceptually, there is no reason to adopt either a narrowly biomedical model or a narrowly social model of disability (Harris 2000; Terzi 2004). Disability, on such an intermediate conception, is the result of both significant impairment and social exclusion, not just one of them. The amount of disadvantage that accompanies impairment is in general significantly influenced by social policies and attitudes. But it is also affected by the type of impairment involved. It is not a case of either/or but of both.

In an earlier WHO conceptualization of disability (1976, 1980), an impairment is viewed as 'an abnormality in the structure of the functioning of the body whether through disease or trauma,' and disability is taken to refer to the 'restriction in the ability to perform tasks' (cited in Terzi 2004: 142). The handicap that accompanies disability refers to the 'social disadvantage that could be associated with either impairment and/or disability.' This WHO conceptualization might be used in a way that views impairment as the sole cause of disability and disadvantage, but there is no reason to think that social policies and attitudes are not also contributing to disadvantage—they most clearly do. If we also take Oliver's proposal seriously, then we should try harder to see the sense in which social policy actually causally contributes to disability or disablement and not merely to disadvantage. (Harris argues that the social model confuses disability with disadvantage, but the point we are exploring is more charitable.) The current WHO International Classification of Functioning conceptualization of disability more explicitly sees disability as the result of the interaction of individuals with some health condition and their social environment.[12]

To see the point, we should take the concept of disability apart and view it as the loss of some abilities relative to what people without a particular impairment or health condition have. An example will help: Suppose someone cannot walk because of a spinal injury and becomes a person with paraplegia. We can call that person's inability to walk a

---

[12] We see our position as supportive of the spirit of the ICF framework but we do not embrace the specific wording of the proposed ICF definition: 'Disability is a difficulty in functioning at the body, person, or societal levels, in one or more life domains, as experienced by an individual with a health condition in interaction with contextual factors.' We agree that a disability is the result of the interaction of a health condition with contextual factors, but we are puzzled at the claim this is a 'difficulty in functioning . . . as experienced by an individual,' which makes disability seem more subjective than it is and more subjective than proponents of the definition intend. See Leonardi et al. 2006.

basic disability. Suppose further that he gets significant rehabilitation of various kinds and that he is also equipped with technologically advanced wheelchairs, both motorized and not. Because of the rehabilitation and technology, he can do more of the things that other people can do despite his physical impairment and basic disability. He can be mobile in many of the ways others can by walking. He can move readily around his (wheelchair-adapted) house, go shopping or to work (assuming proper ramps, doors, and other accommodations for people like him), or even engage in sports that involve mobility. He may not be capable of a basic function such as walking, but he is functionally mobile in many of the ways people who walk are.

There are, however, still some things he cannot do, such as accompany his child through the woods near his home to her school. Because the trail in the woods is not accessible to wheelchairs, he is unable to do what other parents in the neighborhood regularly do. We can think of this inability to get his child to school by accompanying her through the woods as a *secondary or consequential disability* that he has compared to others without the impairment that results in his basic disability. So far, it looks as if his impairment is 'the' cause of his disability, now conceived of as the union of his basic and consequential disabilities—but this is misleading.

However, suppose his neighborhood is very cohesive. Other parents and children care about his inability to get his child to school in the company of other children walking through the woods. They offset his secondary disability by walking his child with theirs to school through the woods. In this way he is no longer disabled relative to others in the ability to get his child to school in the way most children get there (although he cannot accompany her personally because he cannot walk and cannot be mobile in the woods in the way he is in other settings). This social cooperation and inclusion reduces his disability, for it removes some forms of disablement from his comprehensive set of basic and secondary disabilities. It does so even as it also reduces his disadvantage relative to others. We could think of this effect as simply reducing his disadvantage, leaving his disability as it was (and of course his impairment as it was). But just as a wheelchair not only reduces his disadvantage but arguably reduces his inability to function as others do—he can shop, move around an (altered) house and place of work—and thus reduces his disability, so too does the effort of his cohesive neighborhood reduce his disability and not just his disadvantage.

Arguably, the problem here is primarily semantic and not real. On one view, the disability we have discussed is adequately described as not being able to walk. Everything else is the social disadvantage that accompanies the disability. That disadvantage is reduced by use of a wheelchair and by helpful neighbors. On the other view, his disability is some set of comparisons of how he can function relative to others. His being unable to walk is one important, basic part of his disability, but his being unable to get his children to school in a standard way is a part of his disability that is only present if his neighbors fail to be as inclusive as they fortunately are. Suppose the town sent a bus for his child instead of the neighborhood effort. Arguably such a disadvantage would be removed just as when his neighbors pitch in, but he is still disabled relative to the ability of other parents to get their children to school by means of a group walk in the woods. In effect, with their help, he is able to get them his child in a typical way and so his disability is reduced. This way of understanding the impact of exclusion on disability (and not just on disadvantage) may be the intuition behind the part of the social model that we are trying to salvage, and it is reflected in the ICF view of disability as arising in the interaction of an individual with a health condition with 'contextual factors.' But it is completely separate from the unsupportable contention that *only* social exclusion creates disability.

In the cases we looked at of brain-injured people with significant impairments, success in adapting varied across individuals. N.E. fared worse than G.Z. And success in adaptation, as in the case of G.Z., does not mean a return to quality of life before injury. G.Z.'s is not the shape and content of his earlier life, nor is it similar to what might be enjoyed by someone who has a motor or sensory deficit but retains full cognitive and emotional capabilities. Indeed, with proper rehabilitation, had G.Z.'s accident resulted in paraplegia or blindness, not brain injury, he might have been able to resume the very plan of life his actual injury ended. Arguably, much of the disadvantage suffered by people with motor or sensory disabilities results from social exclusion, since so many of their other capabilities remain intact and allow them to perform the full array of complex cognitive and social tasks involved in work and other parts of life. But just as clearly, people with significant brain injuries or depression or other forms of mental illness may be disabled and disadvantaged not only by social exclusion but also by their cognitive and emotional impairments. Arguably, the impairments may be the more important factor in many of these disabilities.

Although some of the force of our argument draws on the contrast of some kinds of disability with others, not all of it does. It is important to remember that even for sensory or motor deficits, presumably included in the standard fare of the standard story, the impairment should not be ignored in thinking about the resulting disability. One strong supporter of the social model criticizes it, as a person with a significant impairment, for not 'including all of our lives,' that is for not recognizing the impact of impairment on disability (Crow 1996). The social model's silence about impairment 'prevents us from dealing effectively with the difficult aspects of impairment. Many of us remain frustrated and disheartened by pain, fatigue, depression, and chronic illness, including the way they prevent us from realizing our potential or railing fully against disability (our experience of exclusion and discrimination)' (Crow 1996). Crow still wants to view disability as the result of exclusion, as the experience of exclusion, but it seems implausible that in an ideal world, with no forms of exclusion, there would be no disability, given the ongoing impairment and its multiple effects.

It might be argued that we have misconstrued the force of the social model. Properly used, it does not ignore impairment and the need for treatment and rehabilitation, contrary to the lament in Crow's discussion. Rather, proper treatment and rehabilitation is a prerequisite for thinking about the impact of social exclusion. If this is the proper way to conceive of the social model, despite the positions taken by some of its original advocates, than we have no complaint. Our position is that disability should be conceived of as caused by both impairment and exclusion, and that view is made more plausible by noting the variability of adaptation across and within disabilities. We take this view to be supportive of the spirit of the ICF framework.

The theory of justice and health developed by one of us (Daniels 2008; 1996) provides a unified account of what we owe each other in responding to both sources of disability and its resulting impact. Since protecting health or normal functioning makes a significant (if limited) contribution to protecting opportunity, then, since we have more general obligations to protect opportunity, we owe each other a distribution of the socially controllable factors, including healthcare, that promote and protect health. Specifically, we owe each other prevention and treatment of pathology that leads to significant impairment, including appropriate rehabilitation. Where we cannot prevent or eliminate impairment or compensate for the loss of function, we owe each other reasonable measures to protect the exercisable opportunity-space of those with disabilities. This means not only reasonable accommodation in the workplace and other public settings, but broader efforts at social inclusion. Far from it being conceptually or normatively an error to admit two basic sources of disability (and disadvantage), doing so shows that we must address both sources of disadvantage because we owe each other the protection of our fair shares of exercisable opportunities.

2.5. Implications for Advocacy

We have noted the positive contribution that the social model makes in focusing the energy of advocates for disability rights on the many forms that social exclusion takes. We have no quarrel with the view that some impairments become disabilities solely as a result of some forms of social exclusion. Our argument, however, is that some impairments are clearly a contributory cause of significant disability and disadvantage. No doubt social exclusion makes these disabilities even worse for those who have them, but, even in the absence of such exclusion, the impairments remain transformative of the capabilities or opportunities it is reasonable for them to exercise. We owe people not just the strong effort at social inclusion but the proper forms of treatment and care—to say nothing of prevention—that can mitigate the degree of disability these impairments involve.

Some of the attraction of the social model may be the result of focusing on a narrow, if prevalent, set of motor and sensory disabilities. Although motor or sensory impairments mean there are some things that people with them cannot do, or cannot do in the same way as people without the impairments, proper forms of social inclusion, combined with some forms of technology where they are available, often open the door to a similar set of exercisable opportunities to that enjoyed by people without the impairments but with similar talents and skills.[13] For significant mental illness and for many brain injuries, neither existing technology nor robust social inclusion can make up for the disability that results. Still, many people with these disabilities could function much better than they do and adapt better to their situations if the intensive and expensive treatment and rehabilitation work they need were accessible to them.

The danger of versions of the purely social model that deny the important contribution of some impairments to disability is that they could lead to failure to advocate for the immediate needs of people with those disabilities. Obviously, however, one of the socially controllable factors that makes disability more severe is neglect of the impairments that also contribute to them. This issue is likely to receive some clear public attention as a result of the dramatic brain injuries suffered by many combatants in Iraq and elsewhere. Many of these thousands of casualties would not have survived in previous wars, but they now must survive in a society that often sorely neglects them, as the recent exposés of the conditions in Walter Reed Hospital and elsewhere have shown (Shane 2007). Desperate mothers of brain-injured soldiers have sought private care for their sons when they believe not enough has been done for them by the military (Winerip 2008). Proper advocacy for the soldiers damaged in a war is essential to reducing their disability and helping them adapt to their radically altered lives.

The problem is hardly isolated to the military. One of us (E.D.Z.) struggles constantly to find reimbursements for the brain-injured patients in the program in which she works. The glaring contrast between what is possible for wealthier patients from around the world and what happens to those without adequate financial or insurance coverage is a constant reminder of the need for more intensive advocacy for proper treatment for certain groups of people with disabilities.

---

[13] Similar but not identical: The person with paraplegia in our earlier example can exercise the opportunity to have his child accompanied through the woods to school, though he cannot accompany the child as some other parents can. The cohesive neighborhood improves the range of opportunities for both the parent with paraplegia and his child but fails to make them strictly identical to what others enjoy.

References

Beck, A. T., and Weishaar, C. R. (1995). Cognitive Therapy. In Raymond J. Corsini and Danny Wedding (eds.), *Current Psychotherapies*, 5th edn. Itasca, Ill.: F. E., Peacock Publishers, 229–60.

Bennett, K. J., Torrance, G. W., Boyle, M. H., and Guscott, R. (2000). Cost–Utility Analysis in Depression: The McSad Utility Measure for Depression Health States. *Psychiatric Services*, 51/9: 1171–6.

Ben-Yishay, Y., and Daniels-Zide, E. (2000). Examined Lives: Outcomes after Holistic Rehabilitation. *Rehabilitative Psychology*, 45/2: 112–29.

Boyd, N. F., Sutherland, H. J., Heasman, K. Z., Tritchler, D. L., and Cummings, B. J. (1990). Whose Utilities for Decision Analysis? *Medical Decision Making*, 10: 58–67.

Brickman, P., Coates, D., and Janoff-Bulman, R. (1978). Lottery Winners and Accident Victims: Is Happiness Relative? *Journal of Personality and Social Psychology*, 36/8: 917–27.

Cantor, J. B., Ashman, T. A., Schwartz, M. E., Gordon, W. A., Hibbard, M. R., Brown, M., Spielman, L., Charatz, H. J., and Cheng, Z. (2005). The Role of Self-Discrepancy Theory in Understanding Post-Traumatic Brain Injury Affective Disorders: A Pilot Study. *Journal of Head Trauma Rehabilitation*, 20/6: 527–43.

Carver, C. S. (1998). Resilience and Thriving: Issues, Models, and Linkages. *Journal of Social Issues*, 54/2: 245–66.

Cella, D. F. (1995) Measuring Quality of Life in Palliative Care. *Seminars in Oncology*, 22/2: 73–81.

Clarke, A. E., Goldstein, M. K., Michelson, D., Garber, A. M., and Lenert, L. A. (1997). The Effect of Assessment Method and Respondent Population on Utilities Elicited for Gaucher Disease. *Quality of Life Research*, 6: 169–84.

Crow, L. (1996). Including All of our Lives: Renewing the Social Model of Disabilities. In Colin Barnes and Geof Mercer (eds.), *Exploring the Divide*, ch. 4., pp. 55–72. Leeds: Disability Press.

Damschroder, L. J., Zikmund-Fisher, B. J., and Ubel, P. A. (2005). The Impact of Considering Adaptation in Health State Valuation. *Social Science & Medicine*, 61: 267–77.

Daniels N. (1996). Mental Disabilities, Equal Opportunity and the ADA. In Bonnie R. J, Monahan J. (eds.), *Mental Disorder, Work Disability, and the Law*. Chicago: University of Chicago Press, 282–97.

——(2008). *Just Health: Meeting Health Needs Fairly*. New York: Cambridge University Press.

De Wit, G. A., Busschbach, J. J. V., and De Charro, F. T. H. (2000). Sensitivity and Perspective in the Valuation of Health Status: Whose Values Count? *Health Economics*, 9: 109–26.

Dolders, M. G. T., Zeegers, M. P. A., Groot, W., and Ament, A. (2006). A Meta-analysis Demonstrates No Significant Differences between Patient and Population Preferences. *Journal of Clinical Epidemiology*, 59: 633–64.

Dominitz, J. A., and Provenzale, D. (1997). Patient Preferences and Quality of Life Associated with Colorectal Cancer Screening. *American Journal of Gastroenterology*, 92: 2171–8.

Dorman, P. J., Waddell, F., Slattery, J., Dennis, M., and Sandercock, P. (1997). Are Proxy Assessments of Health Status after Stroke with the EuroQol Questionnaire Feasible, Accurate, and Unbiased? *Stroke*, 28: 1883–7.

Fox, D., and Leichter, H. M.(1993). The Ups and Downs of Oregon's Rationing Plan. *Health Affairs*, 12/2: 66–70.

Froberg, D. G., and Kane, R. L. (1989). Methodology for Measuring Health-State Preferences—III: Population and Context Effects. *Journal of Clinical Epidemiology*, 42/6: 585–92.

Hall, J., Gerard, K., Salkeld, G., and Richardson, J. (1992). A Cost Utility Analysis of Mammography Screening in Australia. *Social Science and Medicine*, 34: 993–1004.

Harris J. (2000). Is there a Coherent Social Conception of Disability? *Journal of Medical Ethics*, 26: 95–100.

Human Rights Commission (1997). Definition of Disability for Human Rights Purposes. www.cupe.bc.ca/files/definition_of_disability_for_human_rights_purposes_nov_06.pdf

Hurst, N. P., Jobanputra, P., Hunter, M., Lambert, M., Lochhead, A., and Brown, H. (1994). Validity of EuroQol—A Generic Health Stature Instrument—in Patients with Rheumatoid Arthritis. *British Journal of Rheumatology*, 33: 655–62.

Johnston, M. V., and Miklos, C. S. (2002). Activity-Related Quality of Life in Rehabilitation and Traumatic Brain Injury. *Archives of Physical Medicine Rehabilitation*, 83 (Suppl 2): S26–S38.

Leonardi, M., Bickenback, J. Ustan, T. B., Kostanjsek, N., and Chaterji, S. (2006). Measurement of Health and Disability. *The Lancet*, 370/9586: 483–4.

Luthar, S. S., Cicchetti, D., and Becker, B. (2000). The Construct of Resilience: A Critical Evaluation and Guidelines for Future Work. *Child Development*, 71/3: 543–62.

O'Connor, A. M. (1989). Effects of Framing and Level of Probability on Patients' Preferences for Cancer Chemotherapy. *Journal of Clinical Epidemiology*, 42: 119–26.

Oliver, M. (1996). *Understanding Disability: From Theory to Practice*. Basingstoke: Palgrave.

Papakostas, G. I., Petersen, T., Mahal, Y., Mischoulon, D., Nierenberg, A. A., and Fava, M. (2004) Quality of Life Assessments in Major Depressive Disorder: A Review of the Literature. *General Hospital Psychiatry*, 26/1:13–17.

Polsky, D., Willke, R. J., Scott, K., Schulman, K. A., and Glick, H. (2001). A Comparison of Scoring Weights for the EuroQol Derived from Patients and the General Public. *Health Economics*, 10: 27–37.

Reindal, S. M. (2000). Disability, Gene Therapy and Eugenics—A Challenge to John Harris. *Journal of Medical Ethics*, 26: 95–100.

Revicki, D. A., and Wood, M. (1998). Patient-Assigned Health State Utilities for Depression-Related Outcomes: Differences by Depression Severity and Antidepressant Medications. *Journal of Affective Disorders*, 48: 25–36.

——— Shakespeare, A., and Kind, P. (1996). Preferences for Schizophrenia-Related Health States: A Comparison of Patients, Caregivers and Psychiatrists. *International Clinical Psychopharmacology*, 11: 101–8.

Riis, J., Loewenstein, G., Baron, J., Jepson, C., Fagerlin, A., and Ubel, P.A. (2005). Ignorance of Hedonic Adaptation to Hemodialysis: A Study Using Ecological Momentary Assessment. *Journal of Experimental Psychology*, 134/1: 3–9.

Sackett, D. L., and Torrance, G. W. (1978). The Utility of Different Health States as Perceived by the General Public. *Journal of Chronic Diseases*, 31: 697–704.

Shane, S. (2007). Panel on Walter Reed Issues Strong Rebuke. *New York Times*, April 12, 2007. Accessed April 19, 2008 at: http://www.nytimes.com/2007/04/12/washington/12medical.html

Slevin, M. L., Stubbs, L., Plant, H. J., Wilson, P., Gregory, W. M., Armes, P. J., and Downer, S. M. (1990). Attitude to Chemotherapy: Comparing Views of Patients with Cancer with those of Doctors, Nurses, and General Public. *British Medical Journal*, 300: 1458–60.

Sprangers, M. A. G., and Schwartz, C. E. (1999). Integrating Response Shift into Health-Related Quality of Life Research: A Theoretical Model. *Social Science & Medicine*, 48: 1507–15.

Stucki G. (2005). International Classification of Functioning, Disability, and Health (ICF): A Promising Framework and Classification for Rehabilitation Medicine. *American Journal of Physical Medicine and Rehabilitation*, 84: 733–40.

Terzi, L. (2004): The Social Model of Disability: A Philosophical Critique. *Journal of Applied Philosophy*, 21/2: 141–57.

Torrance, G. W. (1986). Measurement of Health State Utilities for Economic Appraisal. *Journal of Health Economics*, 5: 1–30.

Ubel, P., Loewenstein, G., and Jepson, C. (2003). Whose Quality of Life? A Commentary Exploring Discrepancies between Health State Evaluations of Patients and the General Public. *Quality of Life Research*, 12: 599–607.

———————(2005). Disability and Sunshine: Can Hedonic Predictions be Improved by Drawing Attention to Focusing Illusions or Emotional Adaptation? *Journal of Experimental Psychology*, 11/2: 111–23.

——— , Hershey, J., Baron, J., Mohr, T., Asch, D. A., and Jepson, C. (2001). Do Nonpatients Underestimate the Quality of Life Associated with Chronic Health Conditions Because of the Focusing Illusion? *Medical Decision Making*, 21: 190–9.

Wallace, C. A., and Bogner, J. (2000). Awareness of Deficits: Emotional Implications for Persons with Brain Injury and their Significant Others. *Brain Injury*, 14/6: 549–62.

Williams, A. (1995). *The Measurement and Valuation of Health: A Chronicle*. Centre for Health Economics, University of York, UK.

Winerip, M. (2008). Holding onto Hope. *New York Times*, February 10, 2008. Accessed April 19, 2008 at: www.nytimes.com/2008/02/10/nyregion/nyregionspecial2/10Rparent.html?pagewanted=print

Wolfson, A. D., Sinclair, A. J., Bombardier, C., and McGeer, A. (1982). Preference Measurements for Functional Status in Stroke Patients: Interrater and Intertechnique Comparisons. In R. L. Kane, and R. A. Kane (eds.), *Values and Longterm Care*. Lexington, Mass.: Lexington Books, 191–214.

World Health Organization (1976). Document A29/INFDOCI/1, Geneva, Switzerland.

World Health Organization (1980). *International Classification of Impairments, Disabilities, and Handicaps: A Manual of Classification Relating to the Consequences of Disease* Geneva, Switzerland.

World Health Organization (2006). *International Classification of Functioning, Disability, and Health, 2001*, Geneva, Switzerland.

3

Vagaries of the Natural Lottery? Human Diversity, Disability, and Justice: A Capability Perspective

LORELLA TERZI

3.1. Introduction

The concept of human diversity plays a central role in contemporary egalitarian theories of justice. These theories engage the questions of what

I began working on the ideas developed in this essay during a Spencer Foundation Scholarship at Stanford University. The essay was subsequently and more recently completed during a HEFCE Fellowship at the Centre for Public Policy Research at King's College, London. I am grateful to both universities and to the named funding institutions for the invaluable opportunities they provided. I also thankfully acknowledge the generous research leave granted by Roehampton University. Several versions of this chapter, at different stages of development, were presented at conferences, seminars, and workshops. I received helpful comments from audiences at Stanford University, the University of Pavia, Italy, the Institute of Education, London, the Accessibility Research Group at the Department for Civil and Environmental Engineering at University College London, and the Centre for Public Policy Research at King's College, London. The workshops on 'Disability and Disadvantage' organized by the editors of this collection at the 2006 Annual Conference of the American Philosophical Association (Pacific Division), and in May 2007 at the Centre for Political Theory at Manchester University provided ideal conditions for in-depth discussions of the arguments presented in this paper. I thank the audiences of both events. I am also extremely grateful for the insights and suggestions received from Louise Archer, Len Barton, Kimberley Brownlee, Dan Brock, Eamonn Callan, Alan Cribb, Adam Cureton, Randall Curren, Peter Duncan, Walter Feinberg, Leslie Francis, Meira Levinson, Mary Mahowald, Terence McLaughlin, Mozaffar Qizilbash, Jonathan Quong, Denis Phillips, Hillel Steiner, and Georgia Testa. Harry Brighouse, as always, generously gave of his time and suggestions, and David Archard and Jonathan Wolff their tacit support. Last, but not least, thanks are due to traits constitute personal advantages and disadvantages, whether these are naturally or socially caused, and why and how diverse personal traits do or do not have to be considered in determining a just distributional scheme. The concept of human diversity applied by these theories in interpersonal comparisons is often informed by an idea of 'normal' or 'average human functioning', which sets a parameter for evaluative purposes. Within this framework, some egalitarian theories refer to disability as a departure from the defined standard functioning, thus equating it with a disadvantageous, non-normal condition, while others consider it a personal deficit, or a clear case of bad luck. Notwithstanding these different meanings, disability is generally evaluated as an individual disadvantage, and as a morally relevant inequality. What justice demands in relation to this inequality is a further matter, mainly addressed in terms of correction or compensation.

Yet disabled people and their political movements strongly emphasize the limited, exclusionary, and mostly oppressive nature of 'idealized' concepts of normal human functioning and of disability as personal disadvantage. They insist on the abandonment of categories of normality and normal species functioning, and advocate a richer and multifaceted understanding of human heterogeneity, where disability is considered a difference among others. In particular, at the core of the social model of disability, the model proposed and supported by disabled people's movements, lies a rejection not only of any necessary causal relation between individual impairment and disability—seen as caused by social structures—but also of any idea of normality, which is regarded as an ideological construction. Further, some perspectives in bioethics and the philosophy of medicine, while endorsing these positions, critique the presumed scientific and biological legitimacy of concepts of normality,[1] which are considered the result of social prejudice against people with atypical modes of functioning. Within this debate interesting attempts have also been made towards formulating a

the editors of this collection, for their invaluable encouragement and helpful criticisms, and to two anonymous referees for their incisive comments. The arguments developed in this chapter are presented more extensively in L. Terzi, *Justice and Equality in Education,* (London and New York: Continuum, forthcoming).

[1] See e.g. R. Amundson, 'Against Normal Function', *Studies in History, Philosophy, Biology & Biomedical Science*, 31 (2000), 33–53, and A. Silvers, 'A Fatal Attraction to Normalizing: Treating Disabilities as Deviations from "Species-Typical" Functioning, in E. Parens (ed.), *Enhancing Human Traits: Ethical and Social Implications* (Washington: Georgetown University Press: 1998).

neutral conception of disability,[2] a conception that does not evaluate it as inherently negative, or as a disadvantage per se.

What insights can be drawn from these perspectives? Certainly, disabled scholars' positions challenge egalitarian theories, in that they urge the formulation of a just response that avoids oversimplified views of disability, as well as inadequate responses to it in terms of compensations for presumed individual deficits.[3] However, since the primary aim of egalitarian theories is the evaluation of individuals' just shares of benefits and burdens, paramount to this task is determining what kind of difference is disability, and what its weight is in a fair social scheme.

In the light of these considerations, my aim in this chapter is to articulate an egalitarian response to the demands of disability in terms of Amartya Sen's capability approach. To this end, I shall consider three distinct, but related, issues. First, I shall address some of the theoretical limits of the social model of disability, and in particular its critique of the idea of normality. Second, in the main section of the essay I shall present elements of a capability perspective on disability. This perspective, I argue, positively responds to the challenges made by disabled scholars, in that it suggests an understanding of disability as inherently relational, in the sense of resulting from the interaction of individual and social elements. Thus, disability is not simply seen as an inherent individual disadvantage. Further, the capability approach helps in determining what is specific to disability as an aspect of human diversity, while evaluating it within an essentially egalitarian framework. Despite these important insights, however, several objections have been raised to the capability approach generally, and more specifically to its understandings of human diversity and disability. While some highlight the vagueness of the idea of capability, and therefore the unspecified character of the approach, others critique its alleged stigmatization of disability as an inferior natural endowment.[4] Since these criticisms have the potential to undermine the legitimacy of

---

[2] See e.g. A. Silvers, 'On the Possibility and Desirability of Constructing a Neutral Conception of Disability', *Theoretical Medicine*, 24 (2003), 471–87.

[3] The question is interestingly raised and articulated by David Wasserman in 'Distributive Justice', in A. Silvers, D. Wasserman, and M. Mahowald (eds.), *Disability, Difference, Discrimination* (Lanham, Md.: Rowman & Littlefield, 1998).

[4] The first critique is raised by Jonathan Wolff in his contribution to this volume, while the second is articulated by Thomas Pogge in a recent article. See J. Wolff, 'Disability among Equals', Ch. 4 below, and T. Pogge, 'Can the Capability Approach be Justified?' *Philosophical Topics*, 30 (2002), 167–228.

the perspective presented here, in the third and final section of this essay I shall address these objections, while providing some arguments in defence of a capability perspective on disability.

3.2. Human Diversity, Normality, and Difference in the Social Model of Disability[5]

The social model of disability has emerged from the political activism of disabled people's movements and the reflection of disabled scholars on their own experience. Originally conceptualized by the sociologist Michael Oliver,[6] the social model plays a major role in disability studies and has influenced the political positions of disability movements, both in the UK and, in different forms, in the US. The fundamental claim that disability results from oppressive and unjust social structures, rather than from individual impairment, underpins the model's various and important internal articulations. These include positions in the UK which emphasize primarily the social causes and the ideological construction of disability, and positions in the US which endorse a more relational view of impairment, disability and the design of social arrangements.

It is perhaps worth reconsidering here the definition originally proposed by Oliver and other social model scholars. According to that definition,

it is not the individual's impairment which causes disability (Impairment → Disability), or which is the disability (Impairment = Disability), and it is not the difficulty of individual functioning with physical, sensory or intellectual impairment which generates the problem of disability.[7]

Disability is instead the result of social arrangements that, by placing and acting as barriers, work to restrict the activities of people with impairments.

---

[5] This section draws extensively on L. Terzi, 'The Social Model of Disability: A Philosophical Critique', *Journal of Applied Philosophy*, 21 (2004), 141–57.

[6] Michael Oliver originally conceptualized the British version of the social model of disability drawing on the *Fundamental Principles of Disability*, produced by the Union of the Physical Impaired against Segregation (UPIAS) in 1976. However, Oliver maintains that he invented the term 'social model of disability'. See M. Oliver, 'The Social Model in Action: If I had a Hammer', in C. Barnes and G. Mercer (eds.), *Implementing the Social Model of Disability: Theory and Research* (Leeds: Disability Press, 2004), 19.

[7] C. Thomas, *Female Forms: Experiencing and Understanding Disability* (Buckingham: Open University Press, 1999), 14.

Disability, ultimately, is 'socially caused (Social barriers → Disability)'.[8] Thus, as Oliver argues, the social model 'does not deny the problem of disability but locates it squarely within society'.[9] Basically, Oliver sees disability, by contrast with impairment, as something imposed on disabled people by oppressive and discriminating social and institutional structures.

The critique of the idea of normality in terms of average human functioning is inscribed in this framework.[10] 'Normality', writes Oliver, 'is a construct imposed on a reality where there is only difference',[11] and the whole ideology of normal function is seen as primarily constructed in order to control and exclude disabled people from active and full participation in social and institutional arrangements which have no interest in accommodating them. Although disabled people's movements and social model scholars generally share the critical rejection of any concept of normality, the debate within Disability Studies encompasses diverse positions on this issue. Recent works by disability scholars[12] have played a central role in reintroducing broader understandings of human diversity and difference into the debate. Feminist disability scholars like Wendell and Morris, for instance, while being well aware of the cultural and social meanings associated with 'normality' and 'abnormality', nevertheless reinstate considerations related to the individual condition of impairment, with its dimensions of restriction of activity, pain, and illness. Thus, Wendell's approach to bodily differences accepts the existence of biological variations among individuals,[13] and highlights the distinctive and valuable

---

[8] C. Thomas, *Female Forms: Experiencing and Understanding Disability* 14.

[9] M. Oliver, *Understanding Disability: From Theory to Practice* (Basingstoke and New York: Palgrave, 1996), 32.

[10] Some might consider the debate on normality totally abstract and therefore almost irrelevant, especially in terms of service provision, since determining 'abnormal functioning' is deemed essential for identifying different needs, and thus providing appropriate aids and services. However, the debate seems indeed to be relevant when considering conceptions of disability and its evaluation within theories of justice, and particularly given the negative connotations associated with the concept of normality. I am grateful to an anonymous referee for raising this point.

[11] Oliver, *Understanding Disability*, 88.

[12] See J. Morris, *Pride against Prejudice: Transforming Attitudes to Disability* (London: Women's Press, 1991); S. Wendell, *The Rejected Body: Feminist Philosophical Reflection on Disability* (London: Routledge, 1996); Thomas, *Female Forms*; and C. Thomas, 'Disability Theory: Key Ideas, Issues and Thinkers', in C. Barnes, M. Oliver, and L. Barton (eds.), *Disability Studies Today* (Cambridge: Polity); C. Thomas, 'How is Disability Understood? An Examination of Sociological Approaches', *Disability and Society*, 19 (2004), 569–83.

[13] Thomas, *Female Forms*, 105.

experience and knowledge arising from these differences. Similarly, Morris maintains that what prevents a value free use of the word 'normal', in terms of 'that which is common', is the prejudice associated with the recognition of difference in terms of all that is 'undesirable, wrong, not admirable, and in general negative'.[14] But, Morris continues, '[w]e are different. We reject the meanings that the non-disabled world attaches to disability, but we do not reject the differences that are such an important part of our identities.'[15] These, and other scholars,[16] assert the value of disability as constitutive of human experience, and as a difference to be celebrated rather than stigmatized. They further advocate an inclusive society with no social, economic, or cultural barriers to participation.

The social model of disability has the legitimacy that comes with expressing disabled people's own experience, reflection and political aims.[17] However, beyond the political appeal and the important reminder of the moral dimension of this debate, the social model has some evident limitations. First, in stating that disability is caused by discriminatory and unjust social and economic structures, the model overstates the social dimension of both sources and causes of disability. It is difficult to see, for instance, how the inability of a visually impaired person to read non-verbal cues in social interactions can be ascribed uniquely to social barriers. Further, it appears also difficult to attribute the restrictions of activities experienced by people with multiple and complex physical and cognitive impairments unilaterally to the unjust and discriminatory design of social arrangements. Second, the model overlooks the complex dimensions of impairment and its possible restricting effects on certain activities and abilities, and hence its relation to disability. For instance, it overlooks the aspects of pain, fatigue and sometimes illness relating to certain impairments

[14] Morris, *Pride against Prejudice*, 15.   [15] Ibid. 17.

[16] See M. Corker, 'Differences, Conflations and Foundations: The Limits to "Accurate" Theoretical Representation of Disabled People's Experience?' *Disability & Society*, 14 (1999), 627–42; S. French, 'Disability, Impairment or Something in Between?', in J. Swain, V. Finkelstein, S. French, and M. Oliver (eds.), *Disabling Barriers—Enabling Environments* (London: Sage, 1993); and T. Shakespeare, 'Cultural Representation of Disabled People: Dustbins of Disavowal?', in L. Barton and M. Oliver (eds.), *Disability Studies: Past, Present and Future* (Leeds: Disability Press, 1997).

[17] While perhaps the model can be critiqued for reflecting only the position of privileged people in highly developed countries, its importance in driving attention to the structural barriers which compound the effects of impairment cannot, and in my view should not be, underestimated. Whether the model has currency in developing countries—without undermining the important issue of medical care for disabled individuals—is a matter for further investigation. I am grateful to an anonymous referee for very critical insights on this point.

and their consequences on the functioning, and more generally on the lives of disabled people. Consequently, the social model ends up overstating the role of society in determining disability, and presents a partial view that needs specifications and extensions.

Furthermore, the advocated 'celebration of differences' as the guiding value for an inclusive society, and the related rejection of ideas of normality and average human functioning yield some problematic results. Certainly, the rejection of normality as a normative concept is important in counteracting its negative and discriminatory connotations and usages. However, this complete dismissal of a guiding concept, even at the level of description, if applied consistently may lead to some untenable theoretical and practical conclusions. If we deny reference to average, thus typical human functioning, how would we evaluate impairment and disability? Would any functioning or lack of functioning be considered equal in a social theory of disability? What would then constitute impairment and what disability? The rejection of descriptive meanings of average functioning could indeed end up creating another category, that of difference, which, ultimately, appears more problematic and less coherent with the very aims of disabled people's movements. Consider for instance the claims of independent living and the demand for personal assistance provided and supplied to disabled people as a matter of rights. It is difficult to sustain these demands while at the same time negating a departure from average human functioning in the case of some impairment and disability. Ultimately, the total rejection of the concept of normality, even in its descriptive sense of average or typical, and either the lack of a reference concept or its substitution with an unspecified idea of difference, show not only theoretical and political limitations, but also a possible mismatch between the theoretical basis of the social model and some of its practical, political aims.

Recent perspectives in bioethics and the philosophy of medicine have proposed more articulated and justified views of the rejection of normality as social construction in relation to disability. Anita Silvers,[18] for instance, critiques the concept of normal species functioning as a parameter for determining disease, and disability as departure from it, and questions related health policies which promote restoring predetermined

---

[18] A. Silvers, 'A Fatal Attraction to Normalizing' (n. 1 above).

'normal' levels and modes of functioning. She rejects 'the assumption that normal functioning is natural and thereby neutral, and . . . the idea that the criteria for determining what functioning is normal are biological rather than social'.[19] Silvers maintains that concepts of normality are meaningless in the light of the vast differences among people and argues that 'the idea, rather than the reality, of non-normal functioning has become the signifier of whether someone is equally well off, or is advantaged in comparison to others'.[20] 'It is far from clear' she insists, 'that deviations from normal functioning mean either lowered productivity or decreased quality of life',[21] and argues that alternative and atypical modes of functioning should be considered equivalent and as effective as the so-called normal species functioning in evaluating people's relative positions. This critique is interrelated with a rejection of the 'normalization' assumptions underpinning perspectives in health care based on liberal political theory. Silvers advances an understanding of disability in terms of atypical modes of functioning, some of which can achieve exactly the same level of functionality as typical ones. Her view 'accounts both for those disabilities that are the result of unjust social structures, and those disabling conditions that are neither caused nor addressed by changes in social arrangements'.[22] She also identifies a group of disabled people who have complex needs rather than being constructed as such, thus responding to more severe forms of impairments and disabilities. Further, this view is open to the possibility of considering impairment, at least descriptively, as departure from an average condition, without encountering the problems that beset less articulated views of the social model. However, more has to be said about justice for individuals with non-typical or alternative forms of functioning.

All these considerations point to the need for a different approach to conceptualizing impairment and disability than that of the social model, an approach which considers disability as a specific variable of human diversity, and evaluates its impact on the positions of individuals within institutional and social arrangements. The capability approach, developed by Amartya Sen, and further articulated by Martha Nussbaum and other

---

[19] Ibid. 99.   [20] Ibid. 115.   [21] Ibid. 118.

[22] I am extremely grateful to Mary Mahowald for providing insightful written comments to a previous draft of this paper. This and further arguments on Silvers draw on her valuable notes: M. Mahowald, APA Pacific Commentary Manuscript (APA, Pacific Division, March 2006), 3.

scholars, is well suited to assessing the relevance of impairment and disability in designing just and inclusive institutional and social arrangements. The approach suggests a view of disability as emerging from the interaction of individual and social elements, without requiring an explicit recourse to notions of normality and abnormality. It also encompasses considerations of alternative and atypical modes of functionings, thus going some way in responding to the questions raised by disabled scholars and disability movements. I shall consider what the capability approach can contribute to our understanding of impairment and disability in more detail in the next section.

3.3. A Capability Perspective on Impairment and Disability[23]

Amartya Sen's work critically engages with the philosophical debate on justice and equality, and develops a complex and important contribution to egalitarianism.[24] Sen maintains that the object of egalitarian concern, rather than consisting in fair shares of resources or in the satisfaction of individual preferences, resides in evaluating people's capability to achieve valued functionings. Functionings are beings and doings constitutive of well-being. Being well nourished, being educated, or participating in public life are all examples of possible functionings. Capability, on the other hand, represent the real opportunities to achieve well-being, or, as Sen says, the 'various combinations of functionings . . . that the person can achieve. Capability is, thus, a set of vectors of functionings, reflecting the person's freedom to lead one type of life or another.'[25] According to Sen, a just institutional order should pay attention to what a person is able to be (for example being well or poorly educated), and to do (for instance, appearing in public without shame, or performing rewarding activities), since this determines her quality of life, and hence her well-being.[26] Capability, therefore, is related to well-being both instrumentally, as a basis

---

[23] This section largely draws on L. Terzi, 'A Capability Perspective on Impairment, Disability and Special Needs: Towards Social Justice in Education', *Theory and Research in Education*, 3 (2005), 197–223.

[24] A. Sen, *Inequality Reexamined* (Oxford: Clarendon Press, 1992).

[25] Ibid. 40.   [26] Ibid. 39.

for judgement about the relative advantage the person has and her place in society, and intrinsically, since achieved well-being in itself depends on the capability to function, and the individual exercise of choice among capabilities has value of its own as part of living.[27]

Sen endorses equality of capability—or, conversely, 'the elimination of unambiguous inequalities in capabilities'[28]—as the appropriate objective of social policy, and asserts the importance of addressing interpersonal comparisons in the space of capability. Central to the capability 'metric' is the concept of human diversity. Sen maintains, 'Human diversity is no secondary complication (to be ignored, or to be introduced "later on"); it is a fundamental aspect of our interest in equality.'[29] Sen's concept of human heterogeneity entails the complex interrelations of personal and external variations, as well as people's different abilities to convert resources into valued objectives. To illustrate this last point, Sen mentions pregnant and lactating women's needs of higher intakes of food, as well as children's requirement for more proteins than adults. Within this view of human diversity as central, the capability approach holds that differences entailed by gender, physical and mental prowess or weakness, climatic zones, and physical environment, and social and cultural arrangements, all have to be accounted for when addressing the demands of equality.

An example taken directly from Sen's work may help to illustrate the use of the capability metric for interpersonal comparisons, and to introduce considerations pertaining to disability that will be expanded later on:

Consider two persons 1 and 2, with 2 disadvantaged in some respect (e.g. physical disability, mental handicap, greater disease proneness). They do not have the same ends or objectives, or the same conception of the good. Person 1 values A more than B, while 2 has the opposite valuation. Each values 2A more than A and 2B more than B. . . . With the given set of primary goods (resources and opportunities) person 1 can achieve 2A or 2B, also—though there may be no great merit in this—A or B. On the other hand, given 2's disadvantage . . . she can achieve only A and B.[30]

It is evident here that person 2 finds herself in a situation of inequality owing to her personal characteristics and how she converts resources into functionings, despite having the same amount of resources or opportunities. Her disability, which is regarded for the purposes of this example

---

[27] Ibid. 42, 62.   [28] Ibid. 7.   [29] Ibid. p. xi.   [30] Ibid. 83.

as an inherent disadvantage, must be taken into account in evaluating equality.

It is this set of considerations regarding human diversity and its centrality in the metric used to compare individual advantages and disadvantages that has ultimately led Sen to conceptualize the space of capabilities and functionings as the relevant one for equality. He identifies the capability approach as a framework of thought, a general approach to the assessment of individual advantage or disadvantage in social schemes, while declining, in light of the variability of human ends, to specify a definitive list of capabilities or functionings. Sen leaves these processes to public choice, reasoning, and democratic procedures that are themselves the most freedom-preserving means by which social policy can be determined.

The unspecified nature of the approach,[31] and the intentional omission of any principles of justice informing it, leads, however, to some problems. Sen recognizes, for instance, that indexing and measuring capabilities are complex matters, and highlights the difficulties in evaluating and comparing different capability sets.[32] Perhaps the most salient problem faced by the approach resides exactly in determining whether a situation is one of equality, given the fact of pluralism and hence the different and often contrasting conceptions of the good endorsed by different people. While I shall leave these problems aside, suffice it to notice that the debate on these and related issues is ongoing, but does not detract from the valuable contribution of the capability approach to egalitarianism.

3.3.1. *Capability and disability*

It is within the ethical framework thus outlined that important insights for a perspective on disability can be developed. In particular, there are two main contributions that Sen's capability approach makes to conceptions of impairment and disability, and their assessment in interpersonal comparisons aiming at equal consideration and freedoms for disabled people. The first insight relates to how we can think of impairment and disability as aspects of human diversity. This entails an understanding of disability as resulting from

---

[31] Sen, A., *Development as Freedom* (Oxford: Oxford University Press, 1999) and I. Robeyns, 'Sen's Capability Approach and Gender Inequality: Selecting Relevant Capabilities', *Feminist Economics*, 9/2−3 (2003), 61−92.

[32] Sen, *Inequality Reexamined* and *Development as Freedom*. I am grateful to Jonathan Wolff for suggesting a more critical position on these issues.

the interaction of personal and circumstantial factors, as well as important considerations of justice for disabled people. The second insight concerns democratic procedures and the active participation of disabled people and their movements in the process of identifying relevant capabilities, and in evaluating how social policies should be designed when aiming at inclusion. Both require some explanation.

The first and main reason for considering the capability approach innovative with respect to current understandings of disability relates to the specific concept of human diversity proposed by Sen, and to its centrality in assessing equality in the space of capability. This entails several important insights. First, in repositioning human diversity as central to the evaluation of individual advantages and disadvantages, Sen's capability approach promotes an egalitarian perspective that deals at its core with the complexities of disability, in terms both of its conception and of considerations of justice. The concepts of functionings and capability are particularly significant to this end, as they can be related in turn to the restrictions in functionings and to the consequent limitations of capability experienced by disabled people.[33] Second, as we have seen, Sen's concept of human diversity, in encompassing personal and external factors as well as an individual conversion factor of resources into well-being, implies an interrelation between personal and circumstantial aspects of human diversity. This opens the way to considerations of impairment and disability as inherently relational, in that disability is seen as one aspect of the complexity of human heterogeneity, and therefore as one aspect of the complexity of individuals in their interaction with their physical, economic, social, and cultural environment. Thus, impairment, with its possible restrictions of functionings, is seen as a personal feature, which may or may not become a disability—an inability to perform some significant functionings on average and typically performed by individuals under common circumstances,[34] and hence a capability limitation—when it interacts with specific social, cultural, and environmental structures. Disability, so defined, is inherently relational and circumstantial, or, in

---

[33] Mozaffar Qizilbash specifies this point in 'Disability and Human Development', Paper read at the 2006 International HDCA Conference, Groningen, available at www.capabilityapproach.com, consulted June 2007. I am grateful to the author for permission to cite his work.

[34] A. Buchanan, D. W. Brock, N. Daniels, and D. Wikler (eds.), *From Chance to Choice: Genetics and Justice* (Cambridge: Cambridge University Press, 2000), 286.

other words, a phenomenon of the interface of the impaired individual with her specific environment. In this sense disability is distinct from impairment and the latter does not always result in a disability. Whether it does or not depends on the design of the physical and structural setting and on whether it is possible or not to overcome the impairment.[35] Third, this relational view enables disability theory, as well as egalitarian positions, to overcome current understandings of disability as unilaterally biologically or socially determined,[36] because disability can be regarded as one of the aspects of individuals emerging from this interlocking of personal and external factors. Moreover, the capability approach goes also in the direction of promoting a conception of disability as one aspect of human diversity, comparable to age and gender, without suggesting monolithic and direct notions of diversity as abnormality, and without any recourse to idealized notions of normality. Further, the approach seems open to considerations of diverse, atypical modes of functioning as well as different levels of functioning. This appears to be fundamental in overcoming the discrimination and oppression denounced by disabled people's movements as inherent in current notions of normality, abnormality, and diversity. Finally, the capability approach provides an egalitarian framework in which entitlement does not depend upon the causal origin of disability. In contrast to other egalitarian perspectives—such as those based on John Rawls's conception of justice as fairness—which question addressing disabilities with a clear natural origin as matters of justice,[37] the capability perspective defends a metric of interpersonal comparisons which evaluates disability as capability failure, and independently from its causal origin. While a just response to disability may take into consideration its origin in suggesting appropriate aids and services, within a capability perspective any disability is a matter of justice.[38] In other words, the approach shifts attention from whether a disability is biologically or social caused as such to the scope of the full set of capabilities—the opportunities for functionings—that a

---

[35] Buchanan et al. provide a very convincing example to illustrate this. They suggest the case of a hearing impaired person who has lost the hearing function with regard to a range of sound frequencies that is detected on average by persons. If the range of sounds undetectable by the impaired person is irrelevant to the functionings in her social environment, then she is not disabled. Ibid. 287.

[36] I owe this observation to discussions with Harry Brighouse.

[37] Among others, Thomas Pogge supports this view. In 'Can the Capability Approach be Justified?' (n. 4 above) 33–4, Pogge defines naturally caused disabilities as those resulting from 'any combination of ordinary genetic variations, self-caused factors and differential luck'.

[38] I am grateful to an anonymous referee for insightful comments on this point.

person can choose from, and the role played by impairment in this set of freedoms. All these considerations have important theoretical and political implications for an egalitarian perspective on disability. However, before addressing some of these in more detail, an example may be useful in illustrating the insights outlined so far.

Walking is a functioning, and so is moving about from one space to another, and it is a functioning that enables other functionings, such as taking one's children to school, or going to work, or serving as a politician. In this sense moving about may be seen as a basic functioning enabling more complex functionings to take place. Now consider an impaired person who uses a wheelchair. In determining the full set of capabilities that a wheelchair user has to achieve her valued ends, the capability approach looks at how this specific functioning (moving about by wheelchair) interacts with circumstantial factors, such as the physical environment where the person lives and the presence of wheelchair accesses to buildings, and how it interacts with personal conversion factors, such as general strength, health, and aspects of attitude. The approach also considers the interplay between wheelchair use and the person's most valuable ends, one of which could be, for example, having an interest in politics and aspiring to serve as a politician. The capability approach suggests that being a wheelchair user may be considered a disadvantage when the wheelchair is not provided or the physical environment is not appropriately designed. In the same way many persons would be disadvantaged were stairs or lifts not to be fitted between flights in buildings, since very few people would be able to move from floor to floor.[39] The provision of a wheelchair and wheelchair accessibility is a matter of justice on the capability approach, because these contribute to the equalization of the capability to pursue and achieve well-being. Moreover, the different mode of functioning is evaluated here in relation to the design of the environment and, as such, may not be seen as an inherent, personal 'deficit'.

Let us continue with this example and consider the achievement of more complex functionings, such as serving as a politician. Let us suppose that acting in her political capacity is fundamental to the achievement of well-being for the physically impaired person considered in this example.

[39] J. Perry, et al. 'Disability, Inability and Cyberspace', in B. Friedman (ed.), *Designing Computers for People: Human Values and the Design of Computer Technology* (Stanford, Calif.: CSLI Publications, 1996), 2.

And let us also assume that the physical environment is designed so as to prevent her from moving about, thus ultimately preventing her from the achievement of some important functionings. This person, although potentially able to exercise her political role, is prevented from achieving her valued end by the interaction of some of her personal features with some of the characteristics of her physical environment. In this case, her well-being appears to be restricted in some fundamental ways, and hence the full set of capabilities available to this person is diminished.

Ultimately, reconsidering impairment and disability within the capability approach implies reframing these concepts in terms of functionings and capabilities. Impairment is a personal feature that may affect certain functionings and, therefore, become a disability. Consequently, disability is a restriction of functionings. This is the result of the interlocking of personal with social and circumstantial features. Since functionings are constitutive of a person's being, and capability represents the various combinations of functionings that a person can achieve, and hence her freedom to choose and to lead one type of life or another,[40] a restriction in functionings results in a restriction of the set of functionings available to the person. Consequently, it results in a narrower range of capability, thus in a kind of difference that has to be addressed as a matter of justice. This is the specific insight provided by a capability perspective on disability.

The second contribution of the capability approach to disability theory pertains to democratic participation in determining relevant capabilities. Here the approach is compatible with the demands of disabled people's movements on the one hand, and with questions of the design of social schemes and policies on the other. Disabled people's organizations have long denounced their de facto exclusion from active participation in society and have reclaimed their role in society as a matter of rights. The capability approach seems to provide a substantive framework to fulfil disabled people's demands. In promoting some forms of public consultations on the choice of relevant capabilities, it commends a participatory democratic process which avoids exclusion and discrimination as a matter of principle. Moreover, in his explicit commitment to forms of participatory and deliberative democratic procedures, Sen endorses the view that people

---

[40] Sen, *Inequality Reexamined*, 39–40.

who are most affected by a decision should be part of the decision making process as well as of its results. This suggests a positive and active role for disabled people in the selection of relevant and valuable capabilities in consultation with 'normal' people. More specifically, this process is envisaged as a form of 'open public reasoning' both for deciding an equality of democratically selected capabilities, and also an equality of agency freedoms.[41] The role accorded to democratic decision, however, if extremely relevant to the agency of disabled people, is problematic in failing to provide sufficient normative guidance for adjudicating the demands of disabled people in relation to the demands of others.[42] Furthermore, choices concerning which capabilities to protect are to be made through democratic processes, but the capabilities essential to democratic participation would themselves need to be protected as a matter of prior constitutional principle, in order to ensure just outcomes.[43]

While these last considerations highlight some problematic aspects of the approach, whose discussion is beyond the immediate scope of this paper, in what follows I will turn my attention to the specific contribution that the approach makes to a criterion of justice for disabled people.

3.3.2. Issues of justice

The capability framework, as we have seen, suggests a conception of disability as inherently relational, as one aspect of human diversity that has to be considered when evaluating the reciprocal positions of individuals and the distribution of benefits and burdens in social arrangements. Two elements appear crucial in positioning a capability perspective on disability with respect to dimensions of justice: the place of disability in the metric chosen in evaluating people's reciprocal positions in social arrangements, and the choice of design of the social framework. I now turn my attention to each of these dimensions.

The capability perspective provides a metric of interpersonal comparison in which the personal characteristics which regulate the conversion of resources and goods into valuable ends should define individual shares. Thus, according to capability theorists, physical and mental impairments

---

[41] D. Croker, 'Sen and Deliberative Democracy', in A. Kaufman (ed.), *Capabilities Equality: Basic Issues and Problems* (London: Routledge, 2006), 190–1.
[42] I address this aspect further on.   [43] I owe this insight to discussions with Eamonn Callan.

should receive attention under a just institutional order and the distribution of resources and goods should be correlated with the distribution of natural features. For instance, as we have seen, the interest of a wheelchair user has to be accounted for in comparisons made in the space of capabilities and, consequently, a wheelchair provided as a matter of justice. Moreover, consideration should be given to the full set of capabilities available to the person using the wheelchair, and when environmental or social barriers hinder her capabilities these should be removed as a matter of justice too. Seeking equality in the space of capability implies using a metric in which disability, considered as one aspect of human diversity and as a limitation on relevant capability, has to be addressed within the distributive pattern of functionings and capabilities. This implies extra provision for disabled people as a matter of justice, and such provision to a large extent does not appear to be a straightforward 'compensation' for some natural individual deficits, since social frameworks are as fundamental to the relational nature of disability as individual traits are.

The second fundamental element of a capability perspective on disability pertains to the criterion of social justice and the design of social arrangements. If we agree that the design of the dominant social framework substantially determines who is included and who is excluded, and whether impairment becomes disability, and hence a limitation of capability, then the burdens of justice must be discharged largely through the choice of appropriate social arrangements. Buchanan et al. define the dominant cooperative framework as the 'institutional infrastructure of social interaction',[44] and describe the framework of most advanced industrialized societies as extremely complex, and involving institutional structures as well as economic ones, highly specified symbolic languages, and the dominance of competitive markets in the private sectors. The demands on individuals in this society are very high and determine a correspondingly high threshold of competence, involving complex arrays of skills and abilities. In placing these demands on individuals, this social framework already implies who is excluded and who is included. The choice of dominant social framework is, according to Buchanan et al., like choosing which game a group of people is going to play. If the game chosen is, say, bridge, then for instance young children will be necessarily excluded from the game. Conversely,

---

[44] Buchanan et al., 288 and 290.

if the game chosen is 'family', then participation by children is certainly possible. The point is that the choice of the framework determines the level of inclusion, and involves competing interests, namely the interests of those able to efficiently participate in the scheme and those potentially excluded from it. The design and choice of a dominant cooperative social framework is consequently a matter of justice, and one that should be guided by a criterion which balances the interests of impaired people with those of 'normal' people. Thus, the slogan of the disabled people's movement, 'change society, not the individual', needs to be evaluated with respect to these considerations, too.

However, the balancing of interests between disabled and non-disabled people and the claim that the burdens of justice should be discharged largely through the adjustment of social and institutional arrangements need further specification.[45] Here the problem consists in determining the demands of justice when provision aimed at 'intervention' on the impaired individual proves not only more efficient, but is also enabling a broader range of opportunities for functionings than the possible changes to social and institutional arrangements. The contentious case of cochlear implants for hearing impaired children is a clear example of the complexity of the issues at stake. Cochlear implants are technological means which overcome deafness through electrical stimulation of the auditory nerve.[46] These implants, which are available both to adults who have lost their hearing and to children born deaf or deafened during early childhood, facilitate the child's learning of spoken language, but significantly curtail the ability to learn Sign Language. What are the implications of the funding for, and the availability of, this treatment? While providing cochlear implants to deaf children certainly complies with the liberal principle of ensuring broader opportunities for effectively functioning in the individuals' dominant social framework, and hence broader capability, such provision is conversely regarded by many within the Deaf Community as a restriction of opportunities for participating in the 'natural' Deaf Community to which these children belong. As it was noted above, the capability criterion of justice presented remains unspecified on the decision of whether to

[45] I am grateful to Kimberley Brownlee, Dan Brock, and Leslie Francis for suggesting this point.
[46] R. Sparrow, 'Defending Deaf Culture: The Case of Cochlear Implants', *Journal of Political Philosophy*, 13 (2005) 135–52 (135).

adjust the social and environmental design, say by generalizing the use of Sign Language, or instead support cochlear implants. A complex evaluation of the interests of disabled and non-disabled people compounds this, as well as similar questions, and a more precise, comprehensive and unified capability criterion of justice than that presented here is therefore needed for adjudicating these cases. Such a criterion would presumably include considerations of respect as well as fairness, and could be envisaged as the result of the processes of open public reasoning advocated by Sen (and Jonathan Wolff in his contribution to this collection, Ch. 4, seems to endorse this point).

Despite these contentious and still open ethical questions, however, there are two compelling reasons for inclusion, and hence for a criterion of social justice that aims at promoting full capability with respect to disability. The first relates to the devastating consequences of exclusion on the lives and well-being of those excluded, not to mention the disrespect that such exclusion shows, and the second relates to the balancing of interests that such a criterion can aspire to. The capability perspective on disability provides important insights towards such a criterion for social justice in evaluating the demands of disability within the space of capability, in considering disability as having a specific place in the metric used to assess individual shares, and in reinstating the importance of the social framework both in influencing disability and in determining inclusion.

Notwithstanding these positive insights, however, several objections have been raised that question the capability approach and its specific understanding of impairment and disability. To two of these critiques I now turn my attention.

3.4. Justifying the Capability Perspective on Impairment and Disability

My analysis has so far attempted to highlight how the capability approach provides a metric for interpersonal comparisons and a conception of disability that make progress towards formulating a just distributive response to disability. However, the approach has been critiqued on several grounds, both in relation to its normative assumptions, and more specifically in relation to its feasibility of offering a positive account and evaluation of disability. As David Wasserman points out,[47] the approach still 'faces formidable challenges in developing a realistic and plausible account of political justice that incorporates people with disabilities'. In this section, I shall analyse and address two of these challenges. The first, proposed by Jonathan Wolff, may be considered more a specification of the approach than a full critique, and concerns the vagueness of the concept of capability, and, consequently, the vagueness of the approach more generally. The second objection, raised by Thomas Pogge, concerns the supposed stigmatization of disability as an inferior natural endowment entailed by the capability metric. My purpose is to argue in defence of the insights of the capability approach and to reassert the value of its positive account of impairment and disability. In particular, I argue that Wolff's specification of the concept of capability is implied in the processes of open public reason advocated by Sen, thus constituting an important clarification of the approach, rather than a full critique. Further, I argue that Pogge's view underestimates the theoretical reach of the capability approach and wrongly ascribes to it stigmatizing connotations. I begin by analysing the first position, namely the unclear meaning of capability.

While acknowledging the value of Sen's view, in his contribution to this volume Jonathan Wolff highlights the vagueness of the concept of capability, and therefore of the capability approach in general. Wolff points out that Sen's understanding of capability in terms of opportunities for functionings is inscribed in a framework which rightly seeks to provide people with the opportunities to achieve certain functionings, namely those they have reason to value, rather than supplying achieved functionings. This is aimed at ensuring that people can exercise degrees of choice and responsibility, thus enacting their specific conception of what constitutes a worthwhile life. However, Wolff maintains that this appealing aim conceals a lack of clarity in the approach, since, generally speaking, 'opportunities are the only kind of goods that governments can legitimately offer'.[48] Furthermore, Wolff connects the unspecified character of the approach to the vagueness of the idea of a capability. An opportunity for functioning, he claims, can become an achieved functioning only upon exercising some actions on the part of the agent, that is, only if this action falls

---

[47] D. Wasserman, 'Disability, Capability, and Thresholds for Distributive Justice', in A. Kaufman (ed.), *Capabilities Equality: Basic Issues and Problems* (London: Routledge, 2006), 215.

[48] J. Wolff, 'Disability among Equals', Section 2.1. (Chapter 4 in this volume.)

within the agent's power. Consequently, in his view the real issue at stake consists in specifying what kind of actions to expect of people in order for them to achieve and enjoy a certain functioning, that is, to have a capability in the relevant sense. Wolff suggests a notion of reasonableness that justifies acting in some ways rather than others, not only at an individual, but also at an interpersonal level. Thus, a person is expected to act on opportunities, and achieve the related functionings, only insofar as this is interpersonally reasonable to expect. This constitutes, in his view, a 'genuine' opportunity for functioning, as distinct, and more specific than, a 'formal' opportunity.

Wolff's critique and further specification of the concept of capability presents a careful and plausible account, which is generally compatible with Sen's endorsement of democratic processes and open public reasoning for selecting capabilities.[49] Moreover, in specifying a notion of interpersonal reasonableness in relation to the achievement of functionings, Wolff provides a much-needed account of the kind of reason required for a capability to count as relevant. Perhaps Wolff's concept of reasonableness, in order to be theoretically and politically fully justified, should be further determined in relation to more explicit criteria of what constitutes reasonableness. As he aptly notices, his account is likely to be contentious, given the different notions of reasonableness that people may have. However, Wolff's is an important clarification and addition to the idea of capability and to the capability framework more generally.

Potentially more problematic is the objection to the capability approach, and specifically to its evaluation of disability, advanced by Thomas Pogge in a recent article. Pogge's critique of the capability approach is based on John Rawls's egalitarian position, and is inscribed in the debate between Rawlsians (or resourcists, as Pogge refers to them) and capability theorists. Without engaging in lengthy expositions of Rawls's complex egalitarianism, or indeed in the debate between the two perspectives, it is worth recalling here some elements of both. According to Rawls, social arrangements should be designed to give people equal holdings of social primary goods, specified as those features of institutions and resources that free and equal citizens need in order to live a complete life.[50] Notably, both Sen and Nussbaum point out how a focus on primary goods, and hence

---

[49] See above, Section 2.   [50] Rawls, *Justice as Fairness*, 58.

ultimately on resources, overlooks fundamental dimensions of inequality, given people's different conversions of resources into valuable functionings. Thus, they contend that what is important, in evaluating individuals' relative positions, is not their shares of primary goods or resources, but what people can actually do with them, and hence the focus on capability. A key difference between the two approaches lies precisely in the element of sensitivity to personal differences in interpersonal comparisons. While the resourcist approach does not take into account personal heterogeneities as relevant factors in determining people's advantages or disadvantages, the capability approach argues instead that these variations are fundamental to the evaluation of relative positions.

Pogge's critique is inscribed in this debate. He maintains that the capability approach is an important and helpful heuristic device, but argues that it does not provide a criterion of social justice that could in any way be considered a valid alternative to the resourcist perspective.[51] The capability approach, in his view, overstates its contribution to the egalitarian debate, and cannot ultimately be justified. In order to substantiate his claims, Pogge challenges the capability approach on several counts, but primarily and powerfully on what he maintains are its serious problems in dealing with 'natural inequalities'. More specifically, he claims, the capability approach, in including individual natural differences among the elements of moral concerns, ends up identifying disability as 'vertical inequalities', and hence in stigmatizing disabled people as overall worse endowed than other people. Conversely, Pogge claims, the resourcist view considers personal endowments irrelevant to moral concerns, thus equating disability to any other natural feature, like the colour of one's eyes, or one's height. These features are considered overall 'horizontal inequalities', and as such do not constitute grounds for additional resources. The resourcist view, Pogge concludes, avoids stigmatizing people on the basis of their natural characteristics, and it is therefore better positioned to respond to disability than the capability approach. As he says,

While the resourcist approach is supported by this conception of natural inequality as horizontal, the capability approach requires that natural inequality be conceived as vertical. When a capability theorist affirms that institutional schemes ought to be biased in favour of certain persons on account of their natural endowments, she

---

[51] Pogge, 'Can the Capability Approach be Justified?', 176.

thereby advocates that these endowments should be characterized as deficient and inferior, and those persons as naturally disfavoured and worse endowed—not just in this or that respect, but overall.[52]

In responding to these critiques, a first consideration refers to a possible agreement between the two approaches in evaluating the impact of the design of social and institutional arrangements on disability. As we have seen, the extent to which impairment becomes a disability relates to the design of social and institutional arrangements. For instance, a mobility impairment becomes a disability when wheelchair accessibility and facilities are unavailable. In this case, both the resourcist and the capability approach would convene on the necessary environmental and institutional adjustments for the elimination of inequalities. However, it is not entirely clear how the resourcist can explain the necessary adjustment in the institutional design in relation to disability without a direct recourse to the notion of functioning. As Unterhalter and Brighouse point out, for instance, the difference between a visually impaired person and a sighted one does not consist in unequal shares of resources, but in their possibility to function in relation to the design of certain arrangements. More specifically, they note, a blind person does not have expensive tastes, thus preferring to read Braille rather than printed material, and this difference can only be explained by appealing to the absence of a certain functioning.[53] Furthermore, the differences between the two perspectives emerge even more starkly when considering cases when inequalities in levels of functionings cannot be addressed with social and environmental changes. Consider, for instance, the restrictions related to visual impairments with respect to the possibilities of recognizing people, or reading social and non-verbal cues in social interactions. A resourcist response would need to consider these restrictions either as socially determined—a position difficult to maintain in this case, as clearly no adjustment can currently be made to address this issue—or as overall irrelevant. However, both positions appear evidently problematic, with the result of serious overlooking substantive inequalities related to certain restrictions in functionings. The capability approach, conversely, captures a fundamental dimension of

---

[52] Pogge, 'Can the Capability Approach be Justified?', 221.

[53] E. Unterhalter and H. Brighouse, 'Distribution for What for Social Justice in Education? The Case of Education for All by 2015', in M. Walker and E. Unterhalter, *Sen's Capability Approach and Social Justice in Education* (London and New York: Palgrave), 96.

justice by pointing our attention to the actual opportunities for functionings of disabled individuals.

Furthermore, since the recognition of the kind of difference entailed by impairment and disability is inscribed in a view of human diversity that encompasses all aspects of diversity, as noted above, the capability approach does not necessarily stigmatize disability in as much as it does not stigmatize pregnant or lactating women. Recognizing that certain personal characteristics, in interacting with environmental and social factors, may lead to a disability, and that the latter has to be considered in interpersonal comparisons, does not establish a necessary causal relation between such inequality and any stigmatizing effect. Instead, it reconsiders them in their specificity and with a view on the person's well-being and her choice over the kind of life she has reason to lead. And undeniably such a choice would be compromised, should disability be addressed in terms of equality of resources only, since in the latter case the person's specific difference and its related possible disadvantage would remain not addressed. Ultimately, in aiming at equality in opportunities for well-being, and in allowing in considerations on valuable different sets of capabilities, not exclusively related to an average person but instead encompassing human heterogeneity, the capability approach is sensitive to issues of positive recognition of differences. It therefore provides a much needed response to the complex demands of justice for disabled people.

References

Amundson, R., 'Against Normal Function', *Studies in History, Philosophy, Biology & Biomedical Science*, 31 (2000), 33–53.

Buchanan, A., Brock, D. W., Daniels, N., Wikler, D. (eds.), *From Chance to Choice: Genetics and Justice* (Cambridge: Cambridge University Press, 2000).

Corker, M., 'Differences, Conflations and Foundations: The Limits to 'Accurate' Theoretical Representation of Disabled People's Experience?', *Disability & Society*, 14 (1999), 627–42.

Croker, D., 'Sen and Deliberative Democracy', in A. Kaufman (ed.), *Capabilities Equality: Basic Issues and Problems* (London: Routledge, 2006) 190–1.

French, S., 'Disability, Impairment or Something in Between?', in J. Swain, V. Finkelstein, S. French, and M. Oliver (eds.), *Disabling Barriers—Enabling Environments* (London: Sage, 1993).

Mahowald, M., APA Pacific Commentary Manuscript (APA, Pacific Division, March 2006), 3.

Morris, J., *Pride against Prejudice: Transforming Attitudes to Disability*, (London: Women's Press, 1991).

Oliver, M., *Understanding Disability: From Theory to Practice* (Basingstoke and New York: Palgrave, 1996).

_____ 'The Social Model in Action: If I had a Hammer', in C. Barnes and G. Mercer, *Implementing the Social Model of Disability: Theory and Research* (Leeds: Disability Press, 2004).

Perry, J., et al. 'Disability, Inability and Cyberspace', in B. Friedman (ed.), *Designing Computers for People: Human Values and the Design of Computer Technology* (Stanford, Calif.: CSLI Publications, 1996).

Pogge, T., 'Can the Capability Approach be Justified?' *Philosophical Topics*, 30 (2002), 167–228.

Qizilbash, M., 'Disability and Human Development', Paper read at the 2006 International HDCA Conference, Groningen, 29 August, 1 September 2006, available at www.capabilityapproach.com consulted June 2007.

Rawls, J., *Justice as Fairness: a Restatement* (Cambridge, Mass.: Harvard University Press, 2001).

Robeyns, I., 'Sen's Capability Approach and Gender Inequality: Selecting Relevant Capabilities', *Feminist Economics*, 9/2–3 (2003), 61–92.

Sen, A., *Inequality Reexamined* (Oxford: Clarendon Press, 1992).

_____ *Development as Freedom* (Oxford: Oxford University Press, 1999).

Shakespeare, T., 'Cultural Representation of Disabled People: Dustbins of Disavowal?, in L. Barton and M. Oliver (eds.), *Disability Studies: Past, Present and Future* (Leeds: Disability Press, 1997).

Silvers, A., 'A Fatal Attraction to Normalizing: Treating Disabilities as Deviations from "Species-Typical" Functioning', in E. Parens (ed.), *Enhancing Human Traits: Ethical and Social Implications* (Washington: Georgetown University Press: 1998).

_____ 'On the Possibility and Desirability of Constructing a Neutral Conception of Disability', *Theoretical Medicine,* 24 (2003), 471–87.

Sparrow, R. 'Defending Deaf Culture: The Case of Cochlear Implants', *Journal of Political Philosophy,* 13 (2005) 135–52.

Terzi, L., 'The Social Model of Disability: A Philosophical Critique', *Journal of Applied Philosophy,* 21 (2004), 141–57.

_____ 'A Capability Perspective on Impairment, Disability and Special Needs: Towards Social Justice in Education', *Theory and Research in Education,* 3 (2005), 197–223.

Thomas, C., 'Disability Theory: Key Ideas, Issues and Thinkers', in C. Barnes, M. Oliver, and L. Barton (eds.), *Disability Studies Today* (Cambridge: Polity, 1997).

———— *Female Forms: Experiencing and Understanding Disability* (Buckingham: Open University Press, 1999).

———— 'How is Disability Understood? An Examination of Sociological Approaches', *Disability and Society,* 19 (2004), 569–83.

Unterhalter, E., and Brighouse, H., 'Distribution for What for Social Justice in Education? The Case of Education for All by 2015', in M. Walker and E. Unterhalter, *Sen's Capability Approach and Social Justice in Education* (London and New York: Palgrave), 67–86.

Wasserman, D., 'Distributive Justice', in A. Silvers, D. Wasserman, and M. Mahowald, *Disability, Difference, Discrimination* (Lanham, Md.: Rowman & Littlefield, 1998).

———— 'Disability, Capability, and Thresholds for Distributive Justice', in A. Kaufman, (ed.), *Capability Equality: Basic Issues and Problems* (London: Routledge, 2006).

Wendell, S., *The Rejected Body: Feminist Philosophical Reflection on Disability* (London: Routledge, 1996).

Wolff, J., 'Disability among Equals', Ch 4 in this volume.

4

Disability among Equals

JONATHAN WOLFF

My task in this paper is to ask what we need to do if we are to construct a society in which people are to be treated as equals, whatever their disability status. I intend to provide a conceptual framework for posing and approaching this question, and to help clarify some policy objectives. My primary reason for taking on this task is that analytical political philosophy seems to have lagged behind social policy on these issues,[1] and the treatment of disability by political philosophers has sometimes seemed insufficiently thought through. I do not deny that there is a great deal of sensitive and important recent work,[2] yet we seem to lack a systematic, plausible approach to the topic. Thus I will attempt to set out the beginnings of an answer

Near and distant relatives of this paper have been presented to many audiences and read and commented on by many people. In particular I would like to acknowledge the help of audiences at Virginia Commonwealth University, the University of New Mexico at Albuquerque, MIT., University College London, the University of Manchester, the University of Southampton, the University of East Anglia, Ben Gurion University of the Negev, National University of Ireland, Galway, the University of Liverpool, the University of Sheffield, and the Kennedy School, Harvard University. I am particularly grateful to Richard Arneson, John Baker, Dan Brock, Alex Brown, G. A. Cohen, Miriam Cohen Christofidis, Roger Crisp, Avner de-Shalit, Simon Duffy, Ronald Dworkin, Alon Harel, John Harris, W. D. Hart, Dan Hausman, Richard Hull, Frances Kamm, Annabelle Lever, Andrew Mason, Trenton Merricks, Veronique Munoz Dardé, Jennifer Nagel, Glen Newey, Michael Otsuka, Janet Radcliffe Richards, Sarah Richmond, John Roemer, Karen Rothstein, Julian Savulescu, Tim Scanlon, Tom Shakespeare, Anita Silvers, Hillel Steiner, Sergio Tenenbaum, Georgia Testa, Nick Tyler, Peter Vallentyne, Alex Voorhoeve, Stuart White, and Andrew Williams for their comments and suggestions. Work on this paper began during a Fulbright Senior Scholarship, while visiting at Columbia University, and the final version was written up during a period of AHRC-funded leave.

[1] For a fascinating sample of theoretical work from scholars active in the disability movement see the essays in Shakespeare 1998, and Tremain 1996.

[2] See, in addition to the other papers in this collection, for example Bickenbach 1993; Silvers et al. 1998; and Buchanan et al. 2000. Rawls, notoriously, deliberately excluded questions of disability from the account of justice set out in *A Theory of Justice* (Rawls 1971). See also Rawls 1999: 259; and Rawls 1982: 168.

to the question of how society should address issues of disability. I seek an answer with credibility from the point of view of both philosophical theory and social policy.

By way of introduction and summary, I shall defend the following claims:

1. Ideally, a good society will meet at least two goals. First it should offer its citizens *genuine opportunities for secure functionings*. Second it should be *a society of equals* in at least the sense that differences between people should be accepted.[3]

2. A person's opportunities in life are determined by three kinds of factor: first, his or her internal resources (Rawlsian natural assets); second, his or her external resources (money, property, and so on); and third, the social, cultural and material structure of that person's society. In attempting to remedy disadvantage a choice will often need to be made between kinds of action corresponding to these kinds of factor.

3. To be disabled is to be in a position where one's internal resources are impaired and do not provide one with adequate genuine opportunities for secure functioning, given the social and material structure in which one lives, together with the external resources at one's disposal.

4. If society were concerned only with enhancing the opportunities of each particular disabled individual, this would generally provide reason to pursue policies of 'personal enhancement' (improving internal resources) or sometimes provision of external resources, rather than material or social change.

5. However, there are often strong reasons for 'status enhancement' (changing social and material structures), connected with the idea of a society of equals. Accepting difference is one reason, avoiding stigmatizing individuals provides another reason, and reducing risks to all provides a third.

6. Social action to address disability needs to be seen in the context of many competing claims on resources, of greater and lesser urgency. Disability typically involves complex limitations on an individual's opportunities for secure functioning. The focus of social concern,

---

[3] This view of a good society is defended in detail in Jonathan Wolff and Avner de-Shalit (2007). This paper applies the analysis of that book to the particular issue of disability, and thus draws heavily on this joint work.

however, is the individual's limited opportunities and not disability in itself.

7. Nevertheless anti-discrimination policy needs to identify a group to be protected. However, the concept of disability is unhelpful in this context and policy should be aimed at avoiding discrimination against people who are impaired in their mental or physical functioning.

These theses will be developed in following sections. First, however, I will explain my claim that much contemporary egalitarian thought suffers through being out of step with social policy concerning disability.

4.1. Egalitarian Thought and Disability Policy

Although increasingly coming under critical scrutiny, much recent thinking about equality has been dominated by what has become termed 'luck egalitarianism'.[4] This sees the goal of egalitarian justice as that of neutralizing the effects of good and bad (brute) luck on individual fortunes. The method by which it is proposed to achieve such neutralization is normally termed 'compensation'. Within this view disability is often regarded as a paradigm of bad luck (either in itself or in its effects), for which, it would immediately follow, compensation is due.

Now it is not always clear what is meant by 'compensation'.[5] Sometimes it appears to be little more than a placeholder for the idea that 'something must be done'. But sometimes compensation is viewed in cash terms, or at least in terms of material goods, the provision of which is regarded as 'making up for' something else which is lost or lacking. There are two quite separate possible rationales for offering disabled people cash compensation, corresponding to the two major currents in contemporary egalitarianism. According to the first—the approach based on the idea of welfare—those who are disabled are thought to suffer from lower

---

[4] Anderson (1999) coined this term. Luck egalitarians, in this sense, include Dworkin, Cohen, and Arneson. For critical discussion see Wolff 1998, Anderson 1999, Hinton 2001, and Scheffler 2003.

[5] A useful attempt at clarification is Robert Goodin's distinction between 'means-substitution' compensation and 'ends-displacement' compensation. See Goodin 1990. For doubts about this distinction and an attempt to replace it with a continuum, while remaining within the spirit of Goodin's suggestion, see Wolff 2002: 209.

levels of welfare (typically preference satisfaction) than others, and so need compensation to bring them to an appropriate welfare level. According to the second—within the theory centred on the idea of resources—those with a disability are conceptualized as lacking 'internal resources' compared to others (irrespective of the effects of this on their welfare) and so should be offered additional 'external resources' to make up for this lack. Both strands can in many circumstances converge on the policy of offering cash compensation for disability, albeit for different reasons.

However, when we turn our attention to real social policy we find that the focus is rather different. While it is true that people with disabilities sometimes seek support from the state in cash form, this, first, is only one of many measures sought, and second is seemingly never claimed as compensation for the special miseries of disability, although the idea that it is required to allow people to overcome a lack of internal resources is more plausible. Even so, many financial claims will normally be based on one or both of two specific reasons. The first is poverty; the consequence of the difficulties disabled people often face in earning an adequate income. The second is the special expenses of medical or other equipment or personal help required simply to get by, which may soak up a large proportion even of an income that would otherwise be adequate. Yet we should note that in reality there are many other possible strategies for addressing disability, aside from cash transfers, such as medical intervention, and technical, social, and cultural change. This will be explored more thoroughly shortly. In the meantime we should note that luck egalitarianism—at least in the forms currently on offer—typically recommends a strategy which is rarely thought of as appropriate, or at least sufficient, for addressing disability.

The point is not that equality of welfare or equality of resources must always offer cash compensation, for there may be contingent reasons why other measures may be used. For example, some forms of collective provision may be a more efficient means of delivering welfare or resources than individual cash compensation. Rather, it is that these views lack a principled reason for preferring other strategies. In my view this is a serious weakness of such theories (although other people might view it as a strength). It appears, then, there is every reason for looking beyond the welfarist and resourcist views which have provided a main strand of luck egalitarianism.

4.2. The Good Society

The failure of luck egalitarianism has been attributed to its excessive concentration on the idea of fairness between individuals, to the exclusion of the idea of creating relations of equality between people.[6] However, it is important not to make the opposite mistake of imagining that all that matters is social relations. Rather, equality is surely a matter both of distribution and of social relations, which need to be integrated into a single scheme. That integrative task will not be attempted here in detail. Nevertheless, as indicated, a background assumption to this discussion is that a good society will meet at least two goals. First it should offer each citizen *genuine opportunities for secure functionings*. Second it should be *a society of equals* at least in the sense that differences between people should be accepted. Consequently, in formulating a theoretical approach to disability policy we have to consider both of these goals. Section 4.2.1 discusses the former at some length, Section 4.2.2 the latter, more briefly.

4.2.1. Genuine Opportunities for Secure Functioning

The view to be developed here owes a good deal to Amartya Sen's well-known 'capability' view, although this is not the place to engage in lengthy exposition of Sen.[7] To lay out the barest bones of Sen's theory, when assessing an individual's well-being we should consider not that person's welfare level, or their resources, but their 'capability to function', where functionings are what a person can 'do or be' and understood to be irreducibly plural in the sense that more of one cannot always make up for less of another.[8] A capability is, it seems, an individual's opportunity to achieve a functioning, and a capability set is an individual's opportunity to achieve a range of different sets of functionings, given that capabilities or opportunities can be used to achieve various different ends. Sen deliberately avoids giving a definitive list of functionings, but in the case of disability the most relevant are likely to include mobility; education; independence; fulfilling leisure; employment; financial well-being; health

---

[6] See Wolff 1998, Anderson 1999, and Scheffler 2003.

[7] For insightful discussion of Sen, see Lorella Terzi's paper in this volume Ch. 3 (Terzi 2009).

[8] Sen's theory is set out over a number of works. For representative samples see Sen 1980 and Sen 1999.

(including freedom from pain); social relations to others, including the ability to express one's care and affection for them; family life; a sense of being valued; and participation in the political life of one's community.

Although Sen's view is extremely helpful, I want here to defend a dual modification; the 'genuine opportunity for secure functionings' view. I will not question the idea of functionings, but rather the shape of the theory in which functionings appear. The first issue centres on the vagueness of the idea of a capability. To explain, within the tradition founded by Sen it is customary to argue that the government's proper role is not to provide functionings for people, but to provide opportunities for functionings, which, as noted, in Sen's terminology is rendered 'capability to function'. The advantage of the capability approach is often thought to be that it creates a space between government and its citizens in which a citizen is able to exercise a significant degree of responsibility for his or her own fate. Accordingly, on such a view, if a government provides for its citizens the proper capabilities to function, citizens have no complaint if, as a result of their own choices, they do not achieve appropriate functionings. And correspondingly no one else has a complaint if an individual manages, through his or her own efforts, a higher level of functioning.

Although this sounds appealing in many respects, the contrast between the idea of a government supplying functionings on the one hand, and capabilities or opportunities on the other, is less clear than is often assumed. For, in general, it is impossible for a government to guarantee the functioning level of its citizens without extreme coercion. The old adage that 'you can take a horse to water but you can't make it drink' applies. Short of force-feeding you cannot guarantee a nutrition level. Short of incarceration you cannot guarantee shelter. In normal circumstances all goods—or at least all the goods a government can legitimately offer—are opportunities.[9]

Yet this also points to the vagueness of the capability approach. If we think of capabilities as opportunities for functionings, then this means that the enjoyment of a functioning will generally be conditional on performing some act—if only an act of speech—normally within the agent's power. Hence the central issue becomes the nature of the actions required of the citizens (or exceptionally by others) to turn their capabilities into

---

[9] However, we should not overlook that some disabled people do not live in normal circumstances. For those in institutions, effective incarceration and force feeding is not unheard of. Giving such individuals more control would be a welcome consequence, it seems, of the capability approach.

functionings. Egalitarian theorists have tended to talk in terms of choices but it is rarely as simple as this. Choices generally require other actions, and actions typically have costs, or, at least, risks. Consequently any capability theorist—and more broadly any theorist who wishes to give responsibility a central place—has to consider which actions, and which costs and risks, should be required of individuals in order for them to enjoy a particular level of functioning. The range of variation is enormous: from a life's effort to the stretching out of a hand. A simple appeal to 'capability' or 'opportunity' will not suffice. It is not acknowledged as often as it should be that capability theory, or any opportunity theory of distributive justice, is under-specified until this is settled.

It seems, then, the government, like the Greek gods, has to decide which tests have to be passed and hurdles jumped over before people can enjoy the goods they seek. Perhaps the most promising approach considers not whether a choice has been made,[10] or whether an individual identifies with their actions,[11] but whether it is reasonable for someone to act one way rather than another. Whether it is reasonable will, in turn, depend on the potential impact of so acting on other aspects of the person's life, and the lives of others, and the potential impact on the person and others of their not acting in a particular way, assuming that society has to come to their aid in some way. Hence the relevant notion of reasonableness is that of interpersonal justifiability, rather than prudential reason. There are numerous ways in which such a theory could be developed, but here I rely on the general idea, realizing that in practice many cases will be contested as different standards of reasonableness will be assumed by different people.

To illustrate the general idea, many may argue, for example, that it is reasonable for an unemployed single mother to turn down a menial, low-paid, full-time job in order to be able to see her young children to school, and look after them in the vacations. If so, it is right that she should continue to receive state support even though she has chosen to reject full-time work, and to identify with her role as an active mother who personally cares for her children. The costs to her (and to her children, although that is a further issue) of taking this job, it can be argued, outweigh the costs to the taxpayer of continuing to support her. This

---

[10] This is the view favoured by Cohen (1989) and Arneson (1989).
[11] This is the view that many associate with Dworkin. See e.g. Cohen 2004: 7.

takes all the impacts—costs and benefits—of potential action and non-action into account when judging whether an individual has a genuine opportunity. It supposes that someone has a genuine opportunity for achieving a functioning when it is interpersonally reasonable to expect him or her to take steps to achieve that functioning. In the above example, it is true that this woman could get a job to pay for rent and food if state support was cut off, and so in some sense she does have an opportunity for achieving the functionings of shelter and nutrition. Yet on the theory of responsibility advanced here the cost of exercising that opportunity is arguably unreasonable to ask, and if it is unreasonable then the opportunity does not exist in the relevant sense. For ease of expression we can adopt the distinction between 'formal opportunity' and 'genuine opportunity' to capture this sense of responsibility.

However, the capability approach requires a further modification in order to capture more of the nature of advantage and disadvantage. Sen provides two examples which bear examination. The first is from the southern edge of Bangladesh and of West Bengal in India, where the Sundarban ('beautiful forest') grows. This is the habitat of the Royal Bengal tiger, which is protected by a hunting ban. The area is also famous for the honey it produces in natural beehives. The people who live in the area are extremely poor, but survive by collecting and selling the honey, for which they can get a relatively high price in the city. However, this is a very dangerous job. Every year some fifty or more of them are killed by tigers.[12] The second case is of Mr Kedra Mia, a Muslim labourer who worked in a Hindu neighbourhood in Dhaka, where Sen grew up as a child. Mr Mia was knifed on the street by Hindus, and later died. While aware of, and deeply concerned about, the risk of working in a Hindu neighbourhood in troubled times, Mr Mia had no other choice but to do so to save his family from malnutrition.[13]

Although Sen does not emphasize the point, the striking thing about these examples is that the primary disadvantage these people suffer is that they are subject to extreme risks. If there were no tigers, or no Hindu knifemen, there would be nothing to distinguish these cases from perhaps hundreds of millions of others. What makes them special, although sadly not uncommon, is that people take a high risk of death in order to put food

---

[12] Sen 1999: 146.   [13] Sen 1999: 8.

on the family table. Of course life can never be risk-free, and security is a matter of degree. Yet in this case we have people who, in order to achieve a basic level of functioning for their families, are forced to take risks which are far more extreme than those regularly taken by others.

Note too that although in both of Sen's cases people die, even those who do not—the surviving honey collectors, other Muslim day labourers in Hindu districts—suffer disadvantage through exposure to risk.[14] What, though, is this disadvantage? It is multi-dimensional, and intuitively we can list many aspects. First, there is the real possibility of actual harm. Second, there is the fear of and anxiety about that harm. Third, there is the 'planning blight' of living with uncertainty in terms of the difficulty of planning one's life under such conditions.[15] Fourth there are the steps one must take to try to mitigate the risks. Some may argue that unless actual harm is suffered the first dimension is illusory: the mere fact of being subject to risks that others are not. To test this, imagine you are a honey collector who is unaware of the risks and lives to a ripe old age. Are you disadvantaged by the fact of facing this risk, even though it has no effect on your mental state or behaviour, and the harm never falls on you? In my view you are, but I have to concede that it is hard to find arguments either way.

Analysing this further, we can see three distinct ways in which function-ings can be at risk, or, as we might say, three ways in which functionings can be, or become, insecure. First there is a risk to a specific function-ing. A day labourer, or, indeed, an adjunct professor, lives constantly under the threat of unemployment, and thus lacks security of employment. Secondly, this risk is likely to spread to other functionings—cross-category risk. Anyone relying on their income to buy food will find that risks to employment generate risks to nutrition among many other things. Third, steps taken to secure one functioning, such as nutrition, may put other functionings at risk, such as health and safety, as in the case of Kadar Mia and the honey gatherers. To secure food for themselves and their families they put their own lives in grave danger. This we could call an 'inverse-cross-category risk'.

---

[14] I owe the insight that risk is a neglected aspect of disadvantage to Avner de-Shalit. This idea is developed in detail in Wolff and de-Shalit 2007.

[15] For a detailed account of the effects of lack of control on health and life-expectancy see Marmot 2004.

These three forms of risk to functioning create vulnerabilities for disabled people. Quite obviously many people with impairments face insecurity of health; far higher than average risk of a worsening of their condition, or new complications. Another example of the same type is that some disabled people are particularly threatened by the possibility of technical change. Anita Silvers points out that when Microsoft changed from DOS to Windows, many visually impaired people who had relied on screen readers could no longer work, or at least not until Windows compatible readers were introduced.[16] Yet even before the technical change, the visually impaired had a perhaps unnoticed vulnerability to technical change. These are both examples of risks within a single functioning.

Cross-category risk is also present. The possibility of deteriorating health, or lack of flexibility in the workplace reduces employment possibilities, and further, as we have already seen, increases risks to anything depending on income. But there is also inverse cross-category risk, where the attempt to secure one functioning places another functioning at risk. Some disabled people who enter the workplace lay themselves open to the upset of routine day-to-day discrimination, whether deliberate or not, which may have been avoided by staying at home. Similarly those disabled people who wish to enter the public arena such as politics face the possibility of routine public humiliation, especially given the unpopularity of the causes which they are likely to advocate. Those who seek to follow recreations enjoyed by others, such as some forms of sports, may put their health at greater risk. Those provided with the services of a carer to ease the routines of daily life face the risk of abuse. And so on.

In sum, the view sketched here is that in providing a complete account of an individual's level of advantage we need to take notice of that person's *genuine opportunity to achieve secure functionings*, where security is understood in terms of absence of exceptional risk.

4.2.2. A Society of Equals

As mentioned above, it has become common in recent discussions of equality to distinguish between a distributive ideal of equality, in which equality requires the equal provision of some good to all, and an ideal of social equality in which equality concerns the relations in which

---

[16] Silvers et al. 1998: 107–10.

people stand to each other. Limited progress, however, has been made in understanding the latter idea, even though it has been at the heart of a certain tradition of thinking about equality for many decades.[17] Most often the idea of social equality is expressed negatively: an opposition to snobbery and servility; and opposition to hierarchy and patterns of deference. Is social equality to be understood merely as the absence of social inequality? That, surely, is part of it, although it seems to leave something out. For absence of inequality is compatible with relations of alienation between individuals, and more than this is required. Yet it seems hard to say exactly what should characterize a society of equals, if only because many different societies could exemplify this idea in different ways, and it seems wrong to be prescriptive.

Perhaps, though, the way to make progress is to argue that the distinction between a distributive ideal of equality and an idea of social equality does not quite cut things the right way. For if distribution concerns individual well-being then it seems that social equality must be about something else. But what? And what is its point if it does not contribute to well-being? Rather, I suggest that we need a more expansive idea of well-being, where understanding oneself as having a 'place in the world' and not having to look up to others or being regarded as a marginal member of society are themselves important functionings and aspects of well-being. This, then, provides a bridge between a distributive idea and a social idea of justice. On such a view the past error of the distributive ideal was simply to have too narrow an understanding of well-being.[18] On a fully expansive conception the goods produced by social equality are enjoyed as individual aspects of well-being.

In the current context the most important aspect of social equality is that if people are not accepted in their differences from each other they will be excluded or marginalized. Of course there are many other ways of being marginalized and excluded, but to attempt to analyse this

[17] See, for a leading example, Tawney 1931. Recent advocates of this idea include Miller (1998) and Norman (1998).

[18] In an earlier paper (Wolff 2001) I made this same mistake myself. I would now say that we must distinguish between something being good for an individual from that individual recognizing that it is good for them. Social equality—non-exclusion—is good for an individual whether or not they recognize it. Consequently, in the ultimate currency of justice there can be no justified levelling down, although, as it were, in the 'penultimate currency' levelling down will be commonplace.

is beyond the scope of this paper. Nevertheless we can conclude that a society of equals is one that accepts people in their differences, and this, as we shall see later, will have widespread positive effects. This, then, completes the initial sketch of the idea of a good society underlying this discussion.

4.3. Creating Opportunities and Remedying Disadvantage

Earlier I discussed the inappropriateness of cash compensation as an 'all-purpose' approach to remedy disability. What other strategies than cash compensation are available? Rather than simply make a list, I would like to propose an analytic framework in which different forms of strategies can be understood and their presuppositions brought out.[19]

To make progress we need to set the discussion of disability into the broader context of the analysis of disadvantage. If advantage is to be understood in terms of genuine opportunities for secure functionings, we must ask what it is that determines an individual's opportunities. Crudely there are two sorts of factors we need to enter into the calculations: what the person has; and what they can do with it. Dworkin's language of resources is a helpful first step in the right direction. For Dworkin this includes both external resources—money, control over parts of the external world etc.—and 'internal resources'—Rawlsian natural assets.[20] However, contrary to the appearance implicitly encouraged by Dworkin, you cannot 'read off' an individual's opportunities from their resources alone. For, as Dworkin would be the first to admit in other contexts, you also need to know facts about the structures operating within that society; laws and customs, the influence of tradition, religion, language, culture, and other social norms; the configuration of the material and natural environment; and perhaps other things too.[21] Slightly misleadingly I shall refer to all of this as 'social and material structure' (sometimes 'social

---

[19] The following analysis draws on Wolff 2002.   [20] Dworkin 1981b.

[21] To be fair to Dworkin, in his third paper on equality, he does incorporate such material and social factors into his understanding of resources: a resource is different under different social, legal, and perhaps material circumstances (Dworkin 2000: 143–5). However, there seem to be powerful analytic advantages in keeping resources and structures separate, as we shall see.

structure' for short). Thus the overall formula comes to this: the interaction of your internal and external resources with the social and material structure within which you find yourself determines your opportunities, creating for you paths of varying cost and difficulty. In short, your resources are what you have to play with; the structure provides the rules of the game.

Accordingly, we can see that if someone is thought to be lacking in opportunities, then, in principle, there are at least three spheres in which we might try to address this: internal resources; external resources; and social structures. An attempt to address disadvantage in the 'space' of internal resources means, in effect, acting on the person (which, of course, is something agents may do for themselves in some cases). This would include education and training as well as medical and surgical intervention. This, for obvious reasons, I call personal enhancement.

Action in the space of external resources can take at least two main forms. One, of course, is cash compensation, in which individuals are given money to spend as they like. Yet we also provide individuals with resources with strings attached. For example, some students with learning disabilities are given cash to spend only on computers, or are given a computer. But this is not the intended as a grant of a piece of private property, with all the rights normally associated, but rather the use of an object for a particular purpose and not for others. There are many similar examples, including the provision of carers who are employed to perform some services but not others, and so, for example, cannot be hired out to the highest bidder. Granting people resources with use restricted in such ways I call a 'targeted resource enhancement'.

Finally there are ways of improving an individual's opportunities without changing their resources. We can, in effect, change the rules of the game so that people can do better with the resources they already have. This could be the result of a change in law, or social attitudes, or a change in the configuration of the material environment. Perhaps no term is perfect for this, but I shall call it a status enhancement. Consequently we have four distinct strategies for attempting to address disadvantage: personal enhancement; cash compensation; targeted resource enhancement; and status enhancement. Recognition of status enhancement is a great achievement and contribution of the social disability movement.

4.4. The Nature of Disability

If it is true that there are several alternative strategies for addressing disadvantage, then it appears that in any case of disadvantage we will, at least in principle, be faced with a choice between potential strategies. However, in this paper we are not directly concerned with disadvantage in general, but with the particular case of disability. But how, on the theory suggested so far, should we understand disability?

Disability, on the view of opportunity presented here, must lie in the intersection between an individual's personal resources and external conditions. To be disabled is to be in a position where one's internal resources do not provide one with sufficient genuine opportunities for secure functionings, given the social and material structure in which one lives (according to whatever social norm of acceptability is in play[22]) and the external resources at one's disposal. This, clearly, is a very rough statement of the view, and two important challenges need discussion.

First, it is important to clarify the role of external resources, which are highly relevant to one's ability to enjoy secure functionings, and thus are relevant to disability. Eyeglasses, for example, are an external resource, and perhaps are the best technology we have yet invented to overcome impairment. Do we want to say that such resources eliminate the disability of imperfect vision, or rather neutralize (most of) its effects? Here the distinction between 'impairment' and 'disability' is helpful. A successful external technology will not normally remove impairment. But it can prevent impairment being a disability, thought of in terms of social functionings. On this view, then, possession of external resources can eliminate disability, understood this way, simply by mitigating (not removing) impairment.

Of course disability cannot always be eliminated by possession of external resources. A very wealthy paraplegic is still disabled, for although money can help with mobility it cannot currently restore it to the level enjoyed by others. A person who functions at a high level, except in areas for which fine-grained mobility is necessary, remains disabled in a particular respect.

---

[22] I do not say anything here about what this complex norm should be, reserving the topic for future work.

Whether this calls for public action is a further issue which will be discussed below.

The second challenge to the rough definition of disability offered above is that there may be many ways in which personal and external features intersect to cause reduced opportunity to achieve secure functionings which, it could be claimed, have nothing to do with disability. Being female or black in a sexist or racist society would be examples; these are ways in which a person's features intersect with the social structure to create reduced capabilities. Indeed, strictly it would even follow that lack of money is, or at least contributes to, a disability. Can this be right?

Two responses to this challenge seem possible. The common-sense approach is to argue that excluding poverty race and sex is part of the ordinary understanding of disability, and so aim to restrict the definition. The radical approach, which has its attractions, is to emphasize the continuity between disability and other forms of disadvantage, including some forms of discrimination and perhaps even poverty, to the point where retaining a distinct concept of disability loses its usefulness.

Support for the radical approach comes from Alasdair MacIntyre.[23] Although dependency is not all there is to disability as commonly understood, it is an important part in many cases. MacIntrye observes that we all come into the world utterly dependent on others, and many of us leave it the same way. In the meantime, although we almost all achieve some degree of independence, there is no such thing as full independence. Throughout, our lives depend on the knowing and unknowing contribution of uncountable numbers of others. Dependence is a matter of degree, not kind. This, of course, does not show that the same is true of disability, but still it may help us to rethink what we want from the concept of disability. Just as it makes little sense to attempt to divide the world into the dependent and the independent, we might question whether it is useful to sort the world into the disabled and the non-disabled, as the common-sense view tries to do.

Nevertheless, it may seem that there are important reasons for retaining such a distinction, and so for attempting to give a more precise version of the common-sense concept. One reason is that anti-discrimination policy appears to need a clear and useful way of picking out a class of people for

---

[23] MacIntyre 1999.

special protection, and, it may seem, the common-sense view is essential. On such a view it seems that there must be some impairment of bodily or mental functioning which figures as part of the explanation of the further lack of capability to achieve secure functionings. (We return to the issue of anti-discrimination policy in Section 4.9.)

Impairment is a normative concept in that it presupposes some norm or standard against which a person fails to achieve. There is more than one way in which this could be developed. Standardly, a notion of 'normal biological functioning' or 'species-typical functioning' is assumed, and a person with an impairment fails to meet this normal level. Alternatively, the idea of impairment could be personalized in that impairment is simply a failure to achieve what is possible for that person. However, this seems to me a substantial revision of the standard concept, over-personalizing it. This may be more enlightened in some respects, but on the common understanding impairment has an ineliminable reference to the normal or typical.

Now impairment is not sufficient for disability, for an impairment of biological functioning that has no effect on a person's ability to achieve secure functionings is no disability. Hence two sorts of 'normal range' of functionings are assumed: what we could call the biological and the social. What it is to be disabled, on the common-sense view, is to find it harder than others to achieve within the normal range of secure social functionings, and part of the explanation of this is a biological impairment—a lack of functioning—defined in terms of species-typical attributes. Here, then, our working definition of disability is in terms of an extension of the common sense notion: to be disabled is to suffer reduced genuine opportunities for secure functionings, where part of the explanation of this reduction in opportunity is mental or physical impairment, given the external recourses at one's disposal and the social and material structure within which one operates. In Sections 4.7 and 4.8 we will return to explore this common-sense notion further.

4.5. Choice of Strategies of Reasons for Personal Enhancement

Disabled people, it has been assumed, should be the focus of special attention. But what sort of attention? In Section 4.3 several different strategies for addressing disadvantage were explained. How should we choose? Sometimes it will be obvious that one strategy is not feasible or its cost is prohibitive. Yet even among feasible options cost may not be the only factor. Sometimes it is not impossible that we might prefer what appears to be a more costly strategy to a less costly one. For different strategies can send different messages, as they can also presuppose different understandings of the human good. If we choose one strategy over another, it may well be because we presume the truth of one particular account of the human good, or, at least, one element in such an account.[24]

In general, the clearest contrast is between the strategy of personal enhancement and the strategy of status enhancement. In the case of disability, what has been called the medical model of disability, in proposing that we act upon the person normally through surgery or other medical attention, provides an example of the strategy of personal enhancement. Opponents of the medical model often point out that it appears essentialist, or, at least, perfectionist. It presupposes that there is a particular way in which people ought to be. Of course it can be replied that at least some forms of personal enhancement are enabling in that they will allow people to pursue many new goals, and in that way are anti-perfectionist. However, this should not be allowed to obscure the point that very often forms of personal enhancement are proposed as ways of bringing people closer to some form of idealized stereotype, if only that of 'normal species functioning'.

In contrast, the social model of disability proposes that we modify not the individual person, but technology or laws, the built environment or public understandings; in my terminology to attempt status enhancements. Status enhancement seems much more tolerant of people in their differences than policies of personal enhancement and so sends much more of a pluralist, inclusive, message. One worry, though, is that it may tolerate too much, in that sometimes it could be worse for someone, or for society generally, if society adjusts to them, rather than they adjust to society. (To take an example from outside the sphere of disability, consider what would be involved in using this strategy for illiteracy.) But a further concern is simply that status enhancement can be incredibly expensive, and often only marginally effectual, at least in the short to medium term.

---

[24] The following paragraphs rely on Wolff 2002 where the argument in elaborated in more detail.

The strategy of targeted resource enhancement can take a variety of forms and may either support people in their differences or give people only those things which will help enable them to achieve certain 'approved' paths or lifestyles. So it is capable of presenting both pluralist and perfectionist messages.

Cash compensation is perfectionist in one way and pluralist in another. It is perfectionist in that it appears to assume that the only good is either some form of money or something that can be acquired through the possession of money, such as preference satisfaction. But it is pluralist in that it does not investigate, or even care about, what people do with the money once they have it. However, the key assumption behind the strategy of cash compensation as a preferred or exclusive approach is that all disadvantage can be made good through awards of cash. As we saw earlier, one theory on which this is so is on a resourcist understanding of advantage, in which external resources are provided to make up for a lack of internal resources. Another is that of subjective preference satisfaction in which all preferences are, in principle, commensurable.

Internal resources, external resources, and social and material structure are the elements, I have suggested, that determine an individual's opportunities in life. I have also suggested that these match against different strategies for remedy, and that these different strategies at least sometimes make different presuppositions about the human good. This, however, is not yet enough to explain why we should choose one strategy over another. How should such a decision be made? It is not an unreasonable assumption that, where there is more than one possible strategy available, we should use the one which is in some sense most effective. Indeed any other approach seems perverse. Why, other things equal, prefer a less effective strategy to a more effective one?

It may seem that it follows very easily from this approach that we should generally prefer personal enhancement, for, it will be argued, giving people mental and physical abilities is the most efficient way of allowing them to achieve secure functionings.[25] Mental and physical abilities are adaptable, multi-purpose, and greatly improve opportunities. Personal enhancement is direct, it can be highly effective, and, although there may be recovery, adaptation and adjustment time, the benefits of personal enhancement for

---

[25] This apparent consequence was pointed out to me by Frances Kamm.

any given person are likely to be enjoyed within a reasonable time frame. Hence, it may be said, this argument also provides a reason to favour medical approaches to disability.

4.6. Reasons for Status Enhancement

However, this appearance of favouring personal enhancement is by no means the whole story. For it leaves out our other goal: creating a society in which people stand as equals to another.[26] This, as suggested above, provides a set of reasons for preferring the strategy of status enhancement, changing society. One is that status enhancement is non-stigmatizing. A second is that it is inclusive. A third is that it benefits everyone.

We can explore these reasons, somewhat indirectly, by considering the issue that where there are two distinct goals of policy—in this case addressing individual disadvantage and creating a society of equals[27]—there is the possibility of conflict, and the question of how to balance the two issues can generate acute, cruel dilemmas in particular cases. Consider, for example, a society in which it is well known that women will only be able to find good jobs if they meet certain norms of physical attractiveness. It may be the case that for some jobs, such as a fashion model, this may be reasonable enough, but for most jobs physical appearance should be irrelevant. Nevertheless, let us assume that this norm has seeped through society as a whole. Women who fail to meet this norm are disadvantaged, and so may seek cosmetic surgery—a personal enhancement. The question that immediately concerns us is not whether cosmetic surgery should be provided at public expense, but whether this is an appropriate way of addressing the disadvantage such women suffer. Surely status enhancement—a change in norms—would generally be agreed to be preferable.

But why would it be preferable? A good society, it may be said, should not contain rigid pressure to conform, but should be tolerant of

---

[26] I thank Alex Voorhoeve for reminding me of the availability of this reply.

[27] Given my argument that the goods of a society of equals can be understood in terms of a wider conception of individual advantage it is more accurate to say that aspects of individual advantage can conflict. However, putting it this way better brings out the nature of the conflict.

difference.[28] Why? Some might argue that difference is good in itself. This seems implausible. We would not, for example, encourage genetic programmes to produce human beings with lilac or magenta skin, or extra limbs, in order to glory in the difference. Rather we want a world in which existing (and anticipated) difference are accepted. But why should any of us want this?

To begin to answer this question, consider another example, this time in relation to disability. One disability activist has sometimes remarked publicly that he 'celebrates' his quadriplegia. This has been taken by some as a shocking, even irresponsible, statement. Is he advocating quadriplegia? Does he want to bring more quadriplegics into the world? Does he think we should be pleased if someone loses the use of their arms and legs? Should we neglect safety, as if becoming quadriplegic doesn't matter? If he could instantly and painlessly be brought to full functioning, would he decline? Would he disapprove of others who chose the cure? In sum, does he think that it is *better* to be quadriplegic? Rather, I imagine, he is trying to make another, quite different, point with a political intent. A society which has adjusted itself to accommodate quadriplegia by means of suitable transport and education policies, tolerant social attitudes, and other imaginative steps, is good for all of us. It is good in at least two ways. First it helps communicate a message that human beings are all equals and should all be included in our social arrangements. Second, any one of us—or our loved ones—may tomorrow suffer an injury which would leave us quadriplegic. A society ready and waiting for us if we do suffer this undoubted misfortune somewhat mitigates some of its effects. Hence the activist's celebration of quadriplegia is a highly altruistic gesture. Making people aware of the lives of quadriplegics may help us steer society and its institutions in the right direction. He has opened himself up to scorn, ridicule, and incomprehension in order to try to make the world a better place for all. (This, indeed, is an example of inverse cross-category risk.)

To put the general point in the terms of this paper: a society which favours status enhancements reduces risk to everyone. It reduces the risk not of becoming quadriplegic but of suffering further losses of functioning consequent on becoming quadriplegic. Hence status enhancement goes

---

[28] For some reflections on the nature of toleration and its relation to the idea of social ethos, see Wolff 2003.

some way to providing secure functionings for all, insofar as this is possible. It makes us all better off, whatever our fate.

Yet it is not always a simple matter. Let us return to the case of female employment and cosmetic surgery. A young graduate, about to enter the job market, but who fails to live up to norms of beauty, may be desperate to undergo cosmetic surgery. At the same time she may completely understand that she is helping to reinforce the obnoxious values of the dominant culture, to the detriment of others like her, who will continue to feel forced to undergo surgery. And these people may include her younger sisters and daughters. But, she may well argue, she has no choice. Her refusal to conform would have no effects on its own. It would be an empty gesture, unless it was part of a mass popular or political movement. Status enhancement is rarely possible on an individual basis, unless one is already a role model of some sort. Here, then, individual functioning and longer-term social progress pull apart. Progress relies on the very public courage of the few. Yet this should not make us turn away from policies of status enhancement. For imagine we have achieved a world in which people are accepted whatever they look like. They never need form the thought that they might not be accepted (except, perhaps, as a rather extraordinary historical observation about how things were in the bad old days), nor do they even need to form the thought that they have benefited from social policy. This, then, is why status enhancement is non-stigmatizing. It does not need to identify which particular individual to help in order to help them. It requires neither pity nor gratitude.

4.7. Disability and Social Policy

What I have just said about the non-stigmatizing benefits of status enhancement may seem to be in tension with the fact that, from the point of view of social policy, we do need to identify people with disabilities. Furthermore, the definition I have offered shows how to do this: a disabled person is someone who lacks genuine opportunity for secure functionings owing (in part) to physical or mental impairment. So there is, it may be argued, both a need to identify disabled people in order to help them, and a means of doing so.

However, this argument presupposes that disabled people need help of some form because they are disabled. On this view, we must attend to the needs of disabled people whatever else is true of them; whether they are wealthy or poor; have a wide and rich social network or are socially isolated, and so on. An alternative view is that disability as such is not the crux of the matter; rather we need to come to an assessment of what we could call someone's total life experience, and those who do worse on this measure have the most urgent social claims. Which view is correct? One argument is that a humane society should attend to each and every need of each and every person, and so all people with disabilities should receive assistance whatever else is true of them. In response it will be argued that resources are limited and we cannot do everything. Consequently what matters is whether or not people have genuine opportunities for secure functioning, and not whether any lack of functioning is attributable to any particular cause. On such a view the idea of mental and physical impairment is strictly speaking irrelevant to social policy: what matters is the most urgent lack of opportunities for secure functionings. Disability gives rise to claims alongside many other calls on scarce resources and must be judged against them.

There seems to be something right about both sides. For example, allowing only those of below average income to use disabled parking bays, on the grounds that the wealthier do not need subsidized parking, is not an attractive social policy. Where a measure is relatively cheap, and beneficial, there seems reason to apply it generally. Yet at the same time it should be possible to have a reasoned debate about whether some measures are over-demanding; for example, building codes for disabled access which make building, say, a new leisure centre prohibitively expensive. This is not to say that such codes must be wrong, but it should be possible to ask such a question with an open mind, taking into account all the consequences. Decisions have their costs and these should be brought into the open, at least at the level of the formulation of general policy.

However, even when we take a 'total life experience' approach, where, strictly speaking, the issue of disability (lack of opportunity through impairment) becomes irrelevant, this does not mean that the concept of disability is irrelevant in practical terms. For some impairments are so devastating that they typically cause a whole set of effects. Indeed many disabled people find a whole range of secure functionings beyond them. Hence the idea of disability remains important as a marker for a constellation of disadvantages, rather than as a disadvantage in itself. Even if, at the most fundamental level, the concept of disability has little or no work to do, in practical terms it is of use.

4.8. Anti-Discrimination

It may be urged that there is one further way in which the concept of disability is required for theoretical purposes, one which renders the radical approach to disability, canvassed in Section 4.4 above, highly problematic. Disability advocates sometimes seem to want to argue both that there is no hard and fast line between able-bodied people and disabled people, yet, at the same time, that disabled people should receive special legal protection. Here, it may seem, disability advocates face a dilemma. If they wish to argue that disabled people need special treatment in legal and social policy, then a clear distinction between the disabled and non-disabled is indispensable. So the radical proposal that disability is, in effect, nothing special cuts away this ground. If there is nothing special about disability, there is nothing special about disability. On the radical view, societies should attempt to remedy disadvantage, whatever its cause. Consequently, as we have seen, aiding some biologically impaired people may turn out to be a low social priority if, for example, their lack of secure social functioning is relatively minor.

In response to this it is tempting to think that a dual view may be the way forward. There is a difference between outright discrimination—whether intentional or negligent—and disadvantage. The common-sense view of disability—or something like it—appears to have an essential role to play in the formation of explicit legislation and policy, protecting people with disabilities against discrimination, on the model of legislation against sexual and racial discrimination. However, from the point of view of distributive justice the concept of disability itself needs no place, except to be recognized as one very common correlate, and probable cause, of social disadvantage; a reduced opportunity to achieve secure functionings. And here too we see the situation parallel to that of race and gender.

Yet on further reflection it is apparent that we do not, after all, need the common-sense view of disability even for anti-discrimination policy. For the parallel to race and gender is not disability but impairment: discriminating against people on the basis of their physical and mental properties, not on their opportunity to achieve secure social functionings. So on the view advocated here, discrimination policy needs the concept of impairment; while social justice needs the concept of advantage understood as the genuine opportunity to achieve secure functionings. Nevertheless the concept of disability remains important. As noted, people with severe impairments often find it difficult to achieve a whole range of secure functionings, and so if someone is impaired to this degree then it is likely that they will need to be the focus of special attention. The term 'disability' has a vital use in identifying particular 'clusters' of disadvantage. However in itself the concept of disability need play no fundamental role formulating the theory behind social policy.

4.9. Conclusion

My task in this paper has been to consider how a society of equals should deal with issues of disability, seeking an answer with credibility from the point of view of both political philosophy and social policy. Rather than attempt to summarize my claims and arguments once more (they are set out in the introduction) I would like to conclude by drawing attention to one central argument of this paper: the advantages of status enhancement as a form of addressing disadvantage. Although those who advocate the social model have long understood and advocated this, it is worth ending with a statement of the three grounds on which, according to the arguments of this paper, it should often be the preferred means of addressing disadvantage, when available. First, it is non-stigmatizing; individuals do not have to be identified in order to be helped. Second, it is inclusive, welcoming people in their differences, rather than attempting to impose a single mould. Third it benefits everyone by reducing risk. For a society of equals this should be an immensely attractive strategy even if it cannot always be achieved in practice.

References

Anderson, Elizabeth (1999). What Is the Point of Equality? *Ethics*, 109: 287–333.

Arneson, Richard (1989). Equality and Equality of Opportunity for Welfare. *Philosophical Studies*, 56: 77–93.

Bickenback, Jerome (1993). *Physical Disability and Social Policy*. Toronto: University of Toronto Press.

Buchanan, A., Brock, D., Daniels N., and Wikler D. (2000). *From Chance to Choice*. Cambridge: Cambridge University Press.

Cohen, G. A. (1989). On the Currency of Egalitarian Justice. *Ethics*, 99: 906–44.

——— (2004). Expensive Tastes Ride Again. In Justine Burley (ed.) *Dworkin and his Critics*. Oxford: Blackwell Publishers, 3–29.

Daniels, Norman (1985). *Just Health Care*. Cambridge: Cambridge University Press.

Dworkin, Ronald (1981a). What is Equality Part 1: Equality of Welfare. *Philosophy and Public Affairs*, 10: 185–246. Reprinted as ch. 1 of Dworkin 2000.

——— (1981b). What is Equality Part 2: Equality of Resources. *Philosophy and Public Affairs*, 10: 283–345. Reprinted as ch. 1 of Dworkin 2000.

——— (1993). Justice in the Distribution of Health Care, *McGill Law Journal*, 38: 883–98.

——— (2000). *Sovereign Virtue*. Cambridge Mass.: Harvard University Press.

Goodin, Robert (1990). Theories of Compensation. In R. G. Frey and C. W Morris (eds.) *Liability: New Essays in Legal Philosophy*. Cambridge: Cambridge University Press, 267–86.

Hinton, Timothy (2001). Must Egalitarians Choose Between Fairness and Respect? *Philosophy and Public Affairs*, 30: 72–87.

MacIntyre, Alasdair (1999). *Dependent Rational Animals*. London: Duckworth.

Marmot, Michael (2004). *Status Syndrome*. London: Bloomsbury.

Miller, David (1998). Equality and Justice. In Andrew Mason (ed.) *Ideals of Equality*. Oxford: Blackwell Publishers, 21–37.

Norman, Richard (1998). The Social Basis of Equality. In Andrew Mason (ed.) *Ideals of Equality*. Oxford: Blackwell Publishers, 37–52.

Nussbaum, Martha (2000). *Women and Human Development*. Cambridge: Cambridge University Press.

Rawls, John (1971 and 1999). *A Theory of Justice*. Oxford: Oxford University Press.

——— (1982). Social Unity and Primary Goods. In Amartya Sen and Bernard Williams (eds.) *Utilitarianism and Beyond*. Cambridge: Cambridge University Press, 159–85.

——— (1999). A Kantian Conception of Equality. In John Rawls *Collected Papers*. Cambridge Mass.: Harvard University Press, 254–66.

Scheffler, Samuel (2003). What is Egalitarianism? *Philosophy and Public Affairs*, 31: 6–35.

Sen, Amartya (1980). Equality of What? In S. McMurrin (ed.) *1980 Tanner Lectures on Human Values*. Cambridge: Cambridge University Press, 195–220.

——(1999). *Development as Freedom*. Oxford: Oxford University Press.

Shakespeare, Tom (ed.) (1998). *The Disability Reader*. London: Cassell.

Silvers, Anita, Wasserman, David, and Mahowald, Mary B. (1998). *Disability, Difference, Discrimination*. Lanham Md.: Rowman & Littlefield.

Tawney, R. H. (1931). *Equality*. London: George Allen & Unwin.

Terzi, Lorella (2009). Vagaries of the Natural Lottery? Human Diversity, Disability, and Justice: A Capability Perspective. This volume, Ch. 3.

Tremain, Shelley (1996). Dworkin on Disablement and Resources, *Canadian Journal of Law and Jurisprudence,* 9: 343–59.

Wolff, Jonathan (1998). Fairness, Respect, and the Egalitarian Ethos. *Philosophy and Public Affairs*, 27: 97–122.

——(2001). Levelling Down. In K. Dowding, J. Hughes, and H. Margetts (eds.) *Challenges to Democracy*. London: Palgrave, 18–32.

——(2002). Addressing Disadvantage and the Human Good. *Journal of Applied Philosophy*, 19: 207–18.

——(2003). Social Ethos and the Dynamics of Toleration. In Catriona McKinnon and Dario Castiglione (eds.) *The Culture of Toleration in Diverse Societies: Reasonable Toleration*. Manchester: Manchester University Press, 147–60.

——and de-Shalit, Avner (2007) *Disadvantage*. Oxford: Oxford University Press.

5

An Inclusive Contractualism: Obligations to the Mentally Disabled

CHRISTIE HARTLEY

Would anyone among us deny that persons with mental disabilities have standing in society as members and that, like other members, these individuals are owed justice? Dispute about this is hard to imagine. It is simply part of our democratic culture.[1] Given this, you would expect that the theories of justice thought to be most promising by political philosophers would be inclusive of the mentally disabled as members of society and responsive to their interests as such. Political philosopher John Rawls has stated that when theorizing about justice, we should begin with our firmly held beliefs and provisionally assume that any acceptable account of justice

I thank Elizabeth Anderson and Stephen Darwall for generous comments on earlier drafts of this paper. Peter Railton, Cynthia Stark, Mary Mahowald, Kimberley Brownlee, and Adam Cureton have also given me very helpful feedback. Earlier versions of this paper were presented at the University of Michigan, the Institute for Research on Women and Gender, Georgia State University, a meeting of the Pacific Division of the American Philosophical Association, and a workshop for this collection held at the Parr Center for Ethics, University of North Carolina at Chapel Hill. I thank the audiences at these places for valuable discussion. While completing this paper, I held an American Fellowship from the American Association of University Women Educational Foundation; I gratefully acknowledge their support.

[1] There is much disagreement about what society owes those with disabilities ranging from the material goods and services society owes to the disabled to the rights and liberties that the disabled should enjoy. I assume all obligations we have to others as members of a state are a matter of justice, not charity, but when we think of ourselves as members of the moral community, we should recognize that we can have both moral obligations of justice and of charity. For an interesting discussion of the distinction between obligations of justice and obligations of virtue, see Onora O'Neill, *Towards Justice and Virtue: A Constructive Account of Practical Reasoning* (Cambridge: Cambridge University Press, 1996).

must respect them.[2] It might then come as a surprise, at least if you have been unaware of recent work by Martha Nussbaum or Eva Feder Kittay,[3] that the most highly regarded theory of justice, Rawls's theory, does not address what is owed to those with severe mental impairments.[4] What's more, Nussbaum and Kittay have raised doubts about whether any contractualist theory like Rawls's can be inclusive of the mentally disabled.[5]

In this essay, I begin to construct a contractualist account of justice that is inclusive of the mentally disabled. I shall argue that when society is cast as a fair system of cooperation, those with mental disabilities should indeed count as members of society since they have the capacity to engage in cooperative projects that are of fundamental importance to contractualist society. Contractualists do not need to recognize merely having needs as an animal or the ability to feel pain as an independent ground for a claim to justice in order to include the mentally disabled within contractualist theory.[6] Rather, contractualists can construct a theory that is inclusive of the mentally disabled by properly appreciating the numerous ways in which persons with mental disabilities make substantial contributions to the creation, establishment, and maintenance of a society based on relations of mutual respect.

For my purposes, I understand a mental disability to be any kind of mental impairment that interferes with someone's ability to form, pursue, or carry out valued projects in society. Such impairments may be developmental or may result from illness or accident. Of course, not all mental impairments raise serious problems for contractualism in its traditional form (e.g. a cognitive impairment that inhibits a person's ability to read but not to

[2] J. Rawls, *Political Liberalism*, paperback edn (New York: Columbia University Press, 1996), 8.
[3] M. C. Nussbaum, 'The Future of Feminist Liberalism,' *Proceedings and Addresses of the American Philosophical Association*, 74 (2000), 47–79; M. C. Nussbaum, 'Beyond the Social Contract: Toward Global Justice,' *The Tanner Lectures on Human Values*, 24, ed. Grethe B. Peterson (Salt Lake City: University of Utah Press, 2004), 413–507; M. C. Nussbaum, *Frontiers of Justice: Disability, Nationality, Species Membership* (Cambridge, Mass.: Belknap Press, 2006); E. F. Kittay, *Love's Labour: Essays on Women, Equality, and Dependency* (New York: Routledge, 1999); E. F. Kittay, 'When Caring is Just and Justice is Caring: Justice and Mental Retardation', *Public Culture*, 13 (2001), 557–79.
[4] Rawls, *Political Liberalism*, 20–1.
[5] See the work of Nussbaum and Kittay referenced in n. 3 above.
[6] Can contractualists recognize claims to justice based solely on these considerations? I cannot explore this issue here. Even if they cannot, members of society can still pass laws and policies regarding the welfare and treatment of animals. However, I believe the contractualist theory I develop suggests that we have duties of justice to at least some nonhuman animals, given that some of these animals make *cooperative* contributions to contractualist society.

communicate verbally or reason). The mental impairments that are of interest to me are those that frustrate a person's capacity to form a rational conception of the good or to develop a sense of justice, since it is thought that one must have these abilities to be a cooperating member of society.

5.1. The Exclusion of the Mentally Disabled

To begin, it is worth considering why Rawls does not address the interests of the mentally disabled in his theory of justice. Importantly, Rawls does not assert that we do not have obligations of any kind to the disabled.[7] Rather, he believes it is useful to temporarily bracket the matter of what we owe to the disabled in order to deal more easily with what he believes to be the fundamental case of justice, which he specifies as 'the terms of social cooperation between citizens regarded as free and equal, and as normal and fully cooperating members of society over a complete life'.[8] Rawls claims that cooperating members of society should be regarded as possessing the two moral powers, that is, the capacity for a sense of justice and the capacity to develop a rational conception of one's good.[9] Cooperation requires that members of society possess these capacities, according to Rawls, because terms of cooperation must be justifiable to all.[10]

However, Rawls's postponement of questions regarding what is owed to the mentally disabled is problematic. First, it runs the risk of suggesting that our obligations to those with the two moral powers are more important than our obligations to the mentally disabled. Second, extending Rawls's view of justice to the mentally disabled is no easy matter. In Rawls's theory of justice, the goods that members of society need access to as a matter of justice are only based on the needs of members with the two

---

[7] Rawls, *Political Liberalism*, 20–1.

[8] Ibid. 20. By this description of the fundamental problem of justice in *Political Liberalism*, Rawls excludes those human beings without the two moral powers as well as those who do not have mental and physical abilities in the normal range. Ibid. 272 n. 10. Yet, in *Political Liberalism*, Rawls also states that the possession of the two moral powers is a necessary and sufficient condition for being a 'full and equal member of society.' Ibid. 302. Regardless of how we should understand Rawls's own view about members' physical abilities, contractualists should treat the possession of the two moral powers as a sufficient condition for being a fully cooperating member of society because of the cooperative contributions to society that persons are able to make through these capacities.

[9] Ibid. 301–2.   [10] Ibid. 300–1.

moral powers. So any attempt to extend Rawls's theory to include those persons without these powers would require some revision to the list of goods that Rawls claims are relevant to justice. Moreover, the principles of justice that govern the distribution of these goods would also have to be modified to ensure both that the needs of the disabled are met and that obligations to the disabled are fairly divided among members of society. Finally, because Rawls thinks social cooperation necessitates the possession of the two moral powers, an extension of Rawls's own view would require a justification for our obligations to the mentally disabled not based on cooperation.

Rawls, in fact, expresses uncertainty about whether his theory of justice as fairness can address questions concerning what we owe to those with temporary or permanent disabilities.[11] Yet, Rawls's failure to address what we owe to those with disabilities may not reflect a limitation of contractualism but may result from particular elements of Rawls's theory that are not necessary to or that are even inimical to contractualism.[12]

5.2. The Nature of Contractualist Cooperation

Instead of trying to extend Rawls's theory of justice to include the mentally disabled, I propose that we return to the core ideas of contractualism to see if there is a way to include the mentally disabled within contractualist theory from the beginning. Rawls, of course, has been crucial to the development of some fundamental contractualist ideas, but, again, perhaps the core ideas of contractualism do not or need not lead to the particular contractualist theory Rawls proposes. Central to contractualist accounts of domestic justice is that society is viewed as a system of cooperation over time. Following Rawls, I take this system to be composed of the principal political, social, and economic institutions in society or, in Rawls's terminology, the basic structure of society.[13] According to contractualists,

---

[11] Ibid. 20–1.

[12] Cynthia Stark claims that Rawls intends to keep some elements of *contractarianism* in his *contractualist* theory. 'Contractarianism and Contribution, Or Why Talents Matter *Somewhat*,' unpublished manuscript. Nussbaum, too, understands Rawls as retaining many elements of contractarianism in his theory, though I think she mistakenly interprets Rawls as proposing a contract for mutual advantage.

[13] Rawls, *Political Liberalism*, 11 and 301.

a society is just when the terms of cooperation are fair and establish a society based on relations of mutual respect among members viewed as free and equal. Fair cooperation, according to Rawls, has three distinct characteristics that set it apart from other kinds of cooperation. First, it is 'guided by publicly recognized rules and procedures that those cooperating accept and regard as properly regulating their conduct'. Second, its concern is with 'terms that each participant may reasonably accept, provided that everyone else likewise accepts them'. According to Rawls, such 'fair terms' of cooperation establish a kind of *reciprocity* among members of society in which 'all who are engaged in cooperation and who do their part as the rules and procedure require, are to benefit in an appropriate way as assessed by a suitable benchmark of comparison'. Finally, fair cooperation includes an 'idea of each participant's rational advantage, or good'.[14] Fair cooperation so understood involves members of society being responsible to each other for maintaining a just society and for respecting other members of society as equal members.

The contractualist idea of fair cooperation should be distinguished from the idea of cooperation for mutual advantage. The latter is the view that cooperation among individuals is rational or justified if prospective cooperators have more to gain by working with others according to rules that are advantageous to everyone than if they abstain from cooperation.[15] This requires that the benefits of including an individual in a cooperative project must offset the cost of her participation. Oftentimes many different terms for cooperation are better for prospective cooperators than no cooperation at all. When this is the case, individuals' particular talents and skills will affect the particular terms for cooperation to which all agree.[16] Those who will be in the worst position if no bargain is struck have an inferior bargaining position relative to others. Because individuals' talents and skills influence the terms of cooperation, the terms that are agreed to be mutually advantageous for all, in the sense of individuals being

[14] Rawls, *Political Liberalism*, 16.

[15] On the distinction between contractualism and contractarianism, see Stephen Darwall's introduction in his edited volume *Contractarianism/Contractualism* (Malden, Mass.: Blackwell Publishing, 2003), 1–8.

[16] What agents can bring to the initial bargaining position is, in most accounts, subject to something like the Lockean proviso, which moral contractarian David Gauthier puts like this: 'the proviso prohibits bettering one's situation through interaction that worsens the situation of another.' D. Gauthier, *Morals by Agreement* (Oxford: Clarendon Press, 1986), 205.

better off by cooperating, may in fact allow for significant inequalities among cooperators. Cooperation for mutual advantage is distinctive of social contract theories in the tradition of Hobbes, sometimes referred to as 'contractarian' in contrast to 'contractualist'. Contractualist theories of cooperation differ from contractarian theories, theories of cooperation for mutual advantage. Contractualists require that terms of cooperation among members of society be reasonable or justifiable to all members viewed as equals and not merely terms that are rationally advantageous to all members in the sense of allowing individuals to better their situation by working together with others. Furthermore, contractualism's endorsement of reciprocity, rather than mutual advantage, does not require that those who count as cooperating members of society be such that their cooperative contributions to society outweigh the costs of their participation.

Although contractualist cooperation is distinct from other conceptions of cooperation because of these characteristics, it is important to keep in mind that cooperation of any kind involves *individuals working together with others for a common end*.[17] For contractualists, this means that members of society must make some kind of cooperative contribution to the relationships or social institutions that allow for relations of mutual respect.[18]

Now, when thinking about cooperation, we often picture individuals working together in the production or distribution of some independently existing product, say, material goods. We tend to focus on the production or distribution of material goods that result from the cooperative project and not on the relationship among those persons who produce them. In fact, we think of the goods of cooperation as external to the relationship of those who cooperate to produce them in the sense that, even though the reason the individuals cooperate is to produce or enjoy certain goods, the goods produced do not determine the nature or the terms of the cooperative relationship among those who produce them. I call this way of thinking about cooperation the production model.

---

[17] The *Oxford English Dictionary* defines cooperation as '[t]he action of co-operating, *i.e.*, of working together towards the same end, purpose, or effect; joint operation'. *Oxford English Dictionary Online*, 2nd edn, s.v. 'cooperation'.

[18] To be more precise, I should say that when society is viewed as a system of cooperation, beings whose claim to membership rests on cooperation must make some kind of cooperative contribution to society. Perhaps contractualists can recognize other grounds for membership even when society is viewed as a fair system of cooperation.

This can be contrasted with another model of cooperation that I call the relationship model. The focus of cooperation in this model is on the development of the relationship between those cooperating. Independently existing goods may be important to the establishment of the relationship in various ways, but the relationship is the primary concern of the cooperative project. Consider friendship. In most cases the point of a friendship is to develop a certain kind of intimate relationship with another. The end of many friendships is, in fact, companionship. By companionship, I neither mean a relationship that is solely composed of one's coordinating one's behaviour with another's (after all, people respond in this way to others when they attempt to avoid running into each other on the street), nor do I mean a relationship that merely involves sharing emotions through, what Stephen Darwall has called, emotional contagion, as when one, for example, becomes happy by simply walking into a room with happy people.[19] The kind of companionship that I intend involves engaging with another in a shared endeavour. It includes one *recognizing* another as a responsive, animate being and communicating with her. Two individuals working together to choose and prepare a meal that is equally desirable to both parties would count as this.

When thinking about the focus of cooperation for contractualists, we should have in mind the relationship model, not the production model. Social cooperation for contractualists is about the establishment of a society based on relations of mutual respect between free and equal members. Its concern is not primarily with the production and distribution of goods but is with the construction of a certain kind of relationship that is itself produced by relating. Elizabeth Anderson's work on equality as a social relationship is helpful when trying to grasp the contractualist conception of cooperation.[20] Anderson notes that some egalitarians think equality amounts to a just pattern of distribution among persons. On these views, equality among individuals consists of their having equal shares of a distributable good (e.g. opportunity for welfare), and social relationships are only important insofar as they influence this.[21] Anderson distinguishes this view of equality from her relational view, which

---

[19] Darwall discusses emotional contagion in his *Welfare and Rational Care* (Princeton: Princeton University Press, 2002), 54–8.

[20] E. Anderson, 'What is the Point of Equality?', *Ethics*, 109 (1999), 287–337.

[21] Ibid. 313.

she calls democratic equality. Anderson describes democratic equality as follows:

democratic equality regards two people as equal when each accepts the obligation to justify their actions by principles acceptable to the other, and in which they take mutual consultation, reciprocation, and recognition for granted. Certain patterns in the distribution of goods may be instrumental to securing such relationships, follow from them, or even be constitutive of them. But democratic egalitarians are fundamentally concerned with the relationships within which goods are distributed, not only with the distribution of the goods themselves.[22]

Likewise, contractualists are fundamentally concerned with social relationships. The terms of social cooperation, as applied to the basic structure, are to establish a society based on mutual respect among members regarded as equals, and members of society are viewed as committed to living on terms of mutual respect with others.

5.3. From Fair Cooperation to Membership in Society

What do these core ideas of contractualism suggest about membership in society? As noted, Rawls thinks the contractualist idea of fair cooperation leads to a conception of societal membership in which members possess the two moral powers, that is, a capacity for a sense of justice and a capacity for a rational conception of the good. He must reason as follows: fair cooperation requires that the terms of social cooperation be justifiable to all members of society; hence, to be a member of society one must possess those capacities that would allow one to assess the justifiability of the terms of cooperation.

However, a society based on fair terms of cooperation does not require that all members possess the capacities that would allow them to assess the justifiability of the terms of cooperation. What is required is that the terms of cooperation be justifiable to those with the two moral powers and that, if there are members without the two moral powers, proper consideration be given to the interests of these individuals as equal members when the terms

---

[22] Ibid. 313–14.

of social cooperation are constructed. For someone who does not possess the two moral powers, terms of cooperation can be judged fair if they are justifiable to a trustee for this individual. The trustee, of course, would be charged with the task of representing the interests of the individual and would assess the reasonableness of the principles of justice given that individual's interests as a member of society.[23]

Now, one might worry, as Nussbaum does, that those with the two moral powers who are trustees for others will inadequately consider the interests of individuals not able to represent themselves given trustees' interest in securing terms of cooperation favourable to themselves. Fair representation for those unable to represent themselves is a serious concern. In contractualist theory, however, members are not viewed as merely self-interested beings who cooperate only for mutual advantage. They are concerned with constructing a society based on fairness and mutual respect. They are fundamentally committed to terms of cooperation that are fair and respectful of all members of society as equal members. Hence, if the disabled (or some subset of the disabled) are not as well off as other members of society in some respect relevant to their objective interests as members of society, members of society will have reason to review the terms of cooperation to see if the interests of the disabled were properly weighed.[24]

We must now address how contractualists should determine who counts as a member of society if fair cooperation does not require that all members of society possess the two moral powers. As I've stated, the concern of justice for contractualists is the establishment of a society based on relations of mutual respect among members viewed as free and equal. Social cooperation is for this end. Contractualists should aim to provide fair terms of cooperation for all those who cooperatively contribute to a society so understood. The capacity for cooperative contribution is the appropriate ground for membership in contractualism.

To decide who counts as a member of society entitled to justice, contractualists must consider all the kinds of cooperative contributions

---

[23] The notion of a trustee is not new to contractualism. Rawls claims that those who choose the principles of justice for fair cooperation behind the veil of ignorance are trustees for all free and equal citizens. *Political Liberalism*, 24.

[24] The objective interests of members of society must not be biased in favour of any particular group. So, we would need to revise Rawls's account of the objective interests of members of society, which is those goods members need 'for developing and exercising the two moral powers and for effectively pursuing conceptions of the good with widely different contents'. *Political Liberalism*, 75–6.

individuals can make to a society based on relations of mutual respect. These cooperative contributions include those made through developing relationships with others and through individuals' abilities to produce other social goods like rights and liberties, opportunities of certain sorts, and the material goods and services that are instrumental to making relations of mutual respect in society possible. The inclusion of those persons who lack the two moral powers as members of society in contractualist theory depends on (1) whether those persons who lack the two moral powers cooperatively contribute to contractualist society and (2) whether we can give a reasonable account of the role of a trustee for these individuals. As I shall argue, one does not need the two moral powers to engage in some of the cooperative projects important to contractualist society.

5.4. Cooperation and the Mentally Disabled

People with mental disabilities, with the exception of those who are comatose or in a completely vegetative condition, are capable of cooperatively contributing to society.[25] For example, many people with mental disabilities are able to work in the labour market in the production of material goods and social services. In 2000, there were 1,823,291 people with mental disabilities of working age in the US labour market,[26] and those who work with persons with mental impairments agree that the current level of labour force participation considerably misrepresents the number of mentally disabled persons able to participate in the labour force if only given training and support.[27] Independent of participation in the

---

[25] Here I am concerned with just those persons with mental disabilities who lack the two moral powers. Of course, not all mental impairments interfere with a person's capacity for the two moral powers (e.g. some cases of dyslexia or autism).

[26] According to the US Census Bureau, in 2000 there were 2,957,923 men in the US age 21 to 64 who were noninstitutionalized and who had a mental disability; of these men, 982,912 were employed in the labour market. According to the same study, there were 3,032,967 women in the US age 21 to 64 who were noninstitutionalized and who had a mental disability; of these women, 840,379 were employed in the labour market. US Bureau of the Census, 'PCT29. Sex by Age by Mental Disability by Employment Status for the Civilian Noninstitutionalized Population 5 Years and Over', *Census 2000, Summary File 3* (available using American Factfinder at www.factfinder.census.gov (2004, April 26)).

[27] See E. E. Castles, *'We're People First': The Social and Emotional Lives of Individuals with Mental Retardation* (Westport, Conn.: Praeger Publishers, 1996), 112–22; J. P. Shapiro, *No Pity: People with Disabilities Forging a New Civil Rights Movement* (New York: Times Books, Random House, 1993), 142–58; J. W. Trent Jr, *Inventing the Feeble Mind: A History of Mental Retardation in the United States*

labour market, many people with disabilities cooperatively contribute to society by performing household work that is crucial to the family, an institution that is part of the basic structure. These contributions to society are important, and contractualists should recognize those who make them as members of society entitled to justice.

Of course, some people with mental disabilities cannot work in the labour market or contribute to household work. Nonetheless, these people, excepting those who are comatose or in a wholly vegetative condition, can cooperatively contribute to society, too, through their capacity for engagement. In what follows, I offer an account of the psychology of engagement and show how the capacity for engagement allows persons with mental disabilities to make cooperative contributions of fundamental importance to contractualist society.

The sort of engagement important for cooperation requires a kind of common recognition between individuals.[28] It involves individuals seeing each other as responsive, animate beings and recognizing the ability of the other to be responsive to what one does. Individuals view each other not simply as able to respond to their environment but as able to respond to something they interpret and recognize as a communication to themselves. The recognition between individuals includes the recognition of the status of the other as a being with whom communication is possible. This recognition must be communicated between individuals through some kind of interaction.

The communication of this recognition, that is, of individuals' recognition of each other as animate, responsive beings, is almost never explicitly stated. It is, however, expressed by any communicative expression between individuals. Communication necessitates that one take another as a responsive, animate being with the ability to respond to what one does. For example, when I direct a question to you, I take it that you can respond to my inquiry. Individuals engage with each other when they make mutual communicative expressions to each other.

(Berkeley: University of California Press, 1994). Trent notes the emergence of schools in the 1840s and 1850s for the purpose of instructing those with mental disabilities in how to be productive citizens in their local communities. Ibid. 7–39. Despite much success, economic and social factors resulted in a move toward custodial institutions in the mid- to late 1800s. Ibid. 60–95.

[28] In developing my account of engagement, I benefited from Stephen Darwall's work on the interpersonal nature of respect. S. Darwall, 'Respect and the Second-Person Standpoint,' *Proceedings and Addresses of the American Philosophical Association*, 78 (2004), 43–59.

An important aspect of engagement is that the individuals communicating are cooperating with each other in a joint project. They are working together at least for the sake of making a communication.[29] When I discuss a philosophical question with a student, I am working with the student to make progress on a philosophical problem, but we're also, in virtue of our attempts at communication, working on communicating with each other. Likewise, when a small child looks at a parent and pushes her food away to communicate that she's not interested and when the parent looks back at her imitating an eating motion, the parent and child are working together on communicating. Moreover, working together with another, as opposed to merely coordinating one's behaviour with another's, *requires* communication. Cooperation of any kind then depends on the capacity for engagement, that is, the ability to recognize others as responsive, animate beings and the ability to communicate one's recognition of this to them.

The capacity for engagement, though, is not only the foundation of any kind of cooperation, but it is also an incipient form of the capacities that make for *fair* cooperation and a society of mutual respect. To see this, we need to understand the nature of respect; I rely on Stephen Darwall's work here. In the construction of a society based on mutual respect, our concern is with a kind of recognition respect. Darwall describes recognition respect, generally, as an attitude one takes toward other beings or things in one's deliberations; it involves attributing to another being or thing its proper value in virtue of the capacities or qualities it has and directing one's conduct accordingly.[30] He claims that recognition respect for persons in particular, though, not only consists of valuing someone appropriately as a person and directing one's conduct accordingly but also involves recognizing that persons as such have the authority to make claims on each other as equals.[31] And Darwall asserts that to have the authority to demand respect as a person from another means that one has standing to make that demand and that one's standing gives the person to whom one's demand is directed a special kind of reason for acting, a reason based on one's authority.[32] This kind

---

[29] Similarly, Philip Pettit and Michael Smith have claimed that to be in an intellectual conversation with another is to be engaged in a joint project concerning what one should believe or desire/do. P. Pettit and M. Smith, 'Freedom in Belief and Desire,' *Journal of Philosophy*, 93 (1996), 429–49.

[30] S. Darwall, 'Two Kinds of Respect,' *Ethics*, 88 (1977), 36–49 (38).

[31] Darwall, 'Respect and the Second-Person Standpoint'.   [32] Ibid.

of reason is a second-personal reason since it requires the presence of an authoritative relationship between the individuals involved. Moreover, as Darwall notes, authority is intimately connected with accountability: the authority to demand respect from another includes the power to make that person accountable to one. Respect for persons then is, fundamentally, interpersonal in nature.

Engagement, like respect, is interpersonal in nature, and it involves a particular way of addressing another. The capacity for engagement does not require that one be able to recognize another as a person, as does recognition respect. However, to engage with another one must communicate with him; this entails that one regard him as having a special kind of *status* or *standing*, the standing of a being with whom one can communicate and share ends. The recognition central to engagement is an incipient form of the recognition characteristic of respect.[33]

Let us now turn to how the capacity to engage with another allows persons with mental disabilities to make cooperative contributions to contractualist society. I'll focus first on how persons with mental disabilities are able to contribute to the family and then show how these persons are also able to make important contributions to society more generally.

Companionship is an essential part of family life. It strengthens bonds of love and connection between family members. It also provides family members with emotional support and strength for tackling problems they'll face within and outside of the family. It plays a crucial role in keeping families together and helping them to function well. Through various modes of communication, persons with mental disabilities cooperatively contribute to society by providing companionship and emotional support to family members.

That cooperation in the form of companionship can be part of a relationship with someone who has profound mental disabilities is obvious from the relationship Eva Kittay describes between herself and her daughter Sesha,

---

[33] Eva Kittay claims that the ability to participate in certain kinds of relationships is important for how we understand personhood for purposes of justice. Kittay has suggested that we define persons as all those with 'the capacity to be in certain relationships with other persons, to sustain contact with other persons, to shape one's own world and the world of others, and to have a life that another person can conceive as an imaginative possibility for him- or herself'. Kittay, 'When Caring is Just and Justice is Caring' (n. 3 above), 568. Kittay notes that she has been influenced by Cora Diamond's work: C. Diamond, 'The Importance of Being Human,' in David Cockburn (ed), *Human Beings* (Cambridge: Cambridge University Press, 1991), 35–62.

who is profoundly retarded.[34] Sesha is not able to communicate through the use of language, and her mother reports that she has no determinable IQ. Despite these impairments, though, Sesha is able to engage with others. She communicates some of her preferences to others, such as when she enjoys a particular piece of music, and she understands some things that are communicated to her. She shares moments of excitement and laughter with others in response to their communications or their shared experiences. And, from Kittay's accounts, it is clear that Sesha enjoys spending time with her family and caregivers from the kisses and hugs that she gives them. Kittay also stresses that her daughter's communication provides her with emotional support. Sesha's companionship is a cooperative contribution to her family.

Persons with mental disabilities also contribute to the family by helping family members develop important values. Consider Sophia Wong's account of a family game of cards that includes her brother Leo, who is mentally retarded.[35] Wong writes,

our [family's] conception of a good game with family friends isn't one in which subtle and brilliant strategies are successfully deployed and glorious battles are won. Instead of learning to react quickly to rapid play, we cultivate good-humoured patience as we wait endless minutes for Leo to sort his cards carefully by suit and number. We develop the ability to speak clearly and concisely as we struggle to explain the rules of the game in terms he can understand easily. In playing with one less cognitively skilled, we restrain our reflex to take advantage of him thoughtlessly ... It is no simple matter to play well with grace, thoughtfulness, empathy, compassion, patience, and presence of mind.[36]

In a family card game, the Wongs realize the importance of patience and compassion from their interaction with Leo. Also by resisting the temptation to take advantage of him and go for a win, the members of Leo's family develop skills that are distinctive of *fair* cooperation. Namely, they learn to resist taking advantage of another simply because they can or because it is in their interest insofar as winning the game goes. Importantly, the development of relationships of mutual respect within the family

---

[34] Kittay, *Love's Labor* (n. 3 above), 147–61, esp. 150–2; E. F. Kittay, 'At Home with My Daughter,' in Leslie Pickering Francis and Anita Silvers (eds.), *Americans with Disabilities: Exploring Implications of the Law for Individuals and Institutions* (New York: Routledge, 2000), 64–80.

[35] S. Wong, 'At Home with Down Syndrome and Gender,' *Hypatia*, 17 (2002), 89–117.

[36] Ibid. 103.

encourages relationships based on respect outside the family, *and*, in a society based on relations of mutual respect, mutual respect must exist in the family. The cooperative contributions of the mentally disabled to family life justify their inclusion as members of society entitled to justice.

One might object to my present argument on the grounds that showing that persons with mental disabilities cooperatively contribute to the family hardly justifies obligations of justice by all members of society to these individuals. When a person's contribution to society is limited to one institution (the family), then all we can establish is that the members of the specific institution (the family members) that enjoy the contribution have obligations to that person.

It is worth reviewing here what makes the family part of the basic structure of a society based on relations of mutual respect. In Western society, the family is a principal institution of social organization for economic, physical, emotional, and moral support. How goods are distributed in society between families as well as how goods are distributed within one's own family have an important influence on how one does in life. And, it is in the family that the majority of individuals in society develop their most intimate social relations, receive care in times of dependency, and do much of their learning about how to relate to others and the world. Indeed, the family plays a crucial role in the development of persons' sense of justice,[37] as illustrated earlier by the values taught through participation in the Wong family card game. As a principal institution of social organization, the family is an institution that must embody relations of mutual respect among its members if society is to be just. Through their contributions to family life, persons with mental disabilities indirectly support institutions and relationships outside of the family, and, because the family is a principal institution of social organization, cooperative contributions to the family are also direct contributions to society.

People with mental disabilities also have valuable relationships with people outside of their families. In these relationships, persons with mental disabilities cooperatively contribute to society by encouraging others to

---

[37] See J. Rawls, *Justice as Fairness: A Restatement*, ed. Erin Kelley (Cambridge, Mass.: Harvard University Press, 2001), 162–3: '[E]ssential to the role of the family is the arrangement in a reasonable and effective way of the raising and caring for children, ensuring their moral development and education into the wider culture'; S. M. Okin, *Justice, Gender and the Family* (New York: Basic Books, 1989).

explore different, beneficial ways of gaining knowledge, by giving others perspective on what's of value in a human life and by helping others gain a clearer understanding of their humanity, which is crucial for the construction of a society based on relations of mutual respect. I shall discuss each of these contributions.

Inclusive schooling illustrates how relationships with mentally disabled persons encourage others to explore new ways of gaining knowledge. Inclusiveness is an approach to education that accepts and values diversity among students,[38] and it involves a commitment to the instruction of all students in one classroom, whenever reasonable and regardless of different learning abilities. The underlying principle of this educational approach is that inclusiveness 'supports and benefits' everyone.[39] To better accommodate an autistic student who had difficulty sitting through standard history lectures without engaging in disruptive behaviour, one instructor developed a project for his history class's unit on Vietnam with the particular needs of his autistic student in mind.[40] The project involved students from the class conducting interviews of individuals who had lived through the Vietnam era. This project encouraged learning not only through the usual modes of reading texts and listening to lectures but also through direct communication with persons who had relevant experiences. The instructor thought that this project better engaged his autistic student and helped all his students develop important skills and gain valuable knowledge.

By pushing others to explore alternative modes of gaining information, persons with mental disabilities make an important contribution to society. Much can be learned about the world and about what is of value from trying new things, and trying new things can help one see the world from another's point of view, a skill important to assessing the reasonableness of social policies.

Inclusiveness in education and elsewhere in society also builds community. When working with others who are different from ourselves, we form connections with them and can more easily see our similarities as opposed to our differences. Community and fellowship with other members of society motivate us to try to maintain civility and good relations

---

[38] See P. Kluth, 'You're Going to Love This Kid!': Teaching Students with Autism in the Inclusive Classroom (Baltimore: Paul H. Brookes Publishing Co., 2003), 23–4.

[39] Ibid. 23.

[40] This story is paraphrased from Kluth, 'You're Going to Love This Kid', 29–31.

with others, which makes relating on terms of mutual respect easier in a diverse, pluralistic society.

To further appreciate how cooperative relationships with the mentally disabled allow persons to gain perspective on what's of value in a human life and to better understand their own humanity, consider the movie *Radio*.[41] Based on a true story, this movie describes the friendship between a man with mental retardation, known as Radio, and the football coach of the local high school, Harold Jones. The movie focuses both on how Coach Jones helps Radio and on how Radio helps Coach Jones and all those around him. Radio is not concerned with material success or social reputation. He isn't arrogant or proud. He is genuinely kind to everyone he meets and is happy to be included in whatever is going on, valuing and making the most of what is before him.[42] Those in Radio's community who develop relationships with him gain a new perspective on what is of value in life.[43]

But, perhaps most notably, Radio humbles those before him who are arrogant or proud. In one scene, the Hanna High football team goes into the locker room during the halftime of a game; Radio accompanies the team as he is a team assistant. The team is losing the game, and the players are frustrated and upset. A particularly frustrated and arrogant player asks the others if there is any chance he can get the ball that evening, implying the incompetence of others' abilities and his high regard for his own. Radio, not quite understanding what the player means, picks up a ball and takes it to the player. Everyone smiles at Radio's gesture. He offers everyone relief from the tension. His gesture also works to humble the disgruntled player in the kindest of ways. Radio reminds the player that he is part of a team. Here, Radio's innocence allows him to reach someone in a way that most of us could not have.

---

[41] M. Tollin, director, *Radio* (United States: Sony Pictures, Columbia Pictures, 2003), motion picture.

[42] Radio was not always this way. When he first met Coach Jones and others at the school, he would not speak and was extremely shy. With tenderness and attention from others, Radio's personality was revealed.

[43] Elaine Castles states that friendships with persons who have mental retardation are beneficial because they 'can help place educational achievement and material success in their proper perspective, demonstrating the pleasure to be had in the "small blessings" of everyday experience'. Castles, *'We're People First'* (n. 27 above), 75. Eva Kittay also observes that persons with mental retardation give us 'rich opportunities for relationships and experiencing new ways of seeing the world'. Kittay, 'When Caring is Just and Justice is Caring' (n. 3 above), 567.

The ability to humble those who are arrogant or proud is an especially important contribution to a contractualist society because of the danger arrogance poses to relationships of mutual respect. Robin Dillon states that interpersonal arrogance involves both a 'claim to greater respect from others than is one's due' and 'the demand that others value themselves less than they deserve, that they not respect their dignity as persons but abase themselves to serve as mere means to the arrogant person's desire for self-exaltation'.[44] Interpersonal arrogance, then, threatens mutual respect because arrogant people do not recognize others as having equal standing in society, and they disregard the terms for cooperation that are justifiable to all. And, as illustrated by Radio above, people with mental disabilities can puncture overly inflated egos. The humility of some can expose others' tendencies to think too highly of themselves and remind others of the humanity they share with the rest of humankind.

I should note here that I intend Sesha, Leo, and Radio as examples of how mentally disabled persons can contribute to society in the general ways I specified given their capacity for engagement. I don't mean to suggest that all mentally disabled people are kind like Radio and contribute the same perspective to society. The contributions of a mentally disabled person will depend on that person's abilities and personality.

Of course, the cooperative contributions that persons with mental disabilities can make to a society based on relations of mutual respect are not limited to those I just discussed. As one example, Anita Silvers and Leslie Pickering Francis recently pointed out that trust is crucial to all cooperative projects, and trusting relationships between those with and without disabilities promote a cooperative, respectful society.[45]

Because my approach to the inclusion of persons with mental disabilities within contractualism is based on the ability of these persons to cooperate, one might wonder how inclusive my view really is when it comes to including all human beings as members of society. Can, for example, persons with mental disabilities who are extremely withdrawn from social life be included in my view? Or, is it possible to include those persons

[44] R. S. Dillon, 'Kant on Arrogance and Self-Respect,' in Cheshire Calhoun (ed.), *Setting the Moral Compass: Essays by Women Philosophers* (Oxford: Oxford University Press, 2004), 191–216 (209). I've also been helped here by Darwall's discussion of Kant, respect and arrogance in his 'Respect and the Second-Person Standpoint' (n. 28 above).

[45] A. Silvers and L. P. Francis, 'Justice through Trust: Disability and the "Outlier Problem" in Social Contract Theory,' *Ethics*, 116 (2005), 40–76.

with profound mental retardation who have extremely limited abilities or those persons who, due to mental illness or emotional disturbance, engage in behaviour that is disruptive of social relationships?

To address these worries I'll focus on some specific mental disabilities. One mental disability that seemingly poses a problem for my view is autism. Characterized by difficulties with social interaction and communication as well as unusual behaviour that is exemplified by narrow interests, repetitiveness, and stereotypical activity,[46] autism is a developmental disorder that affects a person's ability to engage in cooperation. It is a disorder, though, that affects persons in different ways and to different degrees of severity. Some persons with autism are very social and seek companionship; others are more socially withdrawn. Some autists seem to have difficulty recognizing or responding to the feelings and interests of others.

Despite the challenge for cooperation that autism can create, it is a mistake to think that persons with autism do not have the capacity for engagement. The social withdrawal by persons with autism is often the result of our own misunderstanding of these persons and of our refusal to abandon modes of communication that are most comfortable to us in order to find mediums of communication that make engagement for autists easier.[47] Donna Williams is an autist who found direct or emotional communication painful and debilitating as she was growing up. When people tried to communicate with her directly or appeal to her on an emotional level, she would often shut down, withdrawing herself from communication. Because of her behaviour, Donna was considered uncooperative and sometimes disruptive. The truth is that Donna was misunderstood. It was not that she could not communicate or that she did not want to communicate. She just could not do it in the typical manner, at least not yet. She needed to communicate with others indirectly and in a way that did not make emotional demands, such as being spoken to through objects or even being spoken about instead of addressed directly.[48] Engagement between individuals does require mutual recognition, but communication and recognition can be indirect.

---

[46] For a thoughtful explanation of autism, see Kluth, 'You're Going to Love This Kid' (n. 38 above), 1–21.

[47] Ibid. 15–16 and 107–34. This is also one of the messages communicated by Donna Williams in her autobiographical account of her struggle with autism: D. Williams, Nobody Nowhere: The Extraordinary Autobiography of an Autistic (New York: Perennial, 1992).

[48] Williams, Nobody Nowhere.

Individuals with extremely limited abilities may also cause doubts about the inclusiveness of my approach. Yet almost all human beings have the capacity for engagement. Sesha, the profoundly mentally retarded woman discussed earlier, has extremely limited abilities. Nonetheless, she is able to communicate some of her emotions and desires to others and is responsive to others to some extent. This allows her to share in some joint projects and to provide companionship to those close to her.

Consideration of persons with very limited abilities brings us to the matter of whether it is appropriate for the state to pass judgment on a person's abilities when the state lacks knowledge about a person's potential for engagement. Contractualists are committed to providing members of society with those goods necessary to create a society based on mutual respect. Due to extremely severe disability, though, it may not be clear whether some persons will be able to develop any of the capacities that allow them to participate in society. Yet, withholding from such persons the goods that could help them to develop capacities for cooperation would prevent many people who could participate in society from doing so. To avoid this, the state must assume persons have the potential to cooperatively contribute to society in cases in which there are questions about a person's potential.

Yet there are some human beings who do not count as members of society on my view. For example, anencephalic infants are born with no potential for developing any of the capacities that allow for cooperation. These infants lack a forebrain and cerebrum at birth. They are never conscious and do not survive more than a couple of days. Perhaps there are other human beings who, from birth, lack any potential for developing the capacity for engagement. These human beings may be 'reflexively' responsive to features of their environment, such as light or sound, or they may be in a persistent vegetative state and exhibit no responsiveness to the environment. Only those human beings who, without question, will not develop and have never possessed the capacity for engagement are outside the scope of justice on my view. This, of course, is not to say that we have no obligations to such individuals. They are members of the moral community, even if not members of political society. Though I cannot argue for this here, we surely have obligations of benevolence to all beings with animals needs, and contractualism is perfectly compatible with recognizing this.

Let us take account of those human beings who are entitled to justice on my view. All human beings with the ability to make cooperative contributions to a society based on relations of mutual respect are members of society entitled to justice. Because human beings are not born with the abilities that allow them to make such contributions but, rather, develop these abilities over time with care, human beings with the potential to develop these abilities must, absent other considerations, have access to those goods that will make possible the development of these abilities. When human beings temporarily lose their abilities to cooperatively contribute to society due to illness or accident, these members of society must receive the care they need to develop their abilities for cooperation. In the course of life some human beings may permanently lose their ability to make cooperative contributions to society; but when this happens, these individuals do not lose their membership in society, since no one who cares for her own well-being could agree to an arrangement in which persons would lose membership in society once they lost the ability to cooperate.

Another worry about the inclusiveness of my approach to justice is whether individuals who are more disruptive of social relationships than supportive can count as members of society. Consider that some persons with schizophrenia experience delusions and hallucinations, which can cause these individuals to be violent and disruptive.[49] However, research suggests that most schizophrenics who engage in disruptive and violent behaviour are not receiving proper medication or are under the influence of illegal drugs or alcohol.[50] Moreover, most people with schizophrenia who have a relapse into a psychotic episode show warning signs that should alert those close to the person to seek help for him or her.[51] While some persons with mental disabilities can be violent and disruptive, making cooperative projects with them extremely difficult or even temporarily impossible, research suggests that this disruptive behaviour can be managed.

Some may worry that my view is too inclusive because just as almost all human beings with severe mental impairments possess the capacity

---

[49] For a good discussion of schizophrenia, see E. F. Torrey, *Surviving Schizophrenia: A Family Manual*, 4th edn (New York: HarperCollins, 2001); K. T. Mueser and S. Gingerich, *Coping with Schizophrenia: A Guide for Families* (Oakland, Calif.: New Harbinger Publications, 1994).

[50] See Torrey, *Surviving Schizophrenia*, 307–9. For a general discussion of medication and symptom control, see Meuser and Gingerich, *Coping with Schizophrenia*, 47–83; Torrey, *Surviving Schizophrenia*, 210–55.

[51] See Torrey, *Surviving Schizophrenia*, 345–8; Meuser and Gingerich, *Coping with Schizophrenia*, 85–101.

for engagement so do some nonhuman animals. I think it is a virtue of my view that it suggests we have duties of justice to some nonhuman animals. The case of nonhuman animals, though, raises a number of difficult issues, which I cannot adequately address here. I can only mention a few important matters to consider. We cannot have cooperative relationships with some nonhuman animals. And some nonhuman animals live outside of human society, even if communication with them is possible. Moreover, some nonhuman animals that live among us do not engage in cooperative relationships with us. Such animals are owed benevolence, not justice. In order to determine what is owed to those nonhuman animals that live among us and with whom we communicate, a number of questions must be answered. Do these nonhuman animals contribute to a society based on relations of mutual respect? What, exactly, are these animals owed? How should we determine their objective interests? As Nussbaum suggests, what is owed to animals is surely species-specific.

Having addressed concerns about the inclusiveness of my approach to justice, I must now consider whether such an inclusive theory is fair. One might claim, for example, that those persons with mental disabilities who are unable to contribute to the labour market or to work in the household do not contribute enough to society to justify their inclusion as members, even if they contribute to social relationships.

This objection stems from the idea, found in some versions of social contract theory, that cooperation in society is based on mutual advantage. Again, this is the idea that cooperation is justified when each party to a cooperative project has more to gain by working with others according to rules that are advantageous to everyone than by going it alone; it requires that a person's benefit to society outweigh the corresponding cost in terms of measurable goods. Contractualists have been careful to reject the idea of mutual advantage as part of their understanding of cooperation in favour of cooperation based on reciprocity. Reciprocity, as explained by Rawls, requires that all those who make cooperative contributions to society benefit in accordance with an 'appropriate benchmark of equality defined with respect to that world'.[52] Understood in this way, reciprocity does not exclude persons from membership in society on the basis of

---

[52] Rawls, *Political Liberalism* (n. 2 above), 17. Correspondence with Cynthia Stark has helped me to better understand Rawls's idea of reciprocity.

how much they are able to contribute; the idea of reciprocity does not demand that the benefits of someone's cooperative contributions to society outweigh the costs of that person's inclusion. What is important is that an individual make some contribution to society. If we understand the end of cooperation for contractualists to be the establishment of a society based on relations of mutual respect, then all who make cooperative contributions to this enterprise should count as members.

Moreover, anyone who would worry that it is not enough to merely contribute to the social relationships that are part of contractualist society misses the point of justice for contractualists. Contractualists have a relational view of justice. A society is just when a relationship of mutual respect holds among all members considered as free and equal. Any cooperative contribution to this relationship is of fundamental importance to contractualists. Now, it is true that more will be asked of some persons in society than is asked of others. For example, those members of society in possession of the two moral powers will be responsible for the distribution of the goods necessary to construct a society of mutual respect; however, others, because of some disabilities, will not be responsible for this. One might suggest that this is unfair. Yet one can't make a legitimate complaint of unfairness with respect to an unequal division of responsibilities among members of society if there is no other way of assigning responsibilities that is more just.[53] On my view, the members of society not assigned more responsibilities are people who either lack the abilities necessary to perform a given task or the abilities necessary to be held accountable for performing it. So, in this case, there is not another distribution that is more just.

Here I am assuming that it is legitimate to discriminate between a person's qualifying for benefits and a person's responsibilities to others. Not everyone who is able to cooperatively contribute to a contractualist society also has the abilities that would make the assignment of certain responsibilities to them reasonable. This fact, however, does not make these persons' cooperative contributions any less valuable. It would be wrong to exclude protection and benefits for these contributors simply because they cannot be assigned responsibilities.[54]

---

[53] I am indebted to Elizabeth Anderson for this point.

[54] Moreover, the assumption that it is legitimate to discriminate between a person's qualifying for benefits and a person's responsibilities to others is widely accepted. Non-disabled children are granted membership in society and enjoy its accompanying benefits. They do not, however, as children have

Earlier I claimed that the inclusion of those with mental disabilities as members of society in a contractualist theory of justice depends on whether those with mental disabilities cooperatively contribute to contractualist society and whether we can give an account of what it would mean for the principles of justice to be justifiable to a trustee for a person who lacks the two moral powers. Let me address the latter issue. What is called for here is a general conception of the interests of members who lack the two moral powers so we can pass judgment on whether a trustee could assess the reasonableness of proposed principles of justice given the interests of her trust. The principles of justice for contractualists concern the distribution of those goods necessary to construct and maintain a society based on relations of mutual respect among free and equal members. The interests of members as such are these goods. Members of society with the capacity for the two moral powers are both cooperative contributors to society and accountable for constructing a society based on mutual respect. These members of society need access to the goods that will allow them to function in these capacities. Those persons in society with the capacity for engagement but who lack the two moral powers are cooperative contributors to society but are not assigned responsibilities in society. These persons need access to the goods that will allow them to function as cooperative contributors in a society based on mutual respect among free and equal members.[55] A reasonable distribution of these goods, given the interests of all members of society, is the concern of a trustee for such a member of society.

5.5. Conclusion

I have argued that the scope of contractualism can and should be expanded to be inclusive of the mentally disabled as members of society since they

obligations to others as a matter of justice. It is expected that one day most of these children will be assigned responsibilities, but the qualification for benefits of these children is not conditioned on this.

[55] Persons who lack the two moral powers are obviously not free in all of the senses in which freedom is important for those with those capacities. Rawls says, '[C]itizens think of themselves as free in three respects: first, as having the moral power to form, to revise, and rationally to pursue a conception of the good; second, as being self-authenticating sources of valid claims; and third, as capable of taking responsibility for their ends'. Rawls, *Political Liberalism*, 72. However, it is important to think of members of society who lack the two moral powers as free in at least the two following senses: (1) as beings who have a 'public identity' as members of society regardless of their particular subjective interests and (2) as beings who are, in some sense, self-originating sources of valid claims.

have the capacity to make cooperative contributions to the establishment of a society based on relations of mutual respect. This is just the first step in creating a contractualist theory of justice that properly addresses the interests of the mentally disabled. We also need to rethink the social goods relevant to justice as well as the terms of cooperation that can deliver justice for all.

6

No Talent? Beyond the Worst Off! A Diverse Theory of Justice for Disability

ANITA SILVERS

Congressional Findings, preamble to the Americans with Disabilities Act (1990): *The Congress finds that ... individuals with disabilities continually encounter various forms of discrimination, including outright intentional exclusion.*

A Proclamation by the President of the United States of America (2007): *On the anniversary of the Americans with Disabilities Act (ADA), we celebrate our progress towards an America where individuals with disabilities are recognized for their talents and contributions to our society.*[1]

(Title 42, Chapter 126, Equal Opportunities for Individuals with Disabilities[2])

This essay furthers the pursuit of justice for outliers. In my usage,[3] outliers are people who depart significantly from the prevailing paradigm for philosophical considerability. Often such individuals are explicitly exempted

---

[1] http://www.whitehouse.gov/news/releases/2007/07/20070724-8.html

[2] http://www.ada.gov/pubs/ada.htm#Anchor-Sec-49575

[3] In Anita Silvers and Leslie P. Francis, 'Justice through Trust: Resolving the "Outlier Problem" in Social Contract Theory,' *Ethics*, 116 (2005) 40–77, Leslie Francis and I explore philosophical approaches to the 'outlier' problem. In our usage, 'outliers are (kinds of) people who are considered beyond the reach of justice, at least as justice is conceived in social contract theory, because they do not participate in cooperatively productive activities.' In our view, the 'outlier' problem misunderstands the nature of social contracts and consequently assigns certain kinds of people to outgroups that are ineligible for contracting.

from philosophy's scope as, for example, when epistemological theory discounts the judgments of blind people as irrelevant or unimportant to philosophical accounts of empirical knowledge.[4]

Between theory-based suppositions and these individuals' realities there often is a lack of fit. To account for the misfit, the testimony of outliers, where it challenges or deviates from theory, typically is disallowed on the ground that to be an outlier is to be inherently flawed. Because the experiences of such individuals are supposed to diverge from normal or (in an older terminology) natural human states, they are dismissed as unimportant, that is, as not rising to philosophical considerability. Such disregard of unusual people impoverishes philosophizing by diminishing the adequacy of philosophical accounts.

An expansive, responsive, and receptive theory of justice can enlarge philosophical awareness by valuing outreach to outliers, thereby increasing the diversity of ways of human functioning that become familiar and more readily available to inform our attentive thought. Understandably, if unaware that such people exist or if unknowledgeable about them, philosophers will hardly be alert to the importance of theorizing that reaches, for example, to the perceptual and cognitive functioning of outliers like people with sensory or intellectual disabilities.[5] In contrast, when moral and political theorizing embraces outliers, other areas of philosophy are enriched, for moral and political theories not only reflect how we do treat each other, but also guide how we ought to value and treat each other.

To be afforded moral and/or political standing thus is to be someone whom others recognize and with whom they are drawn to interact. Absent persuasive and powerful principles of justice to bring outliers of every sort into interaction with the rest of society, philosophers, like other citizens, are likely to remain ignorant about and dismissive of them, an arrangement that depletes philosophy as much as every other human practice. Principles of justice are important in encouraging philosophers in every field of the discipline to recognize human differences represented by various kinds of

---

[4] See e.g. the dialogue between Martin Milligan and Brian Magee, in the book *On Blindness* (Oxford: Oxford University Press, 1995), regarding epistemology and the relevance of blindness.

[5] Normative epistemologies may set standards that rule out some kinds of people as knowers. For example, some epistemologies declare blind-from-birth individuals to be incapable of understanding a crucial subset of our concepts about the world. On the other hand, naturalizing epistemologies will miss out on practices that enable some kinds of people to be knowers. For example, some epistemologies take the practices familiar in making visual judgments as the paradigm for knowledge of the world.

outliers. Accordingly, for philosophers an urgency that reaches beyond traditional interests for pursuing moral and political philosophy attaches to the call for fully inclusive philosophical accounts of justice.

6.1. Outlying

Those of us who take inclusiveness to be a virtue in theories of justice should want to know what approach to formulating a philosophical account of justice best addresses the challenge posed by being committed to embrace outliers. In this essay I examine several familiar strategies for bringing outliers to the centre of a political or social philosophy of justice. The aim is to identify a powerfully inclusive approach to justice, from practice and policy to principle to the grounds from which principles arise.

Collectively, the several definitions of 'outlier' suggest why traditional theorizing about justice has been disposed to disregard individuals who are thought to depart significantly from their theoretical paradigms for moral and political considerability. An outlier is, variously, a person or thing that lives or is located outside of, or is separated from, the locus of productive activity or where others mainly are found, or an extreme deviation from the mean, or a value far from most others in a set of data.[6] By definition outliers are so different from most people as to be distanced from society's centre.

Outliers are situated at their society's boundary-lines because they are regarded as so divergent or odd as to verge on being alien. Characterizing people as outliers thus turns on their perceived dissimilarities. Disparities of pigmentation, sex-related traits or behaviors, modes and levels of physical or cognitive functioning, origin or heritage, linguistic or religious practice, talent, and wealth are among the familiar considerations that have resulted in people being treated as outliers. Not unsurprisingly, outliers may be resistant to being pressed into conformity by generalizations or principles, for the very idea of being an outlier evokes departing from the rule.

For this reason, traditional philosophical accounts of justice have overlooked outliers, or at least have omitted concern for people whom they designate as such. Theories of justice traditionally are designed to foreground

---

[6] See http://dictionary.reference.com/browse/outlier

what is common to, or commonly agreed upon or accepted by, ordinary people. Traditional accounts usually start from the centre, or from the easy case, developing basic political principles with an eye to what is necessary for typical people to flourish, or for ideal people to do so. They therefore deny that the state of being different is in and by itself of significance for justice.

Despite their being outcasts in theory, outliers in fact are not always found bound to the lowest level of scales or rankings of wellbeing. For example, as I adduced a decade ago in exploring criteria for prioritizing reparative biomedical interventions,[7] people with albinism in Zimbabwe (a national population with many variations of both ty-pos and ty-neg albinism in its gene pool) experience social ostracism that sharply reduces their access to social interaction and family life. Nevertheless, and in part as a result of the same stereotyping that deprives them of human intimacy, in Zimbabwe the population of people with albinism enjoys appreciable economic security and success.[8] Of course, being treated as an outlier means being distanced from at least some social processes and, consequently, raises the likelihood of being deprived of the benefits social inclusion bestows and secures. This explains why properties that are taken to characterize outliers also often are associated with deficiencies of wellbeing to the point of being identified as defects.

How then to extend justice to outliers? Justice should not in principle be indifferent to difference, for justice should be understood and dispensed in light of the realities that characterize and are experienced by all, not just some, who need justice. Yet which differences should matter for justice, and how they should be addressed when justice is the goal, are far from clear. While recent moral, social, and political philosophy is rich with theories that argue for acknowledging one or another specific difference as crucial to justice, much less thought has been devoted to the question on which this essay is designed to shed some light, namely, how to distinguish

---

[7] Anita Silvers, 'A Fatal Attraction to Normalizing: Treating Disabilities as Deviations from "Species-Typical" Functioning,' in Eric Parens (ed.), *Enhancing Human Traits: Conceptual Complexities and Ethical Implications* (Washington: Georgetown University Press, 1998), 95–123.

[8] Ibid. One reason why people with albinism, as a class, have successful businesses in Zimbabwe is that they are stereotyped as being witches: the dangers of cheating witches in business deals are well known. Another reason is that, as a class, their education level is higher than other people's: this phenomenon is attributed to their need to stay indoors and, hence, the disposition of families to let them remain in school rather than send them out to do unskilled work at an early age.

the kinds of differences that should matter for justice, and how to delineate the difference(s) for justice these should make.

The study begins with a historical note indicating why difference has been posed as a dilemma for justice policy. I next turn to delineating differences about difference that have inspired different policies for pursuing justice. From the level of policy I proceed to the level of fundamental principle, considering how to systematize conduct sufficiently inclusively to do justice to outliers' different kinds of difference. Finally, I discuss meta-theoretical questions about shaping, supporting, and propelling inclusive approaches to justice. The aim is to advance moral and political theory that can appreciate the enormous diversity that characterizes human beings.[9]

6.2. The Dilemma

In the late twentieth century, moral and political progress toward equality foundered on what Martha Minow famously described as 'the dilemma of difference.' Minow's influential account explored why blatantly antithetical approaches to remedying minority exclusion nevertheless seemed to have matching flaws.[10] She pointed out how policies legislating homogeneous treatment and policies legislating special treatment for stigmatized populations equally have resulted in devaluing these populations and thereby in fueling their exclusion.

Minow laid out the dilemma of difference as follows: 'when does treating people differently emphasize their differences and stigmatize or hinder them on that basis? And when does treating people the same become insensitive to their difference and likely to stigmatize or hinder them on that basis?'[11] Rights analysis cannot resolve these questions, which re-emerge on the philosophical level in weighing alternative characterizations of the principle on which excluded minority claims to equality should be based. Is the

---

[9] Some readers may recognize the (perhaps attenuated) kinship of this last stated, meta-theoretical aim to the traditional liberal commitment to a pluralistic account of the Good. For a responsively inclusive account of the latter pertaining to people with disabilities, see Leslie Pickering Francis and Anita Silvers, 'Liberalism and Individually Scripted Ideas of the Good: Meeting the Challenge of Dependent Agency,' *Social Theory and Practice*, 33/2, (2007), 311−34.

[10] Martha Minow, *Making All the Difference: Inclusion, Exclusion and American Law* (Ithaca, NY: Cornell University Press, 1991), 40.

[11] Ibid. 20.

obligation to recognize excluded groups' moral and political equality properly expressed as a claim to extend to them the provisions normally made to address basic human needs? Or is the obligation instead an acknowledgement of their claim to exceptional provisions made to serve their peculiar needs?[12]

The former understanding is broadly unresponsive to the stigmatizing processes that cause minorities' or depreciated groups' exclusion and therefore neither engages with their being rejected nor eliminates it. Minow worries that by focusing on the absense of formal equality of rights, such equal rights mandates trivialize and therefore fail to address the causes of inequality. Programs to ensure equal rights thereby tend to obscure the disadvantageous difference in substantive circumstances between these people whose status justice is needed to elevate the rest of the population.

The latter understanding is narrowly unresponsive to a prevailing cause of stigmatization, namely, that people welcome policies privileging (people like) themselves, but resent policies privileging individuals different from themselves. Minow worries that by privileging a sub-group's needs, such special rights mandates highlight how their beneficiaries differ from other people. Programs to assign special rights thereby tend to preempt the pursuit of equality for those people whose status justice is needed to elevate by dividing them from the rest of the population.

Thus neither of these antithetical interpretations of what is owed to minorities appears to offer a sound or effective basis for progress toward inclusion. Minow traces this problem to the law's tendency to embed norms without justifying them, that is, to a conceptual proclivity embedded in jurisprudential practice. She recommends a dialogical process whereby prospective excluders interact with the excluded and thereby reduce the distance between them. She takes this 'social-relations' approach to be preferable to traditional legal treatments of difference. Her alternative approach emphasizes learning the perspectives of others as a practical solution for including them.[13]

---

[12] Martha Minow, 103.

[13] Ibid. 379. For an account to which I subscribe of the problems with thinking that people can judge from the perspectives of others different from themselves, see Iris Marion Young, 'Asymmetrical Reciprocity: On Moral Respect, Wonder, and Enlarged Thought,' in Ronald Beiner and Jennifer Nedelsky (eds.), *Judgment, Imagination, and Politics* (New York: Rowman & Littlefield, 2001), 205–28.

But if, as Minow correctly concludes, the problem is conceptual, this solution does not respond to it or to anywhere near it. Minow's analysis of the dilemma calls for a conceptualization of difference adequate to advance justice, but she does not construct the needed normative theory. Her discussion establishes that the way law and policy understand difference affects their impact on a diverse population. Of course, urging engagement with unfamiliar kinds of people invites taking a practical step toward greater inclusion, but, absent serious improvement through reconceptualization, her social relations approach is neither a giant step nor the final step toward the goal.

As proposed in Section 6.1 above, being drawn to interact with certain others is both conceptually and causally consequent upon affording them moral and political standing. Interacting with members of an outgroup at least opens the question of whether these outliers have moral and political standing but does not settle it. By itself, therefore, interacting with outliers is insufficient to effect inclusion, for rendering a kind of difference more familiar does not necessarily reduce contempt for it.

6.3. Three Strategies for Justice

I now examine three categories of difference that have prompted discrete strategies for achieving justice. These are (1) differences that should be denied, (2) differences that should be mitigated, and (3) differences that should be embraced. In the first category are stereotypical differences used as pretexts. In the second are differences that are deemed to be deficiencies or defects. In the third are differences that are acknowledged to be special talents. The conceptualizations expressed in this typology of difference prompt very different policies which often are taken to be incompatible and therefore to be in competition with one another to guide us in the search for justice.

To be sure, conflating the categories can confuse claims about justice, for without clarifying them conclusions appropriate to one category can be misapplied as counterexamples to cases proper to another category. Nevertheless, these strategies should not be portrayed as invoking antithetical theories of justice, nor should we think that we must choose just one and apply it categorically. I will show that doing so is counterintuitive and, accordingly, that each strategy has its place within the frame of a properly comprehensive theory of justice.

Some, but not all, of the observations I will apply to the first two categories are familiar. But discussion of them will be helpful because even well-known philosophical positions may expand their influence when juxtaposed unexpectedly or applied in a somewhat novel way. Exploration of the third category introduces a more novel way of thinking about difference and disability because it focuses on talent rather than loss.

Finally, to understand how these different kinds of difference (difference as illusory, as deficiency, and as talent) can be compatible within the proper justice-theoretical frame, I will advert to a recently developed theory of justice, the approach through trust. Unlike traditional social contract theory (at least on some influential readings of the tradition), justice through trust does not take the key to robust social cooperation to lie in preventing or prohibiting or at least regulating advantage.[14] This approach to justice theory therefore does not confront people's differences suspiciously, querying what unfair advantage(s) or disadvantage(s) they might confer. For justice through trust, the spotlight is on enriching cooperation by fairly facilitating diversity of advantage, that is, by cultivating people's different advantages rather than by equating fairness with people's being the same.

That people differ from one another is an obvious—indeed, an inescapable—fact. Justice through trust supposes that strong and stable cooperative schemes must develop practices enabling diverse individuals to approach each other cooperatively because of, rather than despite, their differences. All three strategies have work to do in shaping just practices like these.

6.3.1. Denying difference (difference as illusory)

The least expansive approach to justice for outliers focuses on preventing the harms occasioned by pretextual stereotyping, where differences that make no relevant difference are portrayed otherwise. Albeit cautious to the point of being minimalist, this is by no means an unimportant strategy.

---

[14] For Hobbes, for example, it is important that individual differences offering advantage to their possessors in the state of nature do not necessarily do so as well under the regulations of a stable society. To give another illustration, Rawls's difference principle concerns the kind(s) of difference that should weigh in allocating advantageous benefits. For a contemporary writer who discusses such a view see Allen Buchanan, 'Justice as Reciprociy versus Subject-Centered Justice,' *Philosophy and Public Affairs*, 19 (1990) 227–52.

In the U.S., for example, it has been crucial to establish that demeaning descriptions of differences in sex-related traits or pigmentation are irrelevant to and should not influence the distribution of central political rights. Clearly, disallowing disadvantageous descriptions of difference that are false is an important prophylactic against injustice.

Yet to do this and nothing more in regard to how justice accommodates to difference too easily invites assimilation strategies even where these are as far from the mark as the stereotypes and consequently mislead. During the Civil Rights era in the second half of the twentieth century, the U.S. Supreme Court famously adopted principles such as the requirement for strict scrutiny when public policy or practice deals differently with people based on variations in their pigmentation. A related idea is that differential treatment prompted by differences in sex-related traits be greeted with only a slightly lowered level of suspicion because, the Court has declared, science shows that in most respects women are as able as men.[15]

These proclamations have been understood to say that differences attendant on pigmentation or sex need not and therefore should not be recognized in the pursuit of justice. Blanket pronouncements and non sequiturs like these are overly abstract and also can be irresponsibly idealized. For there are at least two sweeping considerations for contending that justice should engage with difference, especially human biological diversity. (Human biological diversity is constituted by those differences among humans that derive from variations or modulations of the life processes or characteristic phenomena of living human organisms.)

Biological differences do sometimes correlate with functional differences, so abstractly formulating difference-blind policies and practices often obscures or defers engaging with an underlying issue, namely, whether there is a sound basis for differential valuations of real variations in abilities and potentials. The presumption of difference-neutrality is that real differences should not matter or, more subtly, differences that should not matter are not real. Hence the precept U.S. Supreme Court Chief Justice Roberts issued in the recent decision in *Community Education* v. *Seattle School District No. 1*, 'The way to stop discrimination on the basis of race

---

[15] '[W]hat differentiates sex from such nonsuspect statutes as intelligence or physical disability . . . is that the sex characteristic [473 U.S. 432, 441] frequently bears no relation to ability to perform or contribute to society.' *Frontiero* v. *Richardson*, 411 U.S. 677, 686 (1973) (plurality opinion).

is to stop discriminating on the basis of race.'[16] This is to say that race is a difference that should not make a difference, that is, for policy purposes racial differences are not allowed to be real. (Justice Kennedy, the swing vote, dissented from this part of the opinion, allowing that there may be circumstances in which policy may give race weight as a differentiating factor.)[17]

Difference-neutrality tends to deny recognition to different abilities, and as a result fails to scrutinize policies and practices that privilege common or familiar levels of ability as the normal and thereby the socially valuable ones. Moreover, even where biological differences are neutral in respect to the capacity to achieve a socially valued level of ability, there may be a history of their being mistakenly assessed as disabling. A striking example is the U.S. Supreme Court decision in *Goeseart*. Here, despite acknowledging that some women could throw troublemakers out of a bar, the Court upheld a state ban on employing women as bartenders on the unsupported presumption that many women by nature could not deal with drunken troublemakers and therefore that permitting women to bartend placed both private property and public safety at undue risk.[18]

These characterizations, which the Court explicitly acknowledged departed from fact, typify the unabashed pretextual stereotyping based on race as well as sex that was rampant in those times. Even where in principle biological differences should not be invoked in policy and practice, a history of their having been may wield continuing influence. Difference-neutrality that disregards the sequelae of such historical differential treatment to avoid invoking biologically based differences therefore may prolong rather than reduce injustice.

6.3.2. Mitigating difference (difference as deficiency)

Versions of the above observations about the defects of indifference to difference, and the flaws in policies of difference neutrality, are often and very widely made. Feminist philosophers rightly point out not only that women are biologically distinct from men, but also that their biological differences lead them into distinctive reproductive roles, which incline them toward distinctive social roles as well. In general, women are society's

---

[16] *Parents Involved in Community Schools* v. *Seattle School District no. 1 et al.*, 127 s.Ct. 2738 (2007).
[17] Ibid.   [18] *Goesaert* v. *Cleary* [335 U.S. 464].

caregivers, although caregiving is not necessarily reserved for women nor are women categorically better caregivers than men. While it may take a village to raise a child, only women bear children. Women find themselves raising children, even in the absence of a maternally inclined village and even when they also must take on other roles. As many feminist philosophers (and others) have made clear, social systems that do not respond supportively to such role differences impose undeserved disadvantage on women.[19]

In the same vein, regardless of whether claims that pigmentation and similar cosmetic products of biological inheritance impair ability now are acknowledged to be patently false, it is doubtful that a social and political system shaped by such claims or developed in the orbit of such claims is free of the biased structures and practices false ideas linking pigmentation and inferiority promote. Philosophers of race rightly point out that minority group members who are caught in this kind of system really are disadvantaged, and do not deserve to be. Like women as a group, disadvantageous differences in the situations and treatment of racial minorities have biological prompts but are rooted in social history. They are as difficult to dislodge and destroy as a deeply tap-rooted weed.

Disability studies scholars invoke historical and cultural biases to explain why people with disabilities, as a group, are badly positioned in society.[20] Disabled people's differences are real, and their inferior situations and treatment are in very large part a result of a history of exclusion, rejection, and disregard. The insufficient responsiveness of the social system to their differences is rejection they do not deserve. Consequently, at least some disability studies scholars have followed along a path toward justice previously trodden by other liberatory theorists. The aim is to develop principles or schemes to compensate for disadvantages occasioned by real biological or social (including historical) differences.

These observations cast light on a second category of difference, namely, disadvantageous real differences (rather than differences that are

---

[19] See e.g. Eva Kittay, *Love's Labor: Essays on Women, Equality, and Dependency* (New York and London: Routledge, 1999). Also see reviews of this volume, such as Rosemarie Tong's at http://www.humboldt.edu/~essays/tongrev.html or Joan Tronto's in *Signs*, 27/4 (summer 2002), 1191–4.

[20] For a summary and explication of these discussions, see Anita Silvers, 'Formal Justice,' in Anita Silvers, David Wasserman, and Mary Mahowald (eds.), *Disability, Difference, Discrimination: Perspectives on Justice in Bioethics and Public Policy* (Lanham, Md.: Rowman & Littlefield, 1998).

pretextual—that is, are simulated or serve as subterfuges).[21] Theories of justice often fasten on specific differences in people's attainment of whatever intrinsic or instrumental value(s) the particular theory embraces. Individuals who are value-deficient because they cannot rise to or instantiate the property(ies) the theory picks out as valuable, or who are reservoirs of properties the theory picks out as disvalues, are likely to be portrayed as outliers.

Singer's utilitarian position, for example, makes neonates, and especially neonates with disabilities, into outliers. His theory values self-awareness (or, more precisely, self-awareness is a necessary condition for achieving the theory-endorsed valuable states). He denies intrinsic moral considerability to neonates because he thinks they have not yet attained self-awareness. His theory despises suffering. So neonates whose physical or mental characteristics dispose them to extraordinary suffering, or who are likely to be the cause of an unusual degree of suffering in others, are thought of as outliers who may be excluded from any social role or interaction with other people—in Singer's well-known account by being prevented from being born, let die, or more actively eliminated. Singer's treatment of disability identifies this difference with deficiency and further declares that individuals who are worst off because their deficiencies are so severe as to be beyond mitigation or irremediable also are beyond justice.

Author, attorney, and disability rights activist Harriet Johnson commented on the underlying presumption after her initial debate with Singer (their debates were reported in a lengthy *New York Times* article): 'To Singer, it's pretty simple: disability makes a person "worse off". Are we worse off? I don't think so. We take constraints that no one would choose and build rich and satisfying lives within them. We enjoy pleasures other people enjoy, and pleasures peculiarly our own.'[22]

A different example, Rawls's theory of justice, advances a very different notion about what to do with individuals who, according to the theory's

---

[21] To illustrate: that women are people who gestate fetuses is a real (although contingent) difference between women and men. It is true now, although may not be true in future if researchers can extend this talent of male seahorses to human males. That women are people too fragile to keep order in a bar is a pretextual difference because it is false of women generally that they cannot quell barroom brawls and false of men generally that they can.

[22] Dennis Hevesi, 'Harriet Johnson, 50, Activist for Disabled, Is Dead,' *New York Times*, 137/54334, Saturday, June 7, 2008, A15. For a critique of the idea that lives without limitations are more valuable or desirable ones, see Anita Silvers, 'Predicting Disability while Commodifying Health,' in David Wasserman, Jerome Bickenbach, and Robert Wachbroit (eds.), *Quality of Life and Human Difference* (New York: Cambridge University Press, 2005), 43–66.

idea of what is good, are worst off. The Difference Principle, a signature element of Rawls's theory, is explicitly designed to bring justice to people who differ from most individuals because they are worst off.

Rawls takes material resources to be a primary good. To be just, he proposes, the procedure that governs dispensing resources should be responsive to the greatest deviations from normal level of resource possession. Other than to acknowledge and compensate for the difference of being worst off materially, the distributive procedure should be uniform. That is, aside from those who are disadvantaged by this difference, everyone should be treated alike with regard to the distribution of income and wealth. Unequal distributions are to be allowed only to benefit whoever is worst off (and only where benefiting the worst off avoids worsening other people's conditions). In part, this may be because Rawls supposes that in a just society being worst off is a condition attributable to misfortunes such as disadvantageous family position, impoverished natural endowments (such as absence of any of talent), and general bad luck, for which neither those who suffer from it nor other people bear responsibility. But unclarities about the dimensions of being worst off and the disadvantages deserving of compensation abound.

As legal theorist Mark Stein has argued, it is unclear whether the aim is to reduce vast differences in resources each person is enabled to command to improve welfare, or instead to reduce vast differences in welfare itself. On the former interpretation, as Stein points out, more resources than a political system normally contributes to normal working people might be distributed to disabled people to compensate them for deficits in ability or opportunity to obtain employment. That is, they would receive resources to help them approach the normal level of income. On the latter interpretation, more resources than a political system normally distributes to healthy people might be distributed to disabled people to compensate for medical services called for by their deficits in health. Very different views about justice for people with disabilities, and very different advantages and disadvantages to people with disabilities, are prompted by these different interpretations of what makes persons worst off.

Some philosophers have proposed interpreting, applying, or extending Rawls's Difference Principle to significant deficits in nonmaterial goods. Norman Daniels, for instance, takes healthcare to be more important than other material goods because, he says, good health is essential to enjoying liberty and making the most of opportunity—that is, for achieving some if not all of the important democratic goods. On this scheme, Rawlsian justice is held to assign at least some priority in the allocation of healthcare resources to those worst off in health. But only those individuals whom medicine can restore to normalcy command priority, for Daniels thinks that only they will be able to pursue the democratic opportunity that is his rationale for allocating healthcare. Whether chronic care needs have equal standing under Daniels's scheme remains unsettled. Despite invoking those who are worst off in health, Daniels's approach thus focuses on individuals who are just temporarily ill and who can be rescued through provision of acute care and restored to species typicality. Only they can regain species typicality and thereby release from being outliers.[23] Justice here does not reach to outliers with health differences like the chronically ill but merely decreases the group of outliers.

Martha Nussbaum's capabilities approach also responds to differences that are cast as deficiencies and thereby as disadvantaging people who consequently are outliers. Her explication of justice in *Frontiers of Justice* is both an appreciation and a critique of Rawls's view. Nussbaum departs from Rawls initially by proposing an alternative account of primary goods. She focuses much more on identifying who is most likely to be deficient in these goods and exploring the reasons for their disadvantage.[24]

After identifying ten capabilities as fundamentally valuable because they are most central to living a dignified human life, Nussbaum points out that different people may need different amounts of resources to attain the same degree of capability because they are differently situated.[25] The familiar example comes from Amartya Sen, who pointed out that individuals unable to walk may need more resources—for instance, wheelchairs—to achieve the basic mobility necessary for an independent and productive life. Sen notes that in such cases equality is preserved despite an unequal distribution of material goods because walkers and wheelchair users are being provided with similar capability, despite the former needing no resources due to

---

[23] See Anita Silvers, 'A Fatal Attraction to Normalizing: Treating Disabilities as Deviations from 'Species-Typical' Functioning,' in Eric Parens (ed.), *Enhancing Human Traits: Conceptual Complexities and Ethical Implications* (Washington: Georgetown University Press, 1998), 95–8, for a more thorough summary and critique of Daniels's position.

[24] Martha Nussbaum, *Frontiers of Justice: Disability, Nationality, Species Membership* (Cambridge, Mass.: Harvard University Press, 2006), *passim.*

[25] Ibid. 85–8.

their having functional legs and feet, but the latter needing considerable expenditures on wheelchairs or other assistive devices, to traverse the same distances.[26]

In the same vein, Nussbaum argues that there is an obligation under justice to ensure that every citizen reaches threshold levels of all the central capabilities (unless in a particular case no amount of resources can affect that goal). Individuals who are in biological deficit typically will need more resources to achieve the species norms of at least some of the capabilities. Nussbaum's approach to justice warrants such distributions, but only insofar as needed to bring these individuals up to the capability thresholds. In justice, no one deserves distributions of resources to rise above threshold capability as long as those resources might be deployed to raise others to that threshold.

Nussbaum's account of justice for difference thus resembles Rawls's by centering on differences that make some people worst off. Some feminist discussions of justice for difference initially may seem to depart from this pattern by directing attention to women's special strengths and roles. These are portrayed as intrinsic or instrumental goods; by no means are women said to be in deficit for possessing or expressing them. But these theories do not invoke justice directly in virtue of the differences pertaining to female character nor to characteristic female social roles. They do so, rather, to remedy the deficiency of recognition society affords these valuable female differences. Women indeed are biologically different from men, but this line of feminist argument attributes their being worst off to social rather than biological differences.

For feminist theory, the subjects for whom special efforts of justice are invoked are not themselves seen as defective in virtue of their differences. Accordingly, a fundamental objective of feminism is to replace discredited attributions of inferiority to women with an appreciation of women's qualities and traits. Nevertheless, feminists point out, women continue to be diminished by deficient treatment because the social system fails to accommodate their differences.[27] Parenthetically, the well-known social model of disability adopts a similar approach. The social model refrains from characterizing individuals' anomalous abilities to move or sense or

---

[26] See Amartya Sen, 'Equality of What?,' in Sterling M. McMurrin (ed.), *Tanner Lectures on Human Values* (Salt Lake City: University of Utah, 1980), 217–18.

[27] Anita Silvers, 'Feminist Theory and Disability,' *Stanford Encyclopedia of Philosophy* (forthcoming).

reason or execute other basic acts as defects, locating deficiency instead in social organization and practice that excludes or is otherwise antithetical to individuals with these anomalies.[28]

The second strategy for doing justice to difference thus focuses on remedying disadvantage attributable to real biological or real social lack, or to inadequacies in the interaction of biological and social processes. There now is an extensive literature devoted to debating the causes of such deficiencies, and the proper targets and distributive priorities for remedying them. For example, claims that disability is socially constructed, and that the disadvantages associated with disability should be addressed by changing society to accommodate people with disabilities rather than by attempting to alter the individuals themselves, prompt adopting the second strategy.

Within the conceptual framework of this well-known social model of disability, the second strategy is deployed to defend distributing resources for, among other things, purchasing personal assistance and assistive devices and providing compensatory income for people whose impairments give them a claim on being worst off. The second strategy is equally amenable, however, to being deployed within the conceptual framework of the medical model, which usually is taken to be the antithesis of the social model. Guided by the presuppositions of the medical model, justice focused on remedying deficiency aims resources at the provision of rehabilitative medical and educational interventions to meet the expectations and demands of the prevailing social organization and practices.[29]

As explanations of why disabled people are disadvantaged, to the extent it is plausible to designate them as being worst off or at least as being very badly off, the medical and social models of disability are not incompatible. The reasons why people are considered or consider themselves disabled almost always emerge at the intersect of biological and social processes. Adherents of both models typically further agree in conceiving of justice as a strategy for addressing disadvantage occasioned by biological or social differences. They agree as well that priority goes to the worst off, or

---

[28] Anita Silvers, 'An Essay on Modeling: The Social Model of Disability,' in Christopher Ralston and Nustin Ho (eds.), *Philosophical Reflections on Disability* (Springer, forthcoming).
[29] For an extensive discussion comparing medical and social models, see Anita Silvers, 'Formal Justice,' in Anita Silvers, David Wasserman, and Mary Mahowald (eds.), *Disability, Difference, Discrimination: Perspectives on Justice in Bioethics and Public Policy* (Lanham, Md.: Rowman & Littlefield, 1998).

more precisely to whomever among the worst off can benefit from extra resources.

Contention arises in regard to who qualifies as worst off, and to how their deficiencies should be ameliorated. One mistake here is to suppose that different ways in which people can be very badly off must be commensurable. Another mistake is to think that policy must exclusively pursue either biological or instead social change. Deep disagreement—indeed, irresoluble dissension—on these points exists not only between the two models' respective adherents but also among those who declare their allegiance to the same model.

6.3.3. What threshold for justice?

A characteristic result of aiming justice systems at remedying the deprivation(s) experienced by the worst off is the ardour with which various individuals and groups pursue being represented as worst off, or at least as much less well off than others. Rather than promoting diversity, this strategy provokes divisiveness instead. On any account of justice that gives priority or preference to the worst off, various kinds of outliers, subject to diverse reasons for their being badly off, will be poised to compete with each other for that designation, which on such accounts is the narrow door to justice. This second strategy therefore complicates the prospect of engaging outliers in cooperative social interaction. This section will further explore difficulties that arise when justice gives primacy to relieving whoever is designated as being worst off.

Rawls and Nussbaum both focus justice for difference on remedying the disadvantage of whoever is, measured by the ideas of the good on which their respective systems are built, worst off. Nussbaum explicitly commits to inclusiveness by extending the umbrella of first-order justice over people with disabilities, while for Rawls disabled people's considerability emerges only after the basic principles of justice have been shaped and put in place. Nussbaum therefore acknowledges more direct obligations of justice to the disabled, which she takes as requiring remediation of the deficiencies of capability that make them worse off than species-typical people. But does her approach suffice to bring justice to these outliers? Consideration of a key U.S. Supreme Court decision illustrates why focusing justice on remediation for the worst off is problematic.

In *Board of Education of the Hendrick Hudson Central School District* v *Rowley*, the parents of a deaf child, Amy Rowley, sued the local school board under recent federal law (then called the Education of the Handicapped Act) that had opened school doors to disabled children.[30] The school board permitted Amy to enrol in regular classes and made some accommodation to her disability but refused to provide a qualified sign-language interpreter in her classes. An excellent lip-reader, Amy was given a hearing aid that amplified sounds 'during certain classroom activities.'[31] She also received one hour of instruction each day from a special tutor for the deaf and three hours a week of speech therapy.

Amy performed better than the average student (maintaining a B grade point average) and advanced from grade to grade with the other children in her age cohort. Yet she understood only about half of what was said in class. A reasonable presumption is that to develop her intellectual abilities fully, she required in-class sign-language interpretation, for, absent access to what went on in the classroom, she suffered from an instructional deficit. With access to only half the instruction and information her peers received in class, she lacked the same opportunity as hearing children to develop her intellectual talents.

While this conclusion about the impact of deficient communication on Amy presumes that a purpose and effect of providing public education is to enable citizens to develop their potential, it is worth noting that alternative views about the reasons for deploying public resources to fund schools generate similar conclusions. If, for example, a major purpose of free schooling is to train skilled workers for our economy, or to shape citizens well enough informed to contribute to democratic political life, lack of access to so much classroom teaching likely would leave Amy unable to approach her potential for contributing as a worker or as a citizen.

Writing for the majority in a 1982 opinion, however, Justice Rehnquist ruled that Amy was not entitled to the requested accommodation because the statutory mandate of a 'free appropriate public education' had been

---

[30] *Board of Education* v. *Rowley*, Supreme Court of the United States. 458 U.S. 176; 102 S. Ct. 3034; 73 L. Ed. 2d 690 (1982).

[31] A qualified sign-language interpreter was placed in Amy's kindergarten class for a 2-week experimental period, but the interpreter had reported that Amy did not need his services at that time. Her individual educational program also provided that Amy should receive instruction from a tutor for the deaf for one hour each day and from a speech therapist for three hours each week. (20 USC § 1400 (2000 & Supp 2004) at 184).

satisfied by allowing Amy to be in class and to learn. So long as she performed at average level, the school had satisfied its burden, for public education did not require the system to give every child with a disability the opportunity to maximize intellectual potential commensurate with the academic opportunities provided to children without disabilities. The opinion stated that the statutory requirement of a 'free appropriate public education' was satisfied as long as the child benefited educationally in some way.[32] The opinion declared that the constitutional provision for equal protection of the laws did not provide for strict equality of opportunity. For handicapped children educated alongside their nondisabled peers, educational benefit was demonstrated by a plan reasonably calculated 'to open the door of public education to handicapped children by means of specialized educational services but not to guarantee any particular substantive level of education once inside.'[33]

Nussbaum's capabilities approach would, by contrast, guarantee a particular substantive level. But her capabilities approach may not even require supporting a level of attainment as high as the *Rowley* Court took to be necessary. According to Nussbaum's scheme, the state's obligation is to distribute resources enabling each person to attain the threshold human capability level, a functional stage Amy Rowley undoubtedly reached or exceeded using a hearing aid and in-class assistance. The Court would not allocate additional resources to give Amy (or other deaf children) the opportunity to exceed average achievement by more fully developing their talents, even though this is an opportunity many of their hearing classmates realize. Nor would Nussbaum, unless resources are so plentiful that some remain in excess after all people who can do so attain threshold levels of all the capabilities.

What Amy is owed on Nussbaum's approach, absent such repleteness of resources, is educational opportunity adequate for a dignified life, which depending on cultural context may not even need to rise to the level of average educational attainment. Thus, what Nussbaum's scheme offers is, at most and only under some circumstances, materially equivalent to Supreme Court jurisprudence. Neither offers disabled children the same level of opportunity that nondisabled children enjoy to acquire for themselves the information and skills taught in public schools. This is because Nussbaum's

---

[32] Ibid. at 203.   [33] Ibid. at 189–90.

capability theory locates justice in the outcomes of resource distribution and specifically in equality of basic outcomes rather than in equality of full access. On this approach, minimum outcomes that are the same for everyone become benchmarks for equality.

Nussbaum's strategy is to identify the basic necessities for dignified human flourishing as the benchmarks of equality. A strength of her scheme therefore is to obligate the state to facilitate disabled people in arriving at these benchmarks regardless of whether they need more resources than other people to do so. The state similarly is obligated to facilitate everybody else in meeting the benchmarks by offering the resources they need to do so. The state's obligation is to ensure that everyone equally reaches the benchmarks, regardless of whether some people require more resources than others to do so, and of whether those who need more resources burden those who don't.

The level of outcome basic to a dignified human life cannot be set arbitrarily, of course. Nussbaum's basis for proposing a standard is an initially plausible one. She appeals to the levels of the basic capabilities that humans typically attain, namely, to what is normal for our species.[34] So on her scheme justice involves deploying greater or fewer resources to individuals depending on how much in deficit from species-typicality they are, and how difficult, given their circumstances, their ascent to species-typicality will be. A species-typical level is a standard that permits individuals to survive, as a species that typically failed to develop individuals' capabilities to the degree necessary for individual survival eventually would encounter population depletion beyond the point of extinction. And, at least on first glance, such a standard appears to give everyone a kind of equality of status, whether achieving species-typical levels of capability is inexpensive and easy, or very costly, for them.[35]

---

[34] Note that the degree of intellectual capability typically developed by children in Amy Rowley's Westchester County, New York, classroom is likely to be greater than what is typical for the worldwide human population, which once again suggests that the U.S. Supreme Court's distributive justice theory is more generous to children like Amy Rowley than Nussbaum's capability theory would be.

[35] In his response to Nussbaum's Tanner Lectures, Peter Singer questions whether Nussbaum's valorization of capability thresholds sometimes may be implausibly extravagant: what of the objection that utilitarianism makes the ethics of these trade-offs dependent on empirical calculations? Here I would say: I certainly hope so! (Nussbaum's denial that empirical calculations are relevant appears to require that if a society has only one member below the minimum entitlement level, it should spend all its resources on bringing that member above the entitlement level before it spends anything at all on raising the welfare level of anyone else, no matter how big a difference the resources could make

A weakness of this capabilities strategy, however, is the absence of obligation to level the playing field for disabled people so their opportunities to exceed basic outcome benchmarks equal those of nondisabled people. Given the predilection of schools for communicating information aurally in the classroom, and absent provision of qualified interpreters or captioners, a deaf child's opportunity to access classroom teaching will not be equal but instead greatly inferior to similarly talented hearing children's opportunities. Inferior access likely will lead to inferior outcome, even if that outcome exceeds the basic level needed for dignity and flourishing.[36] Such an approach can doom entire classes of outliers to inferior economic and social status, for even extraordinary talent cannot overcome neglect. Without equality of opportunity, disabled and nondisabled children of similar intellectual talents and dispositions are unlikely to achieve parity in their ultimate educational achievements.[37] While such disparate impact might be acceptable if solely due to differences in individual talent, a system where the state creates differential outcomes by privileging ordinary children with access to all instruction while denying equal access to outlying youth seems wrong.

Advocates of the capabilities approach likely would agree that if excess or abundant resources exist, the degree of capability development a state is obligated to support in all its citizens should be raised. But this will not resolve the underlying difficulty, Nondisabled students will continue to enjoy greater opportunity to maximize their potential, and greater likelihood for high status and great success, than disabled students, who still will be deficient in opportunity to achieve a better than average educational result.

to everyone else in society. That, surely, is an absurdity.) Text of Singer's response to Nussbaum is available at http://www.utilitarian.net/singer/by/20021113.htm

[36] Of course, schools could equalize the situation for deaf children in other ways, e.g. by offering all instruction to all children online in the form of text. In this case, hearing and deaf children would be treated identically in that the visual mode of instruction is equally accessible to them.

[37] Although the values promoted by the capabilities approach might be thought to entail a directive to maximize people's capabilities to the fullest extent, this is not so. Nussbaum eschews such a consequentialist thrust (*Frontiers*, 338–42) Construing maximizing capabilities as a political obligation faces practical difficulties as well by requiring much greater resources than just bringing everyone's capabilities to the species-typical threshold. Some might object that state support enabling Amy to develop her intellectual capability fully is unfair because the disparity between Amy and less capable disabled children would widen, making the latter even worse off. But a policy that explicitly deprives Amy of capability levels the state engenders in nondisabled children also seems unfair.

Any pursuit of justice through special distributions aimed at mitigating or compensating for deficits will encounter similar or related difficulties. Deficit is a comparative notion, and therefore by definition is a condition that some but not all people suffer. Erasing the disadvantage of deficit is a principle that must acknowledge and defer to a ceiling above which justice no longer cares whether individuals rise, even if they have the potential to do so, because they no longer are perceived as being in deficit.

A distinction may help to point the way out of the quandary here. Justice should extend to and embrace whoever is worst off, and a justice theory's failure to do so is compelling evidence of its inadequacy. Doing so is quite different, however, from focusing justice on the worst off and delineating it in terms of procedures for elevating whoever is so designated to an improved level. Justice undoubtedly sometimes may be secured through remediation. But justice is not exhausted by remediation, nor should the difference of being very badly or worst off be either the definitive concern or preeminent for justice.

6.3.4. *Embracing difference (difference as talent)*

Where opportunity is open not to ability but rather to privilege that is accorded social position (even to the position of being worst off), aspiration turns to justice for talent. This section advances several reasons for thinking that justice for outliers to develop and express their talents is and should be as much a value as remedying their deficiencies. So the discussion here indicates that the strategy of aiming justice at the worst off passes by a powerful and important route to justice.

We begin with an empirical reason to think that justice for outliers should be sensitive to talent. Then we will turn to the conceptual dimension of calling for justice for talent. The empirical argument appeals to how courts and legislators responded to the *Rowley* Court's dismissal of the proposition that talent deserves fair treatment.[38] Their intuitions about justice do not seem to agree that children with disabilities have no claim on opportunity to excel. The Court in *Rowley* was not moved to extend principles of equality of opportunity or equal protection to disabled children who, as

---

[38] The argument over the next few pages draws from Anita Silvers and Michael Ashley Stein, 'Disability and the Social Contract', *University of Chicago Law Review*, 74/4, 1615–40 (Fall 2007).

outliers, were deprived of talent-developing instruction offered as a matter of course to nondisabled children. Practice subsequent to *Rowley*, however, has eschewed this precedent and instead has taken a progressive approach to the issue of fair opportunity for talent development.

The Individuals with Disabilities Education Act (IDEA) was the successor statute to the Education for the Handicapped Act (EHA) of Rowley's day. As part of IDEA-mandated individualized education plans for disabled children, lower courts now often provide sufficient funds to enable these children to develop their talents as the education system enables nondisabled children to do theirs.[39] Thus, in *Hall* v. *Vance County Board of Education*,[40] the Fourth Circuit acknowledged that while minimal outcomes (like passing from grade to grade) might be expected for 'the most severely handicapped children,' the provision for individualized education plans meant that minimal results 'would be insufficient' for most other children.[41] This is a direct rejection of the standard invoked by the *Rowley* precedent. Writing eight years after *Rowley*, Mark Weber points out how other courts had achieved similar results by upholding the mainstreaming duty explicitly imposed in the EHA and its successors, as opposed to the appropriate education standard of *Rowley*.[42] Noting that this practice is 'a stronger egalitarian idea than that applied in the *Rowley* opinion,' Weber correctly proposes a corollary, namely, that 'schools should affirmatively provide the services to enable handicapped children to prosper in settings from which they have been unlawfully barred.'[43]

That the weak egalitarianism of *Rowley* does not rise to current American moral and political intuitions about justice is further evidenced by the application of the Americans with Disabilities Act (ADA)[44] to public education. Title II of the statute, which prohibits discrimination in the

---

[39] Some commentators argue that ultimately *Rowley* was undone by a 1997 amendment to the IDEA's preamble, 20 USC § 1400(c)(5)(A) (2000 & Supp 2004), which references meeting developmental goals 'to the maximum extent possible' and thus meeting 'the challenging expectations . . . established for all children.' For this reading, see *J.L.* v. *Mercer Island School District*, 2006 US Dist LEXIS 89492, *11 (WD Wash) But see *Lieutenant T.B.* v. *Warwick School Committee*, 361 F3d 80, 83 (1st Cir 2004) (holding that the amended language does not overrule *Rowley*). A second rationale is that 20 USC § 1414(d)(3)(B)(iv) (2000 & Supp 2004) mandates that individual education plans consider the 'full range of needs' and 'opportunities.' For purposes of our discussion, whether public policy overrules *Rowley* or sidesteps it is immaterial.

[40] 774 F2d 629 (4th Cir 1985).   [41] Ibid. at 636.

[42] See Mark C. Weber, 'The Transformation of the Education of the Handicapped Act: A Study in the Interpretation of Radical Statutes,' 24 *UC Davis L Rev* 349, 390–2 (1990) ('The court supported its holding with the plain language of the Act.').

[43] Ibid. at 393.   [44] 42 USC §§ 12101–12213 (2000).

provision of state and local government services, is understood to entitle deaf students to qualified sign-language interpreters if needed to give them full and meaningful access to any school program or activity.[45] Indeed, from Amy Rowley's day, when the issue was whether sign-language interpretation must be provided, controversy now has shifted to the qualifications interpreters must meet to give deaf children meaningful access to the subject matter of their specific courses.[46] State legislation addressing appropriate qualifications for sign-language interpretation for specialized and advanced courses in the public schools is not unusual,[47] offering more evidence of the value United States public policy attributes to equality of opportunity,[48] here instantiated as equality of meaningful access to the content of instruction appropriate to developing students' talents whether or not they have disabilities.[49]

Rowley founders on a classic dilemma in theorizing the state's obligations under justice: should equality of opportunity, which permits differential outcomes responsive to differences of talent and effort, be prior or subsidiary to equality understood as similarity or identity of outcomes? In *Rowley* the Supreme Court opted for the latter understanding, designating the relevant outcome as passing from grade to grade, but subsequent public policy and practice appear to have gone the other way. Yet Nussbaum's capability theory does not appear able to account for, align with, or support the progressive jurisprudence and statutes that disregard or depart from *Rowley* by attending to equality of opportunity, and thereby to fair treatment, for children with disabilities. In regard to education, her theory does not

---

[45] For a detailed account, see the legal memorandum posted by the National Association of the Deaf, *online at* http://www.nad.org/publicschools (visited Apr. 21, 2007).

[46] See generally Chalk Talk, Malicia Hitch, *Educational Interpreters: Certified or Uncertified?*, 34 *J L & Educ* 161 (2005). http://www.law.louisville.edu/students/jle/2006-2007-editorial-staff-and-bio-graphies/ and http://www.kyoba.org/kyoba/bar%20results/pass%20lists%20with%20names/july%20 2005%20pass%20list%20with%20names.html

[47] See e.g. Utah Code Ann §§ 53A–26a–301, 53A–26a–201 (2006) (requiring certification by the Interpreters Certification Board); Minn Stat Ann § 122A.31 (West 2000 & Supp 2007) (requiring certification from the Registry of Interpreters for the Deaf, the National Association of the Deaf, or state commissioner of education)

[48] Ironically, the Supreme Court recognized this point while under Chief Justice Rehnquist (who had written the majority opinion in *Rowley*) by holding in *Cleveland* v. *Policy Mgmt. Sys. Corp.*, 526 U.S. 795, 801 (1999), that 'The ADA seeks to eliminate unwarranted discrimination against disabled individuals in order both to guarantee those individuals equal opportunity and to provide the Nation with the benefit of their consequently increased productivity.'

[49] For a critique of the ADA on the ground that it does not reach equality of opportunity in many contexts, see Michael Ashley Stein and Penelope J. S. Stein, 'Beyond Disability Civil Rights,' 58 *Hastings L J*, June (2007).

seem to add anything to disabled children's flourishing beyond resources to achieve very basic outcomes and could result in lower distributions (as *Rowley* decrees) than existing practice.

That intuitions about (in)justice were strong enough to have deflected the *Rowley* precedent is evidence of the importance we assign to fair responsiveness to people's differences. The *Rowley* aftermath indicates at least as much indignation at inequality imposed to curtail some people's potential for strengths and virtues as at inequality imposed in regard to some people's weaknesses or defects. Theories of justice aimed at mitigating the disadvantage of the worst off face difficulties in accounting for disapprobation of this sort. Focused on deficiency, they neglect Amy and those like her whose losses, however unfair, do not depress their wellbeing drastically.

A further complexity is that individuals in deficit on one scale (for instance, in the ability to hear) may be elevated on some other scales (for instance, in intelligence) and so may truly (but confusingly) be both worse and better off. This consideration helps to explain why the negative impact of biases blocking talent is likely to be ignored by theories that aim improvement procured in the name of justice first and foremost at the worst off. Improving the situations of globally worst off people may not provoke resentment from those not quite as badly off, but improving the situations of people well off in some respects very likely will. Although worse off than similarly talented people who enjoy all the support an accommodating society supplies, talented outliers are unlikely to be worse off than every one else. To hearing students who usually received 'Cs' Amy Rowley no doubt appeared quite fortunate because she received 'Bs' and undeserving of any accommodation that would enable her to surpass them even more.

There are also conceptual arguments for supposing that potential as well as deficiency calls for justice. A familiar contemporary precept advances the advice that you should become all you can be, a notion aligned with traditional philosophical views about the value of self-development. A Platonic variation is that individuals are harmed when their maturation is stymied, and an Aristotelian version locates harm in diversions of individuals' growth from their normal end or aim. Kant's argument that developing one's talents is an imperfect duty is well known: the logic of affirming that happiness is one's end demands at least intermittent attention and effort applied to cultivating one's fullest powers. How unjust it then must be, given these ideas about the value of talent, for social arrangements to ignore or impede outliers in fully realizing the potential their endowments could bestow if the majority of the population has the opportunity to do so. Such a situation would have the state harming outliers, but not others, by denying them full human maturation or the satisfaction of their natural aim, or by standing between outlier agents and their duty.

Reflection on the debates about admitting golfer Casey Martin and sprinter Oscar Pistorius to the highest level of competition in their respective sports further elucidates the appeal for justice for talent. A congenital circulatory impairment leaves Martin requiring a golf cart to travel around a golf course's eighteen holes, an accommodation banned in the U.S. Open. Double-amputation below the knee eleven months after birth leaves Pistorius running on artificial feet, an accommodation that initially was banned in the Olympics as falling under a prohibition against track athletes racing on springs or wheels (prosthetic running feet are neither). Martin and Pistorius both compete well against nondisabled athletes, but individuals who oppose their inclusion unrelentingly try to rationalize their success as being due to their impairments' being accommodated rather than to their talent.[50]

The Professional Golfers' Association (PGA) pursued its claim that riding a golf cart privileged Martin by allowing him to rest all the way to the U.S. Supreme Court, where passionate golfers Justices O'Connor and Stevens led the majority who rejected the PGA's claim.[51] The prevailing opinion

---

[50] Among the objections to Pistorius were the following: 'It affects the purity of sport. Next will be another device where people can fly with something on their back' (Elio Locatelli of Italy, the director of development for the IAAF); 'The rule book says a foot has to be in contact with the starting block...What is the definition of a foot? Is a prosthetic device a foot, or is it an actual foot?' (Leon Fleiser, a general manager of the South African Olympic Committee); 'Pistorius could topple over, obstructing others or injuring himself and fellow competitors' (IAAF officials); '[Allowing Pistorius to compete could cause] athletes to do something as seemingly radical as having their healthy natural limbs replaced by artificial ones? Is it self-mutilation when you're getting a better limb?' (George Dvorsky, Institute for Ethics and Emerging Technologies). From Jere Longman, 'An Amputee Sprinter: Is He Disabled or Too-Abled?,' New York Times, May 15, 2007. www.nytimes.com/2007/05/15/sports/othersports/15runner.htm. See also http://www.finding dulcinea.com/news/sports/Amputee-Sprinter-Eligible-For-Olympics.html for links to many interesting commentaries.

[51] PGA Tour, Inc. v. Martin, (00–24) 532 U.S. 661 (2001) 204 F.3d 994 And for discussion see links at http://sportsillustrated.cnn.com/golf/news/2001/05/29/martin_decision_ap/

noted the absence of evidence that top golfers' performance is impinged by an eighteen hole stroll and the presence of evidence that Martin's difficulty walking on impaired limbs caused sufficient exhaustion to offset any restful riding. To the majority, Martin's success at golf appeared to be his own, his talent, and not the result of his being privileged by having a ride.

In a somewhat similarly sequenced story, of nearly two hundred respondents who emailed the *New York Times* after the story of Oscar Pistorius was published, almost all those objecting to his competing in the Olympics dismissed his documented speed and wins against nondisabled competitors as artefacts of technology rather than products of his own talent. So did dismissive track officials quoted in the story. Despite Oscar's demonstrated success in both disabled and nondisabled racing, a racing official even portrayed him to be so untalented as to pose a danger to other competitors by toppling over on them during a race. Apparently unaware that a gymnast with a wooden leg was a gold medalist in the 1904 Olympics, another official worried that admitting an athlete with artificial legs would contaminate the purity of sport. Nay-sayers strenuously created such strained objections to dismiss Oscar's running talent and thus avoid having to engage with difference because of a talented outlier.[52]

Officials of the International Association of Athletics Federations (IAAF), the international governing body for track and field, ruled that Oscar must be banned to avoid disadvantaging flesh-footed competitors. His prosthetic feet are longer than fleshly feet, and he appears to use about one-fourth less lower leg energy when matched with runners with fleshly feet over a similar distance at similar speed. That finding must be contextualized, however, as is evident from the fact that Oscar has no lower legs and therefore cannot be energizing in the same way as fleshly footed individuals. Ordinarily, the knee, calf, and ankle work together to absorb energy when a runner steps down on his fleshly foot, and when that foot pushes off again the lower leg

---

[52] The vehemence felt by those who object to letting a runner with no feet compete in the Olympics manifests in the sequence of online responses readers sent the *Times*. For example, several early commentators who supported Pistorius's inclusion proposed facetiously that competitors who believed themselves disadvantaged by running against Pistorius's prosthetic feet could have their own feet amputated and don Cheetahs. As the online commenting went on, however, nay-sayers began speculating seriously and with alarm that athletes would be likely to do so (for the same motivation some do blood doping). Another official opined that Pistorius cannot obey the usual rule requiring the runner's foot to touch the starting block, apparently neglecting to notice that sprinters do not usually run barefooted, and therefore that runners with fleshly feet actually touch the starting block with their shoes, which are engineered and selected to give them the most advantage. (See n. 50 for sources.)

generates more than twice the energy that was stored when the foot struck down.

In contrast, when Oscar Pistorius steps down his weight and momentum compress his blade, which thereby stores energy. As the energy reaches the forward edge of the blade, his hip generates twice as much energy as a fleshly footed runner's hip, and when the blade decompresses it returns only four-fifths of the stored energy. In other words, Oscar *is* using less lower leg energy than the standard-issue runner, but he is using more hip energy. As the Court of Arbitration for Sport ruled in overturning the IAAF's ban, the IAAF unfairly tested Oscar's energy expenditure only at the point in his stride when he is most stabilized. There is no evidence that Pistorius has any overall unfair advantage, the Court stated.[53]

One way to characterize the appeals court's principle is as an application of just recognition and respect for talent. Oscar's talent for lower extremity mobilizing is less than typical for Olympic-level racers, but he exceeds others in talented use of his hips. Arbitrarily considering runners' lower leg activity to be the sole locus of talent, the IAAF declared Oscar insufficiently talented to participate in Olympic competition. The appeals court, however, decided that just because lower leg power typically is the source of talented runners' power should not rule out individuals whose unusually talented hips enable them to function similarly well.

Bernard Boxill likewise invokes the value of talent in arguing for the justice of difference-responsive policies that do not treat everybody the same. Boxill rejects the proposal that affirmative action is inherently unjust, observing:

adopting a colour-blind principle entails adopting a talent-blind principle, and since the latter is absurd, so is the former. Or, in other words, differences in talent and differences in colour are on a par.... Colour-conscious policies can conceivably be just, just as talent-conscious policies can conceivably be—and often are—just. It depends on the circumstances.[54]

---

[53] Joshua Robinson and Alan Schwarz, 'Olympic Dream Stays Alive, on Synthetic Legs,' *New York Times*, 157/54313, May 17, 2008, A1, B13.

[54] Bernard Boxill, *Blacks and Social Justice* (Totowa, NJ.: Rowman & Allanheld, 1984), 18. In my view, Boxill's intuition about strategies for justice is validated by the U.S. Supreme Court's decision in *Grutte* v. *Bollinger*, the 2003 case that affirmed the race-conscious admission policy at the University of Michigan Law School. The importance of justice for talent for the national interest is emphasized by Justice O'Connor in her majority opinion: 'In order to cultivate a set of leaders with legitimacy in the eyes of the citizenry, it is necessary that the path to leadership be visibly open to talented and qualified

Boxill's claim is that denying considerability to talent in formulating the principles that regulate our treatment of one another is absurd. Similarly absurd would be denying appreciation, and consequently preference, to talent just because we believe ridiculing and ridding ourselves of the untalented to be wrong.

It does not follow from the iniquity of excluding people based on color that all consideration of color is wrong, nor does it follow from the wrongness of depreciating people because of their disabilities that appreciating people in virtue of their abilities is wrong. Boxill's argument rests on the observation that preference for talent seems patently acceptable to justice and is a principle endorsed by both proponents and opponents of race-based affirmative action. Not only do neither proponents nor opponents object to preference for talent, but both seem to take as intuitive the supposition that that kind of preference is all right. The adversaries' difference arises primarily about the practical matter of when to apply such preference: are advantageous differences in talent to be identified for preference before, or only after, disadvantageous differences attributable to a history of oppression can be resolved?

Nonetheless, in an otherwise admiring review of Boxill's book, Laurence Thomas demurs about the analogy between talent-consciousness and race-consciousness, which to him is not convincing. Thomas rightly notes that 'talent-conscious policies are not intended to be corrective ones. They are intended to serve the ends of excellence rather than justice.' Thomas sees affirmative color-conscious policies as a means of attaining just ends, but does not imagine talent-conscious policies serving similarly.[55]

Thomas's complaint would be correct if achieving justice for outliers is restricted to the two strategies we have already explored: justice for differences that should be denied and justice for differences that should be mitigated. Considerability granted to being talented is no evident feature of theories of justice focused on ignoring differences or on improving the lot of the worst off. In the next section, therefore, we turn to an alternative

individuals of every race and ethnicity. . . . Access to legal education (and thus the legal profession) must be inclusive of talented and qualified individuals of every race and ethnicity, so that all members of our heterogeneous society may participate in the educational institutions that provide the training and education necessary to succeed in America.' *Grutter* v. *Bollinger* (02–241) 539 U.S. 306 (2003) 288 F.3d 732, affirmed at http://www.law.cornell.edu/supct/html/02–241.ZO.html

[55] Review of *Blacks and Social Justice, Law and Philosophy*, 5/1 (Apr. 1986), 121–34 (122–3).

account of justice, one that propels an imperative for cultivating talent in outliers as emphatically as the theories of justice examined previously urge disregarding that they are different or regarding with preference those whose difference results in their being less than average or worst off.

6.4. Justice for Talent

Although justice for talent has been a powerful call in American political development, philosophical scholarship has paid much less attention to the value of exercising talent and to the enabling role justice sometimes is called upon to play so that outliers can do so. What is the value of developing talent, and why should fair and inclusive provisions for exercising talent be a concern for justice? Social support for doing so engenders personal benefits by cultivating individuals' incentive and self-esteem. Perhaps more important, social arrangements that impede people's doing so impoverish productive cooperative social interactions. Further, outliers' prospects for philosophical considerability are likely to be depressed if their differences are obscured or deplored, but to be elevated by a justice theory that foregrounds differences as strengths.

By grounding principles of justice in agreement among so-called normal agents, traditional social contract theory falls short in being responsive to the differences of people whom paradigms of normalcy do not represent.[56] The two strategies for justice examined in earlier sections of this essay proceed from the standpoint of normalcy. The first is an assimilation policy that interdicts attention to anomaly, and the second is a compensation policy that rejects anomaly and deploys resources for its repair. Both take justice to be a matter of advancing outliers to normalcy.

In contrast, the strategy for justice proposed in this section accepts outliers as immutably anomalous. In 'Justice through Trust: Disability and the "Outlier" Problem in Social Contract Theory,'[57] Leslie Francis and I introduced a new approach that grounds social contract theory in the facts of human diversity rather than the fiction of a homogeneous humanity. Justice

---

[56] See Anita Silvers and Leslie Francis, 'Justice through Trust: Disability and the "Outlier Problem," ' *Ethics* 116 (2005), for a review of arguments made by various scholars for this claim.
[57] Ibid.

through trust calls for principles aimed directly at facilitating cooperative interaction among different kinds of people rather than among people who are the same.

Justice through trust endorses three principles crucial to agreement[58] between parties who are of different kinds or occupy different positions. These three principles shape practices that enable agreement to be initiated and regulate practices to sustain that agreement:

One . . . is that procedure and practices should be inclusive, for to trust an agreement the parties must have standing in its development. Second, procedure and practices should recognize and respond to people's differences without disadvantaging them for being so, for to trust an agreement the parties must feel free to be (and reveal) who they are while participating in its development. Third, procedure and practices should enable participants to strengthen each other's involvement and commitment, for the parties need to embrace principles that enable their interactions to be ongoing. To trust an agreement the parties thus must be able to promote the stability of its influence.[59]

These principles nourish each other: all advance people's engaging in approach behaviour, and all reduce their inclination to retreat from individuals disturbingly different from themselves.

The initial principle of justice through trust, necessitating full standing for outliers and therefore sweeping inclusion of them, has been invoked during our discussion of the three strategies for justice. We now turn to a brief exploration of how the latter two principles of justice, which build out on the necessity of inclusiveness to justice, apply. Inclusion through social practices that facilitate people's interacting cooperatively with one another is the theme that links the three principles.

Traditional social contract theory takes fair cooperation among agents to depend on formulating principled practices for allocating benefits and burdens that people (in many versions, rational people only) would accept. Agreeing on (in many versions, bargaining about) what will constitute fair allocation, or even on what should be allocated, seems too sophisticated a

---

[58] To short-circuit any fear that the expression 'agreement' rules out participation by individuals who cannot articulate their intentions (and perhaps do not engage in processes classifiable as forming intentions), see passages of 'Justice through Trust' describing how familiar interactions where responsiveness patterns have evolved fall under a plausibly expansive account of agreement between parties who do not speak the same language because at least one does not speak at all. Thanks to Jeff McMahan for suggesting this line of thought.

[59] Ibid. 66.

process to be conducted fairly prior to the initiation of justice, however. Therefore justice through trust supposes that noncoercive interactive practices must be in place to launch development of sophisticated verbalized principles of justice.

These are practices of bringing and keeping people together so cooperation is launched and then sustained through growing trust. The three principles express ideals for inspiring practices that do so. As the practices gain stability and strength, articulation of the principles that shape them sharpens. But people need not be able to articulate these principles, or to ponder them, to be committed to them. Contracting through trust emphasizes that cooperation-facilitating conditions develop over time, as social activity evolves to strengthen and systematize people's natural proclivities to depend on each other. Contrary to the traditional model on which principles of justice are formulated as conclusions reached through bargaining among equals, justice through trust construes social contracting as evolving rather than as a "one shot" deal, and the account is "constructivist" in the quite literal sense of a building process.[60]

When individuals do not approach each other,[61] but instead fight or flee, the possibility of cooperative interaction is undermined. Facilitating the trust that enables individuals to join together in cooperative interactions, instead of putting distance between themselves and other potential cooperators, calls for practices that encourage cooperators to reveal themselves. For whenever we must hide some essential properties of ourselves, we also must prepare ourselves, if discovered, to flee. Such holding back of one's self attenuates cooperation.[62] Hence the second principle.

---

[60] Ibid. 65.

[61] Approach for cooperation need not be physical. People can cooperate without ever being in each other's presence. Some people even cooperate with unseen spirits whom they believe to exist on an immaterial plane, provided we are convinced these (a) assign standing or considerability to us, (b) know us for who we are, and (c) make covenants with us or otherwise behave in systematic ways toward us. And yes, trusting this way does make us vulnerable, as many commentators on trust emphasize. There is also the Kierkegaardian idea that persevering in trust despite the violation of principle 3 is a test of faith. Justice is not a matter of faith, however, but rather of viscerally plausible expectations.

[62] There is a proviso to the initial principle's valuation of inclusion. Interaction among people that satisfies the standard of full inclusion may not be unavoidably harmful simply in virtue of bringing people together. Without this proviso, nay-sayers could object that the second principle undercuts the first by requiring, in justice, practices in which sadists, cannibals, and others whose other-regarding behavior is dangerous and destructive impose these differences on others. Not so, for such an interpretation of the principles would be self-defeating. Relationships in which one party eats the other are hardly cooperation-sustaining ones. Implementing this proviso correctly calls for applying the first strategy for justice, namely, dispelling pretextual stereotyping. The idea that Pistorius, an experienced competitor

Merely approaching to initiate contact is necessary but does not suffice, however. Practices that reinforce rather than undermine participants' commitment to each other, or at least to their joint enterprises, also are needed. For without feedback that keeps cooperators engaging with one another, joint enterprises are likely to grind to a halt, or else to need so much regulation of people's conduct to be put in place that cooperative relationships recede, banished by interaction driven by oppression and coercion. Hence the third principle.

Justice through trust thus identifies standards for practice that invite and enable people with differences to come together to cooperate. Taken together, the thrust of the three principles is to reposition being worst off (in wealth, health, wellbeing, or on one of the other life quality scales) as just one among various kinds of differences that may cause people to be perceived as outliers and for that reason have an especially urgent call on justice.

People may deviate from normality by being extremely well off, or else by being impoverished, and in various ways. Usually the differences of the kinds of individuals we characterize as outliers in need of justice are thought of as residing in the latter rather than the former direction. Justice in their cases therefore is presumed to aim at erasing (the first strategy we considered) or mitigating (the second strategy we considered) their deficits, relieving their (literal or figurative) suffering so as to elevate them, as much as possible, to a position of fair advantage comparable to everyone else.

Justice for talent is difficult to fit into this frame, however. We think of being talented as having been favored rather than as a state to be ignored or regretted. Where justice is framed in terms usual to the first two strategies for addressing difference, therefore, justice for talent appears to be an unneeded, uncomfortable, or incompatible response. For there seemingly should be no need either to erase or to amplify advantage for those favored with talent.

By noticing how the usual conceptualization circumscribes justice's responsiveness to difference, we can better understand why Oscar's and

---

in both paralympic and nondisabled track competitions, should be excluded from the Olympics because he could topple over on other runners exemplifies a pretextual invocation of the first principle's proviso. As well, see 'Justice through Trust' for a discussion about the impropriety of objecting that the inclusion, through accommodating difference, of outliers necessarily harms previously privileged people by altering their accustomed competitive position.

Amy's situations might be thought not to call for justice. Developing and applying their talents would not decrease the kinds of advantages species-typical individuals have over them but instead could increase their advantageous differences over other people. But how can advantaging one person over another be a requirement of justice when the usual call upon justice is to rectify such asymmetry?

On the approach advanced by justice through trust, reparative action still is owed those very badly off. But the reason is that extraordinary deprivation impedes their coming together through non-coercive, non-oppressive processes with everyone else in productive cooperation. Individuals perceived as unusually well off in some respect also sometimes are excluded from cooperative activities, and in justice their situation calls for redress as well. Thus, talented and untalented both may struggle with social or even natural barriers that impede their fitting in. Valuing inclusion with and through difference, even more than valuing inclusion despite difference, prizes strategies that foreground different kinds of difference rather than just the single difference of being worst (or really badly) off, or the single difference of being different.

What of Amy's case if justice is to be pursued through nourishing trust? According to the principles for achieving justice through trust, just practice requires invigorating the approach behaviors that will facilitate cooperation between Amy and other people. Cooperative interaction is unlikely to flourish if Amy is merely dropped off at an open school door and treated as if her deafness does not make a real difference between her and her classmates.[63] That she might be worst off among her peers in regard to the ability to hear is relevant but should not have circumscribed her call on justice. Taking her claim on justice to arise from her being worst off severely limited the strength of her claim because the strength of her intellect mitigated her disadvantage. In contrast, she has a potent protest based on being excluded from collaborative human activities where she has strengths, but ones she cannot develop and exercise absent full access to information such as correspondingly gifted hearing children enjoy.

---

[63] A personal note: most people with mobility or sensory disabilities are not thrilled to hear the familiar refrain 'I don't think of you as different.' This disclaimer usually is accompanied by failures to accommodate and, consequently, by exclusion of individuals whose disabilities make them different regardless of other people's determination not to interact with them as they really are.

Talent also should command justice. Accommodating alterations in communications practice are called for not only to enable Amy to gain an average education while within the school house, but also to prepare her, like the other children, to cooperate at a highly developed level throughout life. On the principles for securing justice through trust, response to Amy's difference—in this case that absent a sign-language interpreter she understands only half of what occurs in class—must not devitalize prospects of cooperatively connecting deaf and hearing people. But how can there be any other result where outliers' differences are made reasons to exclude them from opportunity offered everyone else, and where those secure in being catered to by the system's practices (as Amy's classmates were) learn to turn their backs on exclusions defended by invoking difference?

What of Amy's case for resources to hire interpreters so she can fully achieve the potential for fruitful interaction with others that is promised by her intellectual talent? What if doing so means other children with disabilities may not be funded for special education, or other gifted children the accelerated instruction that can actualize their potential for cooperative flourishing? This question confronts the familiar fear that accommodating one child with a disability means depriving some other disabled or nondisabled children of resources they need, thus unfairly disadvantaging them.[64]

Traditional social contract theory adherents may crave principles that pre-determine decisively an order of preference for justice deserved. But neither justice through trust nor any other justice theory should try to answer such questions in the abstract. Fears about resource depletion cannot be resolved with generalities. Knowing what kinds of costs might be incurred to remedy exclusion, or even if material resources are needed to do so, requires conscientious case by case investigation.

In this regard, justice through trust departs from many other theories of justice by recognizing that strategies for justice are various and that deploying compensatory resources has no necessary priority among them. For example, in *Rowley* the school district focused on reducing the differences between Amy and other children, making the former more like the latter by providing a hearing aid and speech therapy, but did not concomitantly

---

[64] For an example of supposing that accommodations to disability entail harms to talent, see Mark Kelman and Gillian Lester, *Jumping the Queue: An Inquiry into the Legal Treatment of Children with Learning Disabilities* (Cambridge Mass.: Harvard University Press, 1997).

explore making the latter more like the former by adjusting instructional practice considerably toward visual modes.[65] Resource allocation might have played out differently under a more imaginatively flexible notion of inclusion, one that engaged with the variety of ways children develop intellectual talent and the contributions of classroom interaction to that end. But such flexibility was precluded by a conceptualization of justice that fixated on owing Amy only the opportunity for average achievement like most other children and never the means to excel.

6.5. Conclusion

Debate about the proper approach to justice for outliers typically advances one of several strategies, casting the others as competing with the favoured one and therefore as being wrong. Denying difference and mitigating difference are strategies for securing justice that seem to exclude embracing difference. The first takes justice to depend on homogeneity, proposing that everyone essentially is alike and should be afforded the same treatment. The second takes justice to seek homogeneity, acknowledging people's differences but then altering them or their situations to make them more alike. But embracing difference requires justice to reject homogeneity, cultivating differences that propel people along different paths, yet enabling cooperative interaction among them. Our investigation here has shown all three to be important techniques for combating exclusion based on disability or on other stigmatized characteristics that have been invoked to distance people and make them into outliers. Jettisoning any of the three strategies cannot help but narrow moral and political protection against the unjust exclusion of outliers.

The alternative is to rethink the conceptualization of justice that makes these strategies seem incompatible. The problem is traceable in part to traditional social contract theory's failure to come to grips with the profound

---

[65] While sign-language interpreters are important in facilitating the learning of deaf users of Sign, providing all students with transcriptions of lecture notes is as important to learning. Doing so ensures that all students start from the same record of what the instructor wants to convey. See Teresa Blankmeyer Burke, 'Seeing Philosophy: Deaf Students and Deaf Philosophers,' in *Teaching Philosophy, Special Issue on Disability in the Philosophy Classroom* (ed. Anita Silvers and Anita Ho), 30/4 (Dec. 2007), for more information on sign-language interpreters and deaf students' access to advanced learning.

diversity of potential cooperators, and also in part to the approach's incomplete analysis of the place of fair apportionment in enabling cooperation. If cooperation rests on the propitious allocation of burdens and benefits, then the three strategies indeed seem exclusive of one another, for they rely on very different reasons for assigning distributive priorities. Moreover, the differences of different cooperators will differ in their command of considerability, depending on which strategy is invoked.

Social contracting to justice through engendering and enlarging trust, to the contrary, takes cooperation to be prior to, rather than the product of, formulating a just distributive scheme. On this account of the basis for justice, spreading benefits and sharing burdens to affect not only fairness but flourishing must respond to both similarities and differences among people, as well as to the experiences and efforts that can be links between different kinds of people. Growing trust among them will sometimes involve highlighting homogeneity, sometimes rendering them more homogeneous, and sometimes building out and articulating their very different strengths. The contextualized account of cooperation nourished by just practices that propagate trust thus calls for a more nuanced application of basic principles than traditional contract theory does. Despite—indeed, in virtue of—not ranking who should enjoy priority in escaping disadvantage, such a rich, yet realistic, approach to justice holds the best promise of having room for every kind of outlier.

7

Understanding Autonomy in Light of Intellectual Disability

LESLIE P. FRANCIS

People with intellectual disabilities, it is often thought, lack autonomy, at least if their disabilities are significantly severe. In this paper, I want to destabilize some aspects of this thought, on several fronts. First, it is important to notice that claims about the absence of autonomy are really a loose family of claims, albeit in a loosely Kantian vein. Second, the claims that interest me, and that are core to some of the consequences that are thought to follow from a lack of autonomy, are descriptive or normative claims, not claims about metaphysical differences in kind. Third, some of these claims at least are generally presented in doubly misleading ways, as features of individuals conceptualized separately from others, and as features that do not admit of degrees. In the final two sections of this paper, I press these observations in light of a theoretical and a practical example. The theoretical example is whether people with intellectual disabilities can be regarded as subjects of justice. The practical example is *Atkins* v. *Virginia*,[1] the case in which the United States Supreme Court held that it is cruel and unusual punishment to impose the death penalty on persons with mental retardation. My goal in this paper is not to argue that persons with intellectual disabilities always have autonomy in the same way that people without such disabilities do. It is instead to argue that what it is to have autonomy in some relevant senses is a complex matter and that judgments

I am grateful to Sorin Baiasu, Kimberly Brownlee, Adam Cureton, Douglas MacLean, Anita Silvers, and the participants in the Manchester workshop on disability for their comments on an earlier draft of this paper.

[1] 536 U.S. 304 (2002).

about the autonomy of people with intellectual disabilities must be complex as well.

7.1. Autonomy Attributes

Many different but related attributes have been thought central to autonomy. Because people with intellectual disabilities experience different types of deficits, to differing degrees, it is important to get clear about at least some of the many different, albeit related, sorts of attributes that have been viewed as autonomy. What follows is a list of some of them. I'm sure there are more, and that these I mention might be formulated in different ways. But these are enough for my purposes here.

1. Having the capacity to value.[2] In her rich and insightful discussion of Alzheimer's patients, Agnieszka Jaworska argues that these patients may continue to have autonomy even though they are no longer fully capable of self-guided action, to the extent that they retain the capacity to value.

2. Having the capacity to understand relevant information and to reason out what actions would accord with one's values. This is something like a standard account of decision making capacity in health care and it is how 'autonomy' is often understood in discussions in bioethics. It may be worth noting, however, that the original introduction of the principle of autonomy into bioethics by Beauchamp and Childress viewed autonomy in terms of a Kantian ideal of self-governance.[3]

3. Having the ability to be the initiator of one's own actions—to be an agent.[4] Here, the idea is that one can put what is going on in one's head, as it were, into action.

4. Engaging in practical reasoning by formulating intentions, plans, and more overarching policies. Michael Bratman, for example, has defended the view that autonomy involves a 'conative hierarchy,' in

---

[2] See e.g. Agnieszka Jaworska, 'Respecting the Margins of Agency: Alzheimer's Patients and the Capacity to Value,' *Philosophy and Public Affairs*, 28/2 (1999), 105–38.

[3] Tom L. Beauchamp and James F. Childress, *Principles of Biomedical Ethics* (New York: Oxford University Press, 1979), ch. 3.

[4] See e.g. Sarah Buss, 'Personal Autonomy,' in *Stanford Encyclopedia of Philosophy* (available at http://plato.stanford.edu/entries/personal-autonomy/).

which one engages in a kind of reflective self-management, following not merely what desire is the strongest but what one views as a coherent structure of a life.[5] Such reflective self-management is one interpretation of what it means to be self-governing.

5. Acting in accord with categorical rather than hypothetical imperatives; that is, acting in accord with a principle that one can will to be a universal law, rather than acting in accord with desires. This view has been attributed to Kant,[6] although controversially.[7]

6. Not being subject to coercion or other, closely related forms of pressure. This is autonomy in the political, not the personal, sense.[8]

7. Participating as an agent in the construction of justice, free of guidance by antecedent principles of right or justice, moved solely by interests in one's own moral powers and by one's concern to advance one's final ends, whatever these may be. This is rational autonomy as employed by Rawls in his Kantian constructivist account of justice.[9] Rawls also believed that people in a well-ordered society—that is, a society ordered by principles of justice—exercise 'full' autonomy in the sense that they comply with the principles of justice they would have adopted in the constructivist project.[10]

These attributes call on different, but related, capacities. They include being able to value, being able to reason, being able to resist impulses, being able to imagine an ordered life, being able to order one's life, being able to put one's plans into practice, being able to participate in moral deliberation of an idealized kind, and being politically free. With the exception of the last of these, autonomy in the political sense, it might appear that people with intellectual disabilities lack the individualized cognitive, intentional, and other psychological powers that are necessary for their exercise. It is this picture that I wish to destabilize, at least

---

[5] See e.g. Michael Bratman, 'Autonomy and Hierarchy,' *Social Philosophy and Policy*, 20/2 (2003), 156–76.

[6] See e.g. Paul Guyer, 'Kant on the Theory and Practice of Autonomy,' *Social Philosophy and Policy*, 20/2 (2003), 70–98.

[7] See Thomas E. Hill, Jr., *Dignity and Practical Reasoning in Kant's Moral Theory* (Ithaca, NY: Cornell University Press, 1992).

[8] See e.g. John Christman, 'Autonomy in Political and Moral Philosophy,' *Stanford Encyclopedia of Philosophy* (available at http://plato.stanford.edu/entries/autonomy-moral/).

[9] John Rawls, 'Kantian Constructivism in Moral Theory,' in *John Rawls: Collected Papers*, Samuel Freeman (Cambridge, Mass.: Harvard University Press, 1999), 303–58.

[10] Ibid. 308.

with respect to people with intellectual disabilities who have recognizable psychological traits.[11]

7.2. Autonomy as Descriptive and Normative, not Metaphysical[12]

Let me start with some descriptive points. Intellectual disability is a multifaceted and variable phenomenon. Some intellectual disabilities are present from birth; some emerge through childhood, as a result of metabolic conditions such as poorly managed PKU, physiologic conditions such as intractable epilepsy, acute infectious conditions such as meningitis, or injuries. Still other intellectual disabilities emerge in adulthood, through injury, infection, or disease processes such as Huntington's disease or Alzheimer's disease. In my discussion here, I want to focus on intellectual disabilities that arise from birth or in childhood, before the person has acquired sufficient psychological development to have been at one point relatively capable of valuing, reasoning, deliberating, planning—that is, being autonomous in the ways outlined above in which we generally attribute autonomy to adult human beings.[13]

Intellectual disabilities that arise at birth or in childhood are themselves a richly varied phenomenon, ranging from anencephaly, to what Jeff McMahan has called 'radical cognitive impairment' (that is, impairment to the extent that cognitive capacities and potential are lower than those characteristic of higher primates),[14] to what is classified as 'mild' mental

---

[11] My discussion in this paper does not apply to people in persistent vegetative states or to people who have such devastating losses that they are virtually unresponsive and that individualized conceptions of the good cannot be constructed for them. Part of my argument to follow, however, is that exact lines here will be arbitrary.

[12] With apologies to Rawls's characterization of justice as fairness as 'political, not metaphysical.' John Rawls, 'Justice as Fairness: Political not Metaphysical,' in Freeman, ed., 388–414.

[13] I focus on this case because it is the most difficult one; when people have lifelong intellectual disabilities, there is no opportunity to begin decision making with a conception of their good that they have formulated earlier in life, and then employ forms of substituted judgment in which these conceptions of their good are applied by others serving as prostheses are not available in this case. By comparison, Douglas MacLean's account of 'Respect without Reason: Relating to Alzheimer's,' Ch. 8 this volume, employs as examples people who once were capable of formulating conceptions of their good—whatever that might mean.

[14] Jeff McMahan, 'Some notes on cognitive disability,' unpublished MS presented at the University of Chicago, April 2007.

retardation. 'Mental retardation' is defined in terms of limits in intellectual ability and adaptive behavior, manifested before adulthood.[15] Estimates for the U.S. are that between 2.5% and 3% of the population (between 6.2 and 7.5 million) are persons with mental retardation.[16] The majority of these (87%) have estimated IQ scores between 50 and 70–75, putting them in the 'mild' range of retardation; persons in this range exhibit a variety of differences in cognitive and adaptive behavior skills.

Among the multiple deficits faced by at least some people with intellectual disabilities, several are particularly relevant to one or another of these autonomy attributes. Some people with intellectual disabilities have difficulty with abstract reasoning. Others have difficulty with impulse control. Still others may have difficulty in planning ahead and in pursuing developed plans.[17] Additionally, problems in social adaptation are a defining feature of 'mental retardation'; these may be manifest as gullibility, naïveté, and the risk of victimization—that is, as forms of increased and potentially problematic dependency on others.[18] Some recent discussions in cognitive science picture the mind as a set of processing systems. Accounts of these systems as modular hold that they can be independently damaged; one illustration is people with Asperger's who lack the ability to identify with the mental states of others.[19] Another illustration is that blindness can occur either from retinal damage or from damage to cortical processing systems. Accounts of the mind that deny massive modularity cite the phenomenon of general mental retardation (such as Down's syndrome) as illustrative.[20] These accounts agree, however, on the presence of some kind of executive processing system; this, too, is a

---

[15] Clifford J. Drew and Michael L. Hardman, *Mental Retardation: A Lifespan Approach to People with Intellectual Disabilities*, 8th edn (Upper Saddle River, NJ: Pearson Prentice Hall, 2004), 18–19. There are notorious difficulties in measuring both IQ and skills in social adaptation. Current work on mental retardation recognizes the extent to which it is a social concept. Ibid. 19. The idea of 'six-hour retardation'—people who function reasonably well in ordinary life, but not in school—emphasizes both cultural factors and the importance of broadening the definition of retardation beyond performance on selected academic tasks. See e.g. Lynda Crane, *Mental Retardation: A Community Integration Approach.* (Belmont, Calif.: Wadsworth Publishing, 2002).

[16] From the ARC web site, http://www.thearc.org/faqs/mrqa.html (accessed June 1, 2004). The estimate of 3% has remained consistent over the past 40 years. See Robert B. Edgerton, *The Cloak of Competence* (Berkeley: University of California Press, revised & updated edn, 1993), 1.

[17] Drew and Hardman, *Mental Retardation*, 39.   [18] Ibid. 29.

[19] Peter Carruthers, 'The Case for Massively Modular Models of Mind,' in Robert J. Stainton (ed.), *Contemporary Debates in Cognitive Science* (Oxford: Blackwell Publishing, 2006), 3–21.

[20] Richard Samuels, 'Is the Human Mind Massively Modular?' in Robert J. Stainton (ed.), *Contemporary Debates in Cognitive Science* (Oxford: Blackwell Publishing, 2006), 37–56.

capacity that people with intellectual disabilities may lack to at least some extent.

Let me turn briefly, now, to a comparison with physical disabilities such as deafness or mobility impairments. We are all familiar with ways in which physical capacities of the individual can be supplemented by various prosthetic devices: eyeglasses, hearing aids, and cochlear implants; 'artificial' limbs; and wheelchairs and other sorts of devices for assistance with mobility. These devices make use of physical features of people with physical disabilities, structuring or enhancing them in some way or another. No one questions whether 'I' am seeing because I wear glasses, although they may of course question the quality of my sight or whether I should be permitted to drive a car or whether it is employment discrimination not to hire me to pilot an airplane.[21] No one questions whether 'I' am running if I have a prosthetic foot, although they may question whether it is fair for me to enter a track competition if my foot is an 'enhancement' or claim an Olympic medal if I run on prosthetic legs.[22] On the other hand, there are forms of assistance from others in cases of physical disability in which it might be questioned whether the characteristic in question is in any sense 'mine': do 'I' see with the eyes of others if I experience the visual world only as they describe it to me? Do 'I' move my hand if someone else picks it up from the bed and places it across my chest, without any associated nervous stimulation of 'my' musculature?

Clark and Chalmers have suggested a parallel analysis for intellectual disabilities.[23] We are all familiar with various assistive devices for mental processing: notebooks, palm pilots, calculators. No one suggests that 'I' haven't remembered my appointments for the day if I consult my calendar to refresh my recollection or that 'I' haven't solved a mathematics problem if I use a calculator—although they surely may challenge whether 'refreshed' recollections are admissible as evidence in a court of law or whether calculators should be permitted in university examinations. The point is that what it is for 'me' to do something—whether it requires certain skills that I exercise independently, for example—is at least partially a matter of the context and goals of the activity in question. More recently, the Memory Assistance Project at the University of Rochester has developed

---

[21] The legal case in the United States is *Sutton* v. *United Airlines*, 527 U.S. 471 (1999).
[22] I owe this example to Anita Silvers.
[23] Andrew Clark and David Chalmers, 'The Extended Mind,' *Analysis*, 58/1 (1998), 7–19.

computer vision technology to enable people with Alzheimer's disease to locate familiar objects around the house by touching a visual screen on which the objects are portrayed.[24] These devices make use of structure and enhance individual psychological capacities. As with physical disabilities, we judge the memory to be 'mine' when, albeit assisted, it is a part of my mental life; it is 'yours' when it is part of your mental life but not of mine, even if it is a memory about me.

I want now to explore the significance of this comparison for an understanding of whether people with intellectual disabilities have one or another of the attributes of autonomy I sketched at the outset. With respect to the capacity to value, Anita Silvers and I have defended elsewhere the possibility of constructing individualized conceptions of their good by, with, and for people with lifelong intellectual disabilities.[25] Our argument there was that conceptions of the good can be individually tailored and rooted in individual psychological states without being arrived at independently. It might be contended, however, that what we provided was an account of the interests of people with lifelong intellectual disabilities and of judgments of their levels of well-being—not an account of how they might be regarded as autonomous in any of the additional senses I have outlined.

But this conclusion is too hasty. Consider, for example, the reasoning needed to judge what courses of action will best realize values. As ordinary agents, we often employ the informational and reasoning skills of other agents as well as computational and other devices. Certain types of reliance or dependence are regarded as a departure from the ideal and are discouraged; for example, a patient who simply asks the physician 'you know me; what should I do?' is thought not to have made a sufficiently autonomous decision, albeit a decision that is individually tailored at least if the physician has sufficient knowledge of her values. To be sure, such a statement might simply represent the judgment that the physician will reflect her values more efficiently than she would herself, with the patient retaining a critical eye all along. If so, the patient is relying on the physician as an effective computational aid. But if the patient is in effect deferring to the physician's judgment without any thought about whether the physician's judgment might reflect her values, this will be regarded as an abdication rather than an exercise of autonomy. Models of the physician–patient relationship that reflect assistance and partnership in reasoning are encouraged as, for example, when physicians help patients to articulate values and judge the relevance of information; on some accounts, this partnered decision-making is the ideal of the physician–patient relationship.[26]

Or consider how we resist impulses. Ropes and the mast were prosthetic devices for Ulysses in his effort to resist the sirens.[27] Antabuse and methadone are chemical prostheses against alcohol and drug use. Other people are prostheses, too: his sailors tied Ulysses to the mast and people often rely on friends or family or support groups to keep them from giving in or giving up. Or consider how we plan the shapes of our lives; the involvement of family or friends or even therapists in articulating self-narratives is both routine and cherished, albeit ethically complex.[28]

The comparison with physical disability suggests several points about these judgments about autonomy—about valuing, reasoned decision-making, impulse-resistance, and planning. First, they are not 'all-or-nothing'; just as physical abilities vary, so do psychological abilities as well. The law may insist on all-or-nothing judgments—a person either has decision-making capacity or she does not—but this may be because the law requires a unique determination of a case. Moreover, it is worth noting that the connection between a unique determination and an all-or-nothing judgment of capacity is tenuous at best; adolescents participate as partners in decisions about their custody or their medical care,[29] and it is certainly possible to develop models of shared decision-making for adults with diminished capacity.[30] Unique judgments, that is, need not be all-or-nothing, even in law.

---

[26] Ezekial J. Emanuel and Linda L. Emanuel, 'Four models of the Doctor–Patient Relationship,' *Journal of the American Medical Association*, 267 (1992), 2067–71.

[27] Ryan Spellecy, 'Reviving Ulysses Contracts,' *Kennedy Institute of Ethics Journal*, 13/4 (2003), 373–92.

[28] C. Thomas Couser, *Vulnerable Subjects: Ethics and Lifewriting* (Ithaca, NY: Cornell University Press, 2004).

[29] See e.g. Leslie Pickering Francis, 'The Role of the Family in Health Care Decisionmaking,' *Utah Law Review* (spring 1992).

[30] As an aside, I would like to see models of shared decision-making developed for people with diminished capacity, as an addition to the all-or-nothing models of full capacity or surrogate and proxy decision-making.

Second, the portrait of capacities as a matter solely of internal psychological states or processes is potentially misleading. We use assistive devices, prostheses, and partners all the time, to varying degrees and ends. Some of these are 'internal'—mnemonic devices such as triggers for people's names—but others are not: notebooks, visual aids, even other people. Consider, for example, the apocryphal executive assistant, organizing appointments and files, writing memos and speeches. No one questions whether 'her' boss has organizational capacities—although people surely might question whether the boss has 'remembered' his wife's birthday if the executive assistant gives the prompt, makes the dinner reservation, and buys the present. My point here is that these questions reflect normative judgments about what the boss 'should' or 'should not' execute personally without depending on anyone else if he is to be regarded as genuinely committed to a spousal relationship, not judgments that remembering a birthday is metaphysically different in kind from remembering an appointment.

Finally, and perhaps most importantly, as this last example indicates, the significance of prostheses and other forms of assistance is normative. The judgment that a value, or a choice, or a plan of action is not sufficiently or appropriately a matter of my individual psychological processing to be regarded as 'mine' is a normative conclusion about how that value, or choice, or plan of action is to be regarded, whether it is to be respected, how I am to be treated in light of it. Let me now test these points out in the theoretical context of being a subject of justice and the practical context of the death penalty.

7.3. Being a Subject of Justice

John Rawls's stipulation that people in the original position choosing principles of justice are 'full cooperators' in the practice of justice is by now both well known and much criticized. Some writers, such as Martha Nussbaum, have drawn the conclusion that we should move away altogether from the social contract as the theoretical basis for justice.[31]

---

[31] Martha Nussbaum, *Frontiers of Justice: Disability, Nationality, Species Membership* (Cambridge, Mass.: Harvard University Press, 2006).

Others, such as Cynthia Stark, have defended Rawls as recognizing the role of reciprocity in theorizing about justice.[32] Anita Silvers and I have argued to the contrary that Rawls's mistake lay not in abandoning the social contract but in modelling the social contract as a bargaining rather than a trust-building enterprise.[33] Here, what I want to consider is the understanding of autonomy as Rawls portrayed it. To participate as a subject in the construction of justice, need one be free of guidance by antecedent principles of right or justice, moved solely by interests in ones own moral powers and by ones concern to advance ones final ends, whatever these may be? Need one be self-representing in this regard, moreover? The answer is 'no,' whether the construction of justice is understood as a hypothetical or as an actual process.

Suppose the construction of justice is understood as a hypothetical process, a process of modelling what principles would be derived from what assumptions about the conditions of choosing justice. In a recent discussion of social contract theory and the severely disabled, Henry Richardson offers variant interpretations of the Rawlsian choice situation that would yield, alternatively, Rawls's principles; Nussbaum's requirement of justice that capabilities be satisfied up to a threshold level; a principle that requires institutions to be arranged so as to assure each citizen, so far as possible, a decent minimum of Rawlsian primary goods; and a principle that requires institutions to be arranged so as to assure each citizen, so far as possible, a threshold level of capabilities. On Richardson's view, participants in the original position are 'theoretically designed entities who will, by stipulation, reason in a certain way.' They are thus all trustees, representatives for each of us. None of us self-represents, each of us is represented, whether or not we have intellectual disabilities. On Richardson's view, the question for such trustees is then what to understand as the motivational assumptions governing those whom they represent, not the capacity for self-representation per se. That is, which principles are chosen depends on the assumptions

---

[32] Cynthia Stark, 'How to Include the Severely Disabled in a Contractarian Theory of Justice,' *Journal of Political Philosophy*, e-pub ahead of print (March 2007); in disagreement, see Henry S. Richardson, 'Rawlsian Social-Contract Theory and the Severely Disabled,' *Journal of Ethics*, 10/4 (2006), 419–62.

[33] Anita Silvers and Leslie P. Francis, 'Justice through Trust: Resolving the Outlier Problem in Social Contract Theory,' *Ethics*, 116 (2005), 40–77.

attributed to the choosers, not on whether choosers are conceptualized as self-representing.

But suppose that a choice situation with respect to justice is understood as an actual process of construction, whether by means of a bargain, by means of a process of justification and rejection, or by means of some other process such as the building of trust. If the process of constructing justice is understood as actualized, should only those who can fully self-represent be included as subjects? Or, should those who cannot fully self-represent be included as represented by trustees, along lines suggested by Scanlon?[34] What of objections such as the concern that any actual trustee will have interests of his/her own, and thus have ineluctable conflicts of interest with those whom they represent?

Here, I think, we should question the assumptions that lie behind the way these questions are put. The questions assume that a line can be drawn between those who can 'fully self-represent' and those who cannot. If I am right in my argument, there is no bright line between full self-representers and others. Instead, there are degrees of self-representation, in different respects. Consider, for example, the role of people with intellectual disabilities in building warranted trust. One aspect of warranted trust requires the ability to process information and to reason: abstract reasoning capabilities, for example, may be needed to work out when someone who appears to be representing the interests of a person with disabilities is siphoning off investments, or when economic institutions could be rearranged in a way that is more favourable to those who are badly off. But there are non-cognitive aspects of warranted trust as well: whether someone else is well- or ill-motivated, favourably or unfavourably disposed, smiling genuinely are falsely, loving or indifferent.[35] These aspects of trust may be accessible, perhaps even more accessible, to people with intellectual disabilities than they are to the more cognitively adept or sophisticated of us.[36]

Moreover, a judgment to the effect that the cognitive aspects of trust are what are important—so that people who lack cognitive capacities

---

[34] T. M. Scanlon, *What We Owe to Each Other* (Cambridge, Mass.: Harvard University Press, 1998), 183.

[35] Trust, according to Annette Baier, is vulnerability to the good will of another. See 'Trust and Antitrust,' *Ethics*, 96/2 (1986), 231–60.

[36] I am happy to admit that these aspects of trust may also be accessible to non-human animals, but this is a topic for a different paper.

cannot self-represent—represents a normative judgment that some aspects of trust are to be privileged over others. Yet if Annette Baier was right, that infant trust is the 'primitive and basic' form of trust,[37] this normative judgment is problematic. Concerns about conflicts of interest might seem the obvious objection here: are not cognitive aspects of trust more important in the detection of exploitation that might result from conflicts of interest? This question is not an easy one, but at least part of the answer lies in my observations that judgments here are neither fully individualized nor all-or-nothing. Ordinary individuals have interests in what happens to them, and they have interests in the interests of others; persons with intellectual disabilities have these interests as well. People come to understand their interests in interconnection with others, as I have argued above; they do not understand these interests purely on their own. 'Self'-representation in the sense of independence is an abstraction, and it requires argument to show that it is an idealization. If correctives to the problems raised by conflicts of interest require skills that may be possessed in different degrees and that may be possessed by people with intellectual disabilities—such as the ability to recognize ill-will in others—then the case for the idealization is undercut. Representation as a subject of justice is a multiple and interconnected affair, not a matter of silo-ed self-interest.

7.4. Autonomy and Responsibility

One of the most contested issues about intellectual disability is its relationship to judgments of responsibility that might be thought to follow from whether or not one is an autonomous actor.[38] To the extent that they lack one or another of the attributes of autonomy, people with intellectual disabilities may be thought not to be responsible for what they do, or at least to be responsible in a diminished sense. Although I think that judgments of diminished responsibility based on one or another of the autonomy attributes I identified are part of the issue here—people with

---

[37] Baier, 'Trust and Antitrust,' 245.
[38] See e.g. S. Jan Brakel, 'Individualizing Justice after *Atkins*,' *Journal of the American Academy of Psychiatry Law*, 34 (2006), 103–4.

diminished capacities for impulse control or diminished abilities to reason or plan are less responsible in these respects—I also think that individualized and all-or-nothing assumptions about autonomy attributes and intellectual disability have functioned in a problematic way in how responsibility judgments have been framed as well. My illustration is the recent Supreme Court decision in the United States holding that it is cruel and unusual punishment to subject people with mental retardation to the death penalty, *Atkins* v. *Virginia.*[39] (Let me preface this discussion by saying that I am isolating the issue of responsibility from the case—I am not a proponent of the death penalty, but on grounds that are not relevant to the discussion here.)

In the opinion for the majority in *Atkins*, Justice Stevens concluded that executing the mentally retarded is cruel and unusual punishment under the current consensus of state law and public opinion in the United States. This consensus, Justice Stevens argued, is supported by the Court's death penalty jurisprudence, because diminished culpability undermines retributivist justifications for the penalty and diminished ability to plan undermines justifications for the penalty based in special deterrence. Fair enough, but the Court then left it up to states to determine when offenders do—or do not—fall within the category of 'mental retardation.'[40] Since the Supreme Court's remand in *Atkins*, the state of Virginia has been fighting out whether or not Atkins' IQ tests confirm a judgment of mental retardation.[41] This treats the question as an all-or-nothing one—was Atkins a person with mental retardation?—not as a question about whether Atkins had sufficient capacities to be determined to be sufficiently culpable for the death penalty or indeed for any other sort of punishment to be appropriate in his case. Now, there may be good reasons in public policy for courts to draw a line somewhere—at an IQ test below a given point, for example—such as that bright line tests are needed correctives for state courts' unfairness in applying criteria for mitigation and aggravation in death penalty judgments.[42] But this is a different point from the point I am

---

[39] 536 U.S. 304 (2002).   [40] 536 U.S. at 317.

[41] *Atkins* v. *Virginia*, 631 S.E.2d 93 (Va. 2006). The Virginia Supreme Court remanded the death penalty verdict on the ground that testimony of a state expert that Atkins was not mentally retarded was error because the expert had not examined Atkins by a recognized measure of adaptive behavior. As of this writing, Atkins is still on death row in Virginia, http://www.prodeathpenalty.com/virginia/row.html (accessed May 2007).

[42] Leaving aside the desirability of abolishing the death penalty on other grounds—a subject for another paper.

exploring here, that the question of whether Atkins had sufficient capacities to be judged responsible is not an all-or-nothing question; responsibility comes in degrees.

There was an additional factor in the Atkins case that was obscured by the focus on whether Atkins was or was not a person with mental retardation. The crimes at issue in the Atkins case were an abduction, armed robbery, and murder committed by Atkins and one William Jones. Atkins and Jones gave similar accounts of the case, with the one crucial difference that Atkins testified that Jones had pulled the trigger, and Jones testified that Atkins had pulled the trigger.[43] As a result of his testimony against Atkins, Jones plea bargained to a charge of first degree murder and was ineligible for the death penalty.[44] At the trial of Atkins, the jury found Jones's testimony more coherent and convincing than Atkins's. At the time of their arrest, Jones had refused to give a statement to the police, but Atkins had given a statement that was inconsistent with his later testimony. Neither of these is surprising, if Atkins's capacities for strategic reasoning and articulation were less than Jones's and if Atkins was as a result less capable of protecting himself in the situation than Jones. As it progressed, the case was thus treated as a matter of the individual responsibility of Atkins rather than as a matter of the collective responsibility or comparative fault of Atkins and Jones.

Suppose, however, we view the case as one in which persons with different capacities cooperated with each other in a murderous act—as I have suggested that we view the exercise of the attributes of autonomy in other circumstances. Viewed in this way, who actually pulled the trigger fades in importance to questions about the relative roles of Atkins and Jones in the decision to force themselves into Eric Nesbitt's truck at a convenience store after Atkins had told Jones that he didn't have enough money to buy beer, to force Nesbitt to withdraw money from an ATM, and to shoot Nesbitt in a field afterwards.[45] It was Atkins who had brought the gun to the convenience store,[46] but in other respects what were the respective roles of Atkins and Jones? Was Atkins an equal participant in deciding to force Nesbitt into his truck? Whether or not

---

[43] 536 U.S. at 307.   [44] 536 U.S. at 307 n. 1.

[45] For this description of the events, see http://www.internationaljusticeproject.org/retardationDatkins.cfm (accessed May 2007).

[46] See http://www.internationaljusticeproject.org/retardationDatkins.cfm (accessed May 2007).

Atkins shot Nesbitt, was Atkins acting more or less as the physical strength of the two, or was it Atkins who decided that the two would be better protected from discovery if Nesbitt did not live? These questions were not central to how the case was positioned as it reached the Supreme Court.

On the view I have been exploring, however, questions about the relative roles of Atkins and Jones are exactly what should have been at the centre of the Atkins case. Instead of a picture of the case in which the question was whether Atkins had 'retardation'—yes or no—and thus whether he was 'responsible,' the case should have been viewed in terms of the relative roles of Adkins and Jones. Perhaps Adkins was the physical strength of the pair, or perhaps viewing him as brawn but not brain is to apply an all-too-frequent stereotype of people with intellectual disabilities.[47] Perhaps Jones gave directions or made the strategic observation that the two might be better off if Nesbitt did not live to testify against them. These are the empirical issues that would have been central if the attributes of autonomy, and hence of responsibility, had not been viewed as a matter solely of the internal and individual characteristics of Atkins.[48]

7.5. Summary

Let me sum up, briefly. There are many different attributes of autonomy. These attributes should not be understood as 'all or nothing.' Nor are they possessed by individuals as entirely separate entities, without aids or the cooperation of others. In these respects, persons with intellectual disabilities are no different from the rest of us, although they may have differing capacities, to differing degrees. Whether these differences matter enters us into a complex set of normative questions, rather than resolving them—as I hope my discussions of being a subject of justice and of responsibility in the *Atkins* case have aptly illustrated. It is a mistake to think that the political and social roles of people with intellectual disabilities

---

[47] See the movie *Hot Fuzz* for a recent example of the genre.
[48] For a classic discussion of collective responsibility in terms of the respective roles of individuals, see Joel Feinberg, 'Collective Responsibility,' *Journal of Philosophy*, 65/21 (1968), 674–88.

turn on whether they can be construed as autonomous—and, if they cannot be so construed, that they lack responsibility and obligations and expectations of reciprocity. Appeals to autonomy cannot resolve these very difficult questions because autonomy is so often a collaborative affair.

8

Respect without Reason: Relating to Alzheimer's

DOUGLAS MACLEAN

In the United States alone, 5.2 million people currently live with demen-tia, the large majority of them suffering from Alzheimer's disease. Over 5 million of these people are older than 65. Roughly half the population of Americans older than 85 live with Azheimer's. By the year 2050, if current trends continue and no cure is found, 11–16 million people in the U.S. will have Alzheimer's.[1] The financial cost of the care involved, by a conservative estimate, is currently between $250 and 300 billion annually and rising rapidly.[2] Those *affected* by the disease, including family members, friends, and caregivers, comprise a much larger population. It includes most of us.

The subject I want to address in this paper is the relationship between those who suffer from Alzheimer's (or other forms of dementia) and those who care for or, more generally, care about them. I want to explore a normative or ethical dimension of this relationship. What attitudes can we have toward those who suffer from Alzheimer's? How ought we to think about them?

For discussions that have helped me in thinking about the themes in this paper, I am especially indebted to Elizabeth Foreman, Leslie Francis, Robin Hill, and Susan Wolf.

[1] These facts and other useful information can be found on several websites. See the National Institute for Aging: www.nia.hih.gov/Alzheimers; also *2008 Alzheimer's Disease Facts and Figures*, a report of the Alzheimer's Association, http://www.alz.org/national/documents/report_alzfactsfigures 2008.pdf.

[2] I have estimated these costs from information in the Alzheimer's Association 2008 report. The costs include an estimate of the value of unpaid care.

8.1. Patients with Mid-Stage Alzheimer's

One immediate difficulty in addressing this subject is the progressive nature of the disease. The Alzheimer's Association describes seven stages of mental deterioration, from normal aging through advanced or late-stage Alzheimer's. Early-stage Alzheimer's—stage 4 in this taxonomy—is marked by some loss of memory and other associated difficulties. People in this stage typically struggle a bit to find the appropriate word; they have trouble remembering the names of people they meet; they may lose or misplace objects; they find it more difficult to comprehend what they read or to make and carry out plans. While these problems can be disturbing and have serious implications, they do not change in any important respects the kind of relationship we have with people who exhibit these symptoms.

The far end of this continuum, stage 7, is late-stage Alzheimer's, a condition in which people lose the ability to respond to their environment. They cannot recognize people; although they may utter words or phrases, they can no longer speak; they need assistance with all activities, including eating and toileting; and they may lose the ability to walk, smile, hold their heads up, or swallow without difficulty. Our connection to people suffering from late-stage Alzheimer's is altogether different from our relationship with people in earlier stages of the disease. We can continue to care for them and try to relieve their suffering. We understand how a spouse or child may feel bound by love to care for a late-stage Alzheimer's patient who is incapable of recognizing or responding to her, but what it means to love someone in this condition raises some difficult and important philosophical questions. Beyond a concern to prevent or relieve suffering, however, the idea of any kind of real human relationship with someone suffering from late-stage Alzheimer's seems impossible or at least deeply problematic. I will not attempt to explore these issues in depth here, but I will return at the end of this essay to comment briefly on the relationship between love and respect that this kind of situation reveals. We might attempt to explain a person's relationship to someone who has late-stage Alzheimer's by referring to commitments that stem from an earlier association; or we might appeal to some idea of moral responsibility that we would need to spell out, such as a duty that attaches to one's role as spouse, child, or guardian. This relationship, however, is in many respects less complicated and problematic than the difficult but common relationships we have with people progressing through stages 5 and 6—the mid-stages—of Alzheimer's. These are the relationships I want to consider here.

As people who are otherwise healthy enter the mid-stages of Alzheimer's, they may continue to dress and feed themselves and perform other ordinary tasks, but their memories and other cognitive abilities are severely impaired. Mid-stage Alzheimer's patients are typically unable to recall clearly events in the recent past; they may become vague about their family members and their own personal history; they may lose the capacity to perform normal complex tasks, like balancing a checkbook, planning a dinner for guests, or keeping a schedule. As the effects of mid-stage Alzheimer's worsen, its victims may lose their ability to recall their own address, telephone number, or other personal data; they become confused about where they are and about days and dates; and they begin to need assistance with what for most of us are routine tasks like choosing proper clothes for the season or the occasion, ordering a meal at a restaurant, or getting to places they need to be. The world inhabited by mid-stage Alzheimer's patients shrinks in time to the present. The past is a blur, the future not something for which they can plan. Often a person suffering from this level of dementia is deemed incompetent to make her own medical or legal decisions, and yet she can understand and respond to questions. Signs of intelligence may still show through the great fog of confusion in which she lives.

Many of the capacities that we associate with moral agency, such as the ability to plan or express one's will or values in actions diminish or disappear with mid-stage Alzheimer's. And yet people in this condition can still talk and carry on simple conversations. It is not unusual for them to be aware of, and frustrated by, the cognitive deficits that are overtaking them, although evidence of this frustration should not mislead us into thinking that the deficits are like other disabilities, such as diminished eyesight or loss of the ability to talk. It is not as if there is a perfectly normal functioning human mind struggling to overcome a barrier that a person now confronts. People living through mid-stage Alzheimer's still have and express desires, and they can appreciate things. To the extent that appreciation is a kind of valuing, they are valuers, but they are valuers in an importantly different and shallower way than ordinary, healthy people or than their earlier healthy selves.

Friends and relatives continue to love people who are living through mid-stage Alzheimer's. We care about their well-being and want what is best for them. But figuring out what this means is precisely the most difficult question. It is the deepest challenge to understanding our moral relationship with people living through the mid-stages of Alzheimer's. Do they still have dignity in the moral sense? What does this mean? Can we respect as well as care for them? Thinking about this kind of relationship may help shed light on how we justify certain attitudes and actions as well as giving us a somewhat clearer sense of the meaning and limits of moral concepts like respect and dignity.

8.2. Relating to Alzheimer's Patients and Relating to Pets

Here is a preliminary attempt to describe the philosophical issue I am trying to bring into focus. I assume that our normal moral relationships with people involve attitudes and actions that express respect. Now, respect is a central concept in Kant's ethics, but it is notoriously difficult to understand precisely what he means by it. And in ordinary language, we use the word "respect" to mean different things and to indicate many different attitudes. We say that people deserve respect, but we also say that a great work of art ought to be respected, which means at least that it ought not to be defaced or mistreated and perhaps also that it deserves the effort required to appreciate it. Here respect seems to refer, in some sense, to the appropriate way of responding to whatever we ought to value as an end or for its own sake. But we might also advise someone setting out in a kayak to show respect for the river's currents, or a coach might remind a boxer to respect his opponent's right hook. These are counsels of prudence that do not refer directly to anything we value as an end. We can respect someone as a gifted writer, even if we deplore him as a callous human being. When we show respect for the dead or for the flag, we may mean that we recognize the appropriateness of using symbolic or ritualistic actions to express different kinds of value. We are certainly not valuing a piece of cloth with an unusual pattern of stars and stripes either prudentially or as an end for its own sake.

I will not attempt here to sort out and analyze the different meanings of respect or to try to define a central moral use of the concept.[3] I will also set aside the ways that we can respect some people but not others for the kinds of moral virtues that are part of their character or for the praiseworthy talents they have developed. It makes sense to talk about respecting someone for her courage or for being an outstanding teacher or a tireless public servant. In this sense we may respect someone we know with Alzheimer's for the intelligence he showed in his career as a businessman or for the skill with which he used to play the banjo, even though those days are long since past. We may also admire and respect him for the courage and cheerful spirit he shows now in confronting the limitations brought on by his increasing dementia.

Setting all of these details aside, we can still agree that some idea of respect is at the heart of moral relationships among persons. I take respect in this area to mean at least recognizing something morally valuable in other people and responding appropriately to that value. Our goal is to try to understand the meaning of respect in this sense clearly enough to see whether and how it applies to relationships with mid-stage Alzheimer's patients.

What are the reasons that lead us to claim that morality requires a kind of respect that we are bound to extend equally to all people? It is this idea of respect that allows us to distinguish our relationships with other humans from our relationships and attitudes toward other living things. To respect someone in this sense typically means something like recognizing that she is an autonomous agent, a person, a being capable of determining her own ends in life and guiding her life by reason and will, as well as desire. When we recognize these capacities in ourselves and others, we see humanity as a source of value, because we see ourselves as creatures who can reason, appreciate, and justify ourselves to others.

The appropriate attitudes and actions that follow from this kind of recognition constitute one of the most fundamental meanings of respect, and our understanding of the importance of basic moral rights flows largely

[3] For examples of some of the most important recent attempts to analyze respect, see Stephen Darwall, "Two Kinds of Respect," *Ethics*, 88 (1977), 36–49; Darwall, *The Second-Person Standpoint: Morality, Respect, and Accountability* (Cambridge, Mass.: Harvard University Press, 2006); and Joseph Raz, *Value, Respect, and Attachment* (Cambridge: Cambridge University Press, 2001).

from this idea. Ronald Dworkin captures part of this idea in the following remark:

Recognizing an individual right of autonomy makes self-creation possible. It allows each of us to be responsible for shaping our lives according to our own coherent or incoherent—but, in any case, distinctive—personality. It allows us to lead our own lives rather than being led along them, so that each of us can be, to the extent a scheme of rights can make this possible, what we have made of ourselves.[4]

Unlike morally relevant character traits, such as courage, and talents like artistic ability, which vary considerably among people and are possessed in great degree by only a few, the ability to be autonomous and to lead one's own life, given the opportunity, is present in most people. This capacity is the basis of the kind of respect that we claim is owed equally to everyone. But this very capacity is diminished or destroyed as Alzheimer's runs its course. Thus the question arises, what basis for recognition respect is present in people who are losing or have lost these capacities?[5] If recognizing a right of autonomy is a basic expression of the moral relationship we have with other people, what happens to that relationship as a person loses the ability to live or act autonomously?

Mid-stage Alzheimer's patients, though severely demented, retain consciousness and are aware of their surroundings. They can suffer, and they can experience enjoyment; they can be happily engaged in activities that constitute a set of interests; and they can interact with others. In these ways, they (and we) share the morally relevant capacities of such non-human animals as pet dogs. A person's moral relationship to his pet dog includes looking after the dog's interests. The dog owner should protect his dog from harm, relieve its suffering, and allow it some freedom to run around, fetch, jump, roll, sniff, scratch, and so on, as dogs are naturally inclined to do. But this freedom is not an expression of autonomy, because a dog's activities are not the product of a will. They may be normal expressions of a dog's nature, but they are not instances of self-governance in the sense we usually assume. They are not responses to principles that the dog accepts as true and which become part of its goals and intentions in acting. Dog activities are not actions that carry out a plan or express a subject's values.

---

[4] Ronald Dworkin, *Life's Dominion* (New York: Vintage Books, 1993), 224.
[5] The phrase "recognition respect" is due to Darwall to identify the kind of respect that is relevant here and to distinguish it from respect for talents, abilities, etc., which he calls "appraisal respect."

For these reasons, most people would agree that although it is easy to love and care for a pet dog, respect is not a concept that characterizes this relationship.

Is this how we should think about people living through mid-stage Alzheimer's? The fact that they can use language, can appreciate and value things and not merely desire them, and can respond to reasons, is enough to show that they are clearly still distinguishable from pets. But two further thoughts are also relevant here. First, these capacities in their diminished state do not give us sufficient reason to regard these people as autonomous in the way we think autonomy applies to ordinary people and grounds our basic rights. I will try later in this essay to justify this claim. Second, as the disease progresses to late-stage Alzheimer's, even these capacities disappear, and yet it still seems that something like respect should guide our relationship with people in this condition. We are clearly bound to look after their interests, to protect them and relieve their suffering, just as we are with pet dogs. But even leaving aside the contrast between the appropriateness of euthanizing pets and euthanizing extremely demented humans, it seems clearly possible to act disrespectfully to a late-stage Alzheimer's patient in ways that do not apply to pet dogs. It would be wrong, for example, to play with their bodies in non-painful ways or to leave them sitting naked in the reception hall. Might it also be disrespectful in some circumstances to keep them alive in a non-suffering state?

8.3. Identity and Advance Directives

The passage from Dworkin quoted above is part of an important argument about the moral status of people with Alzheimer's.[6] The argument is couched in a broader discussion of the value of human life and the morality of killing. It begins by distinguishing three values: the idea of autonomy, the idea of what is in a person's best interests, and the intrinsic value of life itself. The intrinsic value of life is important for Dworkin's argument about the morality of controversial practices like euthanasia, allowing people to die, and physician-assisted suicide. It is not relevant to

---

[6] Dworkin, *Life's Dominion*, esp. 218–41.

the issues that arise with mid-stage Alzheimer's patients, so we can leave it aside.[7]

The part of Dworkin's argument that is most important for these issues concerns the meaning of a person's good or best interests. The interpretation of these concepts is controversial, especially when we are thinking of them as they apply to a person living through Alzheimer's disease. The controversy comes clearly to the surface in a philosophical debate surrounding an example that raises questions about the moral importance of personal identity. The example asks us to consider the case of a person who, before showing any symptoms of Alzheimer's, signed an advance directive which states that, should he become legally incompetent, he wants to receive no medical treatment that aims to prolong his life. He is now in the range of advanced mid-stage to early late-stage Alzheimer's, and his condition is severe enough for him to be declared incompetent to make his own medical decisions. But he is otherwise happy and content to engage in the simple activities available to him, such as sitting in the garden on a sunny day, watching television, or joining in group activities with others in his condition. Then he develops an illness that can be treated but will hasten his death if left untreated. The question is whether the advance directive should be honored.

Those who take one side in this debate appeal to ideas of the person's good or best interests to argue that the advance directive should be ignored. The person who is now ill continues to lead a life in some recognizably human sense, to have some capacity for valuing, and to have a desire to continue living. This person, who is quite different from his earlier self, should not be bound by the earlier will or advance directive. Heeding values that a person no longer holds is not to act in a person's best interests.

In other situations, this argument is compelling. Imagine, for example, that when I was in my mid-twenties I was a political radical who opposed capitalism, private property, and especially the way these political and economic forces corrupt the moral characters of most people who live in capitalist societies. Suppose that I vowed at that time to remain true to my radical values, and as a commitment to that vow I shared with my comrades my sincere wish that they should kill me if I ever betrayed these

---

[7] I have addressed this issue in "Valuing Human Life," in Dorothy Zinberg (ed.), *Uncertain Power: The Struggle for a National Energy Policy* (New York: Pergamon Press, 1983), 93–111.

radical ideals. I talked boldly about preferring death to living a life in which I craved middle-class luxuries like expensive wine or worried more about how the stock market was affecting my 401K retirement plan than about how capitalism exploits the working class. Should one of those comrades come knocking at my door today, of course, I would ask him to please wipe his feet before walking on my new rug and then hasten to explain that I've changed my views and modified some of the values I held then but now think were hopelessly naïve. Surely my rights that are grounded in my autonomy allow me to reject my earlier "advance directive" if I have revised my youthful values and chosen in middle age to shape my life differently. Changing my values changes what counts as being in my best interests. My current self may be corrupt, but it is nevertheless competent to reconsider and overrule my earlier judgment about the kind of person I want to be.

In the most radical statement of the "different person" argument, some writers have argued that the Alzheimer's patient is no longer identical with the earlier, physically continuous person who issued the directive.[8] Assuming the non-identity of the earlier and later selves, we might insist that it is no more reasonable to allow the values and wishes of the earlier self to determine what to do to the later self whose interests are very different (and hard for an earlier self to imagine) than it would be to allow the values of one person alone to determine how we ought to treat a different person. To respect the advance directive would be to allow one person's interests to determine the fate of another person in a manner contrary to that person's interests. This would constitute a form of disrespect to the later person.

This argument has an undeniable intuitive appeal. How can a decent caregiver ignore the needs and desires of someone capable of experiencing pleasure and pain for the sake of a value he no longer holds? One problem with the "different person" interpretation of this argument, however, is that it relies on a controversial metaphysical view about the nature of personal identity. Before getting deeply immersed in arguments about whether personal identity should be seen as a matter of psychological connectedness, physical continuity, or some other criterion, I would begin by pointing

---

[8] See Rebecca Dresser, "Life, Death, and Incompetent Patients: Conceptual Infirmities and Hidden Values in the Law," *Arizona Law Review*, 28 (1986), 373–405.

out one way in which this particular example seems to reveal how the parties to the debate have largely ignored aspects of the social contribution to determining a person's identity. There is, in particular, a question about property rights, which are essentially social properties. Thus, if we were to take seriously the idea that a demented later self is a different person from the competent earlier self who wrote the advance directive, we should also wonder how the later self comes to acquire any rights to the savings and other property that the earlier self had acquired and asked to be disposed of according to the terms of his will together with his advance directive. The earlier self may have written the advance directive precisely because he wanted to see his estate go to his children or to his preferred charity rather than to the support and care of this different later self.

Dworkin defends the authority of advance directives, but he does so in a way that avoids engaging metaphysical issues of personal identity or the boundaries of property rights. He has in mind cases involving very advanced dementia and comatose patients, so he simply assumes that the people to whom advance directives apply are no longer autonomous. The question for him comes down to an argument about their interests and the relation between their interests and their (earlier) autonomy. His argument rests on distinguishing the different kinds of interests that we find in competent and demented subjects.

The strands of memory and planning in healthy people, which we use to establish at least part of our sense of personal identity over time, are also crucial to understanding the nature of human interests in normal, competent people. Normal human memory, and specifically the way it determines mental capacities such as anticipation, intention, and imagination, is essential to the way we distinguish ourselves and our moral status from other animals. When these mental or cognitive abilities are severely diminished, a person may still have interests in an obvious and ethically relevant sense, just as our pet dogs have interests, but his moral status and the relationship of his earlier self to his current situation raise difficult questions about the meaning of his good, meaning the good of *his life*, as opposed to the good of only the last segment of his life.

Dworkin develops this point by distinguishing between what he calls a person's experiential interests and his critical interests. The value of a person's life, he argues, depends not only on the quality of the experiences that make up that life but also on the degree to which the life meets certain critical standards. It depends, for example, on the way a person lives up to his ideals, or the level of his accomplishments, or the virtues he has mastered, or the degree to which he has lived independently or has been a loyal friend. People differ in the particular critical standards that they want their lives to meet, but almost everyone recognizes some standards and views the worth of his life in part by his success in meeting them.

If we believed that only experiential interests matter in assessing the quality of a person's life, then we could make no sense of the interests of people who struggle to survive in the face of great adversity and suffering. Nor would it matter whether or not a person is kept alive in a persistent vegetative state. Considering only a person's experiential interests, this kind of life and death decision would be a matter of indifference. But most people are not indifferent about what happens to them in these circumstances. Death is significant, as Dworkin explains, not only because it brings experience to an end, but also because the manner in which a person dies can affect the quality of his life as measured by his critical standards.

If the person who issued the advance directive cared that his life has some meaning, shape, or narrative structure—or even if he simply valued his sense of dignity in the way he lived and believed that his dignity is incompatible with the loss of abilities that were important for him and allowed him to live in ways that express his independence—then refusing to honor his advance directive would seem like allowing others to write the last chapter of his life according to their own values and sense of meaning. His will is being overridden by others for the sake of another person's good, or at least for the sake of the caretaker's sense of his good.

In Dworkin's view, respect for autonomy implies respect for a person's critical interests. Continued life may be in the experiential best interests of the demented person, but given the importance of a person's critical interests, our experiential best interests do not settle the question about respecting or ignoring advance directives. If continuing to live means continuing a slide into deeper levels of dementia and dependency, then it may not be in a person's best interests to continue to live in a demented state, however pleasant his day-to-day existence may seem. Dworkin concludes:

Someone anxious to ensure that his life is not then prolonged by medical treatment is worried precisely because he thinks that the character of his life would be compromised if it were. He is in the same position as people who sign living wills asking not to be kept alive in a hopeless medical condition or when permanently vegetative. If we respect *their* past requests, as the Supreme Court has decided American states must do, then we have the same reasons for respecting the wishes not to be kept alive of someone . . . who dreads not unconsciousness but dementia.[9]

Having come to this conclusion, however, Dworkin also shrinks from its implications, which he acknowledges are "very troubling." The dilemma is even more poignant in the case of mid-stage Alzheimer's patients who can talk and interact with us than it is in the case of late-stage Alzheimer's or people living unconsciously or in permanent vegetative states.

8.4. Autonomy and Critical Interests

Autonomy for Dworkin is to be understood as the capacity to form and act on critical interests. This is the capacity that allows us to "lead our own lives rather than be led along them." In order for this argument to support the conclusion that advance directives should have authority over the experiential interests of a demented later self, Dworkin restricts his discussion, as I have said, to people with advanced dementia or late-stage Alzheimer's. He also assumes that there is a sharp distinction between experiential and critical interests and that critical interests constitute a particularly strong interest in shaping a life or realizing a narrative that guides the values and decisions of most normal people. For example, he writes:

Even a seriously demented person . . . has experiential interests. . . . But by the time the dementia has become advanced, Alzheimer's victims have lost the capacity to think about how to make their lives more successful on the whole. They are ignorant of self—not as an amnesiac is, not simply because they cannot identify their pasts—but, more fundamentally, because they have no sense of a whole life, a past joined to a future, that could be the object of any evaluation or concern as a whole. They cannot have projects or plans of the kind that leading a critical life requires. They therefore have no contemporary opinion about their critical interests.[10]

[9] Dworkin, *Life's Dominion*, 228.   [10] Ibid. 229–30.

We might nevertheless doubt that the distinction between experiential and critical interests is as sharp as Dworkin assumes it is, and we might also question whether critical interests in the sense of having a sense of and wanting to shape one's life "as a whole" is a necessary condition of autonomy.

Dworkin's criterion for leading a meaningful or autonomous life seems instead to be a condition that is rarely met even by fully competent people. This point has been made by T. M. Scanlon, who questions Dworkin's identification of a person's best interests with what makes her life best according to her critical standards. Scanlon plausibly suggests that, "Judgments of [this] kind, in which one views one's life as a whole and asks how best to perfect it, are quite intelligible, but only a few people give such judgments a dominant role in their lives."[11] It is far from obvious that our moral relationships with other people normally require that we do what we can to help them realize their life's plan. Few people, I suspect, have constructed such narratives for themselves which they aim to realize. Dworkin's assumptions about critical interests and their connection to autonomy thus seem too strong.

Scanlon goes on to remark that this kind of assumption might be appropriate for someone like Nietzsche, "but for the rest of us the idea of doing what is 'in our best interests' may point more humbly in the direction of comfort and reassurance insofar as these can be provided."[12] Of course it is in the best interests of all of us that we receive comfort and reassurance from others, and in the case of the most seriously demented people, this may be all we can do for them. But if we reject Dworkin's 'life-span' criterion of critical interests and put something more modest in its place, then questions about the implications of this view for the capacity for autonomy in mid-stage Alzheimer's patients loom large. Even if Dworkin's distinctions in this argument are implausibly sharp and his assumptions too strong, however, simply dismissing them unfortunately deflects attention away from the crucial questions involving our relationship with mid-stage Alzheimer's patients: Do these memory-impaired people still have the capacity to form critical interests? Should we still regard them as autonomous?

---

[11] Scanlon makes this criticism in an otherwise sympathetic review of Dworkin's book, "Partisan for Life," *New York Review of Books*, July 15, 1993: 45–50 (49).

[12] Ibid.

8.5. Autonomy and the Capacity to Value

In an important and subtle article, Agnieszka Jaworska addresses these questions. She argues that the potential for autonomy should be associated primarily with the capacity to value, and the concept of well-being should be understood as the capacity to live according with one's values.[13] The role of critical interests for Dworkin is replaced in her account by a person's capacity to value. This capacity in turn is sufficient for autonomy, and it is possessed by most people with mid-stage Alzheimer's.

Jaworska claims that Dworkin's analysis stands or falls with the assumption that demented patients can no longer form critical interests. In order to be autonomous, however, she regards it as sufficient that a person's desires stem "simply from convictions about what is good to have, which do not require the ability to grasp or review one's whole life."[14] These convictions constitute values, in Jaworska's view, and a person "can value something at a given time, without referring this value to his conception of his life as a whole."[15]

Now in order for this view to be made convincing and to answer the troubling questions about the status and capacity for autonomy in people living with mid-stage Alzheimer's, two issues need to be addressed. First, how should we understand the connection between valuing and autonomy? And second, can people who are afflicted with mid-stage Alzheimer's still be valuers?

According to Jaworska, what happens as dementia increases in a person is that some of the person's values disappear but others remain intact. Presumably some values require the kind of cognitive skills and demands on memory that are lost with dementia, and these values disappear as Alzheimer's progresses. Another loss that accompanies Alzheimer's is the capacity to reason in ways that allow someone to translate values into actions in the ways that normal competent people do. This is all quite plausible. To carry our values into practice often requires planning and means—end reasoning, which require memory and other mental capacities that are lost as dementia increases.

---

[13] Agnieszka Jaworska, "Respecting the Margins of Agency: Alzheimer's Patients and the Capacity to Value," *Philosophy & Public Affairs*, 28 (1999), 105–38.

[14] Ibid. 113.   [15] Ibid.

This kind of cognitive loss explains why a person with mid-stage Alzheimer's can no longer carry out many tasks that used to be routine. She cannot now perform without assistance any but the most routine tasks if they require more than one or two steps. When she goes to the bank to get cash, she may need assistance in writing a check and balancing her checkbook. But Jaworska insists that the capacity for means–end reasoning, which may be essential for carrying values into action, is not necessarily required for having values at all. Thus, if a demented person is still capable of having values, she may nevertheless need help in enacting them. If enacting values is sufficient for autonomy, then it may be possible to give Alzheimer's patients the assistance needed to remain autonomous.

Loss of the capacity for means–end reasoning, assuming other mental abilities are still intact, seems on this view to regard Alzheimer's as not so different from physical impairments. People who are seriously disabled in many different ways can remain autonomous if they are provided the necessary assistance to carry their values into practice[16]. This is how Jaworska views the impairment caused by Alzheimer's. She writes: "The essence of the capacity for autonomy consists in the ability to lay down the principles that will govern one's actions, and not in the ability to devise and carry out the means and plans for following these principles."[17] But to this point her argument begs the question about whether it makes sense to see Alzheimer's like a physical disability. How can we decide if people in this condition (which typically is also progressing toward more severe dementia) are capable of "laying down the principles" that, with assistance from others, will govern their activities?

We are thus left with the question of the point at which Alzheimer's robs its victims of the capacity to value in the sense necessary to regard them as being autonomous or having a will. We are granting, of course, that Alzheimer's patients have interests. They are subjects of experience, so they at least have interests in avoiding pain and suffering, being comfortable, and having the kinds of happy and pleasant experiences that remain within their capacities. If the moral status of demented human beings is substantially different from the moral status of our pet dogs, however, we need to show that these humans are capable of valuing things in a way that is distinct from merely having desires. For Jaworska, valuing is the necessary condition of

---

[16] See Leslie P. Francis, "Understanding Autonomy in Light of Intellectual Disability" (ch. 7 in this volume).

[17] Jaworska, "Respecting the Margins of Agency" 128–9.

autonomy, just as for Dworkin critical interests are its necessary condition. For her, valuing constitutes the basis for the respect as well as the concern we owe to demented people.

8.6. Valuing, Memory, and a Normative Conception of Oneself

Jaworska lists three characteristics that distinguish valuing from merely desiring.[18] First, we think it would be a mistake to lose our current values. I take this to mean that, if we value something, then we are not indifferent between satisfying our desire for it and eliminating the desire. Second, we hold our values to be correct, or at least correct for us. This condition requires the capacity to make some judgment about what we value, which of course is not a necessary property of all desires. Third, Jaworska insists that we can usually give a rationale for what we value, as she puts it, "by situating the value in a larger normative framework." Elsewhere she says that to be a valuer a being must have a "normative conception of oneself" or a "practical identity." She explains this as meaning that a valuer "seems to uphold a conception of himself, a set of ideals in terms of which he perceives his own values."[19] She also claims that the features that are "essential to, or strongly indicative of, valuing" include that for the valuer, "the importance of achieving what she wants, is tied up with her sense of self-worth; and the importance of achieving what she wants is, for her, independent of her own experience."[20]

Jaworska's brief discussion of the conditions for valuing may not be entirely clear and convincing to everyone, but suppose we grant that they constitute a reasonable set of necessary and sufficient conditions. The question I want to press is whether it makes sense to claim that mid-stage Alzheimer's patients satisfy these conditions. Jaworska insists that the requirements of valuing do not imply that one must have a grasp of the narrative of one's whole life, as Dworkin seems to maintain. We have already acknowledged that most people do not let the plan or narrative of their lives play a dominant role in determining their own best interests. It is even controversial, I believe, to claim as a normative

[18] Ibid. 115.   [19] Ibid. 119.   [20] Ibid. 116.

ideal for a fully competent rational person that one's life should have a narrative structure to it.[21] But do Alzheimer's patients satisfy Jaworska's less demanding requirements for valuing?

Her argument at this point rests on descriptions and sensitive interpretations of the desires of a number of Alzheimer's patients that she has encountered. My problem as I read these descriptions is that I find myself less convinced or clear than Jaworska that the people she describes satisfy her own conditions for valuing. Jaworska's descriptions, like my own encounters with people living with mid-stage Alzheimer's, often leave me unsure what to think about their attitudes, beliefs, and capacities. Here I can only illlustrate these doubts by giving a crude summary of some of Jaworska's own brief descriptions.

Dr B, who scored low on all cognitive tests nevertheless was keen on participating in a research study of Alzheimer's patients. He didn't understand the research design, but he claimed to feel that the project was important. He preferred spending his time on the project to the other "filler" activities in his institution. Jaworska says that the fact that Dr B's "role in the project could so alter his self-image demonstrates most poignantly that he valued the project."[22]

Mrs Rogoff used to pride herself in her talent for cooking and being a hostess. Now she lives alone, dependent on a caregiver, Fran, whom she is always happy to see. Mrs Rogoff "invariably gets upset and agitated seeing Fran usurp the mastery of the kitchen. . . . At such times Fran arranges small make-work kitchen tasks that appease Mrs Rogoff." Jaworska concludes from this story that "the clearest indication of retained values comes from visible effects on the person's self-esteem. Mrs Rogoff's self-image suffers whenever she realizes that Fran has taken over as a culinary expert, and these effects can be mitigated, at least temporarily, by semblance of participation in culinary affairs."[23]

Mr O'Connor was a religious man "for whom thoughts of taking his own life or of withholding lifesaving measures for whatever reason were completely unacceptable." In his seventies he developed Alzheimer's, lost his ability to do many of the things he most cared about, and finally could not recognize members of his family, began to mistake characters on

---

[21] See Galen Strawson, "Against Narrativity," *Ratio*, 16 (2004), 428–52.
[22] Jaworska, "Respecting the Margins of Agency," 119.   [23] Ibid. 120.

television for his daughters, and believed that the Rockefellers would take care of his finances. After his wife died, Mr O'Connor began saying that he did not want to continue to live and would not want to receive medical treatment aimed at prolonging his life. Jaworska remarks, "The fact that he wanted to die after she was gone strongly indicates that his feelings for her did not focus primarily on his own experience, and thus that he truly valued her."[24]

Jaworska claims that each of these people, along with others whose conditions she also describes, continues to be a valuer. With assistance, each can retain his or her autonomy. Thus, she writes:

The intensity with which [Dr. B, Mrs. Rogoff, and Mr. O'Connor] communicated [their] values . . . convinces us that these are very authentic ideals. At the same time, Dr. B, with his tenuous grasp of intellectual constructs, could not have taken part in a "real good big project" without the researcher's help; likewise, Mrs. Rogoff could not have held on to her self-image as a prominent player in culinary affairs without significant help from Fran; and Mr. O'Connor . . . would have certainly needed assistance with concrete decisions reflecting his feelings about his wife's death. Given the help, however, they all can live up to their own ideals again, and to that extent exercise autonomy.[25]

Based on the descriptions that Jaworska gives us, there can be little doubt that Dr B, Mrs Rogoff, and Mr O'Connor have strong desires, and that these desires are connected in important ways with values they had earlier in their lives, before Alzheimer's, when they were fully competent. But the capacity to be autonomous in their current situations depends, on Jaworska's own account, on recognizing these desires as values that each still holds. Are the criteria for valuing satisfied? When I think about these cases, I confess that I simply do not know. A certain amount of skepticism seems warranted.

Of the three cases that I am considering from Jaworska's account, Dr B's preference for participating in the research study to spending time on other "filler" activities seems to me to be the clearest case of valuing. But even here I think that calling this preference a value is questionable. Can Dr B explain to us why he thinks it is correct for him to have this preference? Can he give a rationale for it? Would he not only be unhappy but think it a mistake for him to lose that preference? If tomorrow he

---

[24] Ibid.   [25] Ibid. 131.

says that he no longer wants anything to do with the study but just wants to be left alone watching television with the other residents, would we be warranted in feeling disappointed in Dr B? Would we chastise him for being weak-willed?

The other cases seem to me even more dubious. Can Mrs Rogoff give a rationale for her agitation when she sees Fran doing all the cooking? Does she have a normative conception of herself, that is, a set of ideals in terms of which she perceives the value of her (now falsely believed) abilities as a cook? Mr O'Connor is clearly and reasonably lonely and unhappy without the company of his wife. His loneliness has led him both to abandon his earlier religious convictions and to wish no longer to live. We may sympathize with his desire, but do we have any reason to conclude that *he* believes himself correct to have it?

The problem in each of these cases is that dementia deprives its subjects of more than the capacity for means–end reasoning or the ability to implement their values. It also diminishes in other ways the ability to think coherently and to explain or justify one's preferences, desires, and fears. We don't need to have control of the narrative of our whole life, despite Dworkin's claim, in order to have critical interests or values. But to be a valuer, we do need to be able to reflect on ourselves, to stand back at least a bit and take up an objective point of view. I suspect that memory plays an essential role in this ability to reflect. It seems plausible, at any rate, that when a person with Alzheimer's reaches the point at which she is confused about the people and things that have mattered most to her throughout her life, when she cannot recall what happened an hour ago and doesn't think clearly about the future, then her ability to reflect in any meaningful way on herself and her desires and beliefs is also called into doubt.

The most important consequences of memory loss in Alzheimer's patients is not the inability to remember names or recall events or even to implement a plan; rather, it is the loss of ability to reflect, to place oneself in time, to detach from the immediate flow of events and apply abstract standards or principles to one's own situation. A working memory seems in this way to be a necessary condition for a person to have a normative conception of herself. If this is right, then even on Jaworska's less demanding account of valuing, Alzheimer's undermines the capacity of people to be valuers in the sense needed for autonomy.

8.7. Respecting Human Beings

Granted that the intuitions that lead me to reject Jaworska's conclusions are highly speculative, I take them nevertheless to be reasons to doubt that the Alzheimer's patients she describes have the capacity to lead autonomous lives. If this is correct—if people with mid-stage Alzheimer's have neither the capacity to form critical interests in Dworkin's sense nor the capacity to lay down principles that will govern their actions in Jaworska's sense—then the conditions for claiming that these people deserve respect as well as concern may not obtain. Like Dworkin, I shrink from this conclusion. But I also think that there is something wrong in the way we have been thinking about this issue. I will conclude this essay with an attempt to explain the mistake I think we tend to make.

As I write this essay, I have in mind my mother, who lives with an advanced form of mid-stage Alzheimer's. We moved her to a nearby assisted living facility several years ago when her memory loss was great enough to make it impossible for her continue to live on her own. I see her often, and we do things together, but I believe she no longer has the capacity to form critical interests or to lay down principles for valuing. Nevertheless, there is an important sense of respect—that seems to me the correct word to describe it—which governs my attitudes and actions in our relationship.

It is significant that my mother can still use language to communicate, for this allows her to have and express interests—even if they are not values—that are not directly related to experiences of pleasure and pain. This in turn makes possible a sense of dignity that she still possesses. It makes possible the risk of humiliation and insult, whether or not she suffers from them. These are opaque remarks, which I will try to explain further with some illustrations.

A person living with Alzheimer's is capable of appreciating things and recognizing that she appreciates. Such a person can enjoy the flowers in the garden outside her window and can appreciate that the garden is there and well tended. She can express that appreciation. She may also have opinions on which prints in the lounge she likes, and which ones she doesn't like. If someone has the capacity to appreciate things, then she is, in some sense, a valuer. This kind of valuing is different from and perhaps not related to the kind of valuing that is necessary for being autonomous, but it is a capacity that is sufficient to distinguish the status of people with dementia from our pet dogs.[26] In this way human beings—even those living through Alzheimer's—are sources of value. This is sufficient to make them appropriate objects of respect, although the ways we respect people who have the capacity to appreciate will inevitably be different from the ways we show respect for people who are also autonomous.

My mother likes to visit Duke Gardens. She does not remember Duke Gardens when I refer to them, and she would never on her own ask me to take her there. It wouldn't occur to her that she was missing something she liked if we never visited Duke Gardens again, and her attention is easily drawn to other pleasant activities, whether or not they are the kinds of activities she genuinely enjoys. But my awareness that she appreciates visits to Duke Gardens is a reason for me to take her there. To simply ignore this reason would be a way of disrespecting her.

I will give one more example. My mother still remains reluctant to admit that she cannot manage her life independently and do the things she used to do. She likes to think that she can take care of herself. This seems to be a value in something close to Jaworska's sense, even though it rests on false assumptions. When my mother needs some toothpaste or some snacks for her room, I take this to be a reason to drive her to the store to buy them if I have the time, rather than simply pick them up for her on my way to visit her. When we are at the store, she is happy, but she easily becomes anxious and confused. Paying for the items she buys is a delicate matter. I help her find the bills and count the change, but I have to be careful not unduly to delay the cashier or the people in line behind us. These other people, as it turns out, nearly invariably seem to understand and do not object to waiting while we complete the transaction. No doubt they are patient out of respect for a woman who is struggling to carry out a routine task. In these situations I feel that I must also be careful not to become impatient and too quick to take over the simple task of finding

---

[26] I am agreeing here with Jeff McMahan, who remarks, "However long I set my dog in front of my print of Goya's *Devota Profesión*, he will never derive the least spark of aesthetic gratification from it. As far as I can tell, my dog is incapable of any sort of aesthetic response, at least to visual phenomena." *The Ethics of Killing* (New York: Oxford University Press, 2002), 149.

the right bill and counting the change, for that would be patronizing to my mother and would make a charade of her doing the shopping. I am trying to act respectfully and to avoid the risk of embarrassing her. I take care not to explain to her that we are causing the line to move slowly, not to force her to notice something that she might find humiliating. Activities like taking her shopping have a ritualistic quality, but they do not seem pointless for that reason. These are the ways I can still attend to her current interests, even those the satisfaction of which make little or no impact on her comfort or happiness.

When we think about respect and its connection to capacities like having critical interests or being autonomous, we are attaching the concept to properties that are commonly possessed by normal human beings. This way of thinking, however, cannot make sense of some of the attitudes we typically have toward human beings, which we also want to defend as appropriate. It cannot explain our reasons for respecting the bodies of the dead, and it cannot explain what sense we make of actions that seem to be motivated by respect for people who are alive but who no longer have the properties that we most commonly appeal to in explaining respect. But human beings are not simply entities that have or lack certain properties. We are living organisms, subjects who exist in time with natural histories of development and decline. When we think about actions that express disrespect toward the dead or toward severely demented or permanently unconscious people, we tend to see these actions either as relating to properties possessed by these beings at the time or as connected by our own memories to these properties in their earlier selves.

An alternative view, which may be more difficult to explain on meta-physical grounds but better captures many of the attitudes we find natural and reasonable, is that respect and disrespect are owed to human beings, but the properties or capacities that make these attitudes appropriate are organic and developmental; they are not always manifested in the individuals that typically display them through large stretches of their existence.[27] Of course this leaves open the possibility that respect for an individual may demand allowing him to die with dignity rather than

---

[27] A similar view, that respect is owed to "creatures, not features," is defended by Elizabeth Foreman in her Ph.D. dissertation "Focusing Respect on Creatures," University of North Carolina at Chapel Hill, 2008.

continuing to live in a way that is contrary to his critical interests. But this view can also explain how we might nevertheless respect or disrespect people whose only remaining interests are experiential. Some moral attitudes may be explained by the properties of people, but they are directed at the people themselves, the living organisms that we have come to love and respect, in part because of the properties and traits that formed their identities and personalities but may now have declined and disappeared.

Perhaps the point I am suggesting can be made a bit clearer by thinking about a person who is a caretaker for someone he has loved. Think about an elderly but fully competent man whose life is now largely devoted to caring for his wife who is living with Alzheimer's. Does he act from love? It is easy to imagine that he still loves this person with whom he has shared much of his life, but it is just as easy to think that he could not have come to love someone in her present condition.[28] Does he act from a sense of duty, a sense perhaps grounded in the commitment to one another that was part of their shared understanding and bond? This would explain his caretaking as a duty of respect. In any event, it also seems implausible to think that most relationships like this are sustained primarily by a sense of duty to a person under the description of Alzheimer's victim. It is just as easy—more natural, perhaps—to think of this kind of care and devotion as motivated by love and respect for the human being who for many years was different from the way she is now.

This, at any rate, is how I am best able to understand my attitudes and make sense of the actions I take out of respect for my mother. I do not think that she is now capable of autonomy of a kind that could justify respect; nor is she capable of forming critical values. Nor do I take myself to be honoring the fully competent person she used to be. I take myself instead to be acting out of the kind of love and sense of duty (motives that I find impossible in this context to disentangle) a son may have for his mother. These also involve a kind of recognition respect that it is reasonable to have for her as a human being. If I ask myself what kind of creature she is, I can think only that she is a person in the twilight of an ordinary human life, someone with a history as well

---

[28] I note, however, that this possibility is explored in a convincing and moving way in Pier Almodóvar's film *Talk to Her*.

as a past, a human being that is an organic time-bound entity of a kind whose natural development and decline makes her importantly different from the kind of organic entity we find in a pet dog. This makes my relationship with mother different from any relationship one could have with a pet dog.

9

Radical Cognitive Limitation

JEFF McMAHAN

9.1. The Radically Cognitively Limited

Suppose that there are human beings whose overall psychological capacities and potential are comparable to or lower than those characteristic of the higher orders of nonhuman animals, such as chimpanzees. And suppose that the limited cognitive capacities of at least some of these human beings are congenital and resulted because the genes that coded for the growth of their brains were different, or operated differently, from those that code for the development of the brain in other human beings. I refer to these human beings as the 'radically cognitively limited'—though for brevity I will often use the abbreviated term the 'cognitively limited'.[1] None of the claims I will make about the radically cognitively limited necessarily apply to human beings who have, or have had, higher psychological capacities, or who have the potential to develop higher psychological capacities.

The radically cognitively limited are considered disabled, and thus in the same moral category as human beings who are physically disabled. They are generally regarded as less fortunate than most other human beings, and to have suffered a grave misfortune in being congenitally endowed with lower psychological capacities. Yet, because they are human beings, they are thought to have the same basic rights as others. They share our moral status, including our claim to inviolability. They are also assumed to come

I am indebted for comments on this paper to Rom Harré, Judith Lichtenberg, and David Wasserman.

[1] I have coined the ugly term, 'radically cognitively limited', in an effort to avoid various pitfalls in this sensitive area. I have, for example, avoided such terms as 'impaired' and 'deficient' in order not to imply any comparison with biological norms characteristic of the human species.

within the scope of relevant distributive principles—principles of justice and equality. My main aim in this paper is to question and challenge these various assumptions.

Some people believe that there is nothing here to discuss because there simply are no human beings who fit the description I have given—or perhaps because we cannot be sure enough that there are such human beings for any discussion of their status to have practical significance. Eva Kittay, for example, questions whether there really are any 'individuals about whom one can say with any certainty that they are both human and have the cognitive capacities of an animal.' Her arguments mainly question the *intelligibility* of such comparisons: 'Are there humans with the cognition of a nonhuman animal? Again, I do not know what that means.'[2] I will try to explain what it means and will also offer reasons to think that the answer is 'yes'.

The brains of fetuses and infants develop gradually, passing through incrementally differentiated levels of psychological capacity from nil to the level of a child who is more intelligent and sensitive than any nonhuman primate. There are no significant discontinuities, no sudden leaps of capacity from one level to a significantly higher level, bypassing intermediate levels. Of course, psychological capacity is multidimensional and there may be no human being who has psychological capacities that are *identical* to those of any animal. But if a conscious human fetus begins with psychological capacities that are uniformly lower than those of an adult chimpanzee and yet within a few years has capacities that are uniformly higher than those of the chimpanzee, it is reasonable to suppose that for some period during its development the human being had psychological capacities broadly comparable to those of the chimpanzee. Even if this is false, it seems undeniable that the psychological capacities of a newly conscious human fetus are *all* lower, or less developed, than those of a higher nonhuman animal. Anyone who would deny this must indicate what psychological capacity it is that a newly conscious fetus has that a chimpanzee lacks.

What is meant by the claim that a conscious 7-month-old fetus has psychological capacities that are lower, or less developed, than those of a normal, adult chimpanzee is that the fetus has no capacity for self-consciousness while the chimpanzee has some, that the fetus has no capacity for understanding words or signs, while the chimpanzee has

---

[2] E. F. Kittay, 'At the Margins of Moral Personhood', *Ethics*, 116 (2005), 130.

some, that the fetus has no capacity for sociality while the chimpanzee has some, that the fetus has no capacity for reasoning about means and ends while the chimpanzee has some, and so on. If there is some psychological capacity that the fetus has but the chimpanzee does not, or that the fetus has to a higher degree than the chimpanzee, it is incumbent on the person who would ground a claim about moral status on this fact to explain why that capacity has moral significance. "For not every psychological capacity is relevant to moral status. There are some psychological capacities that a human being might congenitally lack without his or her moral status being affected."

Such a human fetus usually though not always has the *potential* to develop levels of psychological capacity higher than those of the chimpanzee, but it is possible that the development of its brain could be irreversibly arrested at 7 months after conception, so that its potential for further psychological development would be lost. That could occur in various ways—for example, through a genetic defect or through injury. The human brain can thus take as its developmentally final form something intermediate between the brain of an anencephalic infant that has no psychological capacity at all and the brain of an adult chimpanzee. A human being to whom this had happened would be radically cognitively limited. She would be aptly described as 'permanently infantile' to indicate that although her body might mature to adulthood, her mind would be permanently arrested at roughly the level of an infant, and below the level of some animals.

9.2. Are Cognitively Limited Human Beings Disabled?

Many writers on ethical issues concerning disability assume that physical and cognitive disability are different dimensions of the same problem. They assume that the disabled form a single unitary group whose moral status is the same and whose claims to justice and equality are all the same. Yet it may be that the physically disabled and the cognitively limited form morally distinct categories. Those with disabilities that are wholly physical in character pose one set of problems about justice, while at least some of those with grave cognitive limitations raise a different set of issues.

One issue that is raised by cognitive limitation but not by physical disability is moral status. When I ask a class of students, as I have done a number of times, why those of us in the room have a higher moral status than the squirrels outside the window, so that it would be more seriously wrong to kill one of us than to kill one of them, the students invariably respond by citing various higher psychological capacities that we have but that squirrels do not: self-consciousness, the ability to plan for the future, the ability to distinguish between right and wrong, free will (by which they generally mean the capacity to deliberate and act on reasons rather than on impulse or instinct), the ability to use language, rationality, and so on. To my surprise, I cannot recall a single instance in which a student has said 'because we are members of the human species', 'because we have immortal souls', or 'because we are made in the image of God'. Perhaps many of them would have offered one of these explanations after reflection, but what they find immediately intuitively compelling is that our mental lives are incomparably higher and richer than that of a squirrel. I believe they are right. Our higher moral status derives from, or supervenes upon, our higher psychological capacities. That we have certain higher psychological capacities makes us beings of a higher sort, with higher worth.

If this is right, persons with disabilities that are only physical must have the same moral status as you and I. But if the cognitively limited have that status as well, it cannot be for the same reason. If they share our moral status, high psychological capacities may be sufficient for high moral status, but they cannot be necessary.

With a bit of prodding, my students can also perceive another important difference between ourselves and animals, one that may also be relevant to moral status. They notice that the psychological capacities that they have cited as relevant to moral status are also necessary for many of the higher goods of human life, such as intimate personal relations based on deep mutual understanding, achievement of difficult and valuable goals, knowledge, aesthetic appreciation, and so on.[3] Our lives would be immeasurably impoverished if they lacked all such goods. That we

---

[3] Kittay notes (ibid. 127–8) that some human beings with severe psychological limitations show unmistakable signs of musical appreciation. If it is true that no animals have this capacity, then those human beings who have it may not count as radically cognitively limited in the sense in which I have defined that phrase. The question remains, of course, whether this psychological capacity is relevant

recognize this is one of the principal reasons why we all dread the prospect of dementia. But these goods are all entirely inaccessible to animals, who lack the psychological capacities necessary for having them. The dimensions of the good that are accessible to animals are much narrower. Many animals enjoy playing, eating, mating, hunting, relaxing, and so on, but no matter how much enjoyment their lives contain, their level of well-being remains well below that of even a barely contented human being, provided that the human being's life contains some of the dimensions of well-being from which animals are excluded by their psychological limitations.

Human beings who are merely physically disabled have the same capacity for well-being that other people have, though their disabilities may impede their ability to achieve the levels of well-being, functioning, or flourishing of which they are otherwise capable. By contrast, the cognitively limited do not have the same capacity for well-being. The levels of well-being that are accessible to them are limited by their psychological capacities in the same way that the levels of well-being that are possible for a comparably endowed animal are.

We classify people with certain physical impairments as disabled if their physical condition constitutes an impediment to their being able to achieve their potential for well-being. But we do not say that animals are disabled because they have psychological capacities that limit their capacity for well-being. This raises the question of why the cognitively limited should be considered disabled. Their inability to achieve the higher levels of well-being accessible to other human beings is not contingent, as it is in the case of the physically disabled. Rather, their limited capacity for well-being is a *feature* of their individual nature, not an impediment to the realization of their nature or potential. So it may seem that the claim that they are disabled suggests or even implies that animals are as well; yet animals are not disabled.

One possibility is that the cognitively limited are disabled while animals are not because their psychological limitations are a misfortune for them in a way that those of animals are not. Because of their limited cognitive capacities, the cognitively limited are dependent on others for their survival and well-being. Animals, by contrast, are adapted for survival with their low

---

to moral status, or whether it alone could give a human being with capacities that are otherwise comparable to those of an animal a higher status than that of the animal.

levels of cognitive capacity. So low cognitive capacities are instrumentally disadvantageous for the cognitively limited in a way that they are not for animals. Perhaps this is what explains and justifies the view that the cognitively limited are disabled while animals with comparable psychological capacities are not.

Yet puzzles remain. Young children are also helpless and dependent in part because of their low cognitive capacities, but we do not on that account regard them as disabled, even temporarily. If the reason why the cognitively limited are disabled while animals are not is that their low cognitive capacities make them dependent, it seems that small children count as disabled as well.

Perhaps the difference between the cognitively limited and children is that dependency is a misfortune for the one but not the other. We see it as natural and appropriate that children should have lower psychological capacities, and thus be helpless and dependent. Many people think it is one of the enviable aspects of childhood that children are relieved of the responsibility of providing for themselves. Dependency is part of what it is to be a small child, just as having limited psychological capacities is part of what it is to be an animal (though being dependent is not). But to have limited psychological capacities and to be helpless and dependent are not part of what it is to be an adult human being and are thus misfortunes for adults. It is thus because psychological limitations are a misfortune for the cognitively limited but not for children and animals that the former are disabled while the latter are not.

This diagnosis would, however, be challenged by those who claim that to be disabled is not a misfortune. Many people, including many disabled people, have made this claim.[4] They argue that, unlike disease, which is bad and for which we should seek a cure, disability is bad only because social conditions make it so, and that we should not seek to 'cure' it but only to provide reasonable social accommodation for the disabled. I have suggested, however, that it may be part of the *concept* of a disability that it is a misfortune. That was supposed to explain why cognitive limitation is a disability in an adult human being but not in an animal. But those who deny that disabilities are misfortunes must reject the suggestion that the reason why the cognitively limited are disabled while comparably endowed

<hr />

[4] H. M. Johnson, 'Unspeakable Conversations', *New York Times Magazine*, 16 February 2003, 79.

animals are not is that their limitations are a misfortune while those of animals are not.

Suppose that it is in fact part of the concept of a disability that it is a misfortune. It is compatible with that that what we refer to as disabilities are not in fact misfortunes. Speakers may in general use the term 'disability' to pick out a range of conditions that they consider to be misfortunes. Provided that the term is used in a uniform way to refer to a relatively fixed set of conditions, it is possible that what people mean by 'disability' is a set of conditions that are misfortunes, even though the conditions to which they apply the term are not in fact misfortunes. So those who deny that disabilities are misfortunes could still accept that the reason why we call the cognitively limited disabled is that we believe, mistakenly, that their limitation is a misfortune. They can even accept that cognitive disability is contingently and instrumentally a misfortune in social conditions such as ours. All they are really committed to denying is that disabilities are intrinsic misfortunes. They might, therefore, consistently argue that the radically cognitively limited are disabled because our society has failed to make reasonable accommodation for them, while neither animals nor children are disabled. Animals are not disabled because they are well adapted to their environment, and children are not disabled because we have always, in general, accommodated them through social norms that assign their care to their parents.

But is it really true that the psychological limitations of the cognitively limited are bad only instrumentally? To test for this, we should imagine external or environmental conditions that would be maximally conducive to the flourishing of the cognitively limited—that is, conditions in which they might continuously sustain the highest level of well-being possible for them on the assumption that their nature and abilities would remain unchanged. Our imagination should not be constrained by what is currently technologically possible. We should imagine the most favourable conceivable environment for them. Then we should compare them in that environment with persons with normal human psychological capacities in the environment in which they could achieve and sustain the highest level of well-being of which they are capable given their nature. This thought-experiment is, of course, only a heuristic device for comparing the highest levels of well-being attainable by each.

Those who claim that disability is only a mismatch between a person's abilities and her environment seem committed to the conclusion that in this thought-experiment, the well-being of the cognitively limited would be as high as that of those with normal psychological capacities. But if what I argued earlier is true—that many of the most important dimensions of well-being are inaccessible to those lacking the higher psychological capacities—then it is impossible that the well-being of the cognitively limited could be as high as that of those with normal capacities. To deny this conclusion one would have to deny that the dimensions of the good that I identified earlier really are irreducible components of the good. Thus, a hedonist of a rather narrow sort might contend that the ideal environment for any sentient being is one that would provide continuous pleasure of the most intense sort. If the cognitively limited have the same capacity for physical pleasure that other people do, their highest possible level of well-being might be the same as ours and any misfortune they suffer in the actual world is potentially remediable by altering the environment. But if that is right because hedonism is true, then because the psychological capacities of the cognitively limited are by definition comparable to those of certain animals, there must be some animals whose well-being could be as high as ours as well.

This is not the place to rehearse the arguments against hedonism, but I believe that they are decisive and that there are dimensions of well-being that are unrecognized by hedonism, or recognized only as instrumental rather than intrinsic. Because some of these dimensions of well-being are necessarily absent from the lives of the cognitively limited, the highest level of well-being attainable by these human beings without augmentation of their psychological capacities is substantially lower than that potentially attainable by persons with normal psychological capacities. If this is a misfortune, it is intrinsic rather than instrumental, though in actual life their misfortunes are instrumental as well. Although their well-being can of course be greatly enhanced by changes in their environment, it is doubtful whether their lives can ever be as good *for them* as a life with a modest level of well-being for a person with normal psychological capacities. Most of us would not trade some fixed number of years of ordinary life with normal psychological capacities for *any* number of years of the most contented life without those capacities and the goods for which they are necessary. As Aristotle says, 'no one would choose to live with the intellect of a child throughout his life, however much he were to be pleased at the things that children are pleased at.'[5] We do of course tend to look back on our childhood with nostalgia, but no one welcomes a return to an analogous state in their 'second childhood'.

That the cognitively limited have lives that, precisely because of their congenital psychological limitations, are substantially less good overall than those of persons with ordinary psychological capacities is regarded by most people as a grave misfortune. We can accept that for the lack of an ability to count as a disability it must be instrumentally disadvantageous, and on that ground accept that the cognitively limited are disabled while animals are not. Yet it also seems to most people that it is a misfortune for the cognitively limited that their limited psychological capacities restrict the range of well-being that is accessible to them. Note that, if this is true, those who claim that disabilities are misfortunes only insofar as social conditions make them so seem driven to accept that radical cognitive limitation is a disease rather than a disability. The challenge, for these theorists of disability and for others, is to explain why having a restricted range of well-being is a misfortune for the cognitively limited but not for animals with comparable psychological capacities. For no one, or virtually no one, thinks that it is a misfortune for an animal not to have the expansive range of well-being that most human beings have.

Most people who have thought about this challenge think it can be easily met because they assume that how well or badly off an individual is is not a function solely of that individual's level of well-being but is instead a function of its level of well-being in relation to some standard for assessing well-being. They further assume that the relevant standard is the range of well-being made possible by the psychological capacities that are normal for the members of an individual's biological species. If an individual is faring well in relation to what is possible for the members of its species, then it is well off, even if its level of well-being is far below that which may be characteristic of the members of another species. A chimpanzee, for example, is well off if it has a good life *for a chimpanzee*, even if a life of the sort it has would be a bad life for a human being. Similarly, a radically cognitively limited human being may be badly off *as a human being* even if a life of the sort she has would be a good one for almost any animal.

---

[5] Aristotle, *Ethica Nicomachea*, trans. W. D. Ross, rev. J. O. Urmson, in *The Works of Aristotle*, ix, ed. W. D. Ross (Oxford: Oxford University Press, 1975), 1174a1–3.

9.3. Misfortune as a Matter of Species Membership

I have criticized this view, which I call the Species Norm Account of how well or badly off an individual is, elsewhere.[6] But there is more to be said about it than is to be found in my earlier criticisms. The assumption on which this view is based is that an individual's intrinsic nature is given by its species. On this assumption, it is in the nature of human beings to have high psychological capacities and therefore the capacity to enjoy high levels of well-being. Any human being who lacks high psychological capacities is failing to realize her own nature, and any human being who falls significantly short of the high levels of well-being attainable by normal members of the species is unfortunate, even if the explanation for the shortfall is that the individual's cognitive capacities exclude the possibility of attaining those levels of well-being.

The problem with this assumption, however, is that it is only statistically in the nature of human beings to have high cognitive capacities. Because there are human beings who lack these capacities, and indeed lack even the potential for having them, the possession of these capacities cannot be essential to membership in the species. It is not part of the individual nature of cognitively limited human beings to have these capacities; indeed, it is their individual nature *not* to have them. So what is the reason for supposing that the capacities are somehow part of their nature as human beings? I suspect the idea here is really that it is in the nature of human beings that they are *supposed to* have various high psychological capacities. Because the cognitively limited are human beings, they are supposed to have these capacities. But they do not, and their failure in this regard is thus a failure to realize their own nature in its fullest form. And this is a misfortune. But this view is explicitly normative rather than biological. If it were biological, it would treat an individual's exemption from the possession of some near-universal *bad* human characteristic as equally a failure to realize her nature. But no proponent of the view would say that. So the Species Norm Account's understanding of the norm for the species is already normative and as such merely begs the question about whether

---

[6] J. McMahan, 'Cognitive Disability, Misfortune, and Justice', *Philosophy and Public Affairs*, 25 (1996), 3–34, and J. McMahan, *The Ethics of Killing: Problems at the Margins of Life* (New York: Oxford University Press, 2002), 145–59.

it is a misfortune to lack certain capacities that are characteristic of the species.

But suppose that I am wrong about this and that whether a human being is well or badly off is determined by where her level of well-being falls along the range of conditions possible for members of the human species generally. What follows about the cognitively limited? It is clear that on this view their psychological limitations are a misfortune, but how bad a misfortune? This cannot be determined just by comparing the cognitively limited with ourselves, for we—human beings with normal psychological capacities who are alive now—do not constitute the whole of the human species. Rather, the human species has existed for a very long time and the nature of its members has changed substantially as it has evolved. Just as there is variation in psychological capacity among the existing normal members of the human species, so there has been even greater variation over time. And just as there is no reason to suppose that my psychological capacities are more representative of our biological kind than yours are, so there is no reason to suppose that ours are more representative of the species than those of our remote ancestors. We have no greater claim than they do to instantiate the nature of our species. Yet the psychological capacities of our remotest ancestors may have been more like those of present-day nonhuman primates than like our own.

What the relevant comparison class is, though, will affect our evaluation of how well or badly off the cognitively limited are. If we compare contemporary cognitively limited human beings with the earliest members of our species, they will emerge as less disabled, and especially less unfortunate, than they would be if we were to compare them with ourselves instead. But since there is no reason to take human beings from *any* historical period as representative of the species over time, perhaps the solution is to take the average or median level of psychological capacity over time as the norm, or perhaps to take the entire range of psychological capacity over the history of the species as the norm. These two suggestions of course give different results, though both imply that our remote ancestors were badly off, though most of their near kin among other primate species were not. And both suggestions imply that our ancestors were worse off than their nonhuman kin even if their absolute level of well-being was higher.

Both these suggestions, moreover, seem arbitrarily limited because they fail to take account of the way in which our species will evolve in the future. The nature of our species is, in other words, still in the making. If we base the norm for our species on the way it has been *up till now*, the norm will be ever-shifting over time. The shifting will, admittedly, be very slow, though it could accelerate when germ-line genetic enhancement of our cognitive capacities becomes a practical possibility. As the norm shifts over time, so does how well or badly off all human beings have been. Assuming that the slow enhancement of our psychological capacities over the course of human evolution has expanded the norm for the species, the lives of our remote ancestors have become worse and worse relative to the evolving species norm. As their descendants' psychological capacities have become increasingly highly developed, and as the range of their descendants' levels of well-being has correspondingly increased, our ancestors' lives have become worse, even though the nonrelational facts about their well-being remain fixed and unalterable. Suppose it were true—and it may be: I do not know the facts here—that for most of the history of the human species, its members have had psychological capacities closer to those of present-day chimpanzees than to those of present-day persons. In that case *we* might constitute a greater deviation from the norm for the human species than the cognitively limited, though of course their lack of instincts for survival is a deviation from the norm for any animal species whose members have the capacity for consciousness.

One might respond to this objection by noting that more human beings have lived since psychological capacities comparable to ours became characteristic of the species than lived during all the preceding time. Assuming that that is true and that the norm for the species is set more by numbers than by the amount of time during which any particular level of capacity prevailed, it seems that the norm for the species should be more reflective of our psychological nature than of the natures of our remote ancestors. Perhaps that is true but it merely serves to accentuate the implausibility of the idea that how well or badly off we are now depends on how our lives and capacities compare with those of our remotest ancestors, and vice versa. For it is hard to see how our being more numerous than our remote ancestors could be relevant to how well or badly off we are.

There are not only variations in psychological capacity among normal human beings now, and even much greater variations among normal human beings over the history of the species, but there are also great variations in psychological capacity within most human lives over time.

We all begin to exist with the most rudimentary possible psychological capacities. Most of us then gradually develop extremely high psychological capacities, and some of us later suffer losses of psychological capacity of varying degrees of severity. The idea that how well or badly off cognitively limited human beings are depends on how they compare with the norm for the human species presupposes that the relevant comparison is between an adult with radical cognitive limitations and a cognitively normal adult. For if one were to compare a newborn infant with radical cognitive limitations with an ordinary newborn infant, there would be little or no difference in psychological capacity. Indeed, if one were to compare an adult human being with radical cognitive limitations with an ordinary infant, there might still be little difference. So the claim that the cognitively limited are unfortunate assumes that the norm for the human species is set by a representative *adult*. Yet if that is right, then it seems that all infants and young children must be badly off[7], as they have limited psychological capacities that in turn limit their access to various dimensions of the good. But most of us, with Aristotle as a possible exception, do not regard them as badly off.

The obvious response to this problem is to relativize the norm not just to species but also to age. On this view, we should evaluate how well or badly off an individual human being is by reference to the norm for human beings of her age. But there are serious problems with this suggestion. It implies, for example, that an individual whose psychological growth is arrested at one year after birth may be well off before the age of 1, but becomes increasingly unfortunate with the passage of time, even if her mental life remains entirely unchanged. Perhaps to many people this will not seem peculiar, but the suggested double relativization has another implication no one is likely to accept.

It is normal, both in human beings and in other animal species, for individuals to experience a decline in various physical and psychological capacities and functions in extreme old age. The facts are depressingly familiar. So if we claim that how well off an individual is must be assessed relative to the norm for individuals of that individual's species *and age*, we will be unable coherently to claim that age-related deterioration is a misfortune, or that we generally become worse off in extreme old age than we were earlier in life.

---

[7] Aristotle writes that 'the life we lead as children is not desirable, for no one in his senses would consent to return again to this.' (*Ethica Eudemia*, trans. J. Solomon, in Ross, *op. cit.*, 1215b23)

Although the Species Norm Account initially seems intuitively plausible, that plausibility appears upon examination to be illusory. But without the Species Norm Account, we have no reason to suppose that congenital cognitive limitation is an intrinsic misfortune for human beings but not for comparably endowed animals.

9.4. Equality and Priority

But suppose that the cognitively limited *are* unfortunate, and that their limitations are bad not only instrumentally but intrinsically as well, as I argued in Section 9.2. What are the moral implications?

Most people believe that the cognitively limited are our moral equals, in the sense that they have the same moral status as all other human beings. Thus, the intentional killing of a cognitively limited human being without one of the standard justifications, such as self-defence, would be murder, though the killing of a chimpanzee with comparable or even higher psychological capacities would not be. But if the cognitively limited are our moral equals, our treatment of them should be governed by the same basic principles of justice and equality that govern our treatment of each other—in other words, the same principles that govern relations among cognitively normal human beings.

Consider, for example, principles of equality. There are various possible currencies of equality—that is, respects in which it is arguable that we ought, ideally, to be equal. Among those for which philosophers have argued are resources, well-being, primary goods, opportunity for well-being, capabilities, and so on. Suppose the proper currency is well-being and that it is lifetime well-being and not just momentary well-being that ought to be equalized. On this view, it would be better if each individual were to get the same amount of good from life, unless perhaps certain inequalities are *deserved*, or result from free choices.

Unless some crude form of hedonism is the correct account of well-being, it is impossible to get the cognitively limited up to the levels of well-being typically enjoyed by most persons with normal psychological capacities in most areas of the world today. But if they come within the scope of the principle of equality of well-being, we have a significant moral reason to try to get them as close as possible—for example, by devoting a disproportionate share of our resources to improving their lives. Or we could achieve greater equality between the cognitively limited and the cognitively normal by 'levelling down'—that is, by deliberately reducing the well-being of the cognitively normal even when this would do nothing to raise the level of the cognitively limited. Most people think that there is *no* moral reason to reduce the well-being of some as a means of reducing unfair inequalities. I disagree. I follow Larry Temkin in thinking that there is a moral reason for levelling down, but that that reason is in most actual cases outweighed by the reason not to harm those whose well-being would be reduced.[8] "If the radically cognitively limited are within the scope of the principle of equality of well-being, we should accept Temkin's view in that case as well. But even if we rule out levelling down as a means of achieving greater equality, that still leaves the option of reducing inequality through transfers of resources that would raise the well-being of the cognitively limited, though by significantly less than they would reduce that of the cognitively normal."

Inequality might also be diminished, or even eradicated, through genetic cognitive enhancement. Most people expect that when genetic cognitive enhancement initially becomes possible, it will work by genetic alteration of the zygote or embryo. But suppose that a genetic therapy is developed that makes it possible to enhance the psychological capacities of adults with radical cognitive limitations. Suppose that it becomes possible by this means to enable the cognitively limited to develop normal cognitive capacities. On some theories of personal identity that treat a certain degree of psychological continuity as necessary to our identity over time, this kind of psychological transformation would be too extensive for the original cognitively limited individual to survive. On these theories, what is thought of as the enhancement of a single cognitively limited individual would really involve causing the original individual to cease to exist and another individual to begin to exist in association with the body of the original. But let us assume that these theories of personal identity are mistaken and that cognitive enhancement of the cognitively limited would be compatible with their continuing to exist. My own view is that, although the radically cognitively limited would survive genetic cognitive enhancement, the psychological discontinuity that it would involve within

---

[8] L. Temkin, 'Egalitarianism Defended,' *Ethics*, 113 (2003), 764–82.

their lives would be so great that we would have little reason to enhance them *for their own sakes, as individuals with radical cognitive limitations*, even though the enhancement would greatly improve their lives as wholes.[9] But this is irrelevant here because our concern is with equality, which is an impersonal value, rather than with beneficence.

The relevant question here is this. If the principle of equality of well-being implies that we would have a reason to enhance the cognitive capacities of radically cognitively limited human beings, why would it not also imply that we have a reason to enhance the cognitive capacities of animals? There are of course various contingent reasons not to enhance the cognitive capacities of animals. And we of course have reasons to enhance the cognitively limited that arise from the ways in which we are specially related to them but not to animals. But none of these considerations has anything to do with equality. The relevant question is why, if there are reasons of *equality* to enhance the cognitive capacities of cognitively limited human beings in order to raise them closer to our level of well-being, there are no reasons of equality to enhance the capacities of animals to raise them closer to our level as well. We naturally assume that principles of equality apply only within our own species, but on reflection that seems entirely arbitrary.

The same question arises with respect to the application of the principle of priority. When people realize that the principle of equality of well-being implies that there can be a moral reason for 'levelling down', they often reject that principle and seek to defend what they took to be egalitarian intuitions by appealing instead to the principle of priority, which holds, roughly, that raising an individual's well-being matters more the lower his level of well-being is. On this view, we should give priority to raising the well-being of those who are worst off. Although the cognitively limited are not in general among the very worst off among human beings, their exclusion from many important dimensions of well-being may place them not very far above those who are worst off. So if they come within the scope of the principle of priority, they should not have first priority, but raising their well-being should have priority over preserving the well-being of most cognitively normal people.

Again, however, if we thought that the cognitively limited have priority because their well-being is low, we would have to explain why animals do not have a similar priority, for their levels of well-being are also low in absolute terms. We would have to explain, in other words, why animals fall outside the scope of the principle of priority while the cognitively limited lie within it. For no one, not even the most ardent proponents of the rights of animals, believes that animals have the kind of moral priority that they would have if they were within the scope of that principle.

It is perhaps revealing that no one really seems to think that the radically cognitively limited come within the scope of the principle of priority either. I do not know of anyone who appeals explicitly to the principle of priority, or indeed to the principle of equality of well-being, to argue that cognitively normal people ought to accept significant sacrifices in their level of well-being in order to raise the well-being of the cognitively limited. Nor do I know of anyone who argues even that resources ought to be devoted disproportionately to increasing the well-being of the cognitively limited, when the same resources could produce more good if devoted to the cognitively normal. That neither egalitarians nor prioritarians are pressing for disproportionate transfers of resources to the radically cognitively limited suggests that the intuition that these human beings have the same moral status as the cognitively normal may not go as deep as some people suppose.

Principles of equality and priority can focus either on lifetime well-being or on well-being at a given time (momentary well-being). There are good reasons why animals lie outside the scope of such principles when they focus on lifetime well-being. In addition to the biologically determined restrictions on both their capacity for momentary well-being and their longevity, there is also a lack of psychological unity and continuity within their lives over time. As Derek Parfit has argued, when the psychological unity within a life over time is less deep, the life *as a whole*—as a unit—matters less than it would if there were greater unity.[10] Equality of lifetime well-being is a significant value only among individuals whose lives matter to the same degree *as wholes*. It simply does not matter whether there is equality of lifetime well-being between individuals whose lives matter greatly as wholes and individuals whose lives matter much less as wholes.

If, however, this shows that animals are not properly within the scope of principles of equality and priority that apply to persons and that focus on

---

[10] D. Parfit, *Reasons and Persons* (Oxford: Clarendon Press, 1984), 329–47, esp. 339.

lifetime well-being, it also shows that the cognitively limited are outside the scope of those principles as well. But it does not follow that there are no principles of equality or priority that have both the cognitively normal and the cognitively limited within their scope. I have suggested that how well or badly off an individual is should be distinguished from what that individual's level of well-being is. As I noted earlier, how well or badly off an individual is seems to be a function of that individual's well-being relative to some standard. Most people assume, as I indicated earlier, that the relevant standard is given by the norms of an individual's species. If that is the correct standard, the situation of the cognitively limited is tragic and, at present, hopeless; their only hope for becoming well off is genetic cognitive enhancement. But suppose that the relevant standard is instead what is possible for them given their own innate individual nature—that is, given their own individual capacities and potential. By that standard they are well off if their well-being is relatively high on the scale that measures the range of well-being accessible to them given their individual psychological capacities and potential. They may thus be well off even if their level of well-being is low in comparison with that of most cognitively normal human beings.

How well or badly off an individual is is a matter of what I call 'fortune'. Fortune depends on well-being but is distinct from it in the way just indicated. My suggestion is that a plausible principle of equality that could encompass both the cognitively normal and the cognitively limited is *equality of fortune*. This principle directs us to aim, not for equality of well-being, either momentary or lifetime well-being, between the cognitively normal and the cognitively limited, but for equality of fortune. It directs us to seek to ensure that the cognitively limited are *as well off* as the cognitively normal. What this means in general terms is that they should do as well by reference to the standard set by their own nature as we are doing by reference to the standard set by our nature. More specifically, there is the appropriate kind of equality between the cognitively limited and cognitively normal human beings if the cognitively limited occupy the same relative position on the scale that measures the range of well-being possible for them that we occupy on our scale.

For the reason given earlier, the principle of equality of fortune is significantly more plausible in its application to the cognitively limited if it focuses on momentary fortune rather than on lifetime fortune. It is enough if moment by moment they are doing as well, relative to what is possible for them, as we are doing relative to what is possible for us. In practice this means that, at any given time, we should seek rough equality of well-being among the cognitively limited themselves, rough equality of well-being among the cognitively normal, and rough equality of fortune between the cognitively limited and the cognitively normal.

The principle of equality of fortune goes naturally with the view that it is not a misfortune for the cognitively limited to be innately endowed with lower psychological capacities. It suggests, rather, that their misfortune, when they are indeed unfortunate, is to fall well below the higher levels of well-being that in ideal conditions they would be capable of reaching.

This seems to be a plausible principle of equality for application across groups of individuals with different capacities for well-being. But it raises further problems. One is of course that if this principle applies to both cognitively normal and cognitively limited human beings, it seems that it should extend to animals as well. We should have the same reason of equality to ensure that animals are doing as well in relation to what is possible for them as the cognitively limited and the cognitively normal are doing in relation to what is possible for them. Most people, however, will be strongly disposed to reject the suggestion that there is any respect in which we ought morally to ensure that animals are equal with us. But perhaps the suggestion will seem less counterintuitive when we note that what seems to be required by the principle of equality of fortune is relatively undemanding. In the case of animals, it seems mainly to require that we simply leave them alone.

A second problem is that if the only principle of equality that applies both to the cognitively normal and to the cognitively limited also applies to animals, this casts doubt on the assumption that the cognitively limited have the same moral status as the cognitively normal. Most people believe that the central feature of the moral status of cognitively normal human beings is inviolability. According to common-sense morality, the cognitively limited share our inviolability, but animals do not.

We are not, however, literally inviolable. There are degrees of violability and we are, among existing beings, the least violable. If, however, there were beings—such as genetically enhanced 'posthumans'—whose psychological capacities were higher than ours by more than ours are higher than those of animals, we might not be the least violable. We might be violable to a greater degree than the posthumans would be. We might, for example, be violable for their sake in much the same way that each of us is now violable for the sake of a great number of other innocent cognitively normal human beings. Perhaps the cognitively limited are more violable than we are, in much the way that we would be more violable than posthumans. But this is, quite literally in this case, a topic for another paper.[11]

[11] J. McMahan, 'Cognitive Disability and Cognitive Enhancement', *Metaphilosophy* (forthcoming).

10

Disability, Discrimination, and Irrelevant Goods

F. M. KAMM

One of the criteria which the World Health Organization (WHO) uses to rate a health care system is 'responsiveness.' This should include the fairness of a health care system, both fairness in how it invests to produce health resources and fairness in its policies for allocating resources that are available. The WHO also recommends the use of Disability Adjusted Life Years (DALYs) in determining the health of individuals and populations. DALYs multiply number of years lived by the degree of disability with which it is lived. The predecessor is the QALYs measurement, which multiplies number of years lived by the quality of the life. DALYs can be used to evaluate the outcomes of various possible health care events on individuals in a population. If it is not unfair to, *at least in part*, use expected outcome in order to decide what health care system to invest in or how to allocate health care resources, may differential reduction in DALYs play a role in deciding how to allocate scarce monetary and health resources?

An earlier article by me discussing many of the issues discussed here was published as 'Deciding Whom to Help, Health Adjusted Life-Years, and Disabilities,' in S. Anand, F. Peter, and A. Sen (eds.), *Public Health, Ethics and Equity* (New York: Oxford University Press, 2004). I discuss some further aspects of the issues discussed in this article in a companion piece, 'Aggregation, Allocating Scarce Resources, and the Disabled' in *Social Philosophy & Policy*, vol. 26, #1, Winter 2009, 148–97. This article makes use of material in these other articles but adds to them. Work on this article was originally supported by the WHO Fairness and Goodness Project.

For comments on earlier versions of this article, I am grateful to audiences at the Kennedy School of Government, the Program in Ethics and Health, and the Law School at Harvard University. I also thank audiences at Amherst College, Georgetown University Law Center, NEH Summer Session on Disability, University of Southern California Law School, and the Pacific Division APA, March 2003. I received additional feedback from the members of Philamore and of the WHO Fairness and Goodness Project, John Broome, James Griffin, Eva Kittay, James Lindeman Nelson, Andrei Marmor, Rosemary Quigley, Gideon Rosen, and Anita Silvers.

How would the use of DALYs bear on the health of disabled people (who, I shall assume, have physical impairments)? DALYs evaluation of their lives could make it clear that their lives are more physically impaired than the lives of the nondisabled, and so health resources should be directed to curing or compensating for their impairment. But suppose we cannot cure or compensate for their disabilities so that their lives are still higher on DALYS ratings.[1] How will they fare in the competition with the nondisabled for other health care resources? Even if we cure their other illnesses or save their lives, we often cannot thereby produce a person with as low a rating for DALYs as if we treat the nondisabled. Our outcomes will often not be as good. If it is not, in general, unfair to consider how good an outcome we will produce in deciding where to use monetary and health resources, is it not unfair to 'discriminate' in such decisions against the disabled? This is the issue with which I shall be concerned.

We can refer to the issue as 'The Problem.' One way it can arise is from the following argument: Disabilities make life worse for the person whose life it is, other things equal. So we try to prevent or correct them (Premise 1). Hence, we will get a worse state of affairs if we help a disabled person whose disability we cannot correct rather than someone else equal in all respects except that he lacks the disability (Premise 2). In deciding whom to help with a scarce resource, we should try to produce the best outcome, at least when other factors are equal (Premise 3). Hence, we should help the nondisabled, other things equal (Conclusion).[2] This conclusion is meant to apply to cases in which we must choose whose life to save as well as cases in which we must decide whose illness to treat when no one's life is at

---

[1] Even if we could only compensate for but not cure their disability, the DALY measure might still be as low as it would be without compensation. This is because the DALY measure does not seem to be a well-being measure but rather a record of a physical problem, whether or not compensation makes it have little impact on well-being. If this is true, it raises concern about the use of the measure. For example, suppose one society decides to spend x amount to compensate for a disability and another society spends the same amount to cure the disability. Well-being levels might be the same in the societies, but one's DALY rating could be much higher than the other's. In such a case, should the DALY rating be at all relevant for deciding whom to help? I shall ignore the issue in this article and just assume for most of this article that higher DALY (and lower QALY) ratings reflect differences in well-being or other forms of goodness in a life.

[2] Peter Singer is a philosopher who accepts this argument and its conclusion, I believe. See his 'Shopping at the Genetic Supermarket' at http://www.petersingerlinks.com/supermarket.htm, and 'Double Jeopardy and the Use of QALYS in Health Care Allocation,' *Journal of Medical Ethics*, 2 (1995), 144–56. I thank Samuel Kerstein for helpful comments on the precise formulation of the argument.

stake. If we deny the conclusion, it seems that we must reject or modify one of the premises.

In this article, I shall examine two different approaches to The Problem and the argument from which it can arise. The first approach (which takes up the bulk of the article) focuses on the third premise. The second approach, taken up in the last section, focuses on the first and second premises. I shall focus on life-and-death cases but also discuss cases in which nonlife-threatening illnesses must be treated.

How we treat the disabled is an important general issue of social policy, affecting macro (large-scale) and micro (personal-level) decision-making. The way in which I shall investigate what general principle should govern our conduct and why will often employ micro allocation cases. But this is just an aid to identifying principles that could be used at the macro level as well.

10.1. General Background to Fairness and Outcome[3]

I shall distinguish between goodness, fairness, and justice. To make these distinctions clearer, consider the following case: A doctor must decide whether to stop a big pain in person A or a small pain in person B. She thinks, correctly, that she will do more good if she helps A. But she also remembers that yesterday B suffered a much *bigger* pain than A will suffer and no one helped B. (A suffered nothing in the past.) So she thinks it would be unfair to let B suffer again, even though she will do less (nonmoral) good if she helps him.[4] If it is overall right to do this, this means she does the morally better thing in helping him, and the state of affairs in which B is helped rather than A is morally better than one in which A is helped. We can even say it has more moral good in it, but this is not because it produces more nonmoral good.

---

[3] This overview is drawn from my *Morality, Mortality, i. Death and Whom to Save from It* (New York: Oxford University Press, 1993). See also my 'Health and Equity,' in C. Murray et al. (eds.), *Summary Measures of Population Health* (WHO, 2002) and my 'Nonconsequentialism,' in H. LaFollette (ed.), *The Blackwell Guide to Ethical Theory* (Oxford: Blackwell, 2000). The overview is intended only to acquaint the reader with some terminology and to introduce certain issues, rather than exhaustively and definitively resolve them.

[4] I am assuming that B does not have lingering effects of yesterday's pain that make his present condition worse than A's.

I distinguish justice from fairness as follows: considerations of fairness are essentially relational, for example, how is A treated relative to B? Justice is concerned with someone getting his due. I can make a situation more just but less fair by giving only one of two people his due when otherwise neither would be given his due. A particular relation between people is equality; sometimes it is fair, but other times, fairness demands inequality—as when individuals have morally relevant characteristics in virtue of which they should be treated differently.

Insofar as respect is owed to each person in virtue of only the characteristics that make her a person, it can be considered a nonrelational requirement. That is, it is owed to each independent of consideration of her relation to others. If each person is owed the respect, they will all (as a side effect) be treated equally in getting what they are owed, but not because the relation of equality between them is owed per se.[5]

An outcome can be evaluated for how fair it is, how just it is, and how much nonmoral good is produced in it. I have said that when we decide how fair an outcome is we judge how individuals fare relative to each other in it. When we consider an outcome for an individual alone, we will only be concerned with how much nonmoral good (including reduction of bad) is produced (and perhaps the justice of this) for the individual, not with the fairness of the outcome.[6] I shall use 'outcome' for individuals to refer to the difference in expected outcome for individuals produced by a resource relative to the expected outcome if it is not used.

Allocation decisions among individuals should be affected, I believe, by the urgency and need of individuals, as well as the outcome that we can produce in each person. 'Urgency' can be used (in a nonstandard way) to refer to how badly someone's life *will* go if he is not helped, and 'need' can be defined as how badly someone's life *will have gone* overall if he is not helped. A could be more urgent in this sense but be less needy than B, for example, if he would die sooner if not treated but after having had a much longer and healthier life. (It should be noted that the standard sense of urgency is probably how soon someone must be helped rather than how

---

[5] Joseph Raz has forcefully distinguished between equality as a side effect and equality as an end. See his *The Morality of Freedom* (New York: Oxford University Press, 1988).

[6] Though, of course, an individual can complain that an outcome is unfair *to him alone* because of how it treats him versus others. Some have argued that we might also consider fairness in connection with how temporal stages of a person fare relative to each other. I disagree and so will omit this consideration.

badly he will fare if not helped. I shall here use 'urgency' to encompass both meanings.)

Suppose we are dealing with two-way micro-conflict cases between equally needy and urgent potential recipients of a scarce resource, who will each give us the same outcome. Fairness, I think, dictates giving each side an equal chance for the resource by using a random decision procedure, because each person is understandably not indifferent as to whether he or someone else is helped. This is so even though the health outcome would be the same even if we were unfair.

But there may be a conflict situation in which *different numbers* of relevantly similar people are on either side and they stand to lose and gain the same thing. I believe it would be a worse state of affairs from an impartial perspective that, for example, B and C die than that A dies. But is it unfair to save the greater number without giving A an equal chance to be saved? What I call the Balancing Argument claims that, in a conflict such as this, fairness demands that each person on one side should have her interests balanced against those of one person on the opposing side; those that are not balanced out in the larger group help determine that the larger group should be saved. Hence, saving the greater number does not conflict with fairness.

An indirect argument for this conclusion is that nonconsequentialists, at least, would not ordinarily override justice or fairness pertaining to whether one person lives just in order to save two other people. For example, they would not kill one person to save two others. Yet many of these same nonconsequentialists intuitively think it is permissible to save two people rather than one. Why would they override fairness in this case but not in others by saving B and C rather than giving A an equal chance to be saved? More likely fairness does not require giving equal chances in the two-versus-one conflict, and so does not have to be overridden.

Consider another case where the interests of two people conflict with the interests of one. The potential loss to A if he dies now (ten years of life) is equal to the potential loss to one of the pair, B, if B dies now. The potential loss to the second person of the pair, C, is very small, for example, a sore throat. (All other things are equal among these people. Call this the Sore Throat Case.) To take away A's 50 percent chance of having ten years of life in order to increase overall good produced by the benefit of a sore throat cure to C fails to show adequate respect for A, I think. This is because from his personal point of view he is not indifferent between his being the one who gets the ten years and someone else getting it. (This was also the account given above for why we should give fair chances to two contestants for a good: each is not indifferent from his partial point of view about who gets the good.) This form of reasoning I am using here to justify *not* maximizing the nonmoral good we produce (by saving B and preventing C's sore throat) gives equal consideration from an impartial point of view to each individual's partial point of view, so I say that it combines objective and subjective perspectives.[7] Hence, I call it *Subjectivity*. It further implies that certain extra goods (like the sore throat cure) can be morally irrelevant, and so supports what I call the Principle of Irrelevant Goods. I think the sore throat in this case is irrelevant, that is, it is a factor that should not be considered; this is stronger than saying it is a factor that should be considered but its significance is overridden by other factors. For the latter might suggest that if more people could each be cured of a sore throat, the argument in favor of depriving A of his equal chance gets stronger. However, I think that no number of people coming into an emergency room needing sore throat cures is relevant to whether we save A's or B's life for ten years.

Whether a good is irrelevant is context-dependent. Curing a sore throat is morally irrelevant when others' lives are at stake, but not when others' earaches are. (This is consistent with a view of reasoning which says that there are background principles that tell us when some consideration which is of a type suitable to be a reason for action (i.e. a prima facie reason) is not in fact a reason in a particular context.[8]) The Sore Throat Case shows that we must refine the claim that what we owe each person is to balance her interests against the equal interests of an opposing person and let the remainder help determine the outcome. Sometimes the remainder is not determinative.

But suppose that the additional lesser loss in C is paraplegia. We should save a person's life rather than prevent someone else's paraplegia when other things are equal and these are the *only* morally relevant choices. However, perhaps it is right to together save one person's life

---

[7] As I use it, it also involves objective constraints on partialist preferences, so if someone unreasonably cares nothing for his life, we can ignore his subjective perspective.

[8] See Thomas Scanlon, *What We Owe to Each Other* (Cambridge, Mass.: Harvard University Press, 1998), 50–5. He also cites the work of Joseph Raz in this connection.

and prevent a second person's paraplegia rather than give a third person an equal chance at having his life saved. This might be because only one life will be saved no matter what we do and the paraplegia is a large loss to one person. If this were right, it would be evidence that giving someone *his equal chance for life* should not receive as much weight from the impartial point of view as saving a life when we would otherwise save no one.

A theory of the fair distribution of scarce resources should also tell us whether the fact that *one candidate* for the resource (rather than a greater number of people together) offers a better outcome than another candidate is morally relevant to deciding who gets the resource as between these two. We have so far considered what to do when additional goods we can achieve if we help one side would be *distributed over* several people. Can we revise what has been said to apply when additional goods we can achieve are *concentrated* in one person rather than another because his outcome would be better?

Some differences in expected outcome between candidates for a scarce resource should be covered by what I have called the Principle of Irrelevant Goods, I think. For example, relative to the fact that each person stands to avoid death and live for ten years, that one of the people would get a somewhat better quality of life or an additional year of life should not determine who is helped, given that each wants what she can get and other factors are equal. One possible explanation for this (which we shall re-examine later) is that *what both are capable of achieving (ten years) is the part of the outcome about which each reasonably cares most in the context*, and each wants to be the one to survive. To take away one person's 50 percent chance of having ten years of life in order to increase overall good produced by the additional year of life in another person (even if it would make the life more worthwhile and not just experientially better) fails to show adequate respect for the person who could only gain ten years. This is because from her *personal point of view*, she is not indifferent between her being the one who gets the ten years and someone else getting it (and more). Again, the form of reasoning I am here using to justify *not* maximizing the good is Sobjectivity. It gives equal consideration from an impartial point of view to each individual's partial point of view, so it combines objective and subjective perspectives. Again, whether an additional good is irrelevant is context-dependent. Getting an extra year is morally irrelevant when each can get ten, but not necessarily when each can get six months. When the extra good in an outcome is morally irrelevant, the extra good is frosting on the cake. The fact that someone might accept an additional risk of death (as in surgery) to achieve the 'cake plus frosting' for himself does not necessarily imply that it is correct to impose an additional risk of death on one person so that another person who stands to get the greater good has a greater chance to live.

In life-and-death decisions, should a *significant* difference between two people in expected outcome correctly play a role in selecting whom to help? It is not easy to explain how this is consistent with fairness, any more than depriving someone of his chance when small differences are at stake. One approach is to say that *society* should bear the loss of a small additional good in outcome for the sake of equal chances between people, but need not bear a large loss in good outcome. But suppose we are not concerned with the benefit *to society*, but only the benefits to the people who can be treated, whose good is an end in itself. Claiming that a large difference in outcome between two people counts may be analogous to the claim made above that if we could save A's life or else B's plus a third person C from paraplegia, we should do the latter. Still, in the two-person case, by contrast with the three-person case, the large additional benefit would be concentrated in the same person, who would already be benefited by having her life saved for at least the same period as the other candidate. Because of this, the additional good may at least count for less in determining who gets the resource than it does when the additional benefit is distributed to a third person, I believe. This may be on account of (1) the diminishing moral value of providing an additional benefit to someone who would already be greatly benefited, (2) the moral value of giving equal chances to different people for the most important part of a good before giving someone more than that, and (3) the lesser moral value of affecting one person rather than positively affecting the lives of more people in a significant way. There is much more to be said about this issue, and it pertains to discussion of the disabled. In particular, if differential outcome ever should make a difference in whom we select to help, it may matter *how* it comes about. For if it comes about in some ways, it may, I think, raise a particular objection, namely discrimination. I shall put off further discussion of some aspects of this issue until Section 10.4.[9]

We have examined some questions about the significance of differential outcome when need and urgency are held constant. What is the moral weight of outcome relative to taking care of the needier or more urgent? That is, what if taking care of the neediest or most urgent conflicts with producing a better outcome in the less needy or less urgent? One argument for taking differential need into account is fairness: give to those who, if not helped, will have had less of the good (e.g. life) that our resource can provide (at least if they are equal on other dimensions) before giving to those who will have had more of the good even if they are not helped. Fairness is a value that depends on comparisons between people. But even if we do not compare candidates because there is only one candidate, it can often be of greater moral value to give a certain good to a person who has had less of it. This is known as giving priority to the worst off. Rather than always favoring those who would be the worst off (a policy known as maximin), we might assign multiplicative factors in accord with the degree of need (and urgency) by which we multiply the expected outcome of the neediest (and urgent). These multiplicative factors represent the greater moral significance of a given outcome going to the neediest (or most urgent) but the nonneediest (and one not most urgent) could still get a resource if her expected outcome was very large. Alternatively, we might give such greater weight to helping the neediest only if they are at a high level of need in absolute terms and not if they are less needy, and if they are at a truly high level of need, producing any reasonably good outcome in them could have lexical priority over helping those significantly less needy.

10.2. QALYs and DALYs

QALYs and DALYs are used to measure the impact illness has on someone in terms of both morbidity and mortality; they also measure the impact of care on someone in terms of reducing both morbidity and mortality. The theory is that we can, for example, do more than merely count the

---

[9] I discuss other aspects of it in 'Aggregation, Allocating Scarce Resources, and the Disabled.'

number of years that will (we expect) be gained as a result of a lifesaving health intervention relative to what would be had without it. We could also count how good these years will be. (Note that even considering number of years is a step beyond merely considering whether a life has been saved but not considering *for how long it will be saved*.) So we may multiply the number of years of life gained by the quality of each year. Alternatively, we may determine how effective aid is by considering how badly someone's life would have gone—or as it is said how disabled he would have been—without the intervention. In this way, we see how much reduction in the disability of years we produce by the intervention. At least, in the case of a single individual, we should aim to increase QALYs and (in a certain sense) decrease DALYs.[10]

How do we measure the quality of a life or the degree to which it is disabled? Philosophers have tried to offer hedonistic, desire-satisfaction, and objective list theories of good and bad lives to answer such questions. That is, they have suggested that a life is of higher or lower quality, depending on how much pleasure/pain there is in it, how many of one's desires (regardless of the object of desire) are satisfied, or how much of certain objective goods (including but not limited to pleasure/no pain) there are in it.[11] But those who use QALYs and DALYs do not use such philosophical theories. They either take surveys of ordinary people (in QALYs) or experts (in DALYs), asking them to rate the quality of various lives with or without various limitations on them. The aim is to assign numbers to conditions. Two tests are often used in achieving this goal: the tradeoff within one life test and the standard gamble test. (I shall deal separately below with the test dealing with tradeoffs between people.) In the first test, we are asked how many years with disability X we would trade for how many years of perfect health. So, if ten years of life as a paralyzed person would be exchanged for five years as a healthy person (ranked at 1), we know, it is suggested, that being paralyzed is to be assigned a .5 quality value.

One problem with this conclusion is that this .5 value derived from 10/5 years may not be consistent over all numbers placed in the same ratio. For example, given a choice between two years paralyzed and one year

---

[10] I say 'in a certain sense,' since the measure must be used so that it does not imply that we should eliminate disabled years by simply eliminating the disabled person when this is not in his interest.

[11] See Derek Parfit, *Reasons and Persons* (New York: Oxford University Press, 1984), appendix.

healthy, one might refuse one year because five years but not one year may be a large enough good to make the exchange worthwhile. So one at least needs to find the cutoff point above which the ratio holds. But above this cutoff point, a similar problem may arise: for once the healthy years gotten are much above five, it may be that someone will accept them, even if the disabled years they give up result in a ratio less than .5. Still, the tradeoff test can make clear that people would exchange some length of life for some increased quality of life (or disability reduction).

The standard gamble test asks one to imagine what risk of death one would take (e.g. in surgery) to exchange some length of life at one level of quality/disability for the same length at a higher quality/lower disability. For example, is a 40 percent chance of death and a 60 percent chance of perfect health equivalent to a 100 percent chance of life with significant paralysis? The greater the chance of death one would take to achieve perfect health, the worse is the state from which one is escaping, presumably.

Let us consider the DALY, in particular. Suppose the following: perfect health is rated at 0; wearing glasses raises one's disability level to .001; severe paralysis (paraplegia) raises one's disability level further so one is disabled to .5.[12] Having this information may be important in deciding not only how much good we can do if we aid (or how much badness will occur if we do not); it may also, some might claim, help us decide whom to aid when we cannot aid everyone. For example, if we think it is fair to give priority to helping the worst off (not necessarily overall worst, but perhaps only healthwise worst), it is important to know that paralysis is worse than wearing eyeglasses. If we ranked paralysis no lower than wearing eyeglasses and DALYs were the only relevant consideration, we could not argue in favor of investing in cures or preventions for paralysis rather than nearsightedness (a macro decision) or treating a person to prevent paralysis in an emergency room rather than prevent nearsightedness (a micro decision). Of course, even if we would reduce DALYs more if we treated paralysis rather than nearsightedness, the cost of doing so may be much greater, and hence the DALYs reduced per dollar (cost effectiveness of allocating) might be greater if we instead treated nearsightedness. (If this were so, it would also imply that for every one paralysis we cure or

---

[12] DALYs will assign a 1 to death; QALYS assigns it a 0. Neither system seems to take account of the fact that some states in life could be worse than death and so deserve a negative number in QALYs and something above 1 in DALYs.

prevent we could cure or prevent hundreds of cases of nearsightedness. I shall return to this issue below.)

Notice that I have mentioned both curing and preventing a disability. It would seem reasonable to think that one would want to avoid (and hence prevent a disability) in accordance with how bad it would be to have the disability, and hence how much one would want to be cured of it if one had it. If one knew that should one fall into state x, there would be no good reason to try to leave it, would it be reasonable to want to avoid it? Surprisingly, the answer might be yes, as going into the state might be disruptive of one's current plans, but once in it one alters one's plan so that there is no more reason to leave state x. Avoiding disruption of current plans might be the only reason to avoid state x. Dan Brock has suggested that this is one reason why nonparalyzed people rank paralysis as worse than people who are already paralyzed.[13] If avoiding disruption of current plans were the only reason, or at least a contributing reason, to avoiding paralysis, it would not be unjust for society to put a higher value on preventing a nonparalyzed person from becoming paralyzed and a lower value on either curing a paralyzed person or preventing paralyses in newborns who had no life plans. (Another less normative and more purely psychological finding might be pointed to in this connection. Psychologists Daniel Kahnemann and Amos Tversky report that subjects ask higher compensation for undergoing an injury ex ante than ex post.[14] That is, when asked how much they would want in order to go through some loss, they ask for more than they ask as compensation once they have suffered the loss.)

However, suppose that those with disabilities had to engage in less intrinsically valuable activities, and/or had diminished freedom to choose among activities because some options were unavailable to them though their remaining options are intrinsically good ones. These might be reasons why a disability is as bad whether one already has it or whether one is still to get it, and they might be reasons why curing a disability is as important as preventing it. In any case, in what follows, I shall assume this is so. Note that the way I would determine that a disability is bad has nothing to do with ranking 'normality' as always good. A normal

[13] See Dan Brock, Working Paper for the Harvard Center for Population and Development, 1997.
[14] See Daniel Kahnemann, 'The Cognitive Psychology of Consequences and Moral Intuition,' Tanner Lectures in Human Values, 1994 (unpublished).

person has only two hands and cannot fly without mechanical assistance. One might have more freedom to engage in worthwhile activities if one had four hands and wings, and so normality is disfavored relative to the enhanced condition.[15]

Some who recommend employing DALYs and QALYs also believe that, in allocating, we should give priority to helping those who are worse off, even if we do not produce as good an outcome (e.g. as much of a reduction in DALYs) as we would achieve if we helped those who would not be as badly off. This could happen if we could not completely alleviate the condition that makes someone be worse off. Hence, concern for lowering DALYs to some degree and helping the worse off are not incompatible. But helping the worse off need not follow *just* from trying to minimize DALYs, if we reduce fewer DALYs in the worse off than in those already better off because we cannot completely cure the worse off.

10.3. The Principle of Irrelevant Goods

But now consider the following scenario: One person is on island A, and another person is on island B. They share all the same properties, except that one just recently lost a hand and the other did not. Because his loss is so recent, they share equally good pasts. We can save the life of either one but not both. Arguably, each will be as badly off as the other if we do not help him since each will be dead, having lived the same length and quality of life. But if we help the person without the hand, we do not produce an outcome with as few DALYs as we would produce if we saved the other person. (*Call this the Islands Case.*) I think it is morally wrong to decide whom to aid on this ground. We cannot rely on the principle of giving priority to the worst off to account for this conclusion, since each would, arguably, be as badly off as the other if not aided. However, the Principle

---

[15] *Wanting* a cure for a longstanding condition could be an indication that the cured life is thought to be better even by the disabled person, though it might just indicate a desire to be like the majority. However, if the majority were disabled and they desired a cure, this would be even stronger evidence that the condition is worse than the nondisabled one. It is possible that some disability makes someone's life worse *physically*, but knowing that she is thought of as a target of cure makes her life *psychologically* worse to an even greater degree. Then it might not be in her overall interest to target funds to cure her. (I thank David Luban for emphasizing the latter point.)

of Irrelevant Goods that I described in Section 10.1 can account for the right decision.

(A somewhat different view of this case stems from the claim that the badness of death as an event depends on how much good it deprives us of. Since the person who has not lost his hand is deprived of a slightly better future, it might be argued that death per se is slightly worse for him, though, of course, this is only because in his case the event of death itself imposes a total loss, a part of which (loss of a hand) the other person has already suffered. If the person who has a hand suffers a worse fate in dying, then helping the person who in this sense will be worse off would also lead us to help him. However, I think that considering how big a loss of future goods someone will suffer in dying is the wrong way to determine who will be worse off. It just tells us who will benefit more from being saved.)

The explanation of the correct decision in the Islands Case may be the same as described in an earlier application of the Principle of Irrelevant Goods: what both people are capable of achieving (and hence the loss they are capable of avoiding) is the part of the outcome about which each reasonably cares most. Put differently, what is reasonably held to be most important to each person can be had by either—long life saved with good quality of life. Furthermore, we should take seriously from an objective point of view the fact that each person, from his subjective perspective, wants to be the one to survive. Fairness may require, therefore, that we not deprive either of his equal chance for the great good of extended survival for the sake of the additional benefit of a hand in one person. This benefit is irrelevant in this context, though perhaps not in another. This is especially true when that one person who would get the additional benefit is someone who would already be getting the other great benefit of additional life. (That is, it is a case of a good concentrated in one of the two rather than dispersed over a third person.) *I shall call this the Major Part Argument*, for either can get the major part of what stands to be gotten.

It might be suggested that an analogy to this case is one in which only one of two people can be chosen to avoid great poverty. Each could reach a high income, but one could become somewhat richer than the other because he has more talent. One might argue that avoiding great poverty by achieving sizable wealth is the major part of what is at stake for each,

each person understandably wants to be the one to be helped, and so the additional wealth that only one can achieve becomes an irrelevant good for purposes of choosing whom to help, at least when we are only concerned with these two people.

This case, of course, is disanalogous in that it does not involve a life-and-death choice. However, it reminds us that the Principle of Irrelevant Good could also be applied to a *nonlife-and-death* case in which we must choose whether to treat a nonlife-threatening illness, such as gastritis, in a disabled person or a nondisabled person. (We are supposing that the drug to treat gastritis is scarce and we cannot treat both patients.) Suppose we could cure this illness as well in the person who lacks a hand as in the person who has two hands. One way to apply the Major Part Argument to this case leads to the conclusion that so long as each will have a life with the major part of what it is reasonable for each to want in life, each should get an equal chance for the treatment.

However, the nonlife-and-death cases also raise other issues. For example, the person who recently lost a hand might be worse off without treatment for gastritis (given that he will then have to deal with *two* problems) than the person with two hands would be.[16] This, it might be suggested, could give one a reason to favor treating the disabled person, even though we could cure the gastritis equally well in both.[17] However, as the disabled person without treatment might still have the major part of what each person wants in life, favoring the worse off person seems to go beyond the Major Part Argument per se.

Most importantly, when we can treat nonlife-threatening illness equally well in a disabled and nondisabled person, the *difference* we make in outcome by treating could be exactly the same, regardless of whom we treat. It is

[16] I first discussed cases of this sort in arguing against Thomas Scanlon's view that it is only how the treatment we have to give bears on the problem it is meant for in each candidate that is relevant to its allocation, in my 'Owing, Justifying, and Rejecting,' *Mind* (2000). Different issues about whether to give priority to helping the worse off person would arise if the person without the hand had lived without it for a long time in the past as well (or even instead). I shall not discuss these different issues in this article.

[17] However, defending such a reason would require showing that it was consistent (*a*) not to hold someone's lacking a hand against him because it is irrelevant and (*b*) to hold his lacking a hand in his favor because it is a relevant burden. For, if (*a*) is correct, why is it not also correct that the person with both hands person has an extra good that is irrelevant when it comes to choosing against him in the matter of preventing gastritus? I was prompted to think of the issue by Carlos Soto's work on the tension between compensating for past disability but ignoring it in future outcomes in life-and-death cases. See his 'Choosing Whom to Save' (unpublished manuscript).

true that if we treat the nondisabled, a person with a 1 QALY ranking may result, and if we treat the disabled instead, a person with no more than a .9 may result. But if we had not treated the nondisabled, he would have been alive with close to 1 ranking anyway.[18] And if we do not treat the disabled, we are left with someone alive with the lower QALY-rated life (at an even lower level than it would be with gastritis treatment). It is only if treating the nondisabled, for example, led to other good effects (healthwise or nonhealthwise) that would not occur in the life of the disabled that there would be a difference in outcome relative to what would occur without treatment.

At the least, on the basis of the Islands Case, we can see that it is compatible with recognizing that not having a hand makes a life worse and makes an outcome worse, other things equal, to also think that, relative to the question of whose life we should save, not having a hand could be a morally irrelevant consideration. Hence, targeting funds to replace a missing hand because life without it is worse (e.g. harder) than life with it, other things equal, is not inconsistent with giving equal weight to saving the lives of the disabled and the nondisabled. This is contrary to what a simple use of DALYs in distributing scarce resources would predict. This way of dealing with The Problem (p. 261 above) accepts the first premise in the argument that gives rise to The Problem, and even the second premise. It rejects the conclusion because it rejects the third premise, as it claims that differences in outcome are not always morally relevant to how we should decide to distribute a scarce resource. Hence, it is part of a nonconsequentialist moral theory which tells us that the right act is not necessarily the one that maximizes good consequences.

10.4. Larger Disabilities and the Principles of Irrelevant Goods and Treatment Aim

A. I applied the Principle of Irrelevant Goods to the Islands Case as an explanation of why we ought not to decide whose life to save in that case

---

[18] Presumably, we are not interested merely in creating perfect specimens, as this would commit us to curing minor conditions in the almost well rather than making big differences to those who are very badly off though they will never be perfect.

on the basis of the fact that one person is disabled and the other is not. Does the principle, in fact, truly account for the range of our judgments about whether disabilities should make a difference to whom we help?

Consider a case involving *a larger disability*. We must choose between saving the life of someone who has just recently become paraplegic (assumed, for sake of argument, to be rated at QALYs .5 on the basis of a tradeoff argument) and a person who would be saved to a perfectly healthy life (QALYs 1). They can live an equal number of years. Suppose we agree that the paraplegic would live a worse life than a nonparalyzed person who merely has to wear glasses, other things equal. Hence, if the issue were whether to give him resources to cure his paraplegia or to provide some other equally costly services to eliminate someone's need for glasses, we should treat the paraplegic. That is, we should move someone up from .5 (given some significant change) before we move someone from .999 up to 1. This is consistent, it might be said, with the claim that when the paralyzed person's life and the perfectly healthy person's life are at stake, the difference in their expected quality of life is morally irrelevant in deciding whom to aid. That is, it might be said that when the prospect each faces is to fall to 0 on a QALYs rating (death), it is a significant good merely to achieve .5, and a person should not be deprived of the equal chance he wants to get that good merely because someone else could achieve that good plus an additional benefit that even brings him to a 1 QALY rating.

Why might this be so? Can we say, in this case, as we could in the Islands Case, that what each would get is at least the major part of what both stand to get, and the difference is frosting on the cake? But if one person can be saved to perfect health and this difference is (assumed to be) equivalent to another .5, does this not mean that the .5 achievable by both is *not* the major part of 1? Of course, one must have traversed from 0 to .5 before he can go further, so .5 is a prior good in that sense. But we cannot say that there is diminishing marginal good in going further than .5, if reaching the top is specifically ranked as twice as good as being at .5.[19] Certainly, it would be reasonable to take a much larger risk of falling from

---

[19] This is compatible with its taking many more goods or avoidance of evils to go from .5 to 1 than it took to go from 0 to .5. In this sense, there may be diminishing marginal good. This is analogous to its taking only $500 to reach level .5 of well-being due to finances but $1,500 to reach to level 1 of well-being due to finances because, once one has $500, it takes much more than an additional $500 to make one twice as well off.

.5 to 0 (dying in surgery) in order to achieve a life rated at 1, than it would be reasonable to take in order to go from .5 to .6 (achieving mere frosting on the cake).

In response, it might be said that it may be morally more important to give someone the basic goods that help him avoid the worst evils and *make a life worth living* than to give him the goods that admittedly double the overall value of his life. Analogously, it may be *morally* more important to give someone their first $500 than to give them whatever amount of additional money (e.g. $1,500) that doubles the value of his life due to finances. Hence, without claiming that a life QALY-rated at 1 provides less than twice the good as .5, we can claim that *moving someone from 0 to .5 is morally more important than moving him from .5 to 1.* Another way of putting this point might be that it is having a life worth living that is of crucial significance, and if paraplegics can have this, they have what is relevant to deciding to give equal chances for life, given that the paraplegic and the normal person, from his personal point of view, each wants to be the one to have a life worth living. I call this argument for giving the disabled and nondisabled equal chances *the Moral Importance Argument* because it emphasizes the moral importance of giving people chances at what is most important in life.

The partially analogous argument in the case of income would claim that avoiding extreme poverty and having a reasonable income is what is most important. Hence, we should give equal chances to escape extreme poverty to someone who will achieve middle-class income and to someone who can, with a combination of what we provide and his superior talent, become a millionaire. This assumes that each wants to be the person chosen and we are only concerned with these two people.

As this is not a life-and-death case, it reminds us of the case of choosing whether to treat a nonlife-threatening illness, such as gastritis, in someone else who has recently become paraplegic or treating the same illness equally successfully in a nondisabled person. One way to apply the Moral Importance Argument to this case implies that as the paraplegic whose illness is treated would have those things that it is most important to have as much as a nondisabled person whose illness is treated, each should be given an equal chance.

It is beyond the scope of the Moral Importance Argument to take account of the possibility that someone who will be paraplegic should be given priority in avoiding the additional burden of the gastritis over someone who will not have the additional problem of paraplegia with which to cope. Taking account of who will be worse off, however, might well be a relevant consideration in deciding whom to aid in this nonlife-and-death case. Again, the most important point in nonlife-and-death situations is that, if we can treat the gastritis as successfully and there are no further differential effects of nongastritis in the disabled and nondisabled, we make the same difference in outcome with treatment relative to what the outcome would have been without treatment whomever we treat.

B. Another argument for sometimes ignoring the move from .5 to 1 in life-and-death cases is as follows. Suppose one can only have a life rated at .5 and not 1, and the alternative is 0 (death), which is very bad. One may reasonably want .5 as much as one would want 1 if one could have it. So, for example, given that .5 is all that one can have and 0 is very bad, one might reasonably do as much to achieve .5 (e.g. spend as much money, suffer as much) as one would do to achieve 1 if one could have it. This is consistent with the willingness to even risk losing .5 and falling to 0 for a chance at 1. That is, the fact that one would risk 0 to get 1 instead of .5 does not show that one would be more likely to risk 0 in other pursuits (e.g. risky leisure activities) because one would only be losing a life rated .5 instead of 1. Hence, a paraplegic might reasonably choose to risk death in order to get a better life for himself as a nonparalyzed person because *he cares more for* (in the sense of prefers) the nonparalyzed life, though he *will not care about* this nonparalyzed life, if he gets it, any more than he *cares about the life he already has*. This shows that 'if one can have only *x*, one cares about it as much as one would care about *y* if one had it' is not equivalent to 'one cares to have *x* as much as one cares to have *y*.'[20] All this may seem

---

[20] This argument implies that when .5 by itself is compared with 0, it is worth some maximal sacrifice x, and when 1 by itself is compared with 0, it too is worth x. This suggests that by the measure of sacrifice, and relative to 0, .5 = 1. But that does not mean that .5 is equivalent to 1 per se on all measures. For example, we could give up .5 for 1 and also risk going from .5 to 0 to get 1, but (obviously) not risk going from 1 to 0 to get .5. This argument could even be taken to generate an intransitivity, that is, .5 = x, 1 = x, −(.5 = 1). But the supposed intransitivity is explicable because of the effects of different contexts; that is, because different alternatives are available: .5 is worth x in a context where 0 is the only alternative, 1 is always worth x, .5 is not worth as much as 1 because when both are alternatives to 0 for a given person, .5 is not worth x, given that sacrifice x should be made to get 1 instead of .5.

paradoxical, yet I think it is true.[21] This supports the claim that willingness to take an intrapersonal risk in order to achieve a better life does not translate into imposing a risk on someone for the sake of achieving that better life in another person.

The failure to appreciate this may be the result of not distinguishing two different notions of the worth of life. First is the notion that involves evaluating lives as better or worse, where all properties of the life are included in this evaluation of the worth of the life. Second is the notion of the worth of life or going on living to someone. Here, the quality of the person's life—which might be referred to as composed of a set of synchronic properties that modify any period of her life—is treated as a background condition, and we ask whether going on living for a certain period of time—which might be referred to as a diachronic property—is worth as much to her as it would be to someone who had different synchronic properties. The claim is that going on living could be worth just as much to someone who has a less favourable set of synchronic/quality properties as to someone who has a more favorable set.[22] This implies that going on living, at least as a self-conscious person, is a separate good for someone to be distinguished from other quality-of-life goods that his life may be instrumental to achieving. The value of the continuing life to a person is not, to a large degree, affected by the instrumental properties of the life.

However, there *are* quality-of-life goods, and someone who lacks them might exchange some length of life to get these goods. This does not mean that he cares less for continuing life per se than someone who already has those quality-of-life goods. There are also some conditions (such as extreme unending suffering) that might negate or override the value of continuing to live as a person.

Notice that some lives are worth living (e.g. an additional three happy months of life), but it might not be reasonable for the person, whose only alternative it was, to sacrifice as much to save it as to save a long life rated 1.[23] Hence, it is not always reasonable to do as much to get one type of

---

[21] I thank Susan Wolf, David Sussman, and other members of Philamore for discussion of this point.

[22] This claim may be in some tension with the view that the badness of death is a function of how much it deprives us of.

[23] I owe this point to David Sussman.

worthwhile life, even if it is all one can get, as it would be reasonable to do to get another type of worthwhile life. Hence, in this additional argument, it is not merely having a life worth living that is crucial. On account of this, I shall call the additional argument the *Sufficiently Good Only Option Argument*. If either the Sufficiently Good Only Option or the Moral Importance Argument is correct, it helps expand the reach of the Principle of Irrelevant Goods. These arguments let us see how the Principle of Irrelevant Goods can be used to argue for treating equally those with large disabilities, even when the Major Part Argument cannot be used to support the Principle of Irrelevant Goods.

What does the Sufficiently Good Only Option Argument imply for cases in which we must decide whether to treat nonlife-threatening gastritis in someone who is recently paraplegic or someone who is nondisabled, other things equal? It seems to imply that if life as a paraplegic without gastritis is a sufficiently good only option, then we should give equal chances to this person and the nondisabled person. It might also be argued that since the paraplegic would have to cope with two problems if he also had gastritis but the nondisabled person would have to deal only with gastritis, we should favour the disabled person when deciding whom to treat. This view, however, goes beyond what the Sufficiently Good Only Option Argument itself implies. Again, in nonlife-and-death cases, the most important point is that if we can treat the gastritis as successfully and there are no further differential effects of nongastritis in the disabled and nondisabled, we make the same difference in outcome with treatment relative to what the outcome would be without treatment whomever we treat.

However, consider a problematic implication of the Major Part, Moral Importance, and Sufficiently Good Only Option Arguments in life-and-death cases: They seem committed to treating sufficiently good diachronic options in the same way as they treat sufficiently good synchronic options. That is, large differences in how long someone can live if we save him could make no more difference to whom we should save than large differences in quality of life, other things equal. For example, suppose one person can be saved to live for five years and another for fifty years and everything else is equal between them. Five years is a very significant good, and, given it is someone's only option, they might well do everything to get it that someone who could live for fifty years would do. Hence, if there is a moral difference between disregarding expected length of life and disregarding disability status (or many other quality-of-life factors), another argument than those we have considered is needed to justify this.

C. Here is one possibility. Each person is entitled to equal respect and (at least for purposes of an impartial distribution of scarce resources) equal concern. That may mean that (at least certain) synchronic properties, such as whether one is paralyzed or not, even assuming that they significantly affect quality of life, should not bear on selection for scarce resources. If these synchronic properties are appropriately thought of as determining one's identity, one might say that equal respect makes identity irrelevant for purposes of allocation. (*Call this the Principle of Irrelevant Identity.*) However, taking into account how long a person can live if he gets a scarce resource is not treating someone differently because of the type of person he is qualitatively; the latter (it is being suggested) is done only if we consider someone's synchronic properties (that provide the character of his time alive). It is compatible with each synchronic type that people could be, that they could have it for longer or shorter amounts of time, at least theoretically. However, this does not rule out that having a certain synchronic property could cause longer or shorter life. For example, having a disability might make impossible doing exercises necessary for longevity. This is what I call linkage—a causal relation between a disability (or any other property) and other effects that are morally relevant to allocation. One does not, I think, hold against someone his synchronic property per se, if one takes account of its causal links. This argument does not focus on the worth of living to someone; it offers an interpretation of meeting the requirements of equal respect and concern, so I shall call it the *Equal Respect Argument*. In another way, it attempts to extend the Principle of Irrelevant Goods while distinguishing quality and quantity considerations.[24]

Does the Equal Respect Argument have implications for cases where we must decide whose nonlife-threatening illness should be treated? One possibility is that equal respect and concern for different types of people

---

[24] How long someone will live is not a quality of a life such that someone might say that we are discriminating against those who will not live long, at least when we are deciding so as to determine whether there will be a long or short life. A context in which we would be discriminating against those who will not live long is refusing them admission to a park more than we refuse admission to those who will live long, even though both can make equally good use of the park.

implies giving equal chances for treatment of gastritis to the disabled and nondisabled person. However, equal respect and concern need not mean equal treatment but rather treatment as an equal. Suppose the disabled person who is to be treated as an equal would suffer more healthwise overall than a nondisabled person if he has gastritis because he also must deal with a disability. Possibly equal respect and concern *itself* implies that the disabled person should be given priority for treatment. Again, it is also important to remember that in nonlife-and-death cases, the difference in outcome with treatment relative to outcome without treatment can be the same, whomever we successfully treat.

D. We have considered the results of the Major Part, Moral Importance, Sufficiently Good Only Option, and Equal Respect Arguments, and the Principle of Irrelevant Goods they support. Are these results consistent with what, I believe, is standardly understood as the correct account of a nondiscriminatory policy? This account says that if a treatment whose aim is to correct a particular problem (e.g. gastritis, upcoming death due to kidney failure) is equally successful in achieving that aim in a disabled and nondisabled person, the difference in outcome represented by the continuing presence of the disability is irrelevant. I shall call this the *Treatment Aim Principle*. It is one way to yield the result noted above, that in nonlife-and-death cases, we can make the same difference in outcome relative to what the outcome would have been without treatment, whether we treat a nonlife-threatening illness in disabled or nondisabled.

However, for various reasons the Treatment Aim Principle differs from the other principles so far considered. First, the Principle of Irrelevant Goods could imply treating candidates equally when the Treatment Aim Principle would distinguish between them. This is because even if the aim of treatment is to correct a particular problem, the Principle of Irrelevant Goods would imply that some differences in the degree to which *that* particular problem is successfully treated could also be morally irrelevant in deciding whom to treat. So, if one person's gastritis could be treated slightly less successfully than another's, this might be morally irrelevant to who gets the treatment. Alternatively, another way to apply the Moral Importance and Sufficiently Good Only Option Arguments is to argue that if the most important part of the good of treatment is possible in either candidate, or if each could get a sufficiently good improvement due to treatment, we should not select on grounds of different success in treating. If this were true of a difference in treatment outcome between two nondisabled candidates, it should also be true that the difference is not what determines a selection between a disabled and nondisabled candidate. A similar conclusion could be drawn about life-and-death cases where one candidate would go on to live somewhat longer than another.

What if we could treat fatal or nonfatal illness much more successfully in one person than in another? The Treatment Aim Principle should favor the person in whom treatment is much more successful. For example, suppose that someone's disability interfered with his doing exercises that needed to accompany a drug that treats gastritis, and so his treatment would not be successful. It takes this as a reason to help the nondisabled person. The other principles I have considered need not lead to this result, if they are combined with giving priority to the worse-off person. But the Treatment Aim Principle is inherently in tension with an argument based on the importance of need in deciding whom to aid (i.e. priority to the worse off) when treatment is less successful. In the case of lifesaving treatment, giving priority to the worse off could direct us to give a successful lifesaving treatment, or even one that is significantly less successful, to the person who would be overall worse off if he did not get it (in terms of years lived) rather than to someone else (who would die at an advanced age, for example). By contrast, the Treatment Aim Principle by itself not only ignores this other consideration but seems to exclude it. It implies that we should just consider what our treatment itself can do for people, rather than considering additional problems (e.g. dying much younger or having an additional problem with which to cope) that one person would have rather than another.

Putting to one side the issue of helping the neediest and continuing our assumption that the disability is recent, let us consider other cases in which treatment of fatal or nonfatal illnesses will be much more successful in the nondisabled than in the disabled person. Then both the Treatment Aim Principle and the other principles I have considered could favour the person in whom treatment is most successful, even if it is due to his disability that the treatment is much less successful in the disabled person. This is an example of linkage—a causal relation between a disability and other effects that are relevant to allocation decisions. Consider first life-and-death cases. Suppose that if we give a scarce, life-saving organ to a nondisabled person, he will live twenty years. If we give it to a disabled person, he will live five years because his disability makes it impossible to do as good surgery on him and/or because he cannot do certain exercises subsequent to surgery. In this case, the Treatment Aim Principle, as well as the Equal Respect Principle, can recommend giving the organ to the nondisabled person. In this sort of linkage case, we are not holding against the disabled person his disability as a lived component of his life but rather considering its causal effects on how many years someone will live if he is treated. This is no different from considering the causal effects of being *non*disabled—a state which is considered preferable to disability in itself—if it were imagined to directly cause a much poorer length-of-life outcome of a lifesaving surgery. In the latter case, according to the Treatment Aim and Equal Respect Principles, the surgery should be performed on the disabled person.

Consider a nonfatal illness. Suppose that someone's disability prevents a successful surgery to correct gastritis. Then the Treatment Aim Principle could recommend allocating the scarce surgery to the nondisabled person. The same conclusion might be yielded by one way of applying the Sufficiently Good Only Option Argument if the outcome of treatment did not make a sufficiently good improvement in the disabled person due to his disability.

However, there is another way linkage can occur and be relevant to allocation of scarce resources and that the Treatment Aim Principle does not capture. Suppose that a disabled person and a nondisabled person each have a fatal disease X and can be treated equally well for it, so that X does not lead to a shorter life in one person than another. However, the disability on its own will result in death shortly after disease X is cured. Strictly speaking, treatment of disease X is equally good in either patient, and so the Treatment Aim Principle should be neutral as to whom we treat. But presumably, it is wrong not to take account of the fact that the very same negative factor that our treatment seeks to avoid—namely, death soon—will occur anyway, though from a different cause. The Treatment Aim Principle by itself does not distinguish between helping someone who will succumb in a few weeks to another illness and someone whose successful treatment implies that he will live for twenty years. By contrast, the other principles that I have discussed can recommend that the nondisabled person get the scarce resource in such a case.

What if a scarce treatment for a nonlife-threatening illness that causes a lot of pain can work equally well in a disabled and nondisabled person, but the disabled person will wind up with the same degree of pain caused by his disability alone. Again, the Treatment Aim Principle, strictly speaking, would recommend not distinguishing between the two candidates, but the principles that I have discussed need not do this.

E. To avoid these problems, we would have to modify the Treatment Aim Principle to what I have called a *Treatment Similarity Principle*, which would focus on whether we could cure a fatal or nonfatal illness without there being conditions similar to the ones we aimed to cure occurring in the patient in any case. (The Treatment Similarity Principle, however, will not correctly deal with a case in which we could successfully treat a *nonfatal* disease equally well in a disabled or nondisabled candidate, but his disability will soon cause the disabled person *to die*. This is because while the soon-to-occur death should undercut the candidacy of the disabled person, this is not because a negative condition *like the one* we are trying to treat will occur in any case from a different cause. Further modification, which I shall forgo, could correct this problem.)

So far, I have discussed the role of linkage in making it permissible to deny a scarce resource to a disabled person, whether we are using the Treatment Aim Principle or other principles I have discussed. But linkage involves a disability having a causal relation to some other property relevant to allocation. The Treatment Similarity Principle shows us a way in which the disability property itself (i.e. the synchronic property) could sometimes be morally relevant to the allocation decision. Suppose a nonfatal disease will cause paraplegia and also pain; and we are interested in treating it in order to prevent both of these bad states. We can prevent the pain equally effectively in either a paraplegic or nonparaplegic candidate, but the fact that we can successfully prevent the disease from attacking the nerves in either candidate results in the prevention of paraplegia only in the candidate who is not already a paraplegic. If avoiding paraplegia is the most important part of our aim, it could be morally correct that the disabled person not be a candidate for the treatment. Furthermore, this is not because of the further causal effects of his disability but simply because of (what I call) the role of disability as a *component of his life*. We have previously seen that the Treatment Similarity Principle extends the limits of the Treatment Aim Principle. Now we see that it also sets a limit to the Principle of Irrelevant Identity (that I introduced in connection with the Equal Respect Argument). It accounts for why it may sometimes be permissible to deny a scarce resource to someone who is disabled because he is disabled per se.

Consider again the Treatment Aim Principle. Arguably, a treatment can be considered less successful even if it achieves its aim, if it has bad enough side effects. Suppose that giving scarce nonlifesaving treatment to a disabled person will result in a bad side effect caused by the interaction of treatment with his disability. The bad effect is not so bad as to totally outweigh the good the treatment does him. A nondisabled person will get the same good effect without the bad side effects. The Treatment Aim Principle might imply that we should help the nondisabled person. The other principles I have discussed could imply the same if the side effects were significant enough.

In the next section, I shall consider further the possible role of side effects of treatments on the allocation of scarce resources to the disabled versus nondisabled.

10.5. More Grounds for not Ignoring Disabilities When Allocating Scarce Resources

A. Suppose that the Principle of Irrelevant Goods implies that we should not prefer saving an unparalyzed person to a paraplegic person (other things equal). Then it would also imply that we should not prefer saving a paraplegic who, as a good side effect of lifesaving treatment, will also be able to walk again, as opposed to a paraplegic who will just as successfully be saved but will remain paraplegic. That is, if we rely on the Principle of Irrelevant Goods to argue for giving equal chances to disabled and nondisabled candidates, despite the difference in possible outcomes represented by the presence of the disability in one candidate, then the Principle will also imply *no role for comparable differences in expected outcome among equally disabled candidates*. It also implies no role for such differences in outcome between equally nondisabled candidates—so if one unparalyzed person would become paraplegic as a bad side effect of lifesaving treatment but another would not, this should make no difference in whom we choose to save. (I call these cases in which the disability condition of a person changes as a result of treatment the Switch Cases.) Are these results correct?

These Switch Cases raise the following possibility: (1) Sometimes a sizable extra good or bad (even of a synchronic property) *that we can produce* in the outcome if we treat one person rather than another can be morally relevant in deciding whom to help. (2) Yet, if candidates for treatment who present themselves have this difference in good or bad between them, and this is why it shows up in the outcome, the extra good or bad should be morally irrelevant in deciding whom we treat.[25] The Principle of Irrelevant Goods cannot account for the simultaneous truth of (1) and (2). I call this the Asymmetry Problem.

Proponents of the view involving both claims (1) and (2) need a principle that will explain why the fact that a person is disabled should be irrelevant in deciding whom to help and if it were relevant this would be (invidiously) discriminatory against the disabled, but the presence of a disability or nondisability in an outcome can sometimes be morally relevant and used nondiscriminatorily in deciding whom to help. A principle that explains it might also imply that it is permissible to save the life of the paraplegic who will, through the procedure that saves him, become nonparaplegic rather than to save the life of the nonparaplegic who will, through the procedure that saves him, become paraplegic.

There could also be Switch Cases and an Asymmetry Problem in nonlife-and-death situations. For example, suppose that a scarce drug that prevents impending blindness will also cure paraplegia in one candidate but not the other. Alternatively, the same scarce drug could be imagined to prevent blindness in either nondisabled candidate but cause paraplegia as a bad side effect in only one candidate. These Switch Cases are meant to contrast with one in which we can prevent blindness in either someone who has recently become paraplegic and will remain so or in someone who will remain nondisabled. In these cases, the principles suggested earlier imply that either equal chances should be given or we should take into account that someone will have a much harder life if he will be both paraplegic and blind rather than just blind. The Principle of Irrelevant Good and other

---

[25] With exceptions already described, such as those explained by the Treatment Similarity Principle. This role for the quality-of-life properties conflicts with the view presented in my *Morality, Mortality, i* (n. 3 above).

principles discussed earlier might be understood to imply that we should ignore the good and bad side effects in allocating the drug, in nonlife and death Switch Cases, at least on the supposition that blindness is a significantly worse fate than paraplegia.[26] Those who support claim (1) and (2) in nonlife-and-death situations will also need a principle that makes these compatible.

Even someone who thought a difference in outcomes such as disability should not matter, regardless of how it comes about, might be interested in seeing if we can distinguish a *discrimination objection* to counting the difference from a more general objection to counting such a difference in outcome based on the Principle of Irrelevant Goods. One claim about these Switch Cases might be that sometimes, even if we incorrectly violate the Principle of Irrelevant Goods in taking account of certain differences in outcomes, we would not be engaged in (invidious) discriminatory conduct. Our conduct might be wrong but not because it involved discrimination.

We have already seen that because the Treatment Aim Principle tells us to ignore disability when the aim of treatment is equally satisfied, it suggests that when disability causes a worse outcome of treatment for another condition, it is not discriminatory to select a nondisabled candidate. We also suggested that the Treatment Similarity Principle implies that when the disability is another cause of the type of condition that we are aiming to treat, or is itself the type of condition we are aiming to treat, it is nondiscriminatory to allocate a drug to the nondisabled person. Nevertheless, favoring the nondisabled person in these cases may still be a mistake, if the differences in outcomes between candidates should be irrelevant goods.

It is important to realize that the Asymmetry Problem raised by the Switch Cases does not depend on another issue I have discussed, that is, the fact that, prior to being disabled, people rate the disabled state as much worse than people do once they are disabled. It might be thought that it is because the disabled person who comes for treatment rates his life equal to the nondisabled person but the nondisabled person rates the same disability we will produce in his future as very bad that an asymmetry problem arises in the Switch Cases, at least when lifesaving

---

[26] If this were not true, we might imagine that the drug prevents impending blindness *and* deafness on the supposition that these together are worse than paraplegia.

treatment would make a nondisabled candidate disabled.[27] But this is not so, because *I am holding constant the negative value of the disability in those already recently disabled and those who will be newly disabled.* So, I am assuming that the life of the already-recently disabled is worse than the life of the nondisabled, other things equal—that is *the reason why* a new disability should be avoided—and yet it could still be wrong to treat differently two people just because one is nondisabled and the other is already-recently disabled. Nevertheless, sometimes, though the continuation of the disability is as bad as its future occurrence, our producing the new disability might provide a reason to favor the candidate who will not be disabled.

B. It will be useful to first present a range of cases and the judgments in each for which I am trying to account. I shall try to defend the judgments, in part, by finding a principle that not only accounts for them but fits with a plausible account of respect for persons. Let 'P' stand for paraplegia and 'U' for unparaplegia in the following cases in which we must decide to whom to give a scarce lifesaving procedure that would be equally good at saving all the lives. Table 10.1 covers Cases 1–3.

In Case 1, a lifesaving procedure will save A or B, but not alter *their* initial status as paraplegic or not. I shall assume (given what was said above) that we should not favor B because a better outcome will result (one with more QALYs) and choosing B for this reason would constitute impermissible discrimination.

In Case 2, we select between nonparaplegic people, but only in the case of C will the lifesaving procedure also cause paraplegia. In this case,

Table 10.1. *Cases 1, 2, and 3*

Persons

A	B	C	D	E	F
P	U	U	U	P	P
↓	↓	↓	↓	↓	↓
P	U	P	U	U	P

Table 10.2. *Case 4*

Persons

C*	D*
U	U
↓↓	↓
P	U

Table 10.3. *Case 5*

Persons

E*	F*
P	P
↓↓	↓
U	P

[27] This explanation would not help with the case in which the paraplegic will become non-paralyzed.

I believe some (who agree with the conclusion in Case 1) might decide it was permissible to save D on the basis of the fact that we would thereby get a better outcome because we would avoid harming someone. (This is so even if one could reasonably want to go on living just as much if one were to be in condition P as if one were to be in condition U.)

In Case 3, we select between two paraplegics, but only in the case of E will the lifesaving procedure have the additional good effect of curing her paraplegia. In this case, I believe some might think it permissible to save E on the basis of the fact that we thereby get a better outcome by producing a cure of paraplegia. (Differentiating between candidates in Case 2 may be less plausible than doing so in Case 3, I think. That is because the harm we would do to C is less than the harm that would befall him if he died.)

Notice that Case 2 differs from Case 4 in Table 10.2. In Case 4, the second arrow leading from U is intended to symbolize the fact that C*'s paraplegia is not caused by the lifesaving procedure, but rather by an independent cause that would have resulted in paraplegia so long as C* lived. It is possible that those who would save D rather than C in Case 2 would nevertheless see Case 4 as morally like Case 1: while the state of person C* when we treat him is unparalyzed, he is the sort of person who, independent of anything that we do, will become paraplegic. I believe that in this case, those whose judgments I am examining would say that we should *not* decide to save D* on the basis of his better outcome.

Similarly, Case 3 differs from Case 5 (Table 10.3). In Case 5, the double-lined arrow leading from P to U is intended to symbolize the fact that E*'s unparalyzed state is not caused by the lifesaving procedure but rather by an independent cause that would have resulted in nonparalysis so long as E* lived. It is possible that those who would save E rather than F would nevertheless see this case as morally like Case 1: while the state of E* when we treat him is paraplegia, he is the sort of person who, independent of anything we do, will be unparalyzed. I believe, in this sort of case, those whose judgments I am considering would say we should *not* decide to save E* on the basis of his expected better outcome. That is, Cases 1 and 5 are morally alike. There should be no difference in how we decide to allocate a lifesaving resource just because one person is permanently paraplegic and the other is only temporarily paraplegic *in this way*. However, to be 'temporarily paraplegic' because our lifesaving cure can also sometimes cure paraplegia has, it might be argued, different moral significance. (Cases analogous to 4 and 5 involving nonlife-and-death situations could be constructed. For example, someone who will become paraplegic independent of what we do is competing for the drug to prevent blindness with someone who will remain nondisabled. And someone who will outgrow his paraplegia is competing for the drug to prevent blindness with someone who will remain paraplegic.[28])

10.6. The Causative Principle

A principle that can account for the responses I have described in the preceding cases can be referred to as the Causative Principle. It tells us to decide which people to help based on the difference we can make to their situations, not on the difference they bring to the situation. (By 'we,' I do not mean doctors in particular, but the health care intervention system generally.) More precisely, the Causative Principle is concerned with the differential effect of our treatment in causing disability or producing nondisability, even though they are just side effects of a treatment meant for other purposes. (The Causative Principle implies that we are entitled (though not obligated) to bring about a better outcome by using our skills in this way. The Causative Principle could also take account of our causing someone to remain U who would otherwise have changed from U to P.) It tells us to ignore these differences in outcome that arise in any other way, whether because the disability inheres in the person or will arise because of what inheres in him, or even will arise from causes outside of him other than the treatment. For example, if we know a criminal will do something to one unparalyzed person to make him paraplegic if he lives, we should ignore it. The difference we make does *not* include every change that will occur in their lives through other causes that follow on what we do to them. This is all against a background in which the outcome that results is still one that is both a life worth living, reasonable for someone to do a great deal to retain, and that can be compared with

---

[28] I have used paraplegia in discussing the Switch Cases. But it is possible that only if we could cure a worse disability (e.g. quadriplegia) would it be appropriate to respond differently to cases in which a better outcome occurs as a result of our curing a disability as opposed to our saving a person who is not disabled. I am only concerned with whether such causation ever matters morally, not so much with when it does.

others for length of life. (See above discussion for a defence of these factors.)

For convenience, I will just say that the Causative Principle tells us to 'ignore who the candidates are, as evidenced by the synchronic properties they have and will have, and look to what we do.' The Causative Principle can be combined with a limited use of the Principle of Irrelevant Goods in that some differences we cause are still morally irrelevant if they are relatively too small.

In Case 1, we save life in the paraplegic person as much—by hypothesis, no more than and no less than in terms of length—as we save life in the nonparaplegic person, and we do not cause nonparaplegia in the nonparaplegic person. By contrast, in Case 3, we cause the additional large good of nonparaplegia in one patient. In doing this, we produce a nonparalyzed life *by saving a life and by making it unparalyzed*. In Case 1, when we save the life of a nonparalyzed person, we produce a nonparalyzed life *by saving a life that is nonparalyzed*; the better outcome *piggybacks* on a property the person brings with him.

In nonlife-and-death cases, there is the comparable difference between (*a*) an outcome in which a person is nonparalyzed and not blind because we piggyback in preventing blindness in a nonparalyzed person and (*b*) an outcome in which a person is nonparalyzed and not blind because we cure paralysis as well as prevent blindness.

One proposed justification of the Causative Principle is that when outcomes are affected by who a person is and/or by what we do, counting only what we do is consistent with respect for different types of persons (described above), at least so long as what we do is significant. Counting the qualitative differences that the people themselves bring is not consistent with respect for different types of persons, *except*, for example, when the difference results in a life below a certain minimum (e.g. not worth living, not worth doing a lot to save) or there is significant conflict with the Treatment Aim and Treatment Similarity Principles. We can reasonably value paraplegia less than nonparaplegia as a state, so as to count it against allocation when we produce it, without treating a person who is or will be (through causes independent of us) in the disvalued state less well because he is in the state. This is like hating the sin, but not the sinner. Admittedly, valuing the nonparaplegic state more than the paraplegic state can have a worse consequence for one person than for another, if we accept the

Causative Principle. For if we use these values to choose whom to aid when we can, for example, do more good for one paralyzed person by making him unparalyzed, the person who will not be cured of paraplegia will not be given the scarce lifesaving or blindness preventing resource. (This contrasts with valuing the nonparaplegic state more than the paraplegic state, and so choosing *to create* a nonparaplegic person rather than a paraplegic person. Here no paraplegic person will exist to be negatively affected by our choice.)

Notice that the Equal Respect Argument said that choosing whom to save based on how long each of the people will live is consistent with respect for different types of people, and no distinction was drawn between extra life being (1) something we produced (e.g. by being able to do a certain type of procedure on one but not another person), and (2) something that results only from what the person brings with him (e.g. extra genetic hardiness). It is only in dealing with the synchronic properties that characterize the time a person lives that, it is suggested, we should distinguish between producing and piggybacking in order to act consistently with equal respect for persons.

Here is an illustration of the Causative Principle on a large scale. Suppose there is a volcano erupting on an island. We could either save 100 people on the left side of the island or 100 on the right, but not both. In Case A, the people on the left are paraplegics, the people on the right are not paralyzed (and the groups are equal in all other respects). The claim is that we should choose randomly if we are not to invidiously discriminate. In Case B, the people on both sides are paraplegics, but because of the peculiar circumstances, if we save the people on the right, we will unparalyze them; if we save the people on the left, we will not unparalyze them. The Causative Principle implies both (*a*) that it is permissible to choose to save the people on the right because they will be unparalyzed by what we do and (*b*) that, even if it were impermissible to do this, it would not be because it discriminates against paraplegics. (It might be impermissible because, for example, the Principle of Irrelevant Goods rules it out on the ground that in a life and death contest, paraplegia is an irrelevant difference.)

We could now re-examine the Islands Case (discussed in Section 10.2) to see whether our judgment there is really best explained by the Causative Principle rather than by the Principle of Irrelevant Goods. The test is to see whether our *correcting* the loss of a hand while saving someone's life could help determine which one of two people we save—one whose lost hand we could not correct and one whose hand we could correct in saving him. If such effectiveness should matter to our choice in this case, then *not* distinguishing between the people in the original Islands Case would only reflect the inappropriateness of distinguishing between people when we do not cause the difference between having a hand or not. By contrast, if the difference in what we can do would not be relevant to our choice, it is the moral irrelevance of the differential good that is crucial. I think the difference between having a hand or not is an irrelevant good in the Islands Case, even when we would correct its absence in one person, and so it is the Principle of Irrelevant Goods rather than the Causative Principle that accounts for our judgment in that case.

10.7. Treatment Aim Principle Modified

As a preface to introducing the Switch Cases, we noted that it is possible that a treatment is often considered more or less successful depending on whether it has bad side effects, even if it achieves the aim of treatment per se. This raises the possibility that the Treatment Aim Principle might also be able to deal with the Asymmetry Problem raised by the Switch Cases.

Suppose that if we use a certain treatment for a deadly heart problem in one paralyzed person, but not if we use it in another, it also cures his paralysis. This was not our original aim. For this reason, the Treatment Aim Principle might seem to be equally satisfied whichever paralyzed person is treated. However, it might be argued that, once we know that the drug can treat two conditions (heart failure and paralysis), we could *aim* at treating them both. Since we cannot achieve both our aims by treating the person who remains paralyzed, this would imply that we do not violate the Treatment Aim Principle in not giving him a chance for treatment of his heart condition. (Another way of looking at this case involves the Treatment Similarity Principle: the person who remains paralyzed has a condition that is like the one we are trying to treat. This could be true if the cause of paralysis in the two people differs.)

But how would the Treatment Aim Principle explain, in a different case, treating the unparalyzed person who will not become paralyzed rather than the one we will paralyze? It might simply be said that successfully treating someone is a function not only of achieving the treatment's aim but also of avoiding bad side effects of treatment. I am not certain that this modification is consistent with the spirit of the Treatment Aim Principle. This is because in this case the bad side effects in one person will not be as bad as the death she will otherwise face, and ordinarily one would not refuse to treat the more serious problem just because a less serious side effect will occur. It is only the fact that someone else will not have the bad side effect that tempts us not to treat.

However, if these modifications were successful, then what I shall call the *Treatment Aim Principle Modified* would result. It may overlap, at least in part, with the Causative Principle. And both have to be constrained by the Principle of Irrelevant Goods, I believe, for minor differences that we cause in treating or achieving the aims of treatment may be morally irrelevant when what is at stake is a chance for a great good that could be had by either patient.

The Treatment Aim Principle Modified could also apply in nonlife-and-death cases. Either we turn the additional large good side effect into a further aim or we judge a treatment more successful if it avoids a significant bad side effect.

10.8. Intrapersonal Quality/Quantity Tradeoffs

Now, consider a further modification of the lifesaving Switch Cases. Suppose that in Case 6, G and H have a disability giving them a QALY rating of .25. We can save G and also undisable him by using a scarce resource in a particular way, but it would reduce the number of years he can live to five. He has the option of going through this procedure or a different lifesaving procedure. The latter is the only one open to H and it uses the scarce resource differently, so that either person could live for twenty years but remain disabled (.25). If G chose the latter, nonswitch option, we should give him and H equal chances for the procedure using the scarce resource. However, it is not unreasonable for G to trade some extra years of life for improved quality of life. If it were true that the disability reduced the QALY rating of a life to .25, then it would not be unreasonable for G to take the switch option with five years of life. Suppose

Table 10.4. *Case 6*

Persons		
G	H	B′
P	P	U
↗ =↓	=↓	>↓
20P 5U	20P	5U

he takes (what I shall call) this *Switch-and-Reduce option*. Should we then continue to give him an equal chance to receive the lifesaving resource? I believe so. After all, it makes it possible to cause in him as much good (though in a different form, combining quality and quantity in a different way) as will be the result of helping H.

Suppose the Causative Principle is correct (or at least not invidiously discriminatory) for some quality properties, and it is also permissible to choose between people on the basis of a big difference in quantity (such as the fact that one will live five years but another will live twenty years), when other things are equal. Then, giving G and H equal chances when G takes the Switch-and-Reduce option is consistent with still *not* giving equal chances to H and B′ in Case 6 (which is a modified version of part of Case 1) when H will be paralyzed but live for twenty years and B′, who is and continues to be *un*paralyzed, will live for only five years. Hence, though G, when he chooses the Switch-and-Reduce option, has the same outcome as B′, he is given an equal chance to be saved relative to H, but B′ would not be given an equal chance relative to H (see Table 10.4). In the case we have considered, when a person chooses a certain quality/quantity tradeoff that we can produce, the higher quality is allowed to compensate for the reduction in quantity. By contrast, the higher quality is not allowed to compensate for the lower quantity when the quality is due to piggybacking, at least according to principles for allocation that I have so far discussed.

What if G had no choice to make between five and twenty years because we could only save him by using the scarce resource in a way that makes him nondisabled (i.e. he goes from .25 to 1) and gives him five years of life? I think that if causation should matter, then this combination of goods, whose quality part, at least, we cause, should result in G having an equal chance relative to H, even if B′ should be disfavoured relative to H.

This would mean that it is not just respect for someone's choosing one option rather than another and giving up longer life that justifies allowing intrapersonal aggregation of quality and quantity to affect interpersonal allocation of lifesaving resources.

If we were able to unparalyze G without reducing his life expectancy from 20 years, he should choose this option over either 20 years paralyzed or 5 years unparalyzed, other things equal. But if either of the latter options merits giving G an *equal chance* for the resource, should not his getting the 20 years unparalyzed that is agreed to be the much better option and whose quality component we cause, imply that we do not discriminate if we favour him for the resource?[29]

There are also Switch-and-Reduce Cases in nonlife-and-death contexts. For example, suppose that one of two paraplegic candidates for a scarce resource that could permanently prevent blindness also has a further option: If we deliver the drug in a certain way, it will also cure his paralysis but at the cost of less successful retention of vision (e.g. he will have only half the years of sightedness of the other candidate). It might well make sense for someone to trade off some vision for some years of free mobility. Each of the candidates should have had an equal chance for the resource if both would remain paralyzed and have as good prevention of blindness. It seems that if a candidate chooses to produce a balance between two aims that makes intrapersonal sense, he should not lose his equal chance for the resource. However, if someone who was all along not paralyzed could be saved from blindness only half as long as a paralyzed candidate for the blindness cure, the principles we considered earlier suggest that he should not get an equal chance for the scarce resource. An outcome that is a result of piggybacking on nonparalysis is treated differently from an outcome one produces, if the Causative Principle is correct.

---

[29] We shall consider G and H again below. The Switch-and-Reduce Cases are derived from my initially considering a scenario in which a paralyzed person who will remain paralyzed and will live twenty years gets a lifesaving resource rather than someone who will remain unparalyzed but live for only five years because we abide by one of the principles discussed in Section 10.3. After getting the resource, the paralyzed person opts for a separate surgery that he knows will cure his paralysis but reduce his life expectancy to five years. Presumably, we would not want to rule out his possibly reasonable choice of the surgery simply on the ground that he is opting for an end state identical to the one that resulted in someone else being deprived of a chance equal to his for the scarce resource. Yet, the case seemed problematic to me.

The Treatment Aim Modified Principle might yield the same conclusions, if producing unparalysis became a second aim of the treatment. It would be considered invidiously discriminatory to give a blindness treatment to a nondisabled person that turns out much better in a disabled person, other things equal. Yet, it seems not to be invidiously discriminatory to give a treatment to a disabled person because we can count the change in his disability status as an aim of treatment that compensates for the reduced effectiveness of treatment for blindness. (If the Treatment Aim Principle were not modified and it focused on only how we achieve the original aims of blindness prevention or life saving, it would not make the same prediction as the Causative Principle.)

To summarize, the Switch Cases and the Causative Principle make it possible for QALYs to be used in allocating scarce lifesaving and nonlifesaving resources interpersonally, even though candidates' expected life years and achievement of original treatment aim were the same, because we could cause a significantly improved quality in one candidate. The Switch-and-Reduce Cases make it possible for QALYs to be used in allocating lifesaving and nonlifesaving scarce resources interpersonally when candidates' expected life years and achievement of original treatment aim are different, if each candidate's outcome is equivalent by the intrapersonal quantity/quality (that-we-cause) tradeoff test.

10.9. Problems for the Causative Principle

Consider Case 7 (Table 10.5). Case 7 is one in which if we save the paraplegic, we will also cure his paralysis, whereas if we save an unparalyzed person we will just save his life, there being no paralysis to cure. Here the outcomes are the same, but *we* produce a significantly larger difference if we treat the paraplegic than if we treat the unparalyzed. Our treatment is, in that sense, more effective with him. The Causative Principle, as presented above, therefore, tells us to save the paralyzed person rather than the unparalyzed. However, I think this is the wrong conclusion and there is no good reason for favoring one over the other.

When the same outcome (U) will come about in the case of the other candidate (albeit not because of our causative power), the benefit of having

Table 10.5. *Case 7*		Table 10.6. *Case 8*	
Persons		Persons	
I	J	K	L
P	U	U	P
↓	↓	↓	↓
U	U	P	P

U as an outcome can be achieved whichever person we choose. This seems morally important, not whether we causally contribute to U. *What motivates the Causative Principle is not pride in our causing more good, but a permission to seek a better outcome for someone when we can cause U without violating moral side constraints.*[30]

Though we achieve the lifesaving aim of treatment equally in both candidates, suppose we acquire two aims once we learn of the additional effect that can be achieved in one patient. Do we then also satisfy the Treatment Aim Principle Modified better if we treat the paralyzed person? One may find it hard to believe that someone who holds the Treatment Aim Principle Modified would claim that his aim of having nonparalyzed people is not satisfied when someone simply remains unparalyzed in the course of treatment. If so, the Treatment Aim Principle Modified would not give weight to how much more good we cause when we treat the paralyzed person in Case 7. On this interpretation of this principle, one's aims can be achieved other than by what one strictly does. This

---

[30] Here is a way in which we should *not* explain our judgments about Case 7: Disaggregate interpersonally and turn the greater difference we make intrapersonally into a greater difference we make interpersonally. If we disaggregate, we claim that the two-person choice case is like the three-person choice case. That is, Case 7 is treated as though it is equivalent to the following case:

$$\begin{array}{ccccc} U & & P1 & + & P2 \\ \downarrow & v & \downarrow & & \downarrow \\ & & & & (\text{core of} \\ & & & & \text{paralysis} \\ & & & & \text{only)} \end{array}$$

In this disaggregated case, we choose between saving the life of an unparalyzed person or saving the life of a paraplegic who remains such and also curing paraplegia in a third person who does not need his life saved. In this case, where the additional good is distributed over a third person, I believe the extra good done could permissibly determine our choice of whom to help. But if this conclusion carried over to Case 7, it would imply that we should save P rather than U, and I think this is wrong.

interpretation of the principle raises a problem, however. For suppose it were true that one of our *aims* would be achieved even by other than what we strictly do. Our original Case 1 involved a paralyzed and unparalyzed person who would remain in each one of those ways if saved. Could we form the aim of having unparalyzed people though we cannot bring nonparalysis about in either but say that our aim is achieved independently of what we strictly do by the person who remains unparalyzed? This would conflict with the assumption that saving the unparalyzed person in such a case is discriminatory. It seems, therefore, that the Treatment Aim Principle Modified faces the same problem with Case 7 as the Causative Principle because, strictly speaking, our treatment does achieve more in the paralyzed than the unparalyzed person.

Now, consider Case 8 (Table 10.6). In this case, we would do harm in the life of an unparalyzed person if we save her when we also cause her to be paraplegic and do no additional harm to an already paraplegic person in saving him. The Causative Principle here tells us to favour treating the paralyzed person, but I think there is no moral reason to do this, since the final outcomes are the same.

Does a similar problem arise for the Treatment Aim Principle Modified? It seeks not to produce bad side effects in treatment and this may imply giving greater weight to paralysis that is a side effect than to the paralysis that remains unchanged with treatment. But one could think that this implication is wrong, for an aim of avoiding paralysis is equally poorly achieved whoever is treated in Case 8. However, suppose we allow bad states that we do not strictly produce to count equally with those that result from our treatment. Then in our original Case 1, where we must choose between saving a paralyzed and unparalyzed person who would each remain so, it might be said that we fail to achieve our aim of unparalyzed people if we save the paralyzed person. But it was assumed that favoring the unparalyzed person in Case 1 would be discriminatory. Hence, the Treatment Aim Principle Modified has to distinguish between caused and not caused states, and this is what leads to a problem with Case 8.

Similar results hold for a nonlife-and-death case. If we can prevent someone from going blind and also cure his paralysis, the Causative Principle and the Treatment Aim Modified Principle seem to imply that we should help him rather than help an unparalyzed person from going blind. However, I think there is no good reason to favor one over the other. In addition, if we can prevent a paralyzed person or an unparalyzed person from going blind, but the cure will cause paralysis in the unparalyzed person, the two principles suggest that we should avoid the treatment that has the worse side effect. Yet, given that both will wind up paralyzed, I think there is no good reason to favor the paralyzed person over the unparalyzed one.

Suppose we accept the implications that the Causative Principle has for cases such as 3, but reject its implications for cases such as 7. Then, we will have to find a principle to account for both sets of judgments.

10.10. The Principle of Irrelevant Identity

What can we substitute for the Causative Principle (and Treatment Aim Principle Modified) that accounts for all the cases? Here is a suggestion: The important point is that what the person is (consisting not only in what he is now but what he would become due to causes independent of us if he survives) should not determine whether he is saved, so long as the outcome that can come about through helping him is significant (e.g. a life for which it is reasonable to take important risks, rather than saving someone already in a permanent coma). This does not mean that the outcome does not matter per se, only that we do not let the differences in what the person is, independent of the change we make, make a difference to whom we save. This has two implications. When the outcomes expected in different individuals are different, to pay attention to anything but the causative difference we make would be to make the difference in them affect our decision of whom to aid. Hence, we can abstract from who they are by attending to the causative component. Or, alternatively, we can imaginatively add the good property that one party is missing into his outcome (or imaginatively subtract the good property the other party has from his outcome total). But when the outcome we expect in different individuals is the same, to attend only to the causative difference we make (from how they were or would have been independent of us) results in the differences in who they are playing a role in deciding whom to treat.

That is, when the bottom line is the same, paying attention to the difference we make is an indirect way of treating people differently on the basis of who they are. Showing that we need do less to reach a given bottom line (outcome) implies that the person had more to begin with, and so the Causative Principle would say, for example, that we should not treat equally someone who had more good to begin with.[31] It holds against the person who is nondisabled the fact that he is nondisabled, since this is what makes there be less of a difference that we make in his being alive and nondisabled. If we do not want who the person is to count against him or for him when outcomes are the same, we could imaginatively add (in our calculation) the disability condition to one person who actually lacks it or take it away from the other who actually has it. Then the causative difference we make would be the same in each. But we achieve the same result by just attending to the fact that the outcomes are the same.

Notice, however, that our cases are consistent with the identity of individuals still making a difference to, for example, how each of two people compare with a third. For example, in Case 1, B, who remains unparalyzed, will not be favoured for the scarce resource over A, who remains paralyzed, but in Case 3, E, whom we switch from P to U, can be favored over someone identical to A. The person who remains U has the same outcome as the person who switches to U, but they have different prospects relative to the someone who remains P. This means that it is only the identity that U and P bring to the circumstances that is determining their differing chances relative to someone who remains paralyzed.[32] This has the result that in 'within-type' contests, for example, between paralyzed people, certain factors, such our making someone unparalyzed in the outcome, can count in favour of a candidate that cannot count in 'between-type' contests. Hence, when we say that 'we do not want who the person is to count against or for him when the outcomes would be the same,' we must mean 'when the outcomes would be the same for the contestants for the resource in a pairwise contest.'

---

[31] It is very important to repeat that I continue to imagine that the disabled person has (only recently) become disabled (and also that the nondisabled person has always been nondisabled). I do this in order to avoid the issue of one candidate being needier than another because, if he is not aided, he will have lived a worse life, other things equal, in having lived for a long time as disabled. If we were to give some priority to helping the person who would be worse off if not aided, this could be a reason to hold someone's having lived a long time nondisabled against him in a choice between him and the disabled. Though this would not be true if only quantity and not quality of life considerations should play a role in evaluation of need in life and death choices. But I have constructed the cases so that this is not a factor.

[32] I owe this point to Gideon Jaffe.

Table 10.7. *Case 9*

Persons		
B	F	E
U	P	P
↓	↓	↓
U	P	U

Similarly, recall that in the Switch-and-Reduce Case 6, B had the same outcome (U for five years) as G (U for five years). They fare differently relative to H (with an outcome of P for twenty years), with B disfavored and G treated equally, if we use the Causative Principle. This is because of their starting points. Yet, if what has been said about Case 7 is correct, if we had to decide whether B or G gets the scarce resource, each should be given an equal chance. One difference that Case 6 introduces is that, when the quality property is something we cause, it can aggregate with quantity to determine the outcome that is relevant to an interpersonal allocation. This is what accounts for equal chances between G and H, even though their outcomes are only alike in QALYs terms.

What if the three types of people in Cases 1 and 3 are present at once? For example, consider Case 9, where each will live equally long (Table 10.7). It would seem that E may be chosen over F on grounds that we cause a better outcome without either one's identity counting for or against him. Then it is a toss-up between B and E, because we would hold the identity of B against him if we favor E. If B wins this fair toss-up, F cannot complain at the lack of an equal chance with B because there is sufficient reason why he is eliminated from the contest by E. Why do we choose this way of proceeding rather than the following way: Start with a toss-up between B and E, which B might win, and then have a toss-up between F and B that F might win? I believe the answer to this is important: We may decide on the basis of which path leads to the best outcome so long as it does not hold anyone's identity for or against him.

Hence, the dominant point of the discussion in this section is that we should treat persons so that who they are (their type-identity, but also more generally, what type they will be independent of the change we make) does not count for or against them, on the assumption of the life being one for which it is worth making sacrifice. This only sometimes commits us to the subsidiary Causative Principle. To capture this dominant point in a principle, I shall use the *Principle of Irrelevant Identity*, which was originally introduced in connection with the Equal Respect Argument. Note that we are concerned with abstracting from what people are, independent of the change we make, though we are still concerned with achieving the best outcome.

Usually, abstracting from characteristics people have or will have independently of what we do and treating them equally is associated with theories of individual rights; they try to capture that it is certain characteristics that all and only persons have which are sufficient for certain forms of treatment (whatever other characteristics the person has). But these theories of rights are also associated with ignoring outcomes entirely. The limited form of abstraction from outcome (i.e. abstraction from what people are independent of what we do) that we are considering contrasts with these rights theories.

Indeed, the fact that we are still concerned with outcome can help us place the point of the Principle of Irrelevant Identity in its proper context. One may put this as follows: (1) We aim at doing what results in the best outcome, (2) on condition that we not hold someone's identity for or against him. [Failing in (2) will defeat our pursuing the aim in (1).] (3) Abiding by the Causative Principle is important when it defeats the charge that we have not met the condition in (2). (That is, the Causative Principle defeats the defeater of (1), thereby allowing us to proceed with (1).) (4) However, if we focus on the Causative Principles more than as a way of meeting (2), we will also violate (2). (These points are reflected in the path that we took in deciding what to do in Case 9.) This all also implies (roughly) that rather than focusing on whether we *cause* a good or bad outcome, we should focus on whether we *cause* a (significantly) better (or worse) outcome than would otherwise exist among any of the candidates. If not, give equal chances. (Determination of whether we cause a better outcome can involve aggregation of quality we cause and quantity as evidenced by the Switch-and-Reduce Cases.)

I have used life-and-death cases in trying to deal with problems raised by the Causative Principle, but the same points apply to nonlife-and-death cases.

10.11. Causal and Component Role of Identity in Relation to the Principle of Irrelevant Identity Once Again

When I originally introduced the Principle of Irrelevant Identity in connection with the Equal Respect Argument, I pointed out that the Principle did not rule out *linkage*, that is, it permitted counting relevant differences causally due to a person's identity. This is quite independent of *our* causing differential effects. I also said that it was a permissible limit on the Principle to take account of the noncausal, component role of who the person is in accordance with the Treatment Similarity Principle. Let us review these points again, now that we have discussed our producing the favored or disfavored conditions.

A. Distinguishing between (*a*) what the person is and (*b*) what results we will produce abstracted from what he is, need not necessarily prevent our attending to results that occur *due to what he is*. The problem of invidious discrimination can arise because of the disability someone brings to the treatment situation as a *component of his life*, without it arising if we do not abstract from its causal role. So, for example, suppose that if we save a paraplegic, he will remain a paraplegic and live two years, but if we save a nonparaplegic, he will remain nonparaplegic and live for ten years. Assume they are alike in all other morally relevant respects. Even if the fewer years alive we can expect from the paraplegic are entirely due to his being paraplegic (i.e. the physical condition affects the success of lifesaving treatment), it need not be discriminatory to take the fewer years into account in the allocation decision. This is linkage. It takes account of paraplegia's effects (its causal role) on quantity of life, but it is consistent with not attending to the synchronic properties of paraplegia (for example, not being able to walk, being in more pain, and whatever else are components of life of the paraplegic in virtue of paraplegia during the years he lives) in deciding how to allocate a scarce lifesaving resource. The causal effects could also include other disabilities. For example, suppose that the drug that could save life causes blindness in the disabled person, but not in the nondisabled person, due to an interaction between the disability and the treatment. This difference in outcome that we can produce in the two candidates might justify giving the scarce resource to one candidate rather than another, and so not constitute invidious discrimination. This is so even though it involves making use of the value judgment that it is worse to be blind than not to be blind when judging the outcome we produce. (It was noted that the Treatment Aim Principle Modified would also take account of bad side effects in deciding whom to treat.)

Obviously, to make this account work, more would have to be done to distinguish the characteristics of a condition from its effects. One cannot just identify effects as those things not distinctive to that condition (i.e. not living long is an effect that has many causes), because characteristics not distinctive of a condition (occurring in other conditions, too) can be components of a condition.

The distinction between the causal role of a disability and its component properties is also crucial in answering one potential objection to the Principle of Irrelevant Identity.[33] It may be said, if our treatment cures paraplegia in addition to saving a life only in one person and not another, this must be because of some difference between the two people, for example, an allergic reaction in the second that blocks a cure. Therefore, to let the difference in outcome count makes the difference between people count, and is that not contrary to the Principle of Irrelevant Identity? But, I would argue, there can be a moral difference between counting against someone his allergy's synchronic properties, as a *component* in his life, and counting the allergy's *causal* effect. Only the former involves treating people differently because we dislike the allergy they have, independently of our causing its presence.

That we are not here holding the disability that someone would have (independently of what we do) against him as a component of his life is further reinforced, I argued earlier, by considering something that improves a life when it is considered as a component. For example, suppose painfreeness adds positively to a life, and yet painfreeness is caused by a protein that interacts badly with our lifesaving treatment and so causes paraplegia or much shorter life. Ignoring painfreeness as a good component

---

[33] The objection was raised by Douglas MacLean and John Broome.

and so not discriminating in favor of the people who have it would be consistent with attending to its effect. Deciding not to help the person with painfreeness because of its causal effects would not constitute discrimination against him on grounds of his painfreeness.

B. I also suggested that there could be cases in which identity as a component feature may permissibly count in selection because the component feature is like one that it is the aim of the treatment in question to deal with. When such identity factors are used as a basis for selection, there may also be no invidious discrimination.

Suppose one candidate is weak due to the effects of kidney disease and the other is hardy since his kidney disease has not progressed as far. We can prevent the kidney diseases from killing each patient equally well but this will (suppose) not reverse past damage. Assume this means that both candidates will live as long, but one will be weakly, the other hardy. Could the Treatment Aim Principle (modified or not) imply that it was permissible to choose the hardy candidate, because it is one aim of fighting kidney disease to stop the loss of hardiness. Selecting the hardy over the nonhardy candidate might be permissible, even if we may not choose just any candidate (e.g. a nonblind over a blind one) who gives us an overall better outcome. If we caused the hardiness in one patient but not in the other, taking account of it could be in accord with the Principle of Irrelevant Identity. But in this case we do not cause the hardiness; the patient is already hardy. However, in curing kidney disease, *we prevent* the loss of hardiness, as (I assume) weakness is one eventual result of not treating the kidney disease. So, in that sense, *we can cause continuation of hardiness* in one patient but not have the same good effect in the other patient. (By contrast, our treatment for kidney disease would do nothing to continue nonblindness in a nonblind patient.) Hence, the Treatment Aim Principle (modified or not) and the Principle of Irrelevant Identity seem to be satisfied if we favor the hardy patient. (This still leaves it open that, relative to death, whether one will be hardy is an irrelevant good.)

Now, suppose that there are two patients who must be treated for fatal kidney disease—a patient who is weak and one who is hardy. The first patient's weakness is not due to the kidney disease. It has another cause that could not have been affected even by a kidney cure that reversed past effects of kidney disease. We can cure the kidney disease equally effectively in both, and this means that we can prevent the weakness *due to kidney disease* equally in both persons. The Principle of Irrelevant Identity seems to imply that we should ignore the weakness that preexists from another cause. The Treatment Aim and Treatment Aim Modified Principles agree; the first because we cure kidney disease as well in each and the second because there are no differential good or bad side effects of our treatment in each.

However, the weakness that has another cause is *like* one of the effects of the disease that we are trying to treat. After all, it may be said, one of the reasons we treat kidney disease is to prevent not only death but continual weakness; we can prevent that state (by stopping the kidney disease) in one patient, but we cannot prevent that state in the other patient because it is overdetermined. (We can stop weakness *from kidney disease* in him but not from the other cause.) The Treatment Similarity Principle says that when we can prevent in one person, but not the other, a state that is like one that gives us a significant reason to try to treat a disease, it is not wrong to ignore the fact that the difference is due to an identity factor. (If this principle has any role to play, it should still be constrained by the Principle of Irrelevant Good, so that at least small differences do not make a moral difference. It remains open that something like curing weakness in one person but not another is too small to make a difference relative to avoiding death.)

Now suppose, counterfactually, that paraplegia was one effect of kidney disease that gave us a reason to prevent the disease. If one candidate were a paraplegic as a result of some other event in his life besides the kidney disease, then our treatment of his kidney disease would not cure or prevent his paraplegia the way it would prevent or cure the paraplegia of a second candidate. Suppose that in our previous case it would be permissible to treat the hardy candidate as opposed to a candidate weak due to causes other than the kidney disease, despite equal success at treating the effects of his kidney problem. Then it would also be permissible to treat the nonparaplegic patient rather than the paraplegic patient in the present example. The Treatment Similarity Principle is here overriding the Treatment Aim and Treatment Aim Modified Principles. However, since we cause the unparalyzed person to remain unparalyzed—he is not merely piggybacking on his initial unparalyzed state—it is consistent with the Principle of Irrelevant Identity.

10.12. Views of Discrimination and a Decision Procedure

The previous discussion implicitly gestures towards *three possible understandings of (invidious) discriminatory conduct*. The *first* possible understanding tells us that acting in any way on the differential value attributed to being nondisabled or disabled is discriminatory. But this would imply that common surgeries undertaken to cure people of paraplegia are discriminatory conduct if we perform them because we think it is better to be unparalyzed than paralyzed. I believe we should reject this first suggestion. Rejecting it helps us see how the claim of discrimination against the disabled differs from the claim of racial discrimination. For a claim of racial discrimination could be supported just by showing that our act was undertaken because we believe it is better to be white than to be black per se (i.e. independent of any other facts, such as having to live with negative social attitudes to blacks). Notice that this discriminatory attitude to blacks relative to whites could be present even if we were deciding *only between blacks* who should get a scarce resource. This would be true, for example, if we decided to give a scarce lifesaving resource to one black person rather than another because it had the side effect of turning him white. (This implies that the fact that we are only choosing between paraplegic people in Case 3 does not, by itself, settle the question of whether we would be engaged in discrimination by deciding to help the person who will stop being paraplegic.)

The *second* possible understanding of discriminatory conduct tells us that acting on the differential value attributed to being nondisabled or disabled when this makes the person who will be disabled worse off than he might otherwise have been (for example, losing a scarce resource he might have gotten on a coin toss) is discriminatory. This understanding of discrimination would rule out the Causative Principle and the Principle of Irrelevant Identity.

If we think this is wrong, we could endorse a *third* possible understanding of discrimination: It is discriminatory to act on the differential value attributed to being able or disabled as a component of someone's life, if that component is not like what we aim to treat, when this makes the disabled person worse off than he might have been because of what he is or would be, independent of what we do. It leaves it open that the value of a component can sometimes count for or against someone if we cause that component (even if this further implies that those in whom we cause a component, for example, are favored relative to someone else when those who have the same component independently of what we do do not get favored in the same way).

Notice that the Treatment Aim and Treatment Similarity Principles can lead to someone being worse off than he would have been because of his disability, but only indirectly because his disability *is disvalued per se* relative to nondisability. For example, it was pointed out that a positively valued state (e.g. hardiness), as much as a disability, could reduce the effectiveness of our ability to treat an illness. And if a disability is another cause of a condition that it is our aim to treat, this could also be true of a positively valued state (e.g. hardiness). Whether the state is negatively or positively valued, the Treatment Aim and Treatment Similarity Principles could prefer the individual without the state that has these effects. However, the disvalue of the disability does come up in deciding what we should treat.

Can we summarize our discussion of principles as a decision procedure (for life-and-death and nonlife-and-death cases) to decide if (the third view of) discrimination is involved? Here is one attempt:

(1) Check the level of well-being (including quantity and quality) to which you can bring someone relative to another;

(2) Check to see if, in reaching this level, counting his starting point (or factor independent of what we do) when it is not similar to a condition we are trying to treat, would make the starting point (or factor independent of what we do) work, as a component feature, in favor of or against him relative to others;

(3) If the answer to (2) is no, deciding whom to help by differences in level of well-being to which you can bring someone will not involve invidious discrimination (on the third view of discrimination). If the answer is yes, deciding whom to help by differences in level of well-being to which you can bring someone will involve such discrimination; and

(4) If avoiding such discrimination is all that should stand in the way of producing best outcomes, decide how to allocate by (1), (2), and (3).[34]

This leaves it open that differences in outcome should not matter because they are morally irrelevant goods, even if attending to the goods would not involve the third view of discrimination. Indeed, my conclusion is that while it may be wrong to ignore the Principle of Irrelevant Goods, doing so need not involve inappropriate discrimination. Hence, some complaints on behalf of the disabled may have to appeal to the Principal of Irrelevant Goods, rather than to a claim of discrimination.

If we decide according to this four-step procedure, it is what we can do for someone in the sense of what level of well-being our behavior will leave him at that will matter, at least so long as making this matter does not involve treating factors (that are unlike those we are trying to treat) beyond what we do as component features in favor of or against some person relative to another.

It is important to remember that this conclusion implies something that may be hard to accept, namely that nondiscriminatory conduct involves treating P → U (i.e. independent of our efforts he will become unparalyzed), no differently from P → P or P → U but permits treating P → U differently from P → P, for U is a better outcome and we produce it. (Analogous results will follow for switches to P.)

One problem with this decision procedure is that it just attends to our treatment of one person relative to another in deciding whether there is invidious discrimination. However, suppose we treat B correctly relative to A and B loses the scarce resource, but we do not treat C correctly relative to A (or D) in order that C not lose the scarce resource. Might not B complain that he is being discriminated against relative to C, for we are holding him to standards to which we do not hold another, and that is enough to support a claim of discrimination?[35] In order to avoid this

[34] Steps (1) and (2) amount to saying that level matters *on condition* that you have brought someone to it, *on further condition* that making level matter does not involve holding good or bad component features not produced by you in favor of or against someone, *on further condition* that the components are not like ones we are trying to treat.

[35] I owe this objection to James Lindeman Nelson. He thinks that 'normal' people have conditions (such as needing to sleep a lot) that make them disabled relative to nonsleepers, yet we would not choose to save the life of one person rather than another because only in him would our life-saving

problem, we might modify step (3) to: If the answer to (2) is no, and the procedure in steps (1) and (2) is applied pairwise generally (or impartially), deciding whom to help by differences in levels of well-being to which you can bring someone will not involve discrimination. If the answer is yes, or procedures in steps (1) and (2) are not applied generally (or impartially), deciding whom to help by differences in this level of well-being will involve discrimination.[36]

In sum, I have argued that there are several ways in which differences between people that we can produce (and sometimes even differences we do not produce) allow us to decide whom to treat without committing the wrong of invidious discrimination. But narrowing the ground on which one may complain of discrimination may only empower the Principle of Irrelevant Goods instead, for it may possibly be called on to prohibit actions that one might have thought could be ruled out on grounds of discrimination.

---

cure also eliminate the need to sleep. Hence, he thinks that we apply a different standard to the disabled and the normal. I think our judgment in this case may be affected by the fact that we think offering an enhancement to normal species functioning is less important than offering treatments for conditions affecting normal species functioning. If this were a morally relevant difference between the case of C versus D and the case of A versus B, then the fact that we did not apply a standard in one selection context that we apply in another may not involve invidious discrimination.

[36] Consider two interesting implications of what we have so far said. Considering the first implication involves examining two more cases. In Case A:

$$
\begin{array}{cc}
U & P \\
\downarrow & \downarrow \\
P & U
\end{array}
$$

the outcomes differ, and in addition to saving lives, we would make a positive difference in P and a negative difference in U. In this case, we may decide on the basis of the difference in outcomes since we produce these in both persons, but the fact that we cause an improvement in one person and a decline in another has no independent weight. That is, it is not the pride and shame a doctor might take in her/his work that should affect our decision but the differential outcome level to which we bring a person (on condition that we produce it). That is, our producing it is a mere side constraint on considering what is important, namely, the differential outcome level. (This could also be said about Case 8, where harming U but not harming P is present, and yet a doctor's disappointment in causing harm should be irrelevant; also in Case 7, where improving P but not improving U takes place and a doctor's pride should be irrelevant.) We may take account of what we do, but not because it is reflecting well or ill *on us*. We may take account of what we do, but not because it is reflecting well or ill *on us*.

Now consider Case B:

$$
\begin{array}{cc}
L_{1(U)} & L_{3(\text{Total Paralysis})} \\
\downarrow & \downarrow \\
L_{2(\text{Paraplegia})} & L_{2(\text{Paraplegia})}
\end{array}
$$

In this case (where L stands for 'level'), we would bring each person to the same level if we save him, but in one case by lowering and in the other case by raising; we also make the same difference to produce the same outcome but in one case negative and in the other positive. These differences should not matter, given that the outcome is the same.

10.13. Intransitivities

A problem that we must be prepared for in using the Causative Principle, the Principle of Irrelevant Identity, and their accompanying decision procedure is apparent intransitivity in choices. We have already discussed this in connection with some Switch-and-Reduce Cases. Let us consider this issue further. My discussion implies that it is nondiscriminatory to prefer a paraplegic candidate (P) who will become unparalyzed (U) as a result of what we do over one who will not, i.e.

$$\begin{pmatrix} A \\ P \to U \end{pmatrix} > \begin{pmatrix} B \\ P \to P \end{pmatrix}$$

Nondiscrimination requires giving equal chances to a paraplegic candidate who will remain that way in a contest with an unparalyzed candidate who will remain that way, i.e.

$$\begin{pmatrix} B \\ P \to P \end{pmatrix} = \begin{pmatrix} C \\ U \to U \end{pmatrix}$$

and it also requires not favoring a paralyzed candidate who will become unparalyzed over someone all along unparalyzed, i.e.

$$-\left[\begin{pmatrix} A \\ P \to U \end{pmatrix} > \begin{pmatrix} C \\ U \to U \end{pmatrix}\right] \text{ (Case 6)}$$

In other words, it would be discriminatory to pick immediately A over C, even though it is nondiscriminatory to pick A over B, and B must be treated as equal to C. (That is, A > B, B = C, −(A > C).)

There is also a second possible intransitivity:

$$\begin{array}{ll} C > D & (U \to U) > (U \to P) \\ D = B & (U \to P) = (P \to P) \\ -(C > B) & -((U \to U) > (P \to P)). \end{array}$$

These apparent intransitivities, however, really raise no deep problem, as the choices are fully explicable on a pairwise basis. Because the pairwise options give rise to different factors that determine our choice in them, we should not expect transitivity. Still, the apparent intransitivities give rise to new questions.

Due to the first 'intransitivity,' it might be said that U has an incentive to paralyze himself prior to our choice, since if he could be made to recover from paralysis, his life will be favored over P and not otherwise. Because of the second intransitivity, U has an incentive to paralyze himself if he knows the lifesaving procedure will paralyze him anyway, since then he will be on an equal footing with U, who will remain U. In sum, the sort of distinctions involved in the Causative Principle and the Principle of Irrelevant Identity give perverse incentives to people. This, however, does not necessarily show them to be wrong. (If affirmative action gave one an incentive to change one's race and doing so were possible, would affirmative action be wrong for that reason?)

What should we do when the three people involved in each triplet present themselves to us at once? As I said above (p. 303), in the first 'intransitivity,' my sense is that nondiscrimination requires us to toss a coin between (P → U) and (U → U), even though, if the coin favors (U → U), this will mean that he is selected over (P → P). This is nondiscriminatory in the context because (P → P) has been *eliminated* as a candidate already not by (U → U) but by (P → U). There is no 'money pump' phenomenon (that is, having to move from selecting U → U to tossing a coin between U → U and P → P) and then favoring P → U to him and onward. This is because one option (P → P) has been eliminated. (Admittedly, the candidate who is eliminated is eliminated by someone who may not ultimately win the contest. Some may say that such phenomena violate Arrow's Principle of Independence of Irrelevant Alternatives, but I think such cases help show that the Principle is either incorrect or its correct interpretation does not conflict with such a result.) In the second 'intransitivity,' we may select (U → U), even if this means he is selected over (P → P), just in case (P → P) loses a fair toss first with (U → P) and is thus eliminated.

10.14. The Supererogation Argument

So far, I have dealt with The Problem by considering reasons to deny or accept Premise 3 in the argument supporting it. Now, I wish to consider a different type of argument that also denies the conclusion that we should help the nondisabled rather than the disabled with scarce resources. This argument raises concerns about Premises 1 and 2 in the argument leading to The Problem. Premise 1 says: 'Disabilities make life worse for the person whose life it is, other things equal, and this is why we try to prevent or correct them.' Embedded in this premise are a proposition and a claim that it explains our behavior. The proposition is that disabilities make life worse for the person whose life it is, other things equal. The behavior it explains is that we try (presumably correctly) to prevent or correct such disabilities.

Premise 2 says, 'Hence, we will get a worse state of affairs if we help a disabled person . . . rather than someone equal in all respects except that he lacks the disability.'

An objection to deriving Premise 2 from Premise 1 is that there is an explanation of why we correctly try to prevent or correct disabilities that is consistent with the view that a disabled life is as good as or even better than a nondisabled life, and so produces even a better state of affairs, other things equal. Further, the life of a disabled person could be as good or even better than the life of a nondisabled person, even if the proposition part of Premise 1 is true (i.e. the disability makes the life in some respect worse). This is because things may not be equal, if there are sources of good in the disabled life not available or not typical in the nondisabled life. Of course, one may doubt that there are such great goods only in the disabled life. My point now is that, even if there were, we could still have reason, all things considered, to try to prevent or cure disabilities.

Our reason for trying to prevent or cure disabilities, as suggested by Premise 1, could be that a disability makes life harder, and so worse, *for someone*, even if it also makes him have a life that is no worse (or even better) than others. Among those who have drawn a distinction relevant to this point are Shelly Kagan and Ronald Dworkin. Kagan, for example, distinguishes between how things are *going for me*—a matter of my well-being—and how my life is going, for example, as a matter of achievement. So my life could be going well, but I might not be doing well.[37] Ronald Dworkin distinguishes between experiential and critical interests, so one's life could be experientially bad but one could still have an important and meaningful life.[38]

---

[37] See his 'Me and My Life,' *Proceedings of the Aristotelian Society*, 94 (1994), 309–24.
[38] See his *Life's Dominion* (London: HarperCollins, 1993). I make a similar distinction in Morality, Mortality, vol. i.

Thus, it could be supererogatory for someone to choose to live a hard life and wrong for us to force such a life on an unconsenting individual, even if it is a good life in terms of meaningfulness and achievement. Analogously, we could know that if someone were left to suffer a great deal of pain rather than be treated for it, he could become a great artist. This would be a better state of affairs than the one that results if he is treated. For then, he will not suffer pain and will live a life of only ordinary insight and achievement. It would be wrong of us (in the absence of his consent) not to treat his pain, and also permissible for him to refuse to suffer the pain, even if he then misses out on extraordinary life. Call this the *Supererogation Argument*.[39]

It accepts Premise 1 but denies that Premise 1 makes Premise 2 relevant. That is, if the lives of the disabled were overall as good as or even better than the nondisabled lives (even if not *for them*) because other things were not equal, this would imply that we would not achieve a worse state of affairs if we helped a disabled person rather than a nondisabled person. This could be true even though Premise 2 is strictly correct, since the premise would just be made irrelevant by the fact that other things are not equal if extra goods occur in the life of the disabled that do not occur in other lives.

The Supererogatory Argument may even apply within the realm of experiential goods alone. This is because, I believe, one need not go through a period of great pain even if this will make possible a future with enough experiential (let alone nonexperiential) goods to make one's life overall have positive value. Analogous to a moral prerogative one has not to make sacrifices to promote what is good for others, one may have a prerogative consistent with self-interested rationality not to do what maximizes one's own experiential good. For example, refusing to go through torture at t_1 in order to achieve subsequent pleasure that outweighs the pain does not seem unreasonable.[40]

If states of affairs could be as good or better if we help the disabled rather than the nondisabled, we can deny the view that we should help the

---

[39] Perhaps another way to make this point is to say that we need not suffer harms for the sake of achieving benefits that consist in more than the avoidance of even greater harms. Some support for this view is to be found in Seana Shiffrin's 'Wrongful Life, Procreative Responsibility, and the Significance of Harm,' *Legal Theory* (June 1999).

[40] On this, see my *Morality, Mortality, i* (n. 3 above).

nondisabled with scarce resources. (But, again, this would be because other things are not strictly equal between able and disabled.) This conclusion is consistent with it being right to try to prevent or cure the disabilities, even if the lives with the disabilities would produce equal or better states of affairs. This is because, as the Supererogation Argument says, it would be supererogatory to choose to live such good lives and wrong for us to impose such good lives on people without their consent.

I think that the Supererogation Argument can help us better understand the debate between Peter Singer and the advocates of the disabled. Singer seems to accept that our preventing and curing disability is evidence for disability being a bad thing, other things equal. He also seems to believe that the fact that a disabled person would seek a cure is evidence that the disability does not lead to other goods that make his life equal to or better than a nondisabled life. As a consequentialist, Singer is interested in producing the best outcome. Therefore, he accepts that scarce resources should go to the nondisabled, other things equal.[41] Some advocates for the disabled answer that their lives are as good as the lives of the nondisabled and hence we produce as good an outcome with a scarce resource. But how can they then explain someone's interest in being cured of the disability? The Supererogation Argument could account for the consistency of the advocates' argument and pinpoint an error in Singer's argument. It does this by saying that some people might not want to pay a price in difficulty for what is as good or even better.

Suppose the Supererogation Argument is valid. Is it sound? That is, is it true that the disabled life is as good or even better than a nondisabled life, in virtue of special features typically lacking in the nondisabled life? I do not believe so. While I cannot here examine this question in great detail, I will consider one aspect of it. Suppose that the special feature is a form of courage or determination that is present when a disabled person accomplishes something with difficulty that a nondisabled person does easily. For example, there may be no special merit in a nondisabled person walking up stairs on his own, while there may be such a merit in a disabled person doing it. Suppose, however, that because basic tasks such as walking up stairs are done easily in the nondisabled life, courage and determination can be exercised in achieving more sophisticated and novel

---

[41] See note 1.

accomplishments. From the point of view of a human ideal, it seems better to exercise courage and determination in achieving nonbasic rather than basic goals. Indeed, it seems like a waste of courage and determination to have to apply them to tasks that could easily be accomplished by people without disabilities, at least on the supposition that these virtues would instead be developed in pursuit of intrinsically higher goals.

Hence, it could be true that if two individuals did no more than walk up stairs, the life of the disabled person who does this may be harder but still more worthwhile than the life of the nondisabled person because the former life exhibits virtues the latter does not. But it would be better still if people were free to do basic things without determination and courage, so that they are free to actually achieve higher goals and still exercise determination and courage in those other pursuits.[42]

---

[42] One alternative objection to Premises (1) and (2) is that if a disabled life is better because other things are not equal, it will not be worse *for the disabled person*, even if it is harder for him. (This is a rejection of Premise 1.) It leaves it open that we could try to prevent disabilities, even though lives with them will be better for *people* with disabilities, because the lives are too hard.

A second alternative objection to Premises (1) and (2) and Singer's use of them assumes something close to the reverse of the assumption of the Supererogation Argument. That is, it assumes that experientially, the lives of the abled and disabled do not differ; the disabled life is not harder due to adaptation. As Singer may be attracted to an analysis of a good life in terms of experiential states, this should lead him to rank their lives equally. However, from the point of view of perfections, or non-experiential goods, having a disability could still make a life worse. It could be for this reason that we prevent or cure disabilities, and that these cures are desired even by the disabled whose lives are not worse experientially in virtue of their disabilities. (Indeed, if we realize the happy disabled would want to be cured, this could be our grounds for preventing disability in someone who is not yet able to have an opinion, such as a child.) On this view, it is only if Singer accepted the nonexperiential measure of a good life that he could argue that we should prevent and cure the disabilities, and that we would get worse outcomes in aiding the disabled rather than nondisabled.

This alternative is suggested by the results of psychologists. For example, Daniel Kahneman reports that, in terms of daily mood, the life of a severely disfigured person (after adaptation) does not differ from that of anyone else. Nevertheless, the same person wishes very much that he could get rid of his disability (independently of the belief that this would improve the experienced quality of his life). Reported by Kahneman in his third Mind, Brain, and Behavior Lecture, Harvard University, April 2008.

11

Ethical Constraints on Allowing or Causing the Existence of People with Disabilities

DAVID WASSERMAN

In 1927 Oliver Wendell Holmes infamously declared that 'three generations of imbeciles are enough.'[1] In comparing surgical sterilization to prevent further generations of imbeciles with a quarantine to stop an epidemic, Holmes made a public-health analogy that now seems strikingly inapt. Yet that analogy expressed a widespread concern of *his* generation, that a spiralling increase in the number and proportion of unfit and defective individuals in a society threatened its health and vigour.

In repudiating *Buck* v. *Bell*, we have rejected the 'science' that linked poverty and underdevelopment to cognitive impairment. We have also recognized the basic right of individuals with limited cognitive ability to have children, a right that 'trumps' any concerns about population fitness that still retain scientific credibility. And we no longer expect individuals to concern themselves with the 'genetic health' of the population in making reproductive decisions. We regard procreative liberty in some form as among the fundamental freedoms of Americans.

Our repudiation of *Buck* v. *Bell* is incomplete and ambiguous, however. While we recognize a right of (almost) *all* prospective parents to have *some* children, if they can do so without technological assistance, we are uncertain

I would like to thank the participants in the Manchester Disability and Disadvantage Workshop, May 2007, for helpful guidance. Adam Cureton, Kimberley Brownlee, Guy Kahane, and Matthew Hanser provided especially valuable criticism and suggestions. Work on this paper was supported by NIH/NHGRI Grant No. 1R03HG004249-01.

[1] *Buck* v. *Bell*, 274 U.S. 200, 207 (1927).

or divided about whether there are moral constraints on the number of children parents may have, and if so, whether those constraints depend upon the parents' means, whether society has an obligation to support parents in having and raising more than a minimum number of children or to subsidize assisted reproduction. Most importantly, we are uncertain or divided about the right to have children with substantial impairments. That issue remained hypothetical as long as a significant probability of having such children was an unavoidable concomitant of the exercise of the right to have children. But with the development of prenatal and, more recently, preimplantation testing for an increasing number of genetically associated impairments, the issue now confronts all prospective parents.

These technologies force us to re-examine the scope of procreative liberty, by making it possible to separate the putative interests of society in the genetic health of the population from the right of adults to bear children. It is no longer necessary, as it was in Holmes's time, to 'cut the fallopian tubes' to reduce the transmission of any condition that can be detected by preimplantation or prenatal testing. The availability of less drastic forms of prevention raises the issues of whether procreative liberty is incompatible with a parental duty to prevent the implantation of embryos or the birth of fetuses with certain genetic features, and whether that liberty encompasses the right of parents to choose not only the number and spacing of their children but also their genetic features.

The speed at which prenatal testing has become a routine part of medical care for prospective mothers, and the frequency with which positive results lead to abortion, has worried many disability advocates and scholars, who see that testing as informed by, and perpetuating, harmful stereotypes about impairments. Some fear that the routinization of prenatal testing is reintroducing eugenics 'though the back door'.[2] For these critics, what was wrong in the eugenics so confidently defended by Holmes was not only its coercive character and invasive methods, but its assertion of an individual and collective duty not to impair the 'genetic health' of the population. They argue that the acceptance of such a duty is even more dangerous now, when the means of preventing the creation of children with disabilities are vastly greater than in the heyday of the old eugenics, and no longer provoke

---

[2] T. Duster, *Backdoor to Eugenics* (New York: Routledge, 1990).

as much resistance from defenders of reproductive autonomy.[3] They view the increasing selectivity of reproductive decisions as threatening a fragile tolerance for diversity and imperfection and as conflicting with a parental ideal of unconditional love.[4]

Yet there is a sharply opposing concern, that genetic technologies will be used 'irresponsibly' to deliberately create children with disabilities. The first well-publicized attempt to select *for* impairment—the selection of a sperm donor with a family history of deafness, to raise the odds of a deaf child—provoked an angry response.[5] Objections to such selection, and to the failure to select against impairments, are not typically framed in the now-unfashionable terms of population fitness. Rather, they make two appeals more congenial to contemporary moral sensibilities: to the welfare, suffering, or rights of the impaired child, and to the injustice of imposing additional burdens on other individuals by the creation and rearing of such a child. Disability advocates question whether these appeals have any greater moral force than Holmes's worry about the threat to the nation's vigour and fitness, or whether they are really the same objections couched in a more acceptable idiom.

The appeal to the child's welfare or suffering confronts two difficult issues, one about life in general, the other about genetic technology. The first is that all human lives contain significant suffering and frustration, and it is unclear whether there is any basis for assuming that a child with an impairment will lead a substantially less happy life than a child without one. The second issue is that, at present, the use of technology to select for genetic features is identity-affecting: the child selected for an impairment, or allowed to be born despite it, could not have existed without it—any embryo or fetus without the relevant genetic features would not have been, or become, *him*. If his life is worth living, any suffering associated with the impairment appears to be well-compensated. This raises a conundrum in moral appraisal that has vexed philosophers for a generation, known as the

---

[3] L. Shepherd, 'Protecting Parents' Freedom to Have Children with Genetic Differences', *University of Illinois Law Review* (1995), 761.

[4] A. Asch, 'Disability Equality and Prenatal Testing: Contradictory or Compatible?', *Florida State University Law Review*, 30 (2003), 315–42; A. Asch and D. Wasserman, 'Where is the Sin in Synecdoche?' in D. Wasserman, J. Bickenbach, and R. Wachbroit (eds.), *Quality of Life and Human Difference: Genetic Testing, Health Care* (New York: Cambridge University Press, 2005).

[5] L. Mundy, 'A World of their Own', *Washington Post Magazine*, 31 March 2002, 22, 24.

'non-identity problem'[6]—Who, if anyone, does a parent harm or wrong in creating an impaired child, if she could have created a child without an impairment? If no one is harmed or wronged, does the parent do anything harmful or wrongful?

The second appeal, to procreative justice, is difficult to assess in part because contemporary theories of justice have trouble with families. It has long been recognized that families help to sustain inequalities that most theories of justice seek to eliminate or reduce, and that the partiality integral to family relationships is often at odds with the impartiality required of citizens.[7] Why should the inequalities and extra costs imposed by parents who select impaired children be more objectionable than the inequalities created by parents who enhance their children's abilities and prospects in myriad ways? Even if the inequality in the latter case is 'offset' by general welfare gains, we should be hesitant to condition procreative freedom on the effects of its exercise on general welfare.

Despite their scepticism about standard objections to creating children with impairments, many disability advocates are reluctant to endorse their deliberate creation. Some of this discomfort reflects misgivings about the selection of a child based on *any* detectable characteristic—impairment, gender, skin- or eye-colour. These misgivings would extend to any means of deliberately raising the odds of having a child with an impairment, from taking mutagenic drugs before conception to choosing a gamete donor with the desired impairment. But many actions undertaken for other purposes may affect the odds of having a child with an impairment. Moreover, the probability of having such a child is likely to depend on somatic and environmental conditions we may one day be able to alter.

These prospects expose divisions among those troubled by prenatal selection. For those who embrace 'disability neutrality'—the view that there is nothing intrinsically or essentially worse about having an impairment than lacking it—there is no obvious reason to oppose conduct that *incidentally* raises the odds of having children with impairments (although, as I will argue, there may be reason to oppose conduct that intentionally does so). Unlike adventitious impairments, congenital impairments do not

---

[6] D. Parfit, *Reasons and Persons* (Oxford: Clarendon Press, 1984).

[7] J. Fishkin, *Justice, Equal Opportunity, and the Family* (New Haven: Yale University Press, 1983).

involve the direct experience of loss or impose what Jeff McMahan calls 'transition costs'.[8]

But not all disability advocates accept neutrality; many believe that it is better, all else being equal, to lack a given impairment than to have one, even if the difference is far less significant than commonly supposed. There is reason to prevent the impairment of an existing fetus, even if it would cause no experience of loss and impose no transition costs, simply because it would be better for the child into whom that fetus would develop not to be impaired. Does support for such preventive measures imply opposition to conduct that incidentally raises the odds of having impaired children?

The non-identity problem highlights one potentially relevant distinction between preventing impairments to existing fetuses and preventing the existence of impaired people. The former makes some actual people better off by keeping them from becoming impaired (assuming, as those who reject disability neutrality do, that all else being equal it is better for someone not be impaired); the latter does not make anyone better off by preventing impairments that he or she could have avoided. If we hold that morality is narrowly person-affecting—very roughly, that something cannot be good or bad unless it is better or worse for some actual individual, then there may be no moral reason to oppose the incidental creation of children with impairments, as long as they are expected to have lives that are good on balance. Even if it is bad for a person with a worthwhile life to have an unavoidable impairment, it is not bad for that person to have been created. Nor does the (assumed) badness of his impairment make it wrong to have created him—assuming, however unrealistically, that there is no harm to others in doing so.

But if we accept, as most people appear to, that there is some moral reason for making better-off people as well as for making people better off (to adapt Jan Narveson's distinction[9])—a reason independent of concerns about justice and harms to third-parties—it appears that there is a reason to support measures to prevent the creation of people with impairments.[10]

---

[8] J. McMahan, 'Preventing the Existence of People with Disabilities', in D. Wasserman, J. Bickenbach, and R. Wachbroit (eds.), *Quality of Life and Human Difference: Genetic Testing, Health Care* (New York: Cambridge University Press, 2005).

[9] J. Narveson, 'Utility and Future Generations', *Mind*, 76 (1967), 62–72.

[10] In *Reasons and Persons*, Parfit offers several examples, such as 'Two Medical Programmes', intended to suggest that we do not recognize any moral difference between otherwise equivalent actions or policies that make people better off and make better-off people. If there is no difference,

Opponents of such measures might claim that this reason was outweighed by reasons opposing *deliberate* selection, which would suggest a moral balancing that might come out the opposite way in some cases. Or they might hold that, whatever force this reason had for other agents, it had none for prospective parents: for them, deliberate selection against impairment was no better than deliberate selection for it, and no reason based on a characteristic (or almost any characteristic) of the future child was a good reason for selection, or even marginally better than any other. I will explore this position below.

The rejection of deliberate selection, however, does not imply that prospective parents lack any moral reason for avoiding conduct that *incidentally* raises the odds of having children with impairments. Moreover, even if parents lacked such a reason, the state might have one—it might have good reason to discourage citizens from engaging in conduct that raised the odds of having children with genetically based impairments, or to reduce those odds by other means.

In this paper, I explore the implications for reproductive decision making of acknowledging a moral asymmetry between actions that raise and actions that lower the odds of having a child with an impairment. I will begin, however, by introducing the ideal of unconditional welcome, which rejects that asymmetry as a basis for reproductive decisions. I argue that this ideal underlies one of the more attractive moral conceptions of the family and one of the most powerful objections to prenatal selection.

I will then consider a hypothetical that appears to compel those who accept that ideal to condone conduct known but not intended to raise the odds of having a child with an impairment. In appraising this challenge, I will present an alternative to unconditional welcome, a view of procreative responsibility that requires parents to be able to justify to their child any serious harm they expect him to suffer, as necessary or unavoidable if he

---

then we must acknowledge the role of impersonal or wide person-affecting principles in our moral thinking—principles that require us to increase the good or reduce the bad in the world (impersonal), or increase the good and reduce the bad for people (wide person-affecting) whether or not, in doing so, we make anyone better or worse off than he or she would have otherwise been. If we acknowledge such principles, we must determine whether they supplement or supersede narrow person-affecting principles, that concern whether we make specific people better off or worse off than they would otherwise have been. One can find *some* difference between the pairs of cases Parfit presents and still conclude that impersonal or wide person-affecting considerations have some moral force.

is to enjoy some greater good. The view holds that they have such a justification only if they regard such harm as necessary for the existence of any child they could have, or of the kind of child they seek to have. While this view recognizes a moral asymmetry between raising and lowering the odds of having a child with an impairment, it does not oppose all conduct that is known to raise those odds. But it also condones many exercises of parental selectivity that the unconditional welcome rationale would condemn.

I conclude by considering whether—despite the preference for private decision making in reproductive matters—it would be less problematic (as well as more effective) for the state to adopt policies, such as environmental regulation, that reduce the odds of parents having impaired children than for parents themselves to reduce those odds by selective procreation.

11.1. The Ideal of Unconditional Welcome

Adrienne Asch and I have argued that preconception and prenatal selection are morally problematic because they are incompatible with the ideal of unconditional welcome to which prospective parents should aspire.[11] This ideal extends the unqualified commitment that parents try to maintain towards their existing children to the onset of the parental project; the point at which a couple or individual decides to bring a child into the family. Under this ideal, any eligibility requirement for family membership, beyond the prospect of a life worth living and the capacity to form intimate relationships, is not compatible with the moral ideal of the family. Both the attempt to prevent and the attempt to cause the existence of future children with impairments, or almost any other characteristic, are at odds with this ideal, which opposes the intentional prevention of a given reproductive outcome as well as the intentional causing of that outcome.[12] Parents who intentionally select an embryo without genetic impairments fail to satisfy that ideal even if they would accept a child with them; they

---

[11] Asch and Wasserman, 'Where is the Sin in Synecdoche?'

[12] Unconditional welcome is consistent with efforts to prevent or treat an embryo or fetus, as long as the prevention or treatment does not alter the identity of the future child, and as long as the willingness to have the child is not conditional on the success of the prevention or treatment.

consign the latter to a kind of waiting list, to be admitted into the family only if no more suitable candidates are available. The (quasi-) random process of fertilization deserves deference not because it is natural, but because it precludes a selectivity that prospective parents ideally should not exercise.

The appropriateness of such selectivity must be assessed in the context of the undertaking prospective parents begin, of creating or expanding a family. Families, particularly contemporary ones, are in one sense very exclusive associations. Family members are expected to have a loyalty and devotion to each other that they have to no one else. When Barack Obama sought to justify his decision to maintain his close association with the Rev. Jeremiah Wright despite his divisive rhetoric, he described him as 'like family;' critics of Obama noted that he nevertheless was not family, and so was not owed the same commitment.

In another sense evoked by the Wright controversy, families are not exclusive—in one familiar phrase, 'they have to take you back'. Because family members will sicken, weaken, stray, and betray, this almost unconditional commitment is difficult to maintain. As a psychological matter, it might be that cohesion would be stronger with greater initial adhesion; if new family members were selected by their parents for their commitment-engendering affinities with existing family members. But just the opposite might be true—that the tighter, stronger bonds could be forged among dissimilar individuals brought together by their membership in the same intimate association; that diversity would breed fraternity.

These opposing claims are both speculative; the stronger case against selectivity rests on the moral character of the association it would create. The more that families were formed on the basis of perceived similarity, the more they would resemble, and compete for, their members' loyalty with, other 'affinity groups'. Those chosen for pre-existing affinities might be able to find associations in which they had even greater affinities. Moreover, their commitment to each other would be strained, morally if not psychologically, by their loss of the affinities that were the basis for their selection. Even if members who lost the traits that were the basis for their initial selection were retained, their sense of full and equal membership would be severely compromised.

Consider a family formed in an era of increasingly refined preimplantation genetic diagnosis. As an embryo, each child was screened for the all the undesirable conditions that were then detectable. Because of rapid progress in genetic diagnosis, each of the older siblings has genetic conditions that would have precluded the implantation of his successors. Each older child (despite receiving a larger share of parental attention than his successors[13]) could reasonably see his membership in the family as less well-grounded than theirs: the eligibility standards for the family go up with improving technology, and he is only a family member because, at the time of his conception, the technology had not improved enough to screen him out. He knows that he is loved as unconditionally as his younger siblings; they, in turn, are loved as unconditionally as those who will be added under even more refined screening techniques. Each nevertheless has a reason to feel like a second-class family member, 'grandfathered in' under a standard that would have excluded him. There is a tension between the unconditional love shown the present child and the conditions imposed on the selection of his siblings, a tension that cannot be easily resolved by recourse to a contrast between ex-ante and ex-post perspectives. The parents' claim, however truthful, that because of their love for the impaired child they actually have they have no regrets that they did not screen for that impairment, is cold comfort when they are now employing that screening to select his future siblings. He experiences, vicariously, the ex-ante perspective on which an impairment like his is a disqualification for family membership.

Compare the alumni of elite colleges who recognize that they would not have been accepted under the far higher admissions standards that now apply. Although that recognition may be humbling, the higher standards that now apply are not in tension with the basic character of the association. An elite university is by design an exclusive club, and its selectivity hardly ends with admission—it grades its students, it confers degrees with varying honours, and it expels students who cannot maintain a minimum grade-point average. A family does not grade its members and, if it imposes minimum standards at all, it is only for qualities it believes every member can maintain, like loyalty and respect.

Admittedly, the scope of unconditional welcome is debatable. We hardly think that a couple who intend to have a child must adopt any baby

---

[13] Ronald M. Green, 'Design: Building Baby from the Genes up', *Washington Post*, April 13, 2008: B1.

left at its doorstep or empty the local orphanages. Parents can certainly limit the number of children they will have, and they can arguably limit their welcome to children who are 'their own' by genetic or biological connection. Thus, they may exclude children for having the characteristic of 'having no genetic connection' or 'being the nth child'. The question is not whether these can be regarded as genuine characteristics, however, but whether selecting on the basis of these characteristics is consistent with the ideal of the family.

Limiting the size of one's family is not only consistent with, but necessary to, that ideal. While a country may be able to admit indefinitely many immigrants, a family cannot become indefinitely large without losing its intimacy. Genetic connection is a more debatable basis for selection. A club which only admitted members with particular pedigrees might seem to be a paradigm of exclusivity. But our paradigm of the family is a genetically based one. While adoption is, or should be, regarded as an equally valid way of forming a family, it is clearly an alternative, atypical means of doing so. On the other hand, genetic connectedness is often, perhaps usually, seen by parents as, in part, a proxy for traits and affinities they might otherwise select for—to want children who are 'flesh of their flesh' may be to desire particular characteristics as well as a particular source. Nevertheless, it seems strained to regard parents who create families in the usual way as engaged in a deliberate act of selection.

11.2. Allowing and Causing Impairment and the Ideal of Unconditional Welcome

Can one oppose prenatal selection against impairments but also oppose conduct that is known to raise the odds of having children with impairments? Jeff McMahan has argued that these positions are inconsistent; that those who oppose conduct that prevents the creation of children with impairments cannot oppose conduct that is known to raise the odds of having such children.[14] He offers a hypothetical, APHRODISIAC, in which a woman takes a drug to enhance her sexual pleasure. That drug also increases fertility

[14] J. McMahan, 'Causing Disabled People to Exist and Causing People to Be Disabled', *Ethics*, 116 (2005), 77–99.

by inducing ovulation and increases the risk of having a child with an impairment: if natural ovulation has recently occurred, it destroys the egg, stimulating the production of another but damaging that egg so that any resulting child will be impaired. The woman wants a child but is indifferent between an impaired and unimpaired one. The substitution caused by the drug is clearly identity-affecting, so McMahan concludes that the woman's action is not worse for her actual child, who will have a life worth living.

McMahan suspects that many people who oppose the prenatal prevention of children with impairments would nevertheless regard the woman as acting wrongly in APRHODISIAC, by increasing the odds of having a child with an impairment in order to enhance her sexual pleasure. He denies that they could defend the consistency of their views by making a distinction between causing and allowing the existence of children with impairments, forbidding the former while requiring the latter. He argues that if it is impermissible not to allow an outcome, it must be permissible to cause it. His 'crucial premise' is that 'if it is impermissible to try to prevent a certain kind of outcome, such as having a disabled rather than a normal child, and if the prevention of that kind of outcome is so objectionable that it is even permissible to deprive people of the means of preventing it, then it ought to be permissible to cause that outcome, provided one does so by otherwise permissible means. In short, if the outcome must be allowed to occur, how could it be impermissible to cause it to occur?'[15]

This should not be taken as a rhetorical question: there may, for example, be processes we are forbidden to interfere with but also forbidden to initiate. McMahan's crucial premise may hold when it is forbidden to prevent an outcome X but not forbidden to prevent $-$ X. But when it is forbidden to prevent X *or* to prevent $-$X, that premise is dubious.[16] The prohibition against selective termination is clearly of the latter sort. Most of those who think it is forbidden to abort a disabled fetus also think it is *forbidden* to abort a non-disabled fetus—if the decision to abort is based on the

---

[15] Ibid. 91. McMahan's doubts about the force of the causing/allowing distinction might seem to be reinforced by the difficulty of even drawing it in the procreative context. Biological parents usually cause the impairment in a fetus they allow to be born, in the sense that they contribute impairment-causing mutations to the fetus's genome. Even parents who employ donor gametes solicit and utilize the donation. Still, there does appear to be a felt difference between (*a*) declining to abort an impaired fetus, however conceived; (*b*) selecting an impaired embryo from an IVF array that includes unimpaired embryos; and (*c*) causing identity-affecting mutations in gametes or an embryo.

[16] Kimberley Brownlee suggested this way of generalizing my objection to McMahan's premise.

characteristics of the fetus, not the readiness of the parents. It may be that what is prohibited is interfering with the outcome of a causal process, not preventing a particular outcome. Thus, some people believe that we should not interfere with certain natural processes, such as the forest fires that break out in dry wilderness areas. On their view, we are forbidden to prevent either the spread of the fire within the wilderness area or its failure to spread. This prohibition on extinguishing forests fires hardly implies a permission to sustain or accelerate their progress.[17]

Moreover, McMahan's critical premise is difficult to assess without some further specification of what is prohibited and permitted, and what qualifies as 'a certain kind of outcome'. If we are forbidden to prevent a harmful outcome just because we can only do so by violating a side-constraint, or by doing something even more harmful, we can hardly infer that we are permitted to cause that outcome.

Even if McMahan's premise is correct, one could consistently oppose *deliberate* action to prevent *or* cause impairment, by denying, in effect, that there are permissible means of doing so under the ideal of unconditional welcome present in the last section.[18] If our objection is to *deliberate* selection or creation, however, why should we condemn the woman in APHRODISIAC, for whom the creation or selection of an impaired child is just an unintended and incidental,[19] only a probable side effect of the pursuit of pleasure? She is not trying to affect the odds of having such a child, just to enhance her pleasure.[20] But we may find a troubling frivolity in letting the

[17] Nor can this be explained by the 'otherwise permissible means' condition. The means of stopping fires in wilderness areas are prohibited even though they are permitted in other settings, such as fighting house fires; the means of sustaining fires are prohibited in wilderness areas even though they are permitted in others settings, such as 'controlled burns'.

[18] It should be noted, however, that many opponents of prenatal testing, including Asch and I, do not seek to deprive parents of the means of obtaining it, only of a clear conscience if they do so.

[19] There would be no tension for those who believed that one should not interfere, *even unintentionally*, with the natural mechanisms for selecting the gametes involved in the reproductive process—something the drug in APHRODISIAC does. But few people who oppose screening show such extreme deference to natural processes.

[20] One feature of the case that may encourage blame is that the drug's action, if not the woman's, may be divisible into identity-affecting and non-affecting parts—the egg-substitution and the egg-damage, respectively. If the damage to the egg occurred in such a way that it did not affect the probability that it would be fertilized by one sperm rather than another, then that damage would arguably not be identity-affecting, and might harm the resulting child in a standard sense. Though the woman could not have prevented damage to the egg without preventing its release, there *could* have been a drug available to her that released the replacement egg without damaging it. That possibility may not be strong or 'real' enough to warrant the claim that she harmed her child by taking the drug she did, but it does make her action in taking the drug look more like a harm-causing than it would if the drug did

pursuit of pleasure determine the kind of child she will have. Even if it is no worse to have an impairment than lack one, or even if it is better not to intentionally select children who have, or who lack, impairments, it may be wrong to let such an important characteristic be determined by such a trivial pursuit.

McMahan could respond that the charge of frivolity overlooks critical differences among the aphrodisiac's possible reproductive effects. Even if the pursuit of pleasure was frivolous, it might be permissible to let it determine the eye or hair colour of the child, or even its sex, in an identity-affecting way (Since sex is determined by the sperm, not the egg, we would obviously have to modify the hypothetical to make the aphrodisiac sex-affecting.) If it is objectionably frivolous to let the pursuit of pleasure raise the odds of disability but not gender-change, it cannot be because disability but not gender is an important characteristic. Rather, it must be because it is disadvantageous to be disabled, but not to be of either sex (at least in contemporary middle-class America).[21] Even if we regard the disadvantages of disability as predominantly social, not medical, this suggests an asymmetry—that it is presumptively or prima-facie wrong to knowingly increase the odds of having a child with an impairment, but not a blond or female child. This is a weak presumption, which can be overcome by the usual reasons women have for delays expected to increase the odds of having an impaired child—for example, the desire to pursue a career before starting a family. But most people, even many of those with doubts about prenatal testing, would not find that presumption overcome by the desire to enhance the pleasure of procreative sex.

not damage any egg, but simply made it more likely that an egg with a pre-existing impairment would be selected. In such a 'pure selection' case, her action might not seem quite as wrong as most people are likely to regard her action in the original case.

But even if we modify APHRODISIAC so that the mechanism selects but does not damage the eggs, another feature of the hypothetical makes the woman's action seem wrong: her attitude toward having a disabled child. McMahan describes her as wanting a child and as regarding the extra burdens of raising a disabled one as compensated for by 'the special bonds that might be forged by the child's greater dependency' (McMahan, 'Causing Disabled People to Exist', 90). If she did not desire dependency for its own sake, she still desired it as a means to intimacy, which seems misguided, if not objectionable.

[21] It might be, however, that disability is disadvantageous only because of the discrimination faced by people with disabilities; that raising the odds of having a child with a significant impairment in contemporary America would be in this respect like raising the odds of having a girl in a harshly misogynist society.

Even a weak presumption, though, would conflict with the ideal of unconditional welcome, since it would still impose a duty of prevention on women who lacked the usual reasons to avoid incidentally creating a child with an impairment. Prospective parents committed to welcoming any child expected to have a worthwhile life and a capacity for intimacy would reject a presumption against creating, even unintentionally, a child with impairments. In rejecting that presumption, they would not need to accept disability-neutrality; they might hold that it was generally worse *for a person* to have than lack an impairment. But for any child expected to enjoy a life worth living, the possibility that he might not have as good a life as some other child his parents might have created would not even count as a prima facie reason for not creating him. Such impersonal or widely person-affecting considerations might have weight in other contexts, but not in reproductive decision making. The imperative to increase total welfare is fundamentally different, and potentially at odds, with the project of adding members to a family that has no, or minimal, conditions for membership.

Proponents of the unconditional welcome rationale, then, would not condemn the woman in APHRODISIAC as long as she had a commitment to loving and raising any child resulting from her drug-enhanced sexual activity, rather than the suspect desire for a dependent child that McMahan describes (at least if that desire did not motivate her to take the drug). If they still had reservations about her conduct, it might be because they were more convinced of her desire to enhance sexual pleasure than of her commitment to welcoming any child. Or it might be because they suspected that her commitment was superficial, based on ignorance or misconceptions about the challenges of raising a child with an impairment.[22] I think these suspicions can be allayed if we imagine a women deeply committed to that ideal, who has repeatedly refused prenatal testing in the past and has an intimate knowledge of the challenges of serious impairments, having one herself or having close relatives with a variety of impairments. If there is something wrong in her conduct, it does not lie in her failure to satisfy the ideal of unconditional welcome.

---

[22] The unconditional welcome rationale clearly would not extend to a woman whose desire for pleasure overcame her considered reservations about having a child with an impairment. Taking the aphrodisiac against her better judgement would show weakness of will, not a commitment to unconditional welcome. Parents should not increase the odds of having any child they are unwilling or reluctant to bear and raise.

11.3. Justifying Unavoidable Impairments

And yet the frivolity of the woman's action in APHRODISIAC may still seem disturbing, even if we are convinced by her avowals of unconditional welcome. For those who reject disability-neutrality, impairments are (presumptively or generally) not a good thing to have. Although it may be reasonable to refuse to select against children with impairments in refusing to select at all, it may still seem insensitive to raise the odds of having such a child merely for one's own transient pleasure. But what can it mean to claim such insensitivity? An impaired child born as a result of the aphrodisiac should not regret a worthwhile life with an unavoidable impairment. The claim that its mother would nevertheless be insensitive to any suffering and limitation associated with her child's impairment may thus appear to concede the moral force of impersonal considerations, since it is not clear that sensitivity to the interests of the future child would oppose its creation.

Yet those impersonal considerations appear to lose some, or most, of their force if the woman sees any suffering and limitation as necessary for the kind of child she wants to have, or the kind of life she wants for it. Many reasons for wanting children of specific kinds, or specific kinds of lives for one's children, are morally suspect, resting on biases, fantasies, or inaccurate, invidious stereotypes. But the moral role these reasons play may depend less on whether they are good reasons than on the extent to which they concern the good of the future child. That role can be seen by examining a relatively appealing reason for wanting a child of a particular kind. Consider DICK AND JANE. Jane is a gay woman planning to inseminate herself with donor sperm. Her closest friend, Dick, recently died of Huntington's, but not before freezing his sperm. Dick had always wanted to have a child, an aspiration he shared with Jane. When he was dying, he asked her if she would be willing to use his sperm to have her child; she said only that she would consider it. Jane ultimately decides to give life to Dick's aspirations, to have and raise a genetic child of Dick's. She wants that child to have a rich, rewarding life, and to come to know and honour the father who posthumously contributed to his life. Dick was homozygous for a dominant Huntington's mutation, so any child created with his sperm will develop Huntington's. Jane is vividly aware of the painful death that Huntington's inevitably causes and has no illusions about the odds of a cure in her child's lifetime. She does believe, however, that the child will have a life well worth living, and she has the means to assure that he receives high-quality care when he becomes incapacitated with Huntington's.

I do not think Jane acts wrongly, or displays insensitivity to the eventual suffering of the child she creates. I think that her conduct is acceptable even if she expects it to bring about less good or more suffering in the world than the choice of a 'normal' sperm from another donor. Although I may be in a minority in finding her conduct permissible, I suspect that most people would find it less objectionable than that of the woman in APHRODISIAC if the latter's pursuit of pleasure created an impairment of comparable magnitude.

There is a difference between the reason Jane has and the usual reasons that overcome the presumption against having, or increasing the odds of having, a child with an impairment. Those reasons concern the woman's right to lead her life as she chooses, or the hardships she would face if she had to alter her life-plans: she should not have to set aside her career, or give up her dream of bearing children, to avoid having a child with an impairment. In contrast, Jane does not need to invoke a right or hardship. She had made no promise to Dick and has no need or deep yearning to bear his child. Her reason for having the child is that she wanted to give life to a child of Dick's, even though that child would enjoy a painfully truncated life. She acts in part for Dick's sake, in part to give life to Dick's child—if not for the sake of such a child, at least for reasons that concern his good. Even if she increases the net suffering in the world by using Dick's sperm instead of sperm free of Huntington's mutations, she acts from a devotion to Dick and from a kind of 'anticipatory partiality' toward the child she creates with his sperm. She is partial in the sense of having a prospective attachment to the as-yet-uncreated child who will develop from the union of their gametes. This is, admittedly, a peculiar kind of partiality, not only because it is directed toward any of the indefinite number of children who might emerge from that union, but because it seeks to favour such a child by bringing it into existence. Proponents of unconditional welcome, as well as those with more conventional views, might deny that such attenuated partiality is morally privileged.

But even if Jane's partiality does not enjoy the same moral status as partiality towards existing children, she can be said to create a child (with an impairment necessary for its existence) for reasons that concern the good of the child. She can treat that child's worthwhile life as justification or compensation for its impairment in a way she could not if giving a child the goods of life was no part, or only an insignificant part, of her reason for having an impaired child. In APHRODISIAC, where enhanced fertility is at best a secondary reason for taking the drug, the woman cannot be said to risk the child's unavoidable impairment for the child's own sake. As I argued in an earlier paper:

Parents' reasons for having a child, or a child of a particular kind, can forge a link between the hardships and the goods of the future child's life. [P]arents cannot love a future child in prospect, as they would love an existing child [citation omitted]; they cannot value his life now as he or they will come to value it, as infinitely dear despite its tribulations. Still, in seeking to give the goods of existence to a child, or a particular kind of child, they treat the unavoidable hardships of his life as necessary for the goods he will enjoy, as offset or subsumed by those goods. In contrast, if they have no reason to want a child who can only exist with certain limitations, that link is not present. They cannot say to the child, 'We saw your limitations as necessary for the kind of child we wanted to bring into being—a child like you.' For parents who were not seeking a child with such unavoidable limitations, that claim would be disingenuous.[23]

There is a sense in which the mother in APHRODISIAC could also offer her child a justification: his life is, after all, well worth living despite, or with, his impairment, and his mother expected such a favourable balance when she took the drug. She is clearly in a better position to claim to have conferred a net benefit on her child than she would be if she had not even expected him to have a life worth living. In that case, she would be like the proverbial taxi driver who negligently causes his passenger to miss a plane that goes on to crash.[24] While the passenger will be relieved at the result of the driver's negligence, he will have no reason to praise or thank him for saving his life. Praise would clearly be due, however, if the driver intentionally conferred that benefit—if, say, he expected the plane to crash, having overhead terrorists plotting its destruction, but knew he would not be believed and did as much as he could by delaying the passenger's arrival at the airport.

---

[23] D. Wasserman, 'The Nonidentity Problem, Disability, and the Role Morality of Prospective Parents', *Ethics*, 116 (2005), 136–52.

[24] One source is J. Feinberg, The Moral Limits of the Criminal Law: Harmless Wrongdoing (Oxford: Oxford University Press, 1990), 20.

But he would not deserve praise if he merely foresaw, without intending, the life-saving benefit of his late arrival. Thus, if he made it a practice to inflate the fare of out-of-town passengers by taking a roundabout route to the airport, the mere knowledge that the scam would save his passenger's life on this occasion would not entitle him to offset that life against the cost and inconvenience of a missed flight. In contrast, the mere expectation that his driving would cause his passenger to miss his flight would make him responsible for that harm as well as the inflated fare. As Matthew Hanser claims, there are asymmetrical responsibility conditions for benefits and harms; the former requires intention; the latter only foresight.[25] (This is not to deny that it is worse to intend harm than to merely foresee it; only to insist that the agent is responsible in either case and must justify his conduct in the latter. The Doctrine of Double Effect denies that he *can* justify his conduct in the former case; I take no position on that.)

In the procreative context, a parent is arguably responsible for any harms that she foresees, or should foresee, her child will suffer, whether associated with an impairment or with the universal conditions of human life, such as pain, illness, loss, and death. (Hanser questions whether a parent is responsible for harmful conditions she merely transmits, but I will assume parental responsibility for the sake of argument.). She is not responsible for the benefits of existence unless she intends to confer them.[26] But intending the benefit is not enough to justify a lesser harm; if it was, then any woman who intends to confer the benefit of existence on a child could justify an unavoidable impairment. The woman in APRHODISIAC intended to give the goods of existence to a child she expected to have an unavoidable impairment. Why can't she justify the latter in terms of the former, since the intended benefits were necessary for the foreseen harms? I think there is an additional condition for justification: the agent must intend to bestow the benefit on someone she believes could not receive it without incurring the harm. If her intention is merely to confer the benefit on *someone*, then it will be equally fulfilled by giving it to an individual who would not suffer

[25] 'Harming Future People', *Philosophy & Public Affairs*, 19 (1990), 47–70. I am not sure of the extent to which the plausibility, and even the coherence, of the claim of asymmetrical standards rests on a non-comparative notion of harm, but I will employ that notion in what follows.

[26] Ibid. That intention need be only one of several intentions underlying the decision to have a child, and need not be one the prospective parents could clearly articulate. Further, It may be manifested as fully in the decision to continue with an accidental pregnancy as in the decision to conceive a child. For more discussion of parental reasons and intentions, see Wasserman, 'Nonidentity Problem'.

the harm, and she will lack a justification for conferring it on someone who would. She will lack a justification even if she knows or expects that the benefit would go to someone with an unavoidable impairment, if it is not her intention to have it go to such a person.

This additional justification requirement may not apply outside the reproductive context, and may therefore seem ad hoc. If I have just one dose of a vaccination against a fatal disease to give to one of several infants, it would be wrong for me to exclude from consideration an infant in whom it would provoke a severe allergic reaction—as long as that reaction was not as bad as the disease and would not block the action of the vaccine. On the other hand, while it might be perverse for me to *select* that infant to receive the vaccine rather than assign it randomly, the recipient would not have a complaint. Indeed, it appears that that infant would be the only one who lacked standing to complain. This suggests that, even if existence can be treated as a benefit, selection for that benefit is morally as well as metaphysically unlike selection for a standard benefit.

While it is misleading to treat the decision about what kind of child to have as a distributional issue, however, it arguably shares one feature with distributional issues. It would not be perverse (although it might not be fair) for me to choose the infant with the allergy to receive the vaccine if that infant was my own child. Now, we obviously cannot have *this* kind of partiality towards a future child: In selecting gametes or an embryo, any one of whom will be our own child, we determine the object of our partiality, and we can hardly justify the selection of one child over another on the basis of that partiality. But we can, and often do, want to give the good of existence to a particular kind of child. The infertility industry caters to the desire to give existence to children with whom a couple will have a genetic connection. Though the desire for such a connection may be suspect, I believe it is fundamentally different than the desire to have a smart or athletic child. In seeking to have a child with a genetic connection, we are seeking to give the benefit of existence to a child (and I will assume without arguing that existence can be treated as a benefit, albeit a unique one) with whom we have a certain affinity, not seeking a 'trophy' child.[27]

---

[27] Of course, parents who select an embryo with a genetic predisposition to intellectual or athletic achievement might not be seeking a trophy child. They might be acting from a misguided conviction

Indeed, parents are sometimes willing to risk having a child with a significant impairment in order to maintain a genetic connection. Even if their reason reflects the sway of adaptive instincts, or a recalcitrant genetic essentialism, it grounds a justification to the child, not an excuse, for any hardship associated with that impairment—they do not need to claim that their desire for a genetic child is intense or overwhelming, merely sincere. In seeking to give the goods of existence to a child who could not exist without an impairment, they act on a reason that enables them to justify any associated hardship to the child.

Similarly, what justifies Jane's decision to have a child with Huntington's is her intention to give the goods of existence to a child of Dick's, a child who could not exist without Huntington's. If Jane had promised Dick to conceive and bear a child from his gametes, that alone would not have given her a reason adequate to justify the hardship of Huntington's disease to the child she had. The intention to fulfil a promise to Dick might in some sense justify her decision to have a child with an impairment, but it would not justify it in the same way as the intention to give the goods of life to a child of Dick's. It is only the latter that would allow her to justify her decision *to* the child; to adduce the benefits of the child's existence to outweigh its unavoidable harms.[28]

that they were pursuing the best interests of 'the child' in picking a smarter or more athletic one. Or they might want to give life to a child who could enjoy the experience of intellectual or athletic achievement, and with whom they could share that experience; perhaps they are ex-athletes who regard their years of competition as the high point of their lives. Although acting on such a desire might seem elitist, that desire arguably concerns the good of the child, and might give the parents a justification for any hardships, genetic, psychological, or social, associated with the child's intellectual or athletic prowess. It would not be necessary that the benefits of that prowess outweigh the harms—they might not—merely that the benefits of the child's life outweigh the harms, since the child could not, ex hypothesi, have enjoyed that life without both those benefits and hardships.

[28] The justification requirement encounters difficulties in assessing 'negligent attempts'—failures to prevent or reduce the likelihood of impairment that do not yield a child with an impairment. If we explain the apparent wrong the woman commits if she has a child with an impairment in terms of the inadequate justification she can offer him, how do we explain the conviction that she does something wrong if she ends up with an unimpaired child? There appears to be a robust intuition that she has acted wrongly by raising the risk of having an impaired child, although in the latter case there is no one she places at risk. But she does not seem to owe a justification to a child who is not impaired: she did not impose any risk on *that* child, except of not being created, a risk she need not justify. But there is no one else to whom she must justify her conduct—her negligence, if that is what it is, does not even have an apparent victim. Since there is no one to justify her conduct to, why should it matter if she has only a weak justification to offer, unless, implausibly, she owes a justification to the world at large, for not acting to maximize good or minimize bad?

11.4. Tension between Unconditional Welcome and Justification

In contrast to the unconditional-welcome ideal, the justification requirement opposes conduct that incidentally raises the odds of having an
impaired child. That requirement would oppose the incidental creation of
impairments, as in APHRODISIAC, because the woman did not take the drug in
order to give the goods of life to a child, or a certain kind of child. Under the
justification requirement, the reason for having or raising the odds of having,
a child with an impairment must concern, at least in part, the good of the
future child. But a prospective parent who, like the woman in APHRODISIAC,
raises the odds of having such a child for reasons unrelated to the child's good
cannot justify a foreseen impairment to the child, even if it is necessary for
his existence. In contrast to Jane, who seeks the good of the child she creates,
the woman in APHRODISIAC seeks her own pleasure by taking the pill, and
she cannot weigh that good against any harm from the child's impairment.[29]

Indeed, the parental justification for having a child with an impairment
might be even stronger if, unlike in DICK AND JANE, the parents *intended* to
have a child with a particular impairment, as in the case of the deaf couple
who sought to have a deaf child. In that case, the parents would have had to
justify any unavoidable hardships associated with deafness by claiming that
those hardships were necessary for the kind of child they wanted to bring
into existence. Admittedly, the possibility of such a justification did not
seem to have affected public opinion, which overwhelmingly condemned
the parents for their course of action. Some of that condemnation may have
been due to the assumption that their 'dysgenic' action imposed significant
costs on society. But it may also have been driven by an impression that the
parents acted in a perversely narcissistic way by seeking a child who would
share their impairment. Their own description of their choice, however,
suggests that they were strongly motivated by the goods they believed a
deaf child would enjoy by being raised in the environment they would
provide, a motive that makes their decision appear at least as child-centred

---

[29] If she was taking a pill to prolong her life rather than increase her pleasure, she might be able to
excuse her failure to prevent the existence of a child with additional hardships that are, from her point
of view, gratuitous. She could deny that that failure reflected a lack of sensitivity to those hardships.
But she could not claim that she exposed the child to those hardships for the sake of a life he could not
have lived without them.

as that of hearing parents seeking a hearing child. The deaf parents did not aim at evil, even if, as they would vehemently deny, being deaf was an evil, but at the good of creating a deaf child—a child expected to have a rich, rewarding life. Any evil in the deafness would have been at most a necessary side-effect of obtaining that good.

The ideal of unconditional welcome, as I noted, rejects the kind of selectivity exercised by the deaf parents. (It is not clear whether it would reject Jane's selectivity, because she sought a child of a particular father, not—even indirectly, through use of that man's gametes—a child with a particular phenotypic trait. Jane can be seen as extending an unconditional welcome *to any child of Dick's*; a restriction on genetic parentage does not seem to condition the welcome, only limit its scope.) The justification requirement conflicts with unconditional welcome just because it demands the kind of selectivity usually condemned by that ideal. Thus, although the women who attempted to have a deaf child because of the life they could give that child might have a justification to give the child, their selectivity made their welcome conditional, even if, as they insisted, they would have welcomed any child.

A further tension between the two rationales is apparent in a variation on APHRODISIAC, in which the drug *reduces* the odds that an egg with an impairment-causing mutation will be released. Clearly, most people would find it acceptable to take such a drug, whether the primary motive was pleasure or 'prevention'. It would not be acceptable under the unconditional-welcome rationale if the woman sought prevention as well as pleasure, but it would escape the justification requirement, since there is no need to justify, to any resulting child, actions that intentionally reduced the odds of having a child with an impairment.[30] That requirement, as noted, creates an asymmetry between actions that increase and actions that decrease the odds of having an impaired child: only the former need to be justified.[31]

---

[30] Similarly, there would be no need to justify actions that raised the odds of having a child with an impairment that was reasonably expected to give her a better life than that of a child lacking one. This may have been the expectation of the deaf couple discussed in the text.

[31] Do the prior or natural odds of impairment set a lower limit on the odds that need to be justified? Does a parent need to justify an action that incidentally *preserves* the odds of having a child with an impairment, e.g. by taking a long-planned vacation that precludes screening? Why, if the baseline odds lack moral significance, shouldn't a parent be required to justify actions that preserve those odds as well as actions that increase them? If the mother's pleasure is not a sufficient justification for the latter, why should her vacation be for the former? The justification rationale can recognize limits to the sacrifices a parent must make to avoid having a child with unavoidable impairment when she has no reason to

No such asymmetry is recognized by the unconditional-welcome rationale: if she merely seeks to enhance her sexual pleasure, neither the woman whose aphrodisiac raises the odds of an impaired child nor the woman whose aphrodisiac lowers it imposes conditions on the kind of child she is willing to have, or tries to affect the odds of having or avoiding a child with a given characteristic. But that rationale opposes her taking either drug *in order* to affect her odds of having an impaired child.

The conflict between the justification rationale and the unconditional-welcome ideal extends far beyond hypothetical cases involving conduct that incidentally increases or reduces the risk of having an impaired child. Parents who have no specific reason to want a child with any of the impairments they decline to screen out lack an appropriate justification to give to the children born with those impairments, even if their reason for declining to screen was to extend an unconditional welcome. They cannot claim that they acted to give the goods of existence to children like them; that certain impairments were unavoidable in the kind of children they wanted to have. Since they would not be able to justify the impairment to the child as something they saw as necessary or likely in order to have a child like him, the justification rationale would require them to take measures to avoid the existence of such children. That rationale would thus require screening in cases—perhaps the large majority—where the parents lacked a reason involving the good of the future child for having, or raising the odds of having, a child with an impairment.

Those attracted to the ideal of unconditional welcome, in turn, would oppose parental selectivity based on the intention to give the goods of existence to a particular kind of child, or a child who would live a particular kind of life—the type of intention held to be critical for an adequate justification. To seek to bring into existence a child with a particular characteristic is to condition's one's welcome, even if one would not reject

want a such a child; such a parent would have an excuse, but not a justification, for failing to take preventative measures that exceeded those limits. An excuse would be needed both for raising the odds of impairment and failing to reduce them. It might seem odd to offer a child an excuse, as opposed to a justification, for features that were necessary for his worthwhile existence. Yet such an excuse would serve to rebut a charge of insensitivity for harms the parent did not see as necessary for the existence of a child she sought to create: even though she did not seek such a child, she could not be expected to make great sacrifices to avoid creating it. A weaker excuse would appear to suffice for unavoidable than avoidable harms; a parent appears obliged to make a greater sacrifice to make a child less badly off than to make a less badly-off child.

a child lacking that characteristic. Selective recruitment compromises an open-door policy, even if the door still remains open to all comers.

11.5. An Additional Challenge for Justified Selectivity

Obviously, the sort of justification explored in the previous section would not pass muster impersonally—it is a justification to the affected child for impairments that are necessary for his existence but that may yield less total well-being than the selection of a different child. Even for the child, however, this justification may be incomplete: he may have other grounds for objecting to the basis for his selection. His parents' desire to have a child with an impairment may conflict with another desire that parents arguably should possess—that things go as well as possible for their child. His complaint would not be for the harm they caused him, but for the attitude they bore him.

Guy Kahane argues that parents who desire to bear and raise a child with a harmful condition generally have a morally defective attitude towards that child.[32] While it is not wrong for parents to desire a child who, they believe, can only exist with a harmful condition, it is wrong for them to desire that that condition continue. Parents should desire that their children's lives go as well as possible, so they should hope that any harmful condition will be corrected, even when that is a practical impossibility.[33] But if they select a child just because he has a given impairment, and not for other attributes associated, however strongly, with that impairment, they will almost always want that impairment to continue, since the elimination of that impairment would defeat their purpose in selecting for it. Even if they have conflicting desires, their hope that the child loses the very characteristic that was the basis for his selection does not make their hope that he retains it morally acceptable. At the very least, the former must be their dominant or overall desire.

As Kahane recognizes, this objection applies only to parents who desire that the child have an impairment, not to those who desire that the child

---

[32] Kahane does not take a position on whether such a morally defective attitude, with the child as its object, wrongs the child or gives him a complaint, but I will assume that it does.

[33] G. Kahane, 'Non-Identity, Self-Defeat, and Attitudes to Future Children', *Philosophical Studies* (forthcoming).

have some characteristic linked with an impairment. Thus, it does not apply to Jane, who wants to have Dick's child, knowing but not hoping that the child will have a Huntington's gene. She need not hope that he retain that gene; she may pray daily for prenatal genetic therapy that would spare him the disease, as long as modifying or replacing the gene would not threaten his identity—an unlikely threat on most accounts of identity. But the objection may apply to a couple who seek a child who is deaf like them—if deafness is regarded as a harmful condition. He is selected for an affinity that he will lose if a treatment becomes available, so they must hope it does not. Even if they hope that the entire family acquires hearing—an unlikely hope for such a couple—their attitude will still be morally defective if they want the child to stay deaf unless they also acquire hearing.

Kahane suggests that the parents' hope that the impairment continues wrongs the child by wishing him ill:

To be sure, it may not make sense for her to complain about, or regret, the fact that she was brought into existence. But she may still legitimately resent her parents for their reasons for bringing her into existence. Even if it was impossible for her to come into existence without being deaf, it was not impossible for her to continue to exist as a hearing child, whether or not correction is available. If someone wishes that you would not recover from a serious illness, it matters little to the moral assessment of that wish whether recovery is possible or not.[34]

Kahane would find the parents' desire objectionable even if it changed once they had the child.

I think there is some merit to Kahane's objection in cases where the impairment itself is the basis for selection. But I would add a couple of significant qualifications. First, I think it is possible to distinguish a desire to have a child with an impairment because of its perceived affinities with the parent from a desire for such a child that arises more or less spontaneously from perceived affinity. In other words, one can desire to have a child because of its condition without desiring to have that child out of a belief that its condition will be a source of affinities. Like Harry Frankfurt's love-before-first-sight for his children, such spontaneous partiality would not rest on a belief about future affinities, although it is certainly compatible with that belief. The prospective parent is simply drawn to a child with

---

[34] Ibid. 17–18.

that characteristic; it is a fondness or attachment unmediated by any belief about how much the parent will enjoy the child's company.

This motivation may be most apparent in selecting *in vitro*—the prospective parents may simply be partial toward an embryo with the genetic basis for a condition that they, their parents, or their siblings have. While they would not feel such partiality towards an embryo lacking that genetic variation, I do not think their partiality must be accompanied by the hope that the future child develop that condition or continue to have it, even if that is virtually certain. They could coherently claim that they selected the child for an affinity that (on reflection) they hoped he would lose—they were simply drawn to the prospect of having such a child, a partiality not conditioned on the child's retaining that affinity. Much as adult love can survive the loss of the characteristic that engendered it, so the love of prospective parents can survive the loss of an affinity that was the basis for their selection. Knowing this, the prospective parents who select a child for an affinity need not hope for its continuation, even if most in fact would.

Parents are often attracted to qualities in children or prospective children that they hope they will not retain. To take the most routine case, parents often adore qualities in their children that they expect and hope will be altered by their maturation—infants into toddlers, tweens into teens. Admittedly, those characteristics are not objectively less good for the children at the time they have them than the characteristics that replace them at a later time. But other qualities that can elicit partiality may be objectively less good ones. Imagine a single prospective father, himself orphaned, looking through an orphanage for a child to adopt. He is drawn to one with a wariness and belligerence that remind him of himself in similar circumstances, and he selects that child on the basis of his powerful identification with him. But he has no desire that the child retain that wariness and belligerence. He has himself spent years trying to lose those qualities, and he wants his son to grow out of them as quickly as possible. Perhaps it is not necessary to understand this parent's attraction to this particular child as a matter of affinity-based partiality. We might put it in terms of an extension of Velleman's Kantian account of love: a variety of conditions may be a basis for selection not because they are believed to be desirable, or predictive of a good 'outcome', but simply because they facilitate the capacity of the prospective parent to apprehend and value the other in prospect as an end-in-himself.

My second qualification concerns prospective parents who do select for an impairment because they expect it to give them an affinity with their future child, and not from unmediated partiality. I think the desire for an affinity, like the desire to give an existing child a sibling, concerns in part the good of the future child, because the goal has an inherent reciprocity. Prospective parents do want to identify with the future child, to share his triumphs and tribulations more keenly than it could if he lacked that affinity. But they want the child to experience this affinity too—the value of the impairment for the child lies in the greater intimacy and shared experience it promises (however falsely) for child as well as parents. So I think that the prospective parents desire an impairment-based affinity for the child as well as for themselves. They need not believe that having the impairment will make the child's life go as well overall as lacking the impairment and the shared experience. But I do not think, and this is my more general qualification, that parents must desire that their children's life go as well as possible, or that it is wrong for them to have certain conflicting desires which motivate them to do less than they possibly could for their children, for the sake of other people or interests.

Consider a parent's desire for his child's company. Such 'consortium', as the law calls it, undoubtedly contributes in most cases to the child's well-being as well as the parent's. But parents often face a dilemma about how much time to spend away from their children at work: they want, for themselves and their children, both the consortium and the income. Assume, not implausibly, that a child's expected well-being would be very low if his parents did not work and spent all their time at home, and if they spent almost all their waking hours at work. The child's expected well-being may be highest at an intermediate point that involves more time away from him than his parents desire. I think it would be fully acceptable for them to choose a point at which they could spend a lot more time with him with only a small drop in his expected well-being. They need not maximize, seek to maximize, or even hope to maximize their child's well-being. (Unless they can hope for what is practically impossible, in which case parents who wish to keep their children in a harmful condition can also hope that they do as well as possible—if we can parse hopes as finely as intentions, then no one except a sadist really hopes that his child have less well-being.) Along with a number of recent writers such as Ruddick, I think parental duties must be interpreted in such a way as to make parenting a (generally or typically) rewarding role, one which rarely requires martyrdom, self-abnegation, or extreme sacrifice. Although parents must satisifice at a high level, I do not believe they must maximize in their actions toward, or desires for, their children.[35] For this reason, I think they have somewhat greater moral latitude in their desires than Kahane may permit them. Whether they have enough latitude to desire to have a child with a significant impairment depends both on how much weight they must give their child's interests and on how adversely the impairment is expected to affect them. Their desire may be morally acceptable even if they do not accept disability-neutrality: if they believe that life with the impairment in question will go worse than a life without it, but also believe that it will still go very well.

11.6. An Additional Challenge for Unconditional Welcome

A significant challenge to the ideal of unconditional welcome arises from the recognition that its appeal, even as an aspiration, may depend on background conditions which ensure that most prospective parents face only slight odds of having a child with a severe impairment. The odds of bearing a child with such an impairment are far less than the odds of conceiving one, in part because of a uterine screening mechanism that detects 'defective' fetuses and aborts up to 78 per cent of all conceptions. Leonard Fleck adduced this phenomenon almost thirty years ago to challenge those who claimed full moral status for the early embryo, arguing that they would have to require prospective mothers to take an 'Omega' pill that would turn off the screening mechanism, to prevent the deaths of all those human lives.[36] The Omega pill poses a challenge to proponents of unconditional welcome as well, even though they need not attribute significant moral status to early embryos. Would the unconditional character of the welcome offered by prospective parents be compromised by the presence of a natural 'bouncer' who screens out most impairment-bearing embryos? While there may be

---

[35] I take no position on whether, in satisficing with respect to their children's well-being, they must be maximizing some composite value.

[36] L. Fleck, 'Abortion, Deformed Fetuses and the Omega Pill', *Philosophical. Studies*, 36 (1979), 3.

nothing insincere about the parents' welcome if they can do nothing to prevent this natural screening, their welcome would look disingenuous if they declined to use the easy means, provided by the Omega pill, to call off the bouncer.

And yet unconditional welcome might seem an impossibly demanding ideal for a family, or a world, in which a high proportion of all children would be born with serious impairments. That ideal emerges from a view of families in which there are usually members with no impairments, or with impairments limited enough to provide support for members with more severe impairments. In a world where the uterine screening mechanism ceased to function, or was suppressed by drugs, would unconditional welcome become, even for its most optimistic proponents, an unsupportable ideal?

There are two reasons why a prospective parent aspiring to that ideal might decline to take the Omega pill. First, it is an ideal for a parent–child relationship, and many of the embryos discarded by the uterine screening mechanism would arguably not be capable of entering into such a relationship. As well as the significant proportion who would be stillborn, there would be many who would not survive more than a few days, weeks, or months after birth and many who would lack even the minimal cognitive requisites for a child–parent relationship—not only ancephalics, but those without the cognitive capacity to form a self-concept or to recognize and re-identify significant others. While a woman or a couple could be custodians to such beings, they could not, in any meaningful sense, be parents. Faced with significant odds of bearing an infant who could not really become a child, and to whom she could not really become a parent, a woman might reasonably refuse to take the Omega pill even if that would result in the spontaneous abortion of many embryos capable of becoming children: not only 'false positives'—'normal' embryos that somehow triggered the rejection mechanism—but also embryos that would develop into impaired children with a full capacity to enter into a parent–child relationship.

A second consideration concerns distributive justice. Our society may currently have, even if it is unwilling to utilize, the resources to secure reasonably fulfilling lives for almost all its severely impaired members without denying fulfilling lives to the rest of its members. It might not have the resources to similarly accommodate a vast upsurge in the population of severely impaired children, at least without substantially compromising the well-being of its existing members, with and without significant impairments. Even if no contemporary theory of justice adequately accommodates families, we may have an overlapping consensus that certain burdens are too great to impose on each other. While, in the shadow of *Buck* v. *Bell*, we are very reluctant to regulate conventional procreative activities, even if they are likely in our current socioeconomic regime to lead to increased social costs or decreased productivity, we might reasonably restrict the use of new drugs that would predictably result, at least in the short term, in a large reduction in the well-being of many third parties. As I will suggest in the Conclusion, it might even be more appropriate for the state to impose such restrictions than for prospective parents to voluntarily adopt them.

Yet the unconditional-welcome rationale still has implications that some disability advocates may find troubling. Although it would not require parents to take the Omega pill, it would give them no reason to avoid measures that caused more modest increases in the odds of less drastic impairments (as some fertility treatments are thought to do) as long as those measures would not cause impairments to children who would otherwise have been born without them. Indeed, without the latter risk, a parent who avoided such measures because of their risk of creating impaired 'multiples' would be conditioning her welcome if her concern was with impairment and not family size.

The Omega pill would pose no temptation for those who accepted the justification requirement. Even if a prospective parent had an appropriate reason for wanting a child with a specific impairment, it would seem irresponsible to slightly increase the odds of having such a child by substantially increasing the odds of having children with a variety of other impairments, children whom the prospective parent did not want and might not be prepared to raise. And it would seem perverse and disrespectful to seek a child with *any* severe impairment, perhaps as a challenge to one's resilience and parenting skills.

11.7. Conclusion

The denial that prospective parents have any obligation to protect the genetic health of the population does not entail that there are no moral constraints on allowing or causing the birth of children with severe impairments. I believe, however, that the most plausible and attractive sources of those constraints are not concerned specifically with impairment or disability. The ideal of unconditional welcome opposes the deliberate creation of children with impairments because it opposes any form of selection among potential children, as long as those children are expected to have lives worth living and the capacity to enter into meaningful relationships with their parents. The justification requirement does not demand so expansive a welcome, but it imposes more stringent constraints. All lives contain serious suffering and limitation, and parents can justify that hardship to a child only if they expose him to it for the sake of a life he could not have enjoyed without it. If parents have no reason to want a child with a given condition—an impairment, a quick temper, or an unpopular skin colour—and they could have had a child without that condition, they cannot justify the distinctive hardships associated with that condition to the child. Neither of these positions on the responsibilities of prospective parents categorically prohibits the knowing creation of a child with an impairment, but neither gives parents licence to create any kind of child they fancy.

Both rationales are informed by implicit role-moralities of parenthood. Those moralities are 'second-order', in requiring the agent not only to act in certain ways but to act with, or without, certain intentions. While the ideal of unconditional welcome may seem to reflect an overly strict or demanding role-morality, its emphasis on the limitation of choice and deference to chance as an essential feature of parenthood appears to have deep resonance in popular thinking. This is how Scully and colleagues interpret the ambivalence about procreative freedom expressed by many participants in their reproductive-technology focus groups:

They were saying that certain kinds of choice that would be legitimate in another context are not merely *inappropriate* if exercised by a parent: they are incompatible with the nature of the good parent–child relationship, as they understood it. The identity of the good parent is constituted by this voluntary self-limitation.[37]

Although the participants were focused on selection for sex, not against impairment, their concern might well have extended to the latter. In most

---

[37] J. Scully, T. Shakespeare, and S. Banks, 'Chance, Choice and Control: Lay Debate on Prenatal Social Sex Selection', *Social Science and Medicine*, 63 (2006), 21–31, 30 (emphasis in text).

of the groups, it did not; perhaps because of the tenacity of the conviction that impairment-screening is undertaken 'for the welfare of the child'. Without that misplaced concern for the child's welfare, it should be easier to see the tension between the self-limitation of the 'good parent' and the exercise of selectivity against future children with impairments.

This raises the intriguing possibility that, contrary to the conventional wisdom of the past two generations, the adoption of certain 'front-door' eugenic policies by the state might be less problematic than the 'back-door' eugenics of parental selectivity. The role-morality of governing is clearly more impartial, and arguably more impersonal, than that of prospective parents; it may not only permit, but require, the consideration of aggregate harms and benefits in certain contexts. For example, it would seem appropriate for the state to impose environmental regulations to reduce the incidence of genetic impairment even if it were problematic for prospective parents to undertake measures for that end. It would seem appropriate for the state to ban production or distribution of the Omega pill, to avoid the prohibitive cost of accommodating a massive upsurge in severely impaired children. In complying with such regulations, prospective parents would not condition their welcome to future children so much as fulfil their duty as citizens to obey the law.

There is precedent for this suggestion in proposals to preserve the integrity of professional roles or relationships in the face of scarce resources by assigning allocation decisions to other agents. Thus, for example, it has been proposed that decisions about the allocation of scarce medical resources be made by some centralized authority, in order to protect doctors from having to engage in a 'bedside rationing' inimical to the physician–patient relationship. Similarly, leaving impairment-reducing measures to the centralized agency of the state would avoid a procreative selectivity that is, arguably, inimical to the parent–child relationship.

There would obviously be the potential for conflict between the role-morality of parents, were it governed by an ideal of unconditional welcome, and the role-morality of citizens. But the degree of conflict would depend on the character of state action to affect the genetic character of the population. On one end of the spectrum, measures to reduce mutagenic emissions and discharges would not require compliance by prospective parents at all (except in their very different capacities as drivers or consumers). On the other end, incentives to use preimplantation genetic diagnosis

(PGD) to detect impairments, or penalties for failing to do so, would, even without any requirement to abort for 'positive' results, deeply intrude upon the decision-making processes of prospective parents and create sharp role-conflicts.

There would be a similar potential for conflict if the role morality of parents incorporated the less-stringent justification requirement. As I suggested earlier, that requirement is consistent with a recognition of the impartial or impersonal concerns that guide state action, but it authorizes parents to ignore those concerns in exercising an 'anticipatory partiality' toward children whose creation may reduce aggregate welfare. State action that tried to limit that parental prerogative, for example by incentives for using PGD or penalties for failing to do so, would create a conflict, but not state action that just made its exercise less likely to yield a child with an impairment, e.g., reducing environmental mutagens—the latter might frustrate, but it would not oppose, the exercise of that prerogative.

There are, of course, intermediate cases. What if the government put anti-mutagenic substances in the water, as it now puts fluoride? While prospective parents would knowingly reduce the odds of having an impaired child every time they drank the water, and arguably do so voluntarily, since they could drink bottled water instead, the interference with their procreative decision making strikes me as fairly slight. Perhaps others would disagree. Does the moral significance of that interference depend on its impact on the probability of having a child with an impairment-causing mutation, or on the extent to which it targets procreative choices, or on both? I am not sure, nor am I sure that I have identified all the morally relevant dimension of the role-conflict. But I do think it is helpful to view conflicts between the state's interest in a genetically healthy population and the ideals and prerogatives of prospective parents, as one aspect of a broader conflict between legitimate state objectives on the one hand and family privacy and parental autonomy on the other.

12

Impairment, Flourishing, and the Moral Nature of Parenthood

ROSALIND McDOUGALL

In this chapter I explore ways in which analysing selection decisions involving impairment can illuminate the moral nature of parenthood. Specifically, I suggest that thinking about the situation of parents with an impairment choosing to create a child with the same impairment highlights an important ambiguity in a virtue-based framework for moral assessment of reproductive actions. I focus on a case of a couple with achondroplasia selecting for a child who is also affected by the condition. Analysing this case brings to the foreground an ambiguity that centres on the concept of a child's flourishing: is there a single universally applicable understanding of the characteristics necessary for a child to flourish or should we take the attributes conducive to flourishing to be specific to a particular family environment? I argue that claiming moral permissibility for couples with an impairment selecting for children with the same impairment points to embracing an environment-specific understanding of the characteristics conducive to a child's flourishing. Embracing such an understanding, however, increases the moral justifiability of a much wider range of reproductive decisions involving selection for parentally desired

For their insightful feedback, I am grateful to the editors and reviewers of this collection and also to the participants at the Disability and Disadvantage Workshop held on 8–9 September 2007 at Chapel Hill, NC.

characteristics. Thinking about selection and impairment thus illuminates not only the ethical considerations involved in this type of situation, but also offers insights about the moral nature of parenthood at a more abstract level.

The chapter is in four sections. In the first section, I outline the analytical framework invoked in this paper, which is a virtue-based approach to the moral assessment of reproductive actions for which I have argued in detail elsewhere. In the second section I describe a situation involving parents with an impairment acting to ensure that their child is similarly impaired, and argue that this type of situation highlights a significant conceptual ambiguity in the approach, specifically around the notion of the characteristics compatible with a child's flourishing. In the third section I unpick this ambiguity, articulating two possible conceptions of the characteristics compatible with a child's flourishing and suggesting that the differing conceptions deliver differing results about the moral status of this couple's action. In the fourth section, I explore the implications of embracing the conception of flourishing that improves the justifiability of the couple's action. I argue that embracing this conception implies that a wide range of selection projects are morally justifiable, including selection *against* impairments and selection for traits such as appearance or sporting ability that are often considered ethically problematic.

I have chosen to write in terms of parents with an impairment selecting to create a child with the same impairment, rather than parents selecting for disability. This is because a central question in this chapter is the extent to which a child's flourishing depends on his or her relationship to the family environment. In the context of Terzi's argument that disability is best understood as 'inherently relational, in the sense of resulting from the interaction of individual and social elements',[1] this central question could be framed as a question of the extent to which a child's impairment is disabling. Hence, by using only the terminology of impairment, I aim to prevent pre-empting discussion of that central question.

---

[1] Terzi, L. 'Vagaries of the Natural Lottery? Human Diversity, Disability, and Justice: A Capability Perspective', (Ch. 3 this volume).

12.1. A Virtue-Based Approach to Reproductive Ethics

I have argued elsewhere for taking a virtue-based approach to the moral assessment of reproductive actions.[2] Such an approach seeks to avoid issues which arise for harm-focused frameworks around the non-identity of the various potential children in question.[3] Reproductive choices are often choices *between* children rather than choices about the characteristics a particular child will have. An individual is not harmed by being brought into existence if he or she has a life worth living. If we accept a harm-based framework then, in light of the non-identity problem, we must also accept the life worth living standard as the appropriate extent to which the welfare of a resultant child should be considered in determining the moral status of a reproductive action; as long as the child produced has a life worth living, his or her predicted quality of life has no further impact on the moral permissibility of the reproductive choice that will bring him or her into existence under a harm-focused framework. For some people, including myself, the intuition that consideration of resultant children's wellbeing beyond the life worth living standard is required is an intuition that must be accommodated in any compelling framework for moral assessment of reproductive actions. The desire to accommodate this intuition while also acknowledging the value of individual liberty in reproductive decision-making motivates the alternative framework for assessing moral status that I put forward. On the parental virtue approach that I suggest, that which determines an act's moral status is the act's compatibility with the set of parental virtues rather than the extent of the harms associated with the act; a parental act is right if and only if it is what a virtuous parent would do.

---

[2] This section draws extensively on two previous papers: R. McDougall, 'Parental Virtue: A New Way of Thinking about the Morality of Reproductive Actions', *Bioethics*, 21/4 (2007), 181–90; and R. McDougall, 'Acting Parentally: An Argument against Sex Selection', *Journal of Medical Ethics*, 31 (2005), 601–5.

[3] The classic description of the non-identity problem is D. Parfit, *Reasons and Persons* (Oxford: Oxford University Press, 1984), ch. 16. For other interesting approaches to avoiding these issues, see D. Wasserman, 'The Nonidentity Problem, Disability, and the Role Morality of Prospective Parents', *Ethics*, 116 (2005), 132–52; and R. Kumar, 'Who Can Be Wronged?', *Philosophy and Public Affairs*, 31/2 (2003), 99–118.

The parental virtue approach is based on parent-specific versions of three neo-Aristotelian claims about right action generally.[4] The general versions of the claims are as follows:

1. The Criterion of Right Action: An action is right if and only if it is what a virtuous person would do in the circumstances.
2. The Nature of the Virtuous Person Claim: A virtuous person is one who has and exercises the virtues.
3. The Nature of the Virtues Claim: Virtues are character traits conducive to human flourishing, taking facts about human life as given.

Versions of these claims can be articulated to apply to the realm of parental action specifically. Thus,

1. The Criterion of Right *Parental* Action: A parental action is right if and only if it is what a virtuous parent would do in the circumstances.
2. The Nature of the Virtuous *Parent* Claim: A virtuous parent is one who has and exercises the parental virtues.
3. The Nature of the *Parental* Virtues Claim: Parental virtues are character traits conducive to the flourishing of the child, taking facts about human reproduction as given.[5]

Obviously, far more needs to be said in order to constitute a comprehensive and robust framework for assessing the moral status of parental actions. A challenge for the approach, for example, is articulating how parental virtue fits with virtue as a person. Like all role-based ethical frameworks, the parental virtues approach faces the problem of the relationship between the role-specific virtues and the general virtues, particularly the potential

---

[4] This neo-Aristotelian account of right action is drawn particularly from the following works: R. Hursthouse, *On Virtue Ethics* (Oxford: Oxford University Press, 1999); R. Hursthouse, *Beginning Lives* (Oxford: Blackwell, 1987); R. Hursthouse, 'Normative Virtue Ethics', in R. Crisp (ed.), *How Should One Live?* (New York: Oxford University Press, 1996); J. Oakley, 'Varieties of Virtue Ethics', *Ratio*, 9 (1996), 128–52; P. Foot, *Natural Goodness* (Oxford: Oxford University Press, 2001).

[5] By 'facts about human reproduction' I refer to things such as human infants' long period of dependence and the conditions necessary to children's physical and psychological development. While I acknowledge that it could be argued that some of the 'facts' about human reproduction are changing in light of exactly the reproductive technologies that the parental virtues framework aims to assess, I suggest that there are a core group of facts about human reproduction that are unchangeable (such as those mentioned above) and that these be used as the basis for deriving parental virtues. (I am grateful to Rebecca Walker for highlighting this issue to me.) It is also important to note that by 'facts about human reproduction' I do not mean the traditional reproductive paradigm of conception via heterosexual intercourse and child-rearing within the heterosexual family.

for conflicts between how I ought to act qua parent and how I ought to act all things considered. In the context of this chapter I will bracket this significant issue, focusing exclusively on how an agent ought to act qua parent. My key claim here is limited to the idea that thinking in terms of these three basic claims offers a useful way of conceptualizing questions in reproductive ethics that avoids problems associated with harm-focused frameworks.

It is worth noting that the parental virtue approach relies on two assumptions. The first is that the primary purpose of parenthood is the flourishing of the child.[6] This assumption does not involve the claim that parenthood ought to be aimed *exclusively* at this end; it is compatible with the idea that parenthood is also partly and justifiably a self-directed project. Positing the flourishing of the child as the primary purpose of parenthood still leaves space for recognizing the importance of the parent's own interests. It is also important to note that the flourishing of the child is taken to be a satisficing rather than a maximizing idea in this context. Positing the primary purpose of parenthood as the *maximal* flourishing of one's child seems obviously implausible. We do not think a parent good if he or she is focused on producing tiny increases in the wellbeing of an already healthy and happy child at great cost to the parent or to other family members. However, the very concept of flourishing involves the idea of a high level of wellbeing; we would not call a child 'flourishing' unless he or she was doing very well. Thus the level to be satisficed in order for a child to be flourishing (while inevitably vague) is intuitively a high one, far higher than the life-worth-living level. On the basis of this assumption about the primary purpose of parenthood, I do not differentiate between maternal and paternal virtues.[7] I take it that both motherhood and fatherhood involve adopting the child's flourishing as a primary aim and thus that parental virtues do not differ between male and female parents.

Positing the parental virtues approach as a framework in *reproductive* ethics involves a further assumption, namely that the realm of parental action includes more than the actions involved in the care of existing

---

[6] Articulating a full account of what it means for a child to flourish is beyond the scope of this chapter but is clearly important in developing the parental virtue approach as a comprehensive framework. For now, I rely on the intuitive understanding that a child's flourishing involves elements including happiness, health, loving relationships, and the development of his or her potential.

[7] I thank Mary Mahowald for drawing my attention to this issue.

children. The idea is that an agent's action can be parental even though the specific child does not yet exist. In the context of the first assumption, understanding the realm of parental action in this broader way makes sense; pre-birth and even pre-conception actions are relevant to a child's flourishing alongside actions once the child is born. The claim is thus that, at least once the project of parenthood has been adopted and conception is imminent, actions can be parental.

I have suggested three parental virtues as the beginnings of a substantive basis for deciding what a virtuous parent would do in particular circumstances: acceptingness (i.e. perceiving acceptingly the characteristics of one's child), committedness (i.e. being deeply committed to fulfilling one's child's physical and emotional needs throughout the child's dependence), and future-agent-focus (i.e. the motivation to behave in ways that promote the development of children into good moral agents). I argued that at least these three parental virtues emerge when we consider the question 'How is one to parent well?' in the context of the relevant facts and a primary aim of flourishing children. Others have suggested further parental virtues. For example, in her work on maternal thinking Sara Ruddick posits humility, cheerfulness, scrutiny, and trustworthiness as virtues.[8] The parental virtue of acceptingness will be a particular focus in this discussion.

It is important to emphasize a point of Hursthouse's (following Aristotle[9]) with respect to virtues in order to prevent a misunderstanding about the nature of parental virtues. Hursthouse argues that the idea of a virtue intrinsically involves the notion of the correct amount; she writes that 'built into each concept of a virtue is the idea of getting things *right*: in the case of generosity giving the *right* amount of things for the *right* reasons on the *right* occasions to the *right* people [Hursthouse's italics]'.[10]

The same needs to be understood of parental virtues. As with the general virtues, the parental virtues involve more than mindlessly maximizing instances of behaviour that could be superficially described by the relevant virtue term. Just as truth-telling at every available opportunity is not equivalent to having the virtue of honesty, accepting each and every

---

[8] S. Ruddick, *Maternal Thinking: Towards a Politics of Peace* (Boston: Beacon Press), 72–9, 118–19. I am grateful to Adrienne Asch and Eva Kittay for directing me to Ruddick's work.

[9] Aristotle, *Nichomachean Ethics,* trans. Terence Irwin, 2nd edn (Indianapolis: Hackett, 1999) II 6, 1106b17–24.

[10] Hursthouse, *Beginning Lives* (n. 4 above), 228–9.

feature of one's child does not amount to having the parental virtue of acceptingness. Keeping in mind the human flourishing aim in the general context and the child's flourishing aim in the parental context facilitates the more appropriately nuanced understanding of the virtues, as will be elaborated further in Section 12.2, where I apply the parental virtue approach to the situation of parents with an impairment selecting for a child who shares their condition. Attempting to ethically analyse this type of situation in terms of parental virtue highlights a significant conceptual ambiguity in the approach as described so far, enabling further development of the framework.

12.2. A Case of Selecting for Impairment

Although selection *against* impairment has engendered significant debate in academic circles, the possibility of parents with impairments deliber- ately choosing *to create* children who share their condition has also been particularly controversial in the public sphere. While, for example, our extensive prenatal screening programs for Down's Syndrome rarely register on the collective public radar, headlines are generated by a Deaf couple's endeavours to ensure their child is deaf.[11] What does a moral framework based on parental virtue have to say about this latter type of situation?

As a focus for answering this question, consider the following specific scenario involving selection for impairment. Imagine a couple, John and Jane, both of whom have achondroplasia. People with achondroplasia have short stature (attaining an adult height of around 4 feet), shortened limbs, and some characteristic facial features; affected children have no cognitive impairment but often have motor delays.[12] It is a heritable condition for which a specific genetic change has been identified, enabling testing of embryos and fetuses.[13] John and Jane decide to use in vitro fertilization (IVF) and preimplantation genetic diagnosis (PGD) to ensure that their

---

[11] See e.g. Anon., 'Baby Gauvin was Born to be Deaf', *Herald-Sun,* Melbourne, 9 April 2002: 7; Anon., 'Couple "Choose" to Have a Deaf Baby', *BBC News,* 8 April 2002,<http://news.bbc.co.uk/hi/english/health/newsid_1916000/1916462.stm> [accessed 18 April 2005].

[12] Little People of America, 'Achondroplasia', http://medical.lpaonline.org/dwarfism_types/resourcelist.php?infotype=dwarftypes&typename=Achondroplasia&id=1 [accessed 19 Feb 2007].

[13] C. Moutou et al., 'Preimplantation Genetic Diagnosis for Achondroplasia: Genetics and Gynae- cological Limits and Difficulties', *Human Reproduction,* 18/3 (2003), 509–14.

child has achondroplasia. They reject embryo Y on the basis that it would most likely have developed into a child of average stature, and choose to implant embryo Z as tests indicate that this embryo will most likely develop into a child with achondroplasia. Nine months later they are thrilled at the arrival of their son Zack who has achondroplasia.

I will assume that John and Jane share the reasoning of Celia, the woman with achondroplasia presented by Davis in her book *Genetic Dilemmas*. Davis writes:

I asked Celia to speak more about their [Celia's and her husband's] reluctance to have a child of average stature . . . She spoke at length of the physical context of her world, in which she and her husband, and other couples like them, had cut down the legs of chairs, designed kitchens with only low cabinets, and in general made their circumstances fit their needs. She talked of how reluctant she would be to change that, and how an average-sized child might not fit in. She also spoke about how hard it would be to carry and care for a child who at age five was as big as its parents. She spoke poignantly of the need she felt every child has to 'look up to' its parents and to feel safe and protected by them physically, and how a child of average stature would not have that experience. She worried that an average-sized child with 'little' parents would feel embarrassed at school . . . Finally, she mentioned how important LPA [Little People of America, an organization that provides support to people of short stature and their families] was in her life.[14]

Celia articulates a range of reasons why people with short stature would want a child who shares their condition, many of which are focused on the potential child: the misalignment between an average-sized child and his or her physical home environment, the difficulty that the parents with achondroplasia could have in fulfilling the physical and emotional needs of an average-sized child, and the problem of isolation from a group central to his or her parents' lives.

Existing analyses would critique John and Jane's decision either on the basis that they are allowing a single characteristic to stand in for the whole,[15] or that their action fails to choose the child expected to have the 'best' life.[16]

---

[14] D. Davis, *Genetic Dilemmas: Reproductive Technology, Parental Choices, and Children's Futures* (New York: Routledge, 2001), 50.

[15] A. Asch, 'Why I Haven't Changed my Mind about Prenatal Diagnosis: Reflections and Refinements', in E. Parens and A. Asch (eds.), *Prenatal Testing and Disability Rights* (Washington: Georgetown University Press), 235–6.

[16] J. Savulescu, 'Procreative Beneficence: Why We Should Select the Best Children', *Bioethics*, 15/5–6 (2001), 413–26.

Taking the parental virtue approach in contrast, we are directed to thinking about whether John and Jane's action would be that of the virtuous parent; according to the Criterion of Right Parental Action, their action is right if and only if it is what a virtuous parent would do in the circumstances. Would a virtuous parent select embryo Z over embryo Y on the basis of Z's status in relation to achondroplasia? Alternative possible actions would be to choose randomly among the embryos or to refrain from IVF and PGD altogether, instead taking the natural lottery.[17] Considering that the virtuous parent is specified as one who has and exercises the parental virtues, we need to consider how well the couple's action aligns with the parental virtues in order to determine its moral status. I will assume throughout the discussion that the preference of the parents with achondroplasia to maintain their current environment is a morally justifiable one. While in some cases parents may be morally required to adjust their environment to accommodate a particular type of child (for example, avoiding all nuts in the home of a child with a life-threatening allergy to peanuts), where the parents themselves require particular concrete features for their own ease of functioning, taking such features as fixed seems morally justifiable.

One of the parental virtues with which John and Jane's action needs to align is acceptingness. Thus far, I have elaborated acceptingness only as 'perceiving acceptingly the characteristics of one's child'. Keeping in mind Hursthouse's claim quoted earlier that virtues conceptually involve getting things right in terms of target, timing, and amount, more needs to be specified about the parental virtue of acceptingness. It seems straightforward that acceptingness cannot involve perceiving acceptingly *all* of one's child's characteristics. It is strongly counterintuitive to think of a parent who accepts his or her child's maliciousness or rudeness as morally admirable. But then we are faced with the question of which characteristics fall within the scope of acceptingness. How do we know if a characteristic is one perceived acceptingly by the virtuous parent? The first assumption outlined above (that the primary purpose of parenthood is the flourishing of the child) suggests the following general test of whether a characteristic falls within

---

[17] The way in which achondroplasia is inherited means that embryos with two affected copies of the gene normally perish in utero. (Individuals with one affected and one unaffected copy of the gene develop the condition.) This would give John and Jane a reason to undergo IVF and PGD even if they did not intend to select for (or against) achondroplasia; they would reject the embryos with two affected copies of the gene, and then choose randomly from among the remaining embryos.

the scope of acceptingness: is the characteristic in question compatible with the child's flourishing? Characteristics that are compatible with a child living a flourishing life would be perceived acceptingly by the virtuous parent, while those that are incompatible with a child's flourishing would fall outside the scope of this parental virtue. This would explain why maliciousness or rudeness are not perceived acceptingly by the virtuous parent; such characteristics have a negative impact on the child's relationships with others, compromising that child's capacity to flourish. Characteristics conducive to flourishing and characteristics which have no effect on flourishing (such as eye colour) are perceived acceptingly by the virtuous parent.

Is the characteristic that John and Jane are rejecting, namely being unaffected by achondroplasia, compatible with the child's flourishing? Positing embryo Y as *unable* to flourish on the basis of a *lack* of impairment is, at least, strongly counterintuitive. But the reasons outlined by Celia highlight plausible ways in which the flourishing of a child without achondroplasia would be importantly compromised by growing up in the home of John and Jane, both because of his or her misalignment with the concrete home environment and because of the relative difference between his or her stature and that of the parents. Although the potential child's ability to function in the average-sized world outside his or her parents' home will of course also have an impact on his or her wellbeing, fitting with his or her family environment seems fundamentally important to his or her flourishing.[18] The compatibility of John and Jane's action with the parental virtue of acceptingness thus seems to depend on how we understand the idea of characteristics compatible with the child's flourishing; are they relative to a particular family environment?

12.3. Two Understandings of the Characteristics Compatible with a Child's Flourishing

Thinking about the moral status of John and Jane's action thus brings out a significant conceptual ambiguity in the parental virtue approach. The

---

[18] Recent sociological work such as that of Annette Lareau supports the claim that it is the family environment that is most powerful in influencing a child's life: A. Lareau, *Unequal Childhoods: Class, Race, and Family Life* (Berkeley: University of California Press, 2003). I thank Lorella Terzi for drawing my attention to this work.

scenario highlights that the concept of characteristics compatible with the child's flourishing can be understood in at least two different ways: as a single universally applicable notion, or as specific to the environment into which a particular child will be born.

The first of these I will call the *universal* understanding. This conception of the characteristics compatible with a child's flourishing takes the idea to be a single universally applicable one. Structurally similar to objective list theories of the good, on the universal understanding there are a particular set of features that constitute a flourishing human life and a correlative fixed set of characteristics that enable an individual to manifest these features in his or her life. The features might include quite vague things such as being part of meaningful human relationships, pursuing knowledge, and acting morally, or far more specific things such as becoming a parent or appreciating music. Although there will be a variety of understandings of flourishing and thus various sets of characteristics posited, the key idea for our purposes here is that any posited set of characteristics will apply identically to all children. The characteristics conducive to a flourishing life for the child of John and Jane will be the same as those conducive to a flourishing life for the child of Russian farmers or the child of an Australian lesbian couple. On this understanding, a parent promoting the child's flourishing involves the parent ensuring that the child has the fixed set of characteristics posited as enabling children to develop the valuable life-features.

An alternative to this universal understanding of the characteristics compatible with a child's flourishing is an understanding in which the set of characteristics compatible with flourishing varies relative to the specific family environment. I will call this the *environment-relative* understanding. On this type of understanding, the attributes compatible with flourishing will vary between children depending on the type of family in which they will grow up. Unlike on the universal understanding, parental characteristics such as being deaf or having achondroplasia are relevant on this understanding, as the parents' way of living determines to a significant extent the kinds of characteristics that the child needs in order to flourish. The parents determine the childhood environment to a vast extent, and it is the child's fit with that environment that impacts his or her flourishing on this understanding. For example, where the parents are part of the Deaf community, hearing ability may be incompatible with flourishing; the child communicates with his or her family and community in sign language. The child's flourishing may be facilitated by the fact that all family members communicate in the same mode, making his or her hearing antithetical to flourishing on this understanding. This way of conceiving the characteristics compatible with a child's flourishing captures the intuition that the child's ability to interact in his or her specific situation contributes to his or her wellbeing.

It is this type of environment-relative understanding of the characteristics compatible with flourishing that is invoked by Celia in the passage quoted earlier, when she suggests that an average-sized child whose parents had achondroplasia would encounter a range of difficulties sufficiently significant to make having achondroplasia preferable. In the John and Jane scenario, for example, a child's lacking achondroplasia precludes flourishing on the environment-relative understanding because the child's physical environment is set up for people with this condition. An average-sized child would literally be a misfit in his or her concrete environment, presumably with negative implications for his or her flourishing. Similarly, it could be argued that John and Jane's short stature means that a child without achondroplasia could not have some of the physical interactions with his or her parents that are conducive to flourishing. Understanding the characteristics compatible with a child's flourishing as environment-relative assumes that the familial environment is substantially fixed (which seems a plausible assumption, particularly in terms of parental characteristics), and that a child's fit with the familial environment has a significant impact on his or her wellbeing.

If we understand the characteristics compatible with a child's flourishing as relativized to the particular family and environment in which that child will live, John and Jane's action aligns with the parental virtue of acceptingness. On this environment-relative understanding, a child's fit with the familial situation into which he or she will be born contributes to that child's flourishing and so a lack of the impairment in question becomes incompatible with the child's flourishing in this situation. On this understanding, John and Jane's selection for impairment aligns with the action of the virtuous parent, at least to the extent that their action is consistent with the specific parental virtue of acceptingness.

However, adopting the universal understanding of the characteristics compatible with a child's flourishing suggests that John and Jane's action is inconsistent with the parental virtue of acceptingness. In rejecting embryo Y on the basis that it would develop into a child who did not have achondroplasia, they fail to perceive acceptingly a characteristic (namely lack of achondroplasia) that is compatible with the child's flourishing. Whatever the specific constituents used to fill out what it means for a child to flourish, it is difficult to imagine a plausible set that being of average stature precludes attaining. On a universal conception of the characteristics compatible with a child's flourishing, the couple's selection looks to be inconsistent with a parental virtue, acceptingness. Lacking achondroplasia is clearly compatible with the child's flourishing on a universal understanding, rendering selection for the impairment a failure to act in accordance with parental virtue. (Of course, it is possible that John and Jane's action may perhaps still be the choice of the virtuous parent overall; ultimately we need to take into account the action's alignment with all of the parental virtues, not just its compatibility or otherwise with acceptingness.)

12.4. Implications Beyond Selection for Impairment

Thus, if we want to argue for a couple's decision to select for impairment as being compatible with acceptingness, we must accept an environment-relative understanding of the characteristics compatible with the child's flourishing. To best align John and Jane's action with that of the virtuous parent, the familial environment must be posited as determining the characteristics a potential child needs in order to flourish. However, understanding children's flourishing in this way has some potentially problematic implications well beyond selection decisions involving impairment. By positing the environment in which the child will live as relevant to the characteristics he or she needs to flourish, a range of other parental selection choices that some would consider ethically worrying are also rendered compatible with acceptingness.

These implications arise partly because an environment-relative understanding of the characteristics compatible with the child's flourishing seems to allow parental preferences to count in measuring potential children's wellbeing. It seems clear that parental preferences as well as their physical characteristics form part of the familial environment in which a potential child will grow up. Alignment with one's parents' values and abilities plausibly increases a child's wellbeing in the same way that fitting the physical home environment does. For example, in the home of bookish academic parents, a bookish, academically able child seems far more likely to flourish than a child lacking any intellectual inclination. This seems particularly likely to be the case when the parents desperately want an academically gifted child. On the environment-relative understanding, having characteristics that fulfil one's parents' deeply held desires is conducive to the potential child's flourishing because these preferences form part of the child's environment. Accepting that a child's misalignment with his or her environment is incompatible with his or her flourishing enables the deeply held desires of a potential child's parents legitimate influence over the characteristics compatible with that child's flourishing. Being the kind of child that one's parents want increases flourishing on the environment-relative conception, a feature that may well count against the acceptability of this conception for some.

Accepting the environment-relative understanding of the characteristics compatible with a child's flourishing therefore implies that the actions of non-impaired parents who select *against* impairment could be consistent with acceptingness. Such parents presumably have a deeply held desire and, in most cases, live in a physical environment which would be incompatible with flourishing for a child with the impairment in question. (Obviously, adjustments to the physical environment can be made in some instances, but where such adjustments make day-to-day living more difficult for the non-disabled parents, these parents' reluctance to make adjustments presumably has the same legitimacy as the reluctance of people with achondroplasia to change their homes to suit a child of average stature.) For example, parents who select against a potential child with achondroplasia could argue that their home environment is set up for people of average stature; just as the child of average stature misaligns with the home of the parents with achondroplasia, the child with achondroplasia misaligns with the home of the average-statured parents. Additionally, if the average-statured parents strongly prefer a child of average stature, this preference also makes up part of the environment into which the child must fit well to flourish. Another example would be the hearing parents who choose to select against a potential child who would be deaf. They could justify their choice on the basis that they greatly value the ability to hear and desperately want a child who has that characteristic. On the environment-relative understanding, these factors contribute to justifying the parents' selection choice because they influence the familial environment. The fit between that environment and any potential child who lacks the desired characteristic determines consistency with acceptingness. Therefore, the understanding of flourishing that enables parents with impairments to select *for* children who share their condition has the implication of rendering similarly morally permissible the actions of non-impaired parents who wish to select *against* the same condition.

Accepting the environment-relative understanding would also imply that various other selection decisions could similarly be consistent with acceptingness. Potential parents could have deeply held desires for characteristics in their children such as high intelligence, heterosexuality, or being a particular sex, for example. If we are claiming that a child who is unaffected by achondroplasia is less likely to flourish in a familial environment based around the condition, it seems equally plausible to claim that a child who lacks sporting ability is less likely to flourish in a familial environment structured around athletic achievement. Just as the flourishing of a child who is unaffected by achondroplasia may be compromised in a family affected by the condition, the child lacking sporting prowess seems unlikely to flourish in a familial ethos structured around athletic achievement, particularly when the parents have a deeply held desire for sporty children. In these cases the parental desire is the key contributor to the potential child's familial environment rather than concrete features of the home. Unlike in the achondroplasia example, it is difficult to conceive of physical features of a familial environment that would be, for example, compatible only with the flourishing of a child of a particular sex, intelligence level, or sporting ability. However if, as suggested earlier, parental desires and preferences form part of that home environment and therefore affect flourishing on the environment-relative understanding, these types of selection choices look morally justifiable at least in terms of their consistency with the parental virtue of acceptingness. Considering the ethically worrying nature of these kinds of selection choices for many people, this result perhaps brings into question the attractiveness of the environment-relative understanding. For those for whom such parental actions are morally unacceptable, the moral status of parents with impairments selecting for children who share their condition must be considered similarly problematic.

12.5. Conclusion

I do not claim that the implications outlined in the previous section show that we ought to reject the environment-relative understanding or, associatedly, that selection for impairment by potential parents with impairments could not be the choice of the virtuous parent. This is for two reasons.

The first is that, as mentioned earlier, the discussion has focused on the parental virtue of acceptingness, alignment with which is not alone determinative of the action of the virtuous parent overall. Even if the environment-relative understanding is rejected and John and Jane's decision deemed incompatible with acceptingness, it may be that consideration of the full range of parental virtues indicates that their choice is the best possible alternative from the virtuous parent's perspective.

The second reason is that the environment-relative understanding of the characteristics compatible with a child's flourishing may ultimately be preferable. Whether the implications outlined are taken as reasons for rejecting the environment-relative understanding will be determined in part by the strength of the intuition that potential parents with impairments are morally entitled to select for children who share their characteristics. Where this intuition is very firmly held, the problematic implications of the environment-relative understanding will be acceptable in the context of the additional positive features of this understanding.

What the discussion in the previous section does show, however, is that the issue of parents with impairments selecting for children who share their impairment cannot be separated from the broader ethical questions around parental selection choices in general. There are ethically important structural similarities to parental selection decisions, whether they involve selection for an impairment or for some other parentally desired characteristic.

Thinking about the moral justifiability from a parental virtue perspective of parents with an impairment selecting for children who share their condition has highlighted both a conceptual ambiguity around the idea of the characteristics compatible with a child's flourishing and the necessity of considering this particular type of selection decision in concert with other types of parental selection choices.

13

Projected Disability and Parental Responsibilities

RICHARD HULL

This paper explores a hybrid view of disability in society in conjunction with the claim that it is wrong to choose to have disabled children. It will be argued that it is hard to say that it is wrong to choose to have disabled children in all but a few cases. A variety of issues encourage that conclusion, including the social aspect of much disability, the non-identity problem, the personal nature of reproductive decisions, and the idea that the separation of 'the disabled' from 'the non-disabled' may no longer be very useful. However, some reproductive possibilities, to say the least, test our moral sensibilities. The rest of the paper explores what we can legitimately say about them.

Before investigating whether having disabled children can be wrongful, a little needs to be said about the approach to disability that is taken here. Many debates about disability have assumed that it is either a purely medical condition or a purely social problem. I have argued at greater length elsewhere that it is generally a bit of both.[1] We should not overlook the fact of physical impairment or functional limitation when we are thinking about disability. Nor should we overlook the role of social structures, attitudes, and arrangements. The problem with the purely medical model of disability is that too strong an emphasis is placed on impairment. Disability is said to *result* from impairment in a way that suggests a direct and inevitable

I am grateful to the editors and to the anonymous OUP referees for their helpful suggestions and comments on an earlier draft of this paper.

[1] R. Hull, 'Defining Disability—A Philosophical Approach', *Res Publica*, 4/2 (1998), and R. Hull, *Deprivation and Freedom* (New York: Routledge, 2007), ch. 2.

connection, but this is simply false in many cases. For example, inadequate welfare measures, education, health and social support services, housing, transport, and built environments do not simply *result* from impairment, nor does institutional or personal discrimination. Yet these are the sorts of things that tend to comprise much of the experience of disability for people with impairments. Rather obviously, they need not just follow or result from the fact of impairment; they depend on how a society responds, or fails to respond, to the needs of some of the people within that society. Thus many disabilities would be much less disabling if society were differently organized. For example, if ramps and lifts were just as common as stairs, people who rely on wheelchairs to get around the built environment would be a lot less disabled than they presently are.

Functional limitation or impairment necessitates disability only if the activity in question requires the use of the functionally limited part or system. Taking the example above, if I cannot walk and rely on wheels to get around, I will clearly be unable to *walk* to the shops. If, however, I cannot get into the shops because they all have steps leading up to them, that is an entirely different matter—and here the disability is dependent on social structures and arrangements, like unsympathetic architectural design. Similarly, if I am colour blind, it is unlikely that I will get a job as a hair colourist in all but the most adventurous of salons, but if I cannot get a variety of other jobs (that do not require being able to distinguish colour accurately) because of the selectors' discriminatory attitudes toward people with impairments, that again is an entirely different matter. In both cases, my experience of disability entails joblessness but, in the latter case, my joblessness is all about a response to my impairment that is far from inevitable or fair. Of course, things are rarely this simple in reality. Disability more often than not involves a highly complex interplay of impairment and social factors. Nonetheless, it is useful to distinguish disabilities that result primarily from impairment from those that result primarily from a socially inadequate or discriminatory response to impairment, when we are thinking about disability issues in the context of present and future reproductive choices. Disability is not just a social phenomenon, but rarely is it a purely medical one either. Each conventional model captures one, but only one, aspect of disability.

Disability tends to concern us because of the impact that it can have on our capacity to flourish as human beings. As Jonathan Glover has recently argued: 'Disability requires failure of functioning. But failure of functioning creates disability only if (on its own or *via* social discrimination) it impairs capacities for human flourishing. It would not be a disability if there were a failure of a system whose only function was to keep toenails growing. With arrested toenail growth, we flourish no less.'[2] Thus, it is the impact that a particular functional limitation has 'either on its own or—more usually—in combination with social disadvantage',[3] on our capacity to flourish as human beings that is critical to the evaluation of how severe a particular disability is and, by implication, whether we should try to do something about it. 'Doing something about it', given the current state of genetic technology, is often taken to mean eradicating disability where we can through preimplantation genetic diagnosis or termination of pregnancy, when functional limitation is identified during that pregnancy. However, given the arguments above, 'doing something about it' could equally mean changing society so that it is much more sympathetic to functional loss. Indeed, removing social disadvantage and implementing the right kinds of changes to social structures and arrangements could render many functional limitations relatively unproblematic, whereupon the functional loss would have much less of an impact on our capacity to flourish. The social aspect of much disability, then, encourages seriously questioning the justice of our present social structures and arrangements. This does not mean that all social barriers or failures bound up with the experience of disability are *necessarily* unjust,[4] but merely that the fact that they are social (and remediable) enables us to question whether we want such conditions to continue. And a variety of theorists converge on the idea, albeit in different ways, that a more inclusive society where disadvantages were reduced and people's capabilities or freedoms were increased would reflect both a defensible and a desirable notion of social justice.[5]

Given the social aspect of much disability, we already have reason to question where the 'wrong' lies, if anywhere, with respect to the choice

---

[2] J. Glover, *Choosing Children* (Oxford: Clarendon Press, 2006), 9. I do not intend to argue for this claim. I am simply accepting it as a very sensible claim to make and attempting to explore some of its implications.

[3] Ibid.

[4] See e.g. the 'bottomless pit' problem. D. W. Brock, 'Cost-Effectiveness and Disability Discrimination', forthcoming in *Economics and Philosophy*.

[5] See e.g. A. De-Shalit and J. Wolff, *Disadvantage* (Oxford: Oxford University Press, 2007); Hull, *Deprivation and Freedom*; and L. Terzi, 'Vagaries of the Natural Lottery? Human Diversity, Disability and Justice: A Capability Perspective', Ch. 3 this volume.

to have a disabled child. For example, the decision to terminate pregnancy because of projected functional limitation could in many cases be made on grounds that primarily reflect a particularly inflexible social structure rather than the particular severity of a medical condition. Here it would seem that if anything is 'wrongful', it is more likely to be our society than it is the anticipated medical condition. In the light of this, adopting a blanket policy of screening with a view to termination in cases of projected disability could be said to be a little hasty. Indeed, with most cases of projected disability, the resulting child will unquestionably have a worthwhile life, which leads many to argue that it could never be wrongful to bring that child into the world.

To claim that it is wrong to have a disabled child is difficult because it usually does not amount to a 'wrongful life' claim. To claim that a life is wrongful is to claim that it would be preferable not to exist than to exist with the kind of life that is subject to the claim. This is considered to apply to particularly severe medical conditions—conditions that are judged to be worse than death. Assuming that we can make sense of that sort of claim, it clearly does not apply to most cases of disability. That is to say, in most cases of disability the person with the disability clearly has a valued and worthwhile life. As such, they would not prefer non-existence to that life—and it would be extremely harsh to argue that they should. Yet often, non-existence is the only alternative to a life with disability, as Buchanan, Brock, Daniels, and Wikler point out.

The special difficulty in wrongful disability cases . . . is that it would not be better for the person with the disability to have had it prevented, since that could only be done by preventing him or her from ever having existed at all. Preventing the disability would deny the disabled individual a worthwhile, although disabled life. That is because the disability could only have been prevented either by conceiving at a different time and/or under different circumstances (in which case a different child would have been conceived) or by terminating the pregnancy . . . None of these possible means of preventing the disability would be better for the child with the disability—all would deny him or her a worthwhile life.[6]

This articulation of Parfit's non-identity problem adds to the question-ability of the claim that it is wrong to choose to have disabled children.

---

[6] A. Buchanan, D. Brock, N. Daniels, and D. Wikler, *From Chance to Choice: Genetics and Justice* (Cambridge: Cambridge University Press, 2000), 245–6.

How can it be wrong to bring a child into the world with a worthwhile existence? Disability here is inextricable from the act of bringing a child into existence with a worthwhile life.[7] Nonetheless, some theorists want to maintain that it is indeed wrong to bring a child into existence with a disability. For example, Buchanan, Brock, Daniels, and Wikler argue that it is wrong to have a disabled child when 'the severity of a genetically transmitted disability [is] great enough that particular parents are morally obligated to prevent it, given the specific means necessary for them to do so'. This is contrasted with disability that is 'sufficiently limited and minor that it need not be prevented, but is instead a condition that the child can be reasonably expected to live with'.[8] However, when the alternative is non-existence, it is not clear how this argument can hold without absurdly raising the threshold of wrongful life.

Buchanan and colleagues follow Parfit by distinguishing 'same person' from 'same number' choices. Our moral choices are most commonly same person choices, where 'the same persons exist in each of the alternative courses of action from which an agent chooses'.[9] So, for example, if a pre- or postnatal intervention with little risk was available to ameliorate an impairment, it seems quite straightforward to contend that it would be wrong not to avail oneself of it, due to the easily preventable effect on the resulting child. Indeed, it is arguable that that would be a clear case of wrongful disability. However, in this case the same person exists throughout. The choice is whether that same person will exist with, with less, or without impairment. That choice is obviously not available in the scenario sketched earlier where the only alternative to a life with disability is no life at all.

Where the only alternative to a life with disability is no life at all, Buchanan and colleagues argue that we are presented with a 'same number' choice, whereupon 'the same number of persons exist in each of the alternative courses of action from which an agent chooses, but the identities of some of the persons—that is, who exists in those alternatives—is affected by the choice'.[10] It follows for them that a moral principle applying to a same number choice will be a non-person-affecting principle, since there is no 'same person' to be affected. It is with this sort of principle that they believe they can maintain that in many cases it is wrong to have

---

[7] Ibid. 246.   [8] Ibid. 243.   [9] Ibid. 248.   [10] Ibid.

disabled children *without* raising the threshold of what is considered to be wrongful life.

The principle that they consider to denote cases where it is wrong to have a disabled child runs as follows:

N: Individuals are morally required not to let any child or other dependent person for whose welfare they are responsible experience serious suffering or limited opportunity or serious loss of happiness or good, if they can act so that, *without affecting the number of persons who will exist* and without imposing substantial burdens or costs or loss of benefits on themselves or others, no child or other dependent person for whose welfare they are responsible will experience serious suffering or limited opportunity or serious loss of happiness or good.[11]

This principle 'allows the child who does not experience the suffering and limited opportunity to be a different person from the child who does'.[12] That is how, according to Buchanan and colleagues, we can say that it is morally wrong to have a disabled child even when it results in preventing that child from having a worthwhile existence. We should substitute it for a non-disabled child who will, presumably, have an even more worthwhile existence.

I have argued elsewhere that the idea of avoidability via substitution has some peculiar implications.[13] Moreover, it is deeply insensitive in at least two respects. First, deciding to terminate pregnancy on the grounds of projected disability can be a very traumatic experience, which can impact on the willingness to try to conceive another child. It can be argued that our moral framework should be wholly sympathetic to such a case, for example, where a couple decide to refrain from bringing about avoidable suffering and, because of their experience, decide not to try to conceive another child. In the light of this kind of case, the moral requirement to substitute can be said to be insensitive. Indeed, principle N implies that the couple's decision, by definition, cannot be justified.[14] However, it could be said to be bizarre to claim that a decision to refrain from bringing about avoidable

---

[11] A. Buchanan, D. Brock, N. Daniels, and D. Wikler, *From Chance to Choice: Genetics and Justice* 249.

[12] Ibid. 249.

[13] R. Hull, 'Cheap Listening? Reflections on the Concept of Wrongful Disability', *Bioethics*, 20/2 (2006).

[14] Hence, Buchanan et al. argue that where parents are unable to have a non-disabled child instead, having a disabled child is not a case of wrongful disability (*From Chance to Choice*, 255). However, it is arguable that any reasons that are strong enough to trigger the motivation to, for example, terminate pregnancy and substitute 'a non-disabled child instead', will likely be reasons to terminate pregnancy

suffering can only be justified by then proceeding to bring about a life of less or no suffering. It is rather like the claim that my decision to refrain from driving a car that pollutes the air obliges me to buy a helium-powered one. Yet it is not at all obvious here that such an obligation follows.

In its defence, the intuition underlying principle N is an admirable one, that 'it is good to prevent suffering and promote happiness (even if doing so reduces no person's suffering and increases no person's happiness)'. Indeed, it could be said that the desire to refrain from bringing about avoidable suffering is a highly understandable reason to consider terminating pregnancy in cases of projected disability. However, that does not mean that a decision to continue with that pregnancy would be necessarily wrong—and this is the second respect in which the idea of avoidability via substitution can be said to be deeply insensitive. That is to say, the moral requirement to substitute is likely to run up against some very personal and deeply held beliefs in many cases.[15] For example, to claim that termination and substitution is 'required' is to wade not very gently into the profoundly personal area of reproductive decision making and, as Jonathan Glover argues, 'there is something to be said for avoiding the intrusion of too many or too stringent moral obligations into an intimate personal decision'.[16] Indeed, many people have deeply held beliefs and convictions with respect to the issue of abortion, which may weigh heavily on their decision making in cases of projected disability. To declare that a decision not to terminate a pregnancy in such cases is *wrong* is unlikely to be at all helpful.[17] Nor is it true if Parfit is right, that a worthwhile although disabled life is better than no life at all.

Given these sorts of difficulties, the idea of avoidability via substitution as a moral requirement is not one with which we should proceed.[18] By

in any circumstances, that is, *whether or not* substitution takes place. If they are not, then availability of substitution must somehow lower the threshold of what is unacceptable.

[15] It could be said that the 'are morally required' part of principle N is too strong and that Buchanan et al. would avoid many problems if they replaced it with 'have moral reason to', because that would allow for stronger moral reasons on the other side. However, the principle would then be a lot less clear about how choosing to have disabled children could be 'wrong'. I am grateful to Jonathan Wolff for pointing this out to me.

[16] Glover, *Choosing Children*, 54.

[17] It is debatable as to whether the same could be said for wrongful life cases.

[18] This is not to deny that the possibility of being able to have a future child without disability may be a legitimate consideration for prospective parents in some cases. It just need not dictate what they do.

implication, problems raised by the non-identity problem remain. Indeed, taking together the social component of much disability, the non-identity problem, the failure of principle N to appropriately address that problem and the intensely personal nature of reproductive decisions, it is hard to see how choosing to have disabled children can be wrong, when the alternative is non-existence.

In addition, it is no longer clear that a rigid distinction between 'the disabled' and 'the non-disabled' is appropriate or useful. It clearly *was* necessary to appeal to what all people with disabilities had in common, in order to build a unified and powerful disability movement. 'The central political concept was that disabled people shared an experience of oppression, originating in the additional burdens—disabilities—imposed on people with impairment by a disabling society. The claim to be a collectivity—like women, black people or the working class—was an explicit aspect of this radical challenge.'[19] However, a powerful disability movement arguably now exists, with much progress being made with respect to issues concerning the experience of disability in society. Questions are now emerging as to whether it is appropriate or useful to continue in the same sort of way.

Tom Shakespeare, for example, raises the question of 'whether the very notion of "disabled people" as a commonality can be sustained'.[20] He argues that the impairment category is particularly complex and multidimensional.

First, impairment may affect different body systems: a particular sense or a set of limbs for example. Some impairments affect multiple systems, others have a singular impact. There is a basic distinction between impairments which are associated with chronic illness and those which affect functioning and appearance, but not health. It is also possible to make basic distinctions between types of impairment: visible and invisible impairments, for example, or impairments which involve pain and impairments which do not. The former will influence the reactions which an individual with impairment receives; the latter will mainly influence the subjective experience of the impairment.[21]

Shakespeare goes on to discuss more complex distinctions and variations, including the age of onset of impairment and the trajectory of impairment. 'Some impairments are static and change little over a lifetime; other

---

[19] T. Shakespeare, 'Categories of Impairment and Disability' (unpublished), 2. See also T. Shakespeare, *Disability Rights and Wrongs* (Abingdon: Routledge, 2006).
[20] Ibid. 6.   [21] Ibid. 7.

impairments may be degenerative, slowly becoming worse; others may be episodic, coming and going in an unpredictable manner; others may be short-lived, with every prospect of recovery'.[22] And while he recognizes the important parallels and similarities with respect to impairments, along with the benefits of working together to understand or combat particular problems, he argues that 'aggregating radically different impairment experiences under the common banner of "disability" is not always useful or insightful, and can sometimes be dangerously misleading'.[23]

The idea that the notion of 'disabled people' as a commonality cannot be sustained and that the term disability is intrinsically fluid and dynamic,[24] fits well with the fact that a raft of different functional losses or limitations can have an impact on our capacity to flourish at one time or another.[25] It also encourages us to cease to view disability issues in terms of 'us' and 'them'. Indeed, as Nancy Ann Davis points out, 'in statistical terms, illness, injury, accident or infirmity beset most of us. And the longer we live, the greater are the odds that we will live some portion of our lives as disabled persons'.[26] Moreover, 'the odds that we will all be related or closely connected to someone who is disabled are overwhelming'.[27] It could be helpful, then, to shift the emphasis of our thinking about disability issues away from rigid categorizations, stereotypes, and separatist political collectivities. An emphasis on the similarities between people rather than the differences, on what we share rather than what sets us apart, might encourage us to become a lot more sympathetic to the experience of functional loss—to current and future people with disabilities. Recognizing that frailty and vulnerability unite us all should also encourage us to change our social structures and arrangements to be more inclusive with respect to people with disabilities. As Davis argues, 'In continuing to advocate—or even tolerate—our society's subscription to a human paradigm that marginalizes disabled persons, and a dominant ideology that pathologizes them, we not only harm those whom we now marginalize but also do something that threatens to make our own lives go less well by our own lights.'[28]

---

[22] Ibid. 7–8.   [23] Ibid. 8.

[24] Ibid. 18. It could be argued that the notion of 'disabled people' as a commonality could be sustained if it includes all of us.

[25] Savulescu and Kahane's paper in this volume (Ch. 1) seems to endorse this view.

[26] N. Ann Davis, 'Invisible Disability', Ethics, 116 (2005), 153–213.   [27] Ibid.   [28] Ibid.

Moreover, we might become less inclined to make hard and fast rules about who should and who should not be born. One of the implications of conceding that disability is fluid and dynamic is that it seems ever so much more difficult to draw a line in the sand denoting which disabilities are wrongful and which are not. Our drive toward screening out dispositions at the genetic level may be further questioned when we acknowledge more fully that many are dispositions that we are likely to share to varying degrees and at different times. Indeed, there is a sense in which we would be condemning ourselves by continuing without pause along such a path.[29] Having said that, recognizing that frailty and vulnerability unite us all is also compatible with a desire not to exacerbate such frailty and vulnerability at the start of life. We could and should become much more sympathetic toward current and future people with disabilities. Yet, at the same time, we could resist the thought of bringing a child into the world who is instantly and considerably compromised. Nevertheless, what the arguments so far suggest is that, however we may fall on this issue, it is hard to say that it is wrong to choose to have disabled children.

What *can* we say about the choice to have disabled children? In a previous paper I argued that, when thinking about reproductive choices, we can legitimately factor in parental aspirations, which tend to be top–down rather than bottom–up.[30] That is, we tend to want to ensure, in as much as we can, fully adequate conditions (social, economic, medical, and emotional) in which to raise a child rather than being satisfied if those conditions are just somewhat above an acceptable minimum. As such, parental aspirations tend to be much higher than the 'better than never having existed at all' threshold set by the non-identity problem. Given that is the case, we can make good sense of some potential parents' desire not to become responsible for creating challenges for their children that lie outside what they perceive to be an acceptable range, even at the cost of creating no life at all. Equally, given the personal nature of reproductive decisions, we should be understanding of those who *are* prepared to take

---

[29] Along these lines, it could be argued that continuing to insist that some disabilities are wrongful would, whether intentionally or otherwise, reinforce arguments in favour of euthanasia. This is not to argue for or against euthanasia, but merely to flag the implication. Davis argues, for example, that a 'society that attaches great importance to meeting able-bodied standards . . . is likely to fail its older members—and our future selves'. N. Ann Davis, 'Invisible Disability', n. 26 above.

[30] Hull, 'Cheap listening?' (n. 13 above), 60.

responsibility for creating avoidable suffering, given the other beliefs that they may deeply hold.

However, I also argued that the more the severity of a projected disability errs toward what could be considered to be wrongful life, the more we can claim that it is irresponsible to bring that life about. Such an idea, of permissible irresponsibility, was an attempt to strike a more sensitive balance between the profoundly personal nature of reproductive decisions and the very serious worries that we can have about some of them, while taking seriously the Parfitian point about non-existence. If we take that point seriously, even though it may sound like the argument of an 'over-ingenious defence lawyer',[31] then we cannot call the creation of disabled children wrong (when the alternative is non-existence) because a child with a worthwhile life is created. The other considerations about disability and the personal nature of reproductive decisions outlined above also encourage that conclusion. However, I want to suggest that we can morally criticize both real choices and hypothetical possibilities that seem to labour the Parfitian point.

Many discussions about reproductive choices focus primarily on the potential child—and understandably so. However, given that, for reasons already explored, it is hard to say that a child is harmed or wronged if it is brought into existence with a worthwhile although disabled life, our unease at some reproductive choices might be better sited elsewhere. The focus that I want to begin to explore here is on the character of the person making the reproductive choice.[32] Using an admittedly crude understanding of Aristotle and virtue theory, it will be seen that, with respect to some procreative decisions, the character of the person making them can be legitimately and forcefully criticized.

There are at least two different ways in which our character can be evaluated with respect to reproductive choices. First, it can be evaluated in the light of the severity of a projected impairment and, we might add, the level of indulgence reflected in a potential selection or enhancement. Secondly, we can evaluate the quality of the choice in question.

---

[31] Glover, *Choosing Children* (n. 2 above), 46.

[32] I am not alone in thinking that this may be a fruitful approach. See e.g. R. McDougall, 'Parental Virtue: A New Way of Thinking about the Morality of Reproductive Actions', *Bioethics*, 21 (2007), 181–90. See also R. McDougall, 'Impairment, Flourishing, and the Moral Nature of Parenthood' (ch. 12 in this volume).

The first category denotes what can be seen to be irresponsible at one end of the scale and, perhaps, over-responsible at the other. It also fits well with the language of deficiency and excess. The argument stated earlier applies here, that the more the severity of a projected disability errs toward what could be considered to be wrongful life, the more we can claim that it is irresponsible (while permissible) to bring that life about. That is to say, one way of articulating our worry about such a choice is to describe it as lacking sufficient concern for the gravity of the impairment that the potential child will face. We clearly need to take great care here if the opposite choice necessitates termination of pregnancy, given the deep beliefs about that issue that some people may hold. However, the more that the gravity of the projected impairment errs toward what could be considered to be wrongful life, the more seriously we might question the character of the person who is prepared to bring that life about, especially if refraining from bringing that life about does not require termination of pregnancy. David Wasserman, for example, discusses the view that parents show deficient concern, 'a carelessness, disrespect, or insensitivity', by causing or allowing children to come into existence with severe hardships.[33] And, while we may resist the implication that the parent thereby harms or wrongs the child for reasons already rehearsed, it is perhaps enough to observe that parents can potentially exhibit a lack of concern for their future child and that that insensitivity can be regarded as a moral fault.[34] We can legitimately worry about and not encourage, then, some kinds of attitudes and their correlative behaviour.

Similarly, while we may understand potential parents' desire to ensure that the child that they have is as healthy as possible,[35] we might worry a lot about parents who attempt to overdetermine the type of child they have via future use of genetic technologies. Indeed, such an attitude toward

[33] D. Wasserman, 'The Nonidentity Problem, Disability, and the Role Morality of Prospective Parents', *Ethics*, 116 (2005), 132–52. Wasserman argues that we should not do 'things as momentous as bringing a child into the world—unless we do them for appropriate reasons'. What I am suggesting is that good reasons and good character are closely connected—and that we need to be able to justify our procreative choices to ourselves in the light of a notion of good character (not excessive or deficient) prior to justifying them to our offspring.

[34] Ibid.

[35] If such a desire is legitimate, then too heavy an emphasis on 'unconditional welcome' could be seen more as unprincipled welcome. For discussion of the idea of unconditional welcome, see D. Wasserman, 'Ethical Constraints on Allowing or Causing the Existence of People with Disabilities', Ch. 11 this volume.

having children could be said to be excessive, reflecting unfavourably on our character as moral agents. Dan Brock observes, for example, that 'in highly competitive societies like our own many parents do already carry the molding, shaping, scheduling, and general controlling of their children's lives to excess in a manner that can verge on tyrannical'.[36] To the extent that such possibilities might increase through the development of genetic technologies, a focus on the character of potential parents enables us to criticize their activities even where there may be no evidence of harm to the resulting child, indeed, even where there may be evidence to the contrary. We can articulate our worry about some forms of selection and enhancement as saying nothing at all complimentary about the type of character who would entertain them.[37]

Of course, these two ends of the scale of potential parental behaviour are extreme. Between them is a huge grey area where 'only a monster of self-confidence would come up with an easy judgment—or a judgment at all',[38] about potential parents' reproductive choices. Having said that, some real or hypothetical possibilities remain that can be deeply unsettling yet may escape criticism on the grounds of excess or deficiency. They are likely to be inconceivable options to most prospective parents and so are highly unlikely. Yet such possibilities exist and it is arguable that what unsettles us about them concerns the quality of the choice bound up with each case.

It was argued earlier that, given the personal nature of reproductive decisions, we should be understanding of those who are prepared to take responsibility for creating avoidable suffering, given the other beliefs that they may deeply hold, most likely about terminating pregnancy. When termination of pregnancy is the only other alternative to having a disabled child, we can see that for many prospective parents the choice, if they believe there is a choice, will be a very difficult one to make. That is, a desire

---

[36] D. W. Brock, 'Shaping Future Children: Parental Rights and Societal Interests', *Journal of Political Philosophy*, 13 (2005) 377–98. Eric Schmidt has recently argued that parental genetic trait selections that shift rather than expand the range of open futures are unacceptable 'because they are an excessive form of parental determination regarding their children's futures'. E. B. Schmidt, 'The Parental Obligation to Expand a Child's Range of Open Futures When Making Genetic Trait Selections for their Child', *Bioethics*, 21 (2007), 191–7.

[37] For example, we might think some choices to be overindulgent or vain.

[38] Glover, *Choosing Children* (n. 2 above), 58. Glover uses this phrase in a slightly different context. I use it here because it brilliantly captures the worry about judging most reproductive decisions too quickly or too harshly.

not to create avoidable suffering may run up against an equally weighty belief about termination; and here I think we would be sympathetic to a decision in either direction. As already suggested, we can judge acts to be morally permissible even though it may be the case that we have some serious worries about them. However, there are other scenarios, real and hypothetical, where choices exist that could be effortlessly made and would bring about less suffering (in a different person, same number sense). Hypothetical examples include Jeff McMahan's APHRODISIAC case and his identity-determining disabling prenatal injury case.[39] Buchanan and colleagues also discuss hypothetical cases, for example, where a prospective mother has a treatable condition that is likely to result in her child having some kind of impairment. If she delays conception for, say, a month, her condition will have cleared up and she will be able to conceive a child who will not have an impairment.[40] In all such cases we are asked to consider how we could possibly object to a prospective mother's choice to deliberately conceive a child with an impairment, even with the ease of the alternatives, given that a child with a worthwhile life will result.

The arguments hitherto presented suggest that it is hard to say that the mother's choice to deliberately conceive a child with an impairment in these types of scenario would be wrong. However, given the undesirability of impairment, we may rightly have a problem with the quality of the choice made given the other options available. That is, unlike the case requiring termination, it is unlikely that there are any reasons that are anywhere near in moral weight to those encouraging that we refrain from bringing about avoidable suffering.[41] With that in mind we can argue that, given the availability and ease of alternative courses of action that do not entail the creation of avoidable suffering, the choice to deliberately conceive a child with an impairment in these types of case is the choice of a character that can clearly and legitimately appal us.

It could be said here that the objectionability of the types of choice described above can be captured by the notions of excess and deficiency. That is, the prospective mother could be said to show deficient care or

---

[39] J. McMahan, 'Causing Disabled People to Exist and Causing People to Be Disabled', *Ethics* 116 (2005), 77–99.
[40] Buchanan et al., *From Chance to Choice* (n. 6 above), 244.
[41] This is not to deny that such reasons might exist in some cases.

concern.[42] However, it does not seem to matter a lot how severe the projected impairment is likely to be. Indeed, it is likely that we would have a problem with these types of choice however minor the impairment that would be created, which suggests that our problem is with the quality of the choice (and the character of the person who makes it) rather than deficient concern for the gravity of the projected impairment. While that could come into it too in some cases, it would seem that the severity of a projected impairment matters less, the more that the quality of a particular choice can be criticized. The clearer the absence of reasons that have competing moral weight to those encouraging us to refrain from creating avoidable suffering, then, the more we might condemn the kind of character that would choose to conceive a child with an impairment of any sort in the above types of case.

While the character of potential parents will more often than not be entirely decent with respect to their reproductive choices, the kind of analysis sketched above enables us to legitimately and forcefully oppose some of the more egregious conclusions that can follow from the non-identity problem as well as some of the less enticing possibilities afforded by the development of genetic technologies. Moreover, if there is anything to the idea that the development of good character gives us a better chance at flourishing, an idea that some initiatives in modern psychology seem to substantiate, then our reproductive choices can be seen to be person affecting even where they result in the birth of a different child, or no child at all. That is to say, our reproductive choices are likely to affect *us* deeply and, by implication, will enhance or diminish our personhood—our own capacity to flourish.[43] And while many claims about character are admittedly highly disputable, it would seem that we should be more than a little bit interested in developing an approach to current and future reproductive choices that will not diminish ourselves.

Having said that, it has been argued throughout that, in all but a few cases, it is hard to say that it is wrong to choose to have disabled children for a variety of reasons. These include the social aspect of much disability,

---

[42] It is arguable that *selecting for* disability could be both excessive and deficient at the same time. It is also worth noting that cases exhibiting deficiency are often likely to be interrelated with worries about quality of choice—and vice versa.

[43] It is arguably highly likely that our flourishing will also be intimately bound up with both the potential for and actual flourishing of our children.

issues raised by the non-identity problem, the intensely personal nature of reproductive decisions, and the idea that disability is intrinsically fluid and dynamic. Most of these reasons also encourage us to become much more sympathetic to and accepting of impairment—and that we make our social structures and arrangements more inclusive with respect to people with disabilities. They need not encourage us, however, to be accepting of *all* present and future reproductive choices that result in the birth of children with impairments, where the alternative is that they do not exist. And, while we may not be able to call those choices wrong, I have argued that we can morally criticize the character of prospective parents in relation to some of them. Indeed, if we don't think seriously in the light of new reproductive technologies about what some of our reproductive choices might say about us, there could be said to be a danger that we will 'remain small together'.[44]

[44] F. Nietzsche, *The Gay Science*, trans. Walter Kaufmann (New York: Random House, 1974), 270.

Index